Genesis Curriculum
The Book of Genesis

Scripture quotations taken from the New American Standard Bible®, Copyright © 1960, 1962, 1963, 1968, 1971, 1972, 1973, 975, 1977, 1995 by The Lockman Foundation Used by permission. (www.Lockman.org) Italics and footnotes have been removed.

Hugh Ross, "Fulfilled Prophecy: Evidence for the Reliability of the Bible," *Reasons to Believe* website, August 22, 2003, http://www.reasons.org/articles/articles/fulfilled-prophecy-evidence-for-the-reliability-of-the-bible. Reprinted with permission.

Where noted (NIV) scripture taken from the Holy Bible, NEW INTERNATIONAL VERSION®, NIV® Copyright © 1973, 1978, 1984, 2011 by Biblica, Inc.®Used by permission. All rights reserved worldwide.

TABLE of CONTENTS

ACKNOWLEDGMENTS

Thank you to Tina Rutherford for seeing editing this work as a ministry.
Cover artwork by Rebecca Giles

Paragraph Writing

Introduction (What's the main idea?)

_____

_____

_____

Detail 1 _____

_____

_____

Detail 2 _____

_____

_____

Detail 3 _____

_____

_____

Conclusion (What's the point?)

_____

_____

_____

Essay Writing Outline (The Plan)

The intro, the three main ideas, and the conclusion will each become a paragraph.

Introduction: What's the main idea?

Get their attention (first sentence): _____

_____

Thesis statement (last sentence): _____

_____

Body: Prove your idea. Give the details that support your thesis.

Main idea 1:_____

_____

Main idea 2:_____

_____

Main idea 3:_____

_____

Conclusion: What's the point?

Restate your thesis in a different way (first sentence): _____

_____

Wrap it up. Why did you write this? So what? What do you have to say about it? (last sentence):

_____

_____

Editing Checklist

Directions: Edit your written work using the Self-Edit columns, fixing any errors you notice. Then, ask someone to complete the Peer Edit column.

	Self-Edit		Peer Edit	
	Checklist Items		Checklist Items	
Punctuation	I read my written piece aloud to see where to stop or pause for periods, question marks, exclamation marks, and commas.		I read the author's piece aloud to see where to stop or pause for periods, question marks, exclamation marks, and commas.	
	Quotation marks are included where needed.		Quotation marks are included where needed.	
Capital Letters	I checked for capitals at the beginning of sentences.		I checked for capitals at the beginning of sentences.	
	Proper nouns begin with capital letters.		Proper nouns begin with capital letters.	
Grammar	My sentences are complete thoughts and contain a noun and a verb.		Sentences are complete thoughts and contain a noun and a verb.	
	I don't have any run-on sentences.		There are no run-on sentences.	
Spelling	I checked spelling and fixed the words that didn't look right.		Spelling is correct.	

Checklist is adapted from Read Write Think. Permission is granted to use for educational purposes.

For paragraphs:

_____ Is there an introduction sentence that states the main idea?

_____ Are there at least three details that tell more about the main idea?

_____ Is there a conclusion sentence that wraps up the idea?

Essay Editing Checklist

Organization

Introduction

_____ Introduction begins with an attention grabber or hook.
_____ Introduction has at least three sentences.
_____ Introduction ends with a clear thesis statement.

Body

_____ There are at least three body paragraphs (each indented).
_____ Each body paragraph has a topic sentence.
_____ Each body paragraph has at least three main ideas.
_____ Each body paragraph has a conclusion sentence.

Conclusion

_____ The conclusion paragraph is at least three sentences.
_____ The conclusion paragraph restates the thesis statement.
_____ The conclusion paragraph answers "So what?" or makes a broad generalization.

Coherence

_____ The ideas flow logically and make sense.
_____ Transitions are used correctly.
_____ There are no awkward parts.
_____ The essay is interesting.

Ideas/Content

_____ Everything in the essay supports the thesis statement (main idea).
_____ There is enough supporting evidence for each body paragraph.
_____ Descriptive and precise words are used.
_____ Sentence structure is varied (a mix of simple, compound, and complex sentences).

Grammar and Mechanics

Point out any of the following that you find:

_____ Misspelled words
_____ Grammatical mistakes
_____ Punctuation errors
_____ Run-on Sentences (more than one sentence smooshed together)
_____ Fragments (incomplete sentences)

Adapted and used with permission from Jimmie's Collage.

How to Use

Thank you for choosing Genesis Curriculum. I hope you have a great year of learning together. That's what Genesis Curriculum is about, learning together. I hope you will learn right along with your children.

As a homeschool curriculum, I encourage you to make this your own. It's prepared and ready to be picked up and used as is, but you are a homeschooler! You get to adapt it to your family however it works best for you. I will walk you through it and give you some ideas for how to use its sections. You might want to come back to this how-to guide occasionally for some pointers you may have forgotten.

Each lesson is written as an outline. You will basically read through the outline to your children. When a line asks a question, stop and let your children answer before you read the answer I give on the next line. Where I include a (Note:) I'm talking to you, and you can just read that to yourself.

Bible

First is the Bible reading. You'll need a Bible to do the readings. These readings go directly through the book of Genesis. I did not include questions with the reading. You can just read it and leave it at that, or you can ask your kids to make observations and ask what they think about it. Do they have any questions? You don't have to have the answers. It's good for them to think and to ask questions and to make decisions about what they believe while you are there to guide them. Some of your questions may be answered in the lesson, but you can always research things together and learn together. That's what GC is all about.

Memory Verses

After the reading is a memory verse. They will have one verse a week. These are from all throughout the Bible but are related to the Genesis readings. They will be reviewing these verses throughout the year and asked sometimes to find the verses in the Bible. On the last day of each week you are to "test yourselves" on the memory verse. It's up to you if you want to give a reward to anyone who can say it from memory.

Language

Next comes the language section. This comes in three parts: handwriting/spelling, vocabulary, and Hebrew.

Handwriting

If you want handwriting practice, I listed a verse number. You could read that out loud and your children could write it as a dictation. Those verses are in the Genesis Curriculum Copywork book. If anything, this might be something you'd want to hold off on until the end if you have younger children who would take a long time to write. A young child could copy the verse while the others do the writing assignment at the end. The Copywork book has enough room to write an additional sentence after the verse as part of the writing assignment. There is also a Tracing book. That has the spelling words for tracing, not the verse.

Spelling

Spelling is also part of this section, and all of the words come from the day's reading. Read the "words to know" one at a time and have the children spell them the best they can, but if I have listed "spelling tips" read the appropriate one when they are attempting that word. The tips are to help them spell successfully, so let them have the tips before they write the word. The tips are listed in order.

Before I created the tracing book, I had my youngest try to hear the first sound of the word and write that letter, upper and lower case, while the others wrote the word. I checked these after we finished the whole lesson and had them rewrite incorrectly spelled words. They will see these words again at the end of the week and during reviews.

You could also do spelling out loud. Sometimes I would ask my first grader to try to give the first two or three letters of a word and then my fourth grader would finish off the word. You can, of course, mix up how you do it too and use any of your own creative ideas.

Vocabulary

Vocabulary is the next section. This is a word from the day's reading. You can see if anyone can define it already. The verse number is listed with the word, so you can read it in context and see what they can guess for the definition. Ask what the part of speech is. (These will be introduced.) Tell them the part of speech and the definition. You can ask someone to repeat the definition. You could ask them to try to come up with a sentence that uses the word. Both the Tracing and Copywork books have the day's vocabulary word, definition, example sentences, and space to illustrate its meaning.

Grammar

As I mentioned, the parts of speech will be introduced and that happens in the vocabulary section. There is some other grammar included in the vocabulary as well. Early on, they learn prepositional phrases, objects of prepositions and direct objects. They don't have to get these the first time they are introduced. They will be brought up with examples over and over again. There will be worksheets on them during the review weeks. If a young child doesn't get these concepts, it's okay. Don't force it. When everyone's learning together, some things the older kids will pick up on that the younger ones won't, but they will be introduced to the concepts which will make it that much easier later on.

Hebrew

The last part of the language section is Hebrew. You will be learning memory verses in Hebrew. This will give you a context to practice vocabulary. You will be learning a little bit of the grammar. Hebrew grammar is very complex. You won't be learning all the ins and outs of it. You will learn the alphabet and practice writing it. Hebrew is a scholarly language, not a spoken language. It doesn't count for some schools' language requirement (just so you know). Learning any language, however, helps in learning any other language. It can only be good for you. ☺ In the back of this book there are lists of all topics covered; the Hebrew page includes a list of the pronunciation tips. You can find helpful links on our site for writing, speaking, and listening practice. Find them on the Online Support page.

Science and Social Studies

Then we come to the meat of the curriculum. Science and social studies topics follow. These were inspired by the day's Scripture reading. Social studies does have some history, but it is much more social studies, the study of humans and their societies. I have included stories of some of my own experiences and observations from my many years of living overseas, most of which has been among Muslims and much of which has been in a Middle Eastern culture. Both science and history are from a definitively young-earth perspective.

Again, when you come to a question in the curriculum with the answer on the next line, stop and have your kids answer with their thoughts. Then you can read my answer and continue on. They don't have to know the answer. They aren't necessarily meant to know the answer, but in asking you are getting their brains turned on and getting them thinking. Let them guess at answers. They don't have to know the right answer in order to speak up.

Show the pictures I included where applicable. The italicized words are defined in the text. When you read a sentence with an italicized word, you can stop and ask them to repeat the word. If you just read what it means, have them tell you what it means. These are words that might show up in their review later. At the end of many of these sections there is a "recall" and "explore more." Ask the recall questions and have them answer to help cement the information in their brains. You could have them write the answers as an assessment. I usually choose who I ask the question to based on whether I think the question is easier or harder. Sometimes I let a younger one try first and then the older ones can answer if the littler ones didn't know.

I wanted to point out one more thing about these lessons and topics. They are different each day. They were inspired by the reading that day, so they aren't in order. You will see how certain topics come up repeatedly, so I don't want you to think that you will never see a topic again just because it didn't continue the next day. Since I wrote all of the lessons, I know what has been covered and can weave threads through the lessons, referring to previous things learned. Some topics are covered multiple times from different angles.

Discussion

The lesson is rounded out with a discussion question. The discussion question is based on the day's lesson. These are open-ended and are meant to make them think. Let each kid give his or her own thoughts and then you can give your own. These aren't right or wrong type questions, so let them express their thoughts without correction. You can give your thoughts, and they will learn from you. This is a great time for instilling wisdom, though some questions are just for fun, like describing a world without gravity.

Writing

The final section is writing. They can then use the discussion question for a writing prompt. They have already thought about it and expressed their ideas, so now they just have to write it down. If your child has other inspiration, you can certainly just let them write on their own topic. This is a free writing time. They are free to write without correction. It's about getting organized thoughts down, not technical perfection.

A younger child might copy the verse. The next youngest (7-9) might write a sentence. A 9-11 year old might write a paragraph. An 11+ child could work on a five-paragraph essay each week. This could be done by using the first topic of the week and on the first day creating a brief outline and writing the introduction. Two paragraphs could be written on each of the next two days. The last day could be for editing just like the others. Once they are proficient at it (maybe it's their second year writing essays), they can start writing a whole essay at once. This is easier if they can type.

I've included paragraph and essay writing instructions with an example using the discussion question from Day 20. That might be a good day to move your child up if they are ready for the next level since you can show them a sample of what's expected. They have paragraph and essay writing worksheets in their workbooks that you could use when getting them started. *See Writing Instruction.

Every five days, they are to edit something they wrote in the last few days. I've included some editing guidelines for that. More of these checklists can be printed from online. They edit and then they are to ask someone older to edit their writing as well. This is the time when you get to make corrections. You don't need to correct everything for younger students, but for instance, after they learn about starting sentences with capital letters (first week), then you should correct that in their writing if they don't. Learn the grammar along with your children so that you can help with editing. I've also included helpful links on our site to help with things such as comma rules and such as well as writing sentences, paragraphs, essays and more.

The first day of each week there is a grammar lesson related to writing with a worksheet to practice. Sometimes I just do the worksheets out loud with my kids. Sometimes I let them work in pairs. Sometimes they do it on their own. (This is homeschool. Do what works for your family.) You may not have a workbook for each child. You need at least one for your family, but maybe you would like to use the Copywork or Tracing books for younger children, and then they can participate orally or with a partner to complete these worksheets.

Review

Also, one day each week there are no new spelling, vocabulary, or Hebrew words. Have the children spell the review words listed. I may just pick out words that I know had caused trouble and have them try those again. You can have them define the vocabulary words out loud. Practice your Hebrew together. Have everyone try to say the memory verses. It's up to you if you want to use this time as an assessment. I just use it as review.

There are five weeks of lessons and then two weeks of review. In the first review week, they have a daily spelling activity. In the second week, you will have vocabulary and grammar review activities. Also on each day there will be either a science or social studies review activity. Many of these activities are found in the workbook. Those you can use as just reviews or you can see them as assessments. Younger children may not remember everything the older kids do. Don't hold everyone to the same standard. My six-year-old is really engaged in this curriculum, but he doesn't remember everything.

In the Tracing and Copywork books I have included one language arts review activity for each of the review days. If there is an activity that the older kids are doing that your younger child wants to do, you can print that sheet off from our site, genesiscurriculum.com. I did include in these workbooks a few favorite activities from the workbook.

Copyright

I decided to not grant photocopy rights. I want to be able to make updates and changes to materials and have everyone use the most recent editions. The workbook is available on our site for printing any extra pages you should need. I've tried to price it so that it's not cheaper to print out. I want to make this easy for you!

Materials List

Where it's marked extra, it's not something that is needed to complete the lesson. It's in the lesson as something additional you could try. An asterisks* marks when something needs to be cut out. If you don't want to cut those pages from your workbook, they can all be printed from our site, genesiscurriculum.com. You can find them through the Online Support page.

1	mirror or any shiny surface for reflecting light
2	mirror, ball that bounces - any size
4	glass of water, pencil or some other straight object to put in water
41	(extra) fan, two plates, water
42	(extra) plate, water, piece of paper, two sponges, salt, cup, sugar cube, colored drink
50	cornstarch, water, bowl
51	food package with label (looking for calorie count)
54	balloon (only if you want to see it for yourself) (extra) plastic bottle with lid, pen or nail; explore more: short tube/hose, stick
57	2 T. white vinegar and ¼ c. skim milk, you can try other types of milk and other acids such as lemon juice and orange juice, (extra) sugar/salt, glass of water
60	biggest screw you have at home; if you have a toy car where you can see where the wheel is attached to the axle; (extra) stick, short tube/hose, strong tape
63	*word parts need cutting out
65	*word strips need cutting
68	*words and definitions need cutting, zip lock bag (or something to save word cards and definitions in)
76	flashlight, pencil with point and eraser, or pen
80	(extra) pencil/pen, cup, thread, paperclip
87	(extra) yarn-just a little piece will do
96	broom (or rake or long-handled scrub brush), string, table that the broom handle reaches across, bucket or basket with handle, something like a big book or weight to go in the basket, (you might need a ruler or wooden spoon and strong tape if your long-handled tool doesn't have a wide place to hold on to securely at the end) See picture on the next page; separately you will need something to act as a wedge such as a long fork or long spoon with a thin edge
97	½ teaspoon dry yeast and ½ cup hydrogen peroxide (alternative: steel wool and vinegar to cover it); plastic cup or glass, a thermometer that can measure room temperature if you have one
98	play dough (clay) in four colors, stick for going through your play dough model (tooth picks or thin skewer, per person)
99	die (If you don't have one, you could write the numbers 1 through 4 on slips of paper and draw them out randomly.)
107	measuring tape
117	rulers with centimeters on them (The kids will be drawing maps and will need to measure centimeters on their papers.)
126	(extra) baking soda, vinegar (or other acid)
131	one apple, salt, cooling rack, four cups or bowls that you can do without for the week, plastic wrap and any tape to seal it shut

132   30 minutes of boiling for: spinach, beets, red cabbage, onion skins; hard boiled eggs for dying, a cup for each dye, white vinegar
*word parts need cutting out

133   paper cups, maybe a few per kid so they can make mistakes (They will put holes in them.)

134   (option 1) baking soda and a variety of things to combine with it for experimentation (solids, liquids, definitely acids like vinegar, orange and lemon juice); (option 2) ice, aluminum foil-could probably use plastic wrap, book, steaming water
*word strips need cutting out – Only need one copy today. They will need these words for Day 138. Hold onto what you cut out.

135   We're going to build a car. Choose your parts. If you can get a variety of sizes of things, then the kids can make different length axles and use different size wheels and test out how it affects the car. You'll need a body: plastic water bottle, toilet paper roll, build a frame out of popsicle sticks, etc. You'll need axles: tooth picks, skewers, hard straws, etc. You will need wheels: bottle caps, wheels from a Lego set, make wheels by slicing off end of toilet paper roll (and then cover openings with masking tape or duct tape.)
(extra) rubber band

137   We're going to draw body diagrams. It would be fun to tape together a bunch of pieces of paper and trace the whole body onto the paper and then draw the bones and organs, etc. onto the body. If you don't want to do this, they will have to draw a body onto a single piece of paper and add in the parts. Just use lines to outline the body to label the parts.

138   *word strips from Spelling Review 19 (Day 134) Each person needs their own or they can work in pairs, etc.

Picture of Day 96 activity

Writing Instruction

Sentence Writing

Students will be practicing grammar throughout the course that will teach correct sentence structure. As each topic is covered, look for those things in their writing. These will include capital letters, punctuation marks, complete sentences with subject and predicate, etc. I will include reminders of what to look for and they will have an editing checklist when they correct their writing.

They will use the discussion question as a writing prompt. Their answer should state the question. You shouldn't have to look at the question to know what they are talking about. Here's an example for the Day 17 writing prompt about a world without gravity.

> I think a world without gravity would be an impossible place to live in because everything would float away.

When they are proficient at the structure, you can encourage longer sentences using commas and conjunctions.

Paragraph Writing

A paragraph is a way to organize your writing. It comes in three parts. The introduction is the main idea of your paragraph. It's what you are going to write about. Then there's the body which should include at least three points to support your idea. These are the facts, the details about your topic. Finally, you have a conclusion sentence that sums up the point. Here's an example with the same discussion question from the curriculum.

> (Introduction) I think a world without gravity would be impossible. (Body-your points) We would have to have belts that harnessed us to something, so we didn't float away. You couldn't play any sports. You wouldn't be able to throw or kick a ball to anyone. You couldn't have food on a plate because it would fly off. You'd have to hold onto to everything, all the time. (Conclusion) I'm glad God thought up gravity to keep us on earth, so we can eat and play and even just be able to walk!

Essay Writing

An essay follows the same structure as a paragraph, but now each sentence is its own paragraph. The introduction should start with an interesting fact or a quote or question.

Something to get the reader's attention. This paragraph ends with your main point. It's called a "thesis statement."

The body should be at least three paragraphs. Each paragraph will be about one of your points that support your topic. Each paragraph should follow the guidelines. The first sentence is the main idea for that paragraph. It is followed by details, more information about it and then a conclusion. In an essay, your conclusion or introduction sentences should transition to the next paragraph.

The last paragraph should start with restating your thesis statement (but not in the same words!) Then sum up why we should care about this topic. What's the point?

Here's an example using the same topic. I took my three details from the paragraph and expanded them into paragraphs. This essay took me fifteen minutes to write. This is about learning how to organize thoughts and to present them in a clear, understandable way.

(introduction) Have you ever wondered what it would be like to float around in space? It's fun to watch videos of astronauts in the space shuttle with their hair sticking up and all their things floating around. What would happen if that was what earth was like? (thesis statement) I think earth without gravity would be an impossible place to live.

(body: main idea 1) Gravity gives us the ability to get around. (details) While we could get around with jet packs, which might be fun for a while, that's only a very limited solution for getting around. We'd have to refuel all the time. If we ran out, we could float away, never to be heard from again. (conclusion) Gravity is what keeps on earth and lets us do the simplest things like walk from here to there.

(transition) Besides getting around, (main idea 2) gravity lets us play our favorite games. (details) Kicking a soccer ball in no gravity would only result in a lost ball. No one could pitch a baseball in zero gravity; the ball would never reach home plate. A game of chess or checkers could work with Velcro pieces and board I guess, but you'd have to sit strapped in to play! (conclusion) The games that we know just can't be played the same way without gravity.

(transition) Maybe even harder (main idea 3) would be trying to eat without gravity. (details) How could you cut up food? You couldn't. French fries? No way! They would have to make dispensers that only let out one at a time. Of course, the ketchup would float right off and up, up and away. Soup would be a wet mess on the ceiling. We'd have to have lids with fat straws on our bowls and then try to keep the soup from floating out through the straw opening! (conclusion) Eating a meal without gravity would not be a relaxed and pleasurable affair.

(Conclusion: restate the thesis) A normal life without gravity is impossible. (sum up and let us know why to care) We rely on gravity for everything, even if we don't realize it. It's enough to keep us from floating away, but not so much that we can't jump, throw a ball, or lift food to our mouths. Earth's gravity is a perfect match for our lives.

Students have an editing checklist in their workbooks for when they edit their writing. They can work on one essay a week, which would be three days for writing and one day for editing. They may eventually be able to do one of these in a single day, especially if you are doing this over multiple years. A high school student would aim to get to that point.

You don't need to start with essays with your older children. Make sure they are proficient in paragraph writing first. Same with your middle children, make sure they are proficient in sentence writing before working on paragraphs. They can use the paragraph and essay writing worksheets to get started. These are in their workbooks as well.

Editing Checklist

Directions: Edit your written work using the Self-Edit columns, fixing any errors you notice. Then, ask someone to complete the Peer Edit column.

	Self-Edit		Peer Edit	
	Checklist Items		Checklist Items	
Punctuation	I read my written piece aloud to see where to stop or pause for periods, question marks, exclamation marks, and commas.		I read the author's piece aloud to see where to stop or pause for periods, question marks, exclamation marks, and commas.	
	Quotation marks are included where needed.		Quotation marks are included where needed.	
Capital Letters	I checked for capitals at the beginning of sentences.		I checked for capitals at the beginning of sentences.	
	Proper nouns begin with capital letters.		Proper nouns begin with capital letters.	
Grammar	My sentences are complete thoughts and contain a noun and a verb.		Sentences are complete thoughts and contain a noun and a verb.	
	I don't have any run-on sentences.		There are no run-on sentences.	
Spelling	I checked spelling and fixed the words that didn't look right.		Spelling is correct.	

Checklist is adapted from Read Write Think. Permission is granted to use for educational purposes.

For paragraphs:

_____ Is there an introduction sentence that states the main idea?

_____ Are there at least three details that tell more about the main idea?

_____ Is there a conclusion sentence that wraps up the idea?

Essay Editing Checklist

Organization

Introduction

_____ Introduction begins with an attention grabber or hook.
_____ Introduction has at least three sentences.
_____ Introduction ends with a clear thesis statement.

Body

_____ There are at least three body paragraphs (each indented).
_____ Each body paragraph has a topic sentence.
_____ Each body paragraph has at least three main ideas.
_____ Each body paragraph has a conclusion sentence.

Conclusion

_____ The conclusion paragraph is at least three sentences.
_____ The conclusion paragraph restates the thesis statement.
_____ The conclusion paragraph answers "So what?" or makes a broad generalization.

Coherence

_____ The ideas flow logically and make sense.
_____ Transitions are used correctly.
_____ There are no awkward parts.
_____ The essay is interesting.

Ideas/Content

_____ Everything in the essay supports the thesis statement (main idea).
_____ There is enough supporting evidence for each body paragraph.
_____ Descriptive and precise words are used.
_____ Sentence structure is varied (a mix of simple, compound, and complex sentences).

Grammar and Mechanics

Point out any of the following that you find:

_____ Misspelled words
_____ Grammatical mistakes
_____ Punctuation errors
_____ Run-on Sentences (sentences smooshed together)
_____ Fragments (incomplete sentences)

Adapted and used with permission from Jimmie's Collage.

Day 1 (check Materials List)

I. Read Genesis 1:1-5.

II. Memory Verse
- o Genesis 1:1
- o In the beginning God created the heavens and the earth.

III. Language
- o Spelling/Handwriting
  - verse 5
  - words to know: formless, void, darkness, moving
  - Spelling tips:
    - Break <u>formless</u> into syllables – form and less.
    - <u>Void</u> has the same vowel spelling pattern as coin and noise.
    - Break <u>darkness</u> into syllables as well – dark and ness.
    - The word <u>moving</u> looks like it could say moe – ving.
- o Vocabulary/Grammar
  - void (vs. 2)
  - completely empty (adjective)
  - other definitions: not valid, empty space
  - An adjective describes. What does void describe? What was void?
    - Void describes what the earth was like.
  - In the beginning of verse 2, what other word is an adjective? What other word describes earth?
    - Formless is another adjective. It's also describing earth.
- o Hebrew
  - God
  - el - o - HEEM
  - Not sure if you pronounced it right? Say "elo" like "hello" without the H.
  - The capital letters tell you where to put the emphasis on the word. It's officially called where the "stress" is in the word. You say that part of the word with a little more umph behind it. You don't even think about it, but you change the volume and pitch of your voice on the stressed syllable. Here are some English words with their emphasis marked to help you understand.
    - DInner (you don't say dinNER)
    - toMORrow (you don't say TOmorrow or tomorROW)
    - toDAY (you don't say TOday)
    - BIble (you don't say biBLE)

IV. Science
- o Light
  - God creates light before He creates the sun and the moon and the other stars.
  - God can do anything. He created the laws of physics, the laws of nature, the laws of how this earth survives and operates, but He can also break them at

any time. (For example, He causes a heavy metal ax head to float, 2 Kings 6:4-6.)
- We're going to look more at what He created when He created light.

o What does light do?
- Jesus is called "the light of the world" (John 8:12).
- Light is what enables us to see. If you are in a room with no light at all, what can you see?
  ▪ You cannot see anything at all.
- When you are looking at something, what you are seeing is the light that is being reflected off of that object. That light bounces off of the object and hits your eyes. Your miraculous brain puts all those light inputs together into the image you "see." And it all happens instantaneously!
- Have you ever reflected light? You can use a mirror or you could try a ring or a watch or any shiny surface. Hold it where a light hits it. Wobble the mirror or other objects and watch the reflection of light move on the wall.

o What is light?
- Light is a dance. Light particles, called *photons,* teeny tiny things in our universe, travel in a straight path, while light from them dances up and down in waves. Light is always moving.
  ▪ If you draw a curvy line, up and down and up and down, that's what a light wave does.
- Light is moving energy. Energy is one of the most important parts of our universe. *Energy* is the ability to do work.
  ▪ So light is moving energy, and in the beginning God created light. I want to tell you something awesome about energy. It cannot be created or destroyed by man! It can only be changed from one form to another. All of the energy that the whole world needs to live and move and have our being was created by God alone on the first day.
  ▪ When people talk of creating energy, they really mean transforming energy. As an example, solar panels don't create energy; they take the sun's energy and convert it into electricity.
- The sun gives energy to the plants which give energy to the animals that eat them. They give you energy when you eat the animal or plant.
- Energy keeps us alive. That light keeps us all alive; it gives us all the energy we need to keep on living.

o Recall: What is light? What is energy?
- Light is moving energy.
- Energy is the ability to do work.

o Explore more: Learn more about light waves and light particles. What is light energy transformed into? How is energy converted?

V. Social Studies
o We call this period of time, early in the earth's existence, prehistory, or the time before recorded history. Recorded history means someone was writing down what happened. The account we have in Genesis was written down by Moses thousands of years after the earth was created. God told him the story and he wrote it down.

- God was the only one there to see and really know what happened when the world was created, so I trust His version of it!
- Who was there in the beginning?
  - We see "God" in verses 1, 3, 4 and 5.
  - We see "Spirit of God" in verse 2.
  - Where was Jesus?
    - Colossians 1:16 says, "For by [Jesus] all things were created, both in the heavens and on earth, visible and invisible, whether thrones or dominions or rulers or authorities—all things have been created through Him and for Him."
      - note: I put [Jesus] in brackets to show that it's not in the text. The verse says "for by him," but I wanted to show clearly the verse is about Jesus.
    - The Hebrew word translated "God" in these verses is actually the plural form of the word, as if it says gods, more than one. Maybe this is out of respect for the one, true, great God, or maybe it's in reference to the trinity. God the Father was not alone.
- Recall: What is prehistory?
  - The time before recorded history

VI. Discussion

- Jesus calls Himself the light of the world (John 8:12).
- What do you think Jesus enables us to see with His light?

VII. Writing

- When you write, you need to make sure your sentences start and end properly. Do you know what I'm talking about?
- Every sentence begins with a capital letter and ends with a punctuation mark. Mostly that means it ends with a period. But maybe you have something to exclaim! Or maybe you need to ask a question?
- Make sure you are starting and ending your sentences the right way.
- Complete Writing Sentences 1 in your workbook.
- (Note: There are some directions at the bottom of the page for Day 2. They shouldn't do that now.)

Day 2 (check Materials List)

I.   Read Genesis 1:6-10.

II. Memory Verse
- Genesis 1:1
- In the beginning God created the heavens and the earth.

III. Language
- Spelling/Handwriting
  - verse 6
  - words to know: dry, expanse, separate, seas
  - spelling tip:
    - The word <u>dry</u> rhymes with try and my and has the same spelling pattern.
    - The word <u>expanse</u> starts with the same letters as exit and extra. It has the word pans in it and ends with a silent E.
    - Say sep-ar-ate when you are trying to spell <u>separate</u>. We pronounce it differently when we speak quickly.
    - The word <u>seas</u> is a homophone. That means that it sounds like another word. This is the seas that you sail boats on. It has the same vowel spelling as tea and real.
- Vocabulary/Grammar
  - expanse (vs. 6, 7, 8)
  - a large, wide, open area of land or water (noun)
  - A noun is a person, place or thing.
  - Verse six also has examples of prepositional phrases. A phrase is just a group of words used together.
    - The words "in the midst" is a prepositional phrase and so is "of the waters" that follows it.
    - The words "of" and "in" are the prepositions. Prepositions mostly tell us the location of things.
    - The words "midst" and "waters" are the objects of the prepositions.
    - The object answers the question "what?"
    - Examples:
      - by the lake – This is a prepositional phrase.
        - By what?
        - the lake – The lake the object of the preposition.
      - around the corner – This is a prepositional phrase.
        - Around what?
        - the corner – The corner is the object of the preposition.
      - on the table – This is a prepositional phrase.
        - On what?
        - the table – The table is the object of the preposition.
    - Go to the Writing Sentences 1 page in your workbook and underline the prepositions.

- (Note: Answers: #1 of, #3 after, #8 in, #11 in)
  - o Hebrew
    - heaven
    - sha-MA-yim
    - When I write a single letter A, that sound is "ah," like going to the dentist "ah." When you see "i," you read it with the short vowel sound. For example from today: yim rhymes with him. The "i" in him has the short vowel sound.

IV. Science
  - o Today we'll look again at light.
  - o On Day 1 we reflected light off of a shiny surface. Today, I want you to look in a mirror, but before we do that, I want you to look at someone else.
    - Stand or sit across from someone else. Touch your right ear.
    - Have the person across from you mirror what you are doing, as if you are looking in the mirror and your partner is your *reflection*.
    - You are touching your right ear. What ear is your partner touching? The left ear! Feel free to play around mirroring each other.
    - Now go look in a mirror. Touch your right ear. The mirror perfectly mirrors you. ☺ The reflection-you is touching the left ear!
    - Why? It has to do with light, of course.
  - o We learned on Day 1 that what we see is the light that bounces off of an object. Light hits the object and then hits our eyes.
  - o What's in the mirror is the light reflecting directly what is in front of it. The light bounces off you and everything else in front of the mirror and you see those reflections.
  - o Let's think about bouncing for a minute. You can bounce a ball directly up and down. It's a little hard to do perfectly up and down. A mirror is perfectly smooth so it bounces light straight back.
    - What happens when you bounce the ball to someone else? If you have a ball handy, you can try it. Pass the ball to each other by bouncing it one time between you.
    - Draw a picture of how the ball bounces when you pass it to someone else. (You don't have to have a ball to do this. Think about it.)
    - It goes down on an angle and then up at the opposite angle.
  - o So, think about what this means for how we see light that bounces off an object. Light is bouncing off everything around you constantly. Every little bit is taking in light and sending off light as it bounces. Isn't it amazing that your brain can take in all of those bits of light simultaneously and continuously and make them into meaningful pictures?
    - Play more with reflection today. Go look at yourself in a teapot or other pot. Look at yourself on the back of a spoon. Why is your image funny? Think about how the light is reflected. Those objects are not flat and smooth like a mirror. The bent surfaces send light out in new directions!
    - Light will be continued.
  - o Recall: How does a mirror work?

- Light bounces perfectly off of it to reflect the light off of what's directly in front of it.
  - Explore more: How do two-way mirrors work? Learn about reflection and concave and convex surfaces.

V. Social Studies
- Learn the names and locations of the continents and oceans. They are found on the Day 2 map of your Map Book.
  - The Pacific Ocean is also the water on the far right side of the map in the middle. Why?
  - The earth is a ball shape, not flat like a map! The two sides of the map are connected to each other.
- How many continents are there?
  - seven
- How many oceans are there?
  - five
- Explore more: What is Pangaea? What does the Bible have to say about it?

VI. Discussion (two choices)
- What do you think is out there beyond what our senses and science can tell us?
  - Our Bible reading today says that God separated the waters by placing the heavens (the vast universe) between them. There are waters above the heavens?
  - Paul writes of a "third heaven" in 2 Corinthians 12.
- How do you think God "gathered the waters"? How did He do it?

VII. Writing
- Use the discussion question as a writing prompt.
- Can you find any prepositions in what you wrote? Get a high five and/or hug if you can.

Day 3

I. Read Genesis 1:11-13.

II. Memory Verse
- o Genesis 1:1
- o In the beginning God created the heavens and the earth.

III. Language
- o Spelling/Handwriting
  - • verse 12
  - • words to know: brought, vegetation, yield, bearing
  - • spelling tips:
    - ▪ The word <u>brought</u> has a tricky vowel-sound spelling. O-U-G-H can have lots of different sounds. Brought is the same as fought and bought.
    - ▪ <u>Vegetation</u> starts like the word vegetables. Think about how you spell veggies.
    - ▪ <u>Yield</u> follows the famous saying, "I before e, except after c."
    - ▪ The word <u>bearing</u> begins with the word bear, the animal. That kind of bear actually contains the word ear.
- o Vocabulary/Grammar
  - • yield (verses 11 and 12)
  - • to produce (verb)
  - • other definitions: to give in to a demand or argument (verb); the full amount produced (noun)
  - • A verb describes an action or a state of being.
    - ▪ Run, jump, talk, eat, etc. are actions and are action verbs.
    - ▪ Here's one we call a *state of being*, I am. "Am" is a verb.
    - ▪ Am, is, are, was, were, will, be, has, been, had, have, become, became are all verbs.
- o Hebrew
  - • earth
  - • A-rets (AH, as in going-to-the-dentist "ah")
  - • The stress is on the A, the first syllable. Here are some words in English that put the emphasis on the first syllable.
    - ▪ trumpet
    - ▪ walking
    - ▪ baker

IV. Science
- o We're going to leave light for today and talk about seeds. Our reading today talked about plants yielding seeds after their own kind. That means that apples produce apple seeds; those apples seeds grow apple trees. Sunflowers produce sunflower seeds that grow more sunflowers.
- o How do seeds work? They die!

- When you eat your fruits and vegetables, be on the lookout for their seeds. Some are harder to find than others. Do you know where banana seeds are? What about carrot seeds?
  - Seeds come in many shapes and sizes. Some plants don't have seeds. A potato is its own seed. You just plant a piece of potato in the ground. If you leave a potato out too long it will start to sprout. It's growing a new plant! (Onions work this way too.)
  - The seed grows inside a plant. Then there are many different ways the seed gets into the ground. They can be planted, but certainly don't have to be. How do you think there are wild flowers and forests? No one planted those. They grew naturally.
  - When a fruit falls off a tree and no one picks it up, what happens to it?
    - When fruit falls to the ground, the fruit will *decompose*, meaning it becomes rotten and decays. Did you ever see a really icky, squishy fruit or vegetable?
    - Fruit that has turned brown and squishy is decomposing. When it does, it leaves a nice environment for a seed to sprout.
    - This can also happen when an animal eats the fruit but the seed comes out the other end unharmed. It's an already fertilized seed! Gross, but a good way for a seed to get growing.
  - Animals may move seeds purposefully or accidentally. Some seeds fly away to new locations. Have you ever blown on dandelion seeds to make them fly away?
    - This is called *seed dispersal*, or how seeds get dispersed, or scattered.
  - The plant has died. The fruit or flower has fallen. It's no longer attached to its life source. The seeds are no longer growing. The seed dies. Then what?
    - It's a mystery. God made it that way. Man can't create life; it can only copy life that God has created.
    - Only God brings life from death. He shows us the resurrection in the life of a plant. We get our life because of the death of Jesus.
  - Here's what we do know. We have a dead seed. It gets a burial. It gets under a little bit of soil. What starts happening to the seed?
    - It gets its nutrients, its food, from that very soil it is under. Those nutrients are taken in by the roots of the plant which start pushing out of the seed when it's ready.
    - While the roots go down deeper into the soil, at the same time, out of the seed green shoots sprout up towards the light.
  - *Germination* is the name of this early growth of a seed plant.
  - The new plant will make its own food from the sun. That's called photosynthesis and that's a lesson for another time.
    - Be on the lookout for seeds and plant some!
  - Recall: What is happening when fruit decomposes? What is happening during seed dispersal? What is germination?
    - It's decaying and going rotten.
    - Seeds are being scattered about.
    - the early growth of a plant (when the plant is first breaking out of a seed)
  - Explore more: How do seeds work? What's the anatomy of a seed?

V. Social Studies
- o Use your map to review continents, oceans.
- o Use the Day 3 map to quiz yourselves on them. I've included a couple of seas on it for you to try to learn if you already know the oceans and continents.
- o Continent Facts (Note: You can do this as a fun quiz and ask your children what they think is the answer to each before you tell them.)
  - Largest: Asia
  - Smallest: Australia
  - Most population: Asia (Half of all the people in the world live here. China and India are the main reason.)
  - Least population: Antarctica (No one lives there.)
  - Most countries: Africa (The number changes more often than you might think as areas declare themselves independent. When I last checked, 55 were officially recognized by world organizations.)
  - Fewest countries: Antarctica (There aren't any countries. Different countries have claimed different areas of Antarctica for scientific research.)
  - Longest river and longest desert are in Africa (Nile, Sahara)
  - The highest point in the world is in Ecuador, South America. Mount Chimborazo will put you closest to space. The peak of Mount Everest will put you the highest from sea level. It just depends on how you are measuring.
- o Explore more: Learn other major bodies of waters, seas and lakes.

VI. Discussion
- o Seeds grow plants "after their own kind," meaning the same kind of plant.
- o When we start a new church, we call it a "church plant."
- o What kind of "seeds" do you think need to be planted to grow a church?
- o Remember, a church is not a building! A church is a group of Christians.

VII. Writing
- o Use the discussion question as a writing prompt.
- o Underline all of the verbs. There is at least one in every sentence. Get a high five and/or hug for each one you find.

Day 4 (Check Materials List)

I. Read Genesis 1:14-19.

II. Memory Verse
- o   Genesis 1:1
- o   In the beginning God created the heavens and the earth.

III. Language
- o   Spelling/Handwriting
  - •   verse 16
  - •   words to know: light, heaven, sign, season
  - •   spelling tips:
    - ▪   Heaven and season use the same "ea" spelling but have different sounds.
    - ▪   Light and sign both have "ig" and the i sound. Signs is a hard one. You can think of it as if it was originally sIGHns with an I-G-H and then the H was dropped.
- o   Vocabulary/Grammar
  - •   govern (vs. 16)
  - •   to rule, to be in control over a group of people (verb)
  - •   The noun form of this word would be government.
  - •   A noun is a person, place, or thing.
  - •   A verb is an action or state of being.
- o   Hebrew
  - •   beginning
  - •   re-SHEET (re, with a short e as in red)
  - •   The e will always have this sound unless I write it as a double ee.

IV. Science
- o   Today we are back to learning about light but in a little bit different way. Let's talk about stars, and most specifically, our sun.
  - •   God placed the perfect sized star in the perfect location to light and warm our planet. He set it all in motion so that we have night and day and summer and winter and springtime and harvest.
  - •   God made the star that we call the sun just right to give us what we need. It's not the biggest star. It's little compared to some, but it's just right to give us the light and warmth we need without baking us!
- o   How fast does light travel? When you turn on a light, how long does it take for the light to fill the room?
  - •   Not long! Light is the fastest physical thing in our universe. Nothing is faster. It travels at an astonishing 300 million meters per second. Take one giant step forward. That's about one meter. Now do that 300 million times in one second!
- o   You might be interested to learn that the famous scientist Albert Einstein wrote this famous equation about energy, $E = mc^2$.
  - •   E stands for energy. C stands for the speed of light.

- o That speed gets the sun's light to us, but how does it warm us?
  - • Everything on earth, even those things not on the earth, is made up of a basic building block called the *atom*. They are things you can't see. They build together in different combinations to make something called *molecules*.
    - ▪ A famous atom you've probably heard of is oxygen, part of what we breathe. You can't see the air you breathe, but it's full of atoms!
      - • A famous molecule you've maybe heard of is H_2O. Do you know what that stands for?
        - ▪ It is the scientific name for a water molecule.
      - • Sometimes you'll hear people call water H_2O. That means that in each water molecule there are two H atoms and one O atom. H stands for hydrogen. Can you guess what kind of atom O stands for?
        - ▪ It's oxygen, so one water molecule is made up of two hydrogen atoms and one oxygen atom.
    - ▪ That means there are three atoms in each water molecule. How many water molecules do you think are in one drop of water?
      - • This is an estimate; it really depends on how big your water drop is, but this is to give you an idea of how small molecules are.
      - • Here's an estimation of the number of water molecules in one drop of water: (That's 400 quintillion, 4 with 20 zeros.)

400,000,000,000,000,000,000

- • Of course atoms are smaller. The number of atoms would be three times that amount because there are three atoms in each molecule of water. What are they? Can you figure out what that number would be?
  - ▪ two hydrogen atoms and an oxygen atom
  - ▪ 12 and 20 zeros
- • So, where were we, ah yes, how the sun's light heats the earth. Have you noticed how much hotter it is in the sun than in the shade? Why is that do you think?
- • When light hits those atoms, it gets them excited, which moves them around. That movement is what produces heat. The light is exciting atoms in the ground and in the walls of buildings and in you!
  - ▪ Do you get hot when you get excited? Not sure? Run around crazy and see if you warm up. ☺
  - ▪ When light hits the atoms, it excites them and gets them moving. Those moving atoms create heat. That heat warms the objects on earth and the earth itself.
- o Let me share one more thing about light. Light can bend. When light hits something that it can travel through such as a window or water, it slows the light down. If the light hits the surface at an angle, it will bend.
  - • This is called *refraction*.

- You can see light bend by sticking a pencil into a glass of water.
  - Does the pencil appear bent? Why?
  - We see the light off of the pencil, not the pencil. The light was bent when it entered through the glass and water.
  - o Recall: What are the basic building blocks of everything? atoms; They combine to make what? Molecules, such as H_2O. What's the fastest physical thing in the universe? light; What is it called when light is bent? refraction
  - o Explore more: Learn about refraction. Try a light experiment. Refraction enables us to have magnifying glasses. How do they work?

V. Social Studies
  - o Our Bible verses say that God gave us the lights in the heavens for signs for seasons, days and years.
  - o We know the sun marks the 24-hour days for us.
  - o As the earth moves in its orbit around the sun, the days get longer and shorter. The longest day of the year marks the beginning of summer. The shortest day of the year marks the beginning of winter. Those days are called the *solstice* and people have often celebrated those days, the change of season when the days start getting longer or shorter.
    - Take a look at the world map on Day 2 and find the *equator*. It's the line that goes between the words "Pacific" and "Ocean" and cuts through the top part of South America. It's an imaginary line, but we use it to divide the world in half. We call those halves *hemispheres*. The top half of the map is the northern hemisphere and the bottom half of the map is the southern hemisphere.
    - In which hemisphere do most people live?
      - In the northern hemisphere
  - o How do the stars mark the seasons?
    - There are stars made into connect-the-dot pictures in the sky. We call these *constellations*.
      - The Bible names a few of them in Job: Orion and Bear and Pleiades. You can find Orion because he wears a belt of three stars in a row.
      - These constellations move through the sky as the year goes on. Well, they stay in one place just like the sun, but as the earth moves through its orbit, they appear to move across the sky.
  - o How have stars been used throughout history for signs?
    - We read in the Bible how the wise men saw the sign of a king in the sky. They were among the first worshipers of Jesus because of it.
    - Sailors and other navigators have used the North Star to find their direction.
    - We can also use the sun by day for direction because it rises in the east and sets in the west.
      - Figure out today, by using the sun, which way is north where you live. (If you point east with your right hand and point west with your left hand, you will be facing north.)
  - o Recall: The equator divides the world into two what? What do we call star pictures?
    - hemispheres
    - constellations

      o Explore more: Learn some of the major constellations and how to tell from where they are in the sky what time of year it is.

VI. Discussion
      o The Bible talks about walking in the light and not in the darkness. Jesus is the light of the world. If you are walking in the darkness, you are not walking with Jesus. If you are walking with Jesus, you cannot walk in darkness.
      o What do you think it means to walk in the light?
      o What do you think it means to walk in the darkness?

VII. Writing
      o Use the discussion questions as a writing prompt.
      o Can you include a vocabulary or spelling word? Get a high five and/or hug for each one you include.

Day 5

I.   Read Genesis 1:20.

II. Memory Verse
- o   Test yourselves.
- o   Say from memory Genesis 1:1.

III. Language
- o   Spelling
  - Test yourselves with the words from Days 1-4.
    - formless, void, darkness, moving
    - dry, expanse, separate, seas
    - brought, vegetation, yield, bearing
    - light, heaven, sign, season
- o   Vocabulary
  - Test yourselves with the words from Days 1-4.
    - void – completely empty
    - expanse -- a large, wide, open area of land or water
    - yield – to produce
    - govern – to rule, to be in control over a group of people
- o   Hebrew
  - Test yourselves with the words from Days 1-4.
    - el – o – HEEM, sha-MA-yim, A-rets, re-SHEET
    - God, heaven, earth, beginning

IV. Science
- o   Today we will learn about birds since we read about God creating them.
- o   How do you know something is a bird? Name the characteristics of birds.
- o   Here's my list of what all birds have in common. How does your list compare?
  - feathers, wings, bills/beaks, lay eggs, two legs
  - They do not have to fly. Some birds such as penguins and ostriches do not fly.
  - They are warm blooded, like humans. That means they generate their own body heat.
  - They are *vertebrates*. That means they have a backbone. So do you!
  - A little note about vertebrates and backbones. Each little bone you feel up the spine is called a *vertebra*. By the way, all of them together are *vertebrae*. That's how you write the plural. You say it with an A sound at the end.
- o   How many different types of birds do you think there are?
  - There are around 10,000 different types of birds. I think God is amazingly creative to make so many different types of animals with so many unique features.
- o   I want to tell you about a special bird, the eagle.
- o   Here are two verses about them.
  - Deuteronomy 32:11 Like an eagle that stirs up its nest, That hovers over its young, He spread His wings and caught them, He carried them on His pinions.

- Pinions are the outer part of a bird's wings including the flight feathers.
  - Isaiah 40:31 Yet those who wait for the LORD will gain new strength; They will mount up with wings like eagles, They will run and not get tired, They will walk and not become weary.
- Let's look at these two verses about eagles.
- How does an eagle stir up its nest?
  - First an eagle takes out all of the soft leaves and feathers that it had put in the nest for the babies' comfort.
    - Why do you think it might do that?
    - It needs to teach the baby to fly. It's time for the young bird to leave the nest.
  - Then the mother will hover over the nest, flapping her wings, demonstrating to the young, getting them to copy her. Their first lift off is in the nest with little hops and flaps.
- What about catching her young and carrying it on her wings?
  - When a young bird leaves the nest, a mother eagle can catch her struggling, learning young and raise it up again.
  - There are many who say eagles never do this. We know at least some or some types must have because it's in the Bible. Here is a quote from someone who has seen it happen.
  - "The mother started from the nest in the crags, and roughly handling the young one, she allowed him to drop, I should say, about ninety feet; then she would swoop down under him, wings spread, and he would alight on her back. She would soar to the top of the range with him and repeat the process. . . . My father and I watched this, spellbound, for over an hour." (*Bulletin of the Smithsonian Institution*, 1937, No. 167, p. 302)
- The second verse talks about eagle's wings and relates it to strength and endurance. Eagles can go up to 75 miles per hour. They also rarely flap their wings on long migration trips. How do you think they can fly so far without flapping?
  - They ride the drafts of wind which hold them up under their large wings which can be up to over a meter long each!
- Recall: Names some characteristics of birds: feathers, wings, bills/beaks, lay eggs, two legs; What does it mean that birds are vertebrates? They have a backbone.
- Explore more: Learn bird anatomy and compare and contrast its body systems to those of humans. Or choose another bird to learn about.

V. Social Studies
- Our verse today says that God created "swarms of living creatures." In science we talked about what makes something a bird. Well, what makes something living? What is life?
- What things are alive? Name the types of things that are alive.
  - Basically there are animals and plants. Can you think of what they have in common?
    - Maybe you thought of how they all need energy to live.
- What makes animals and people different from plants?
  - Why will some people eat plants but not animals?

- Are animals more important than plants? Why or why not? If you think one is more important than the other, what would happen if you didn't have the other?
  - What makes animals different from people?
    - Are people more important than animals? Why or why not?
  - Some people think we should have fewer people on earth so that we don't destroy so much of our planet, our natural resources. They think we should have fewer people on earth in order to protect our plants and animals. What do you think?
    - We should care for our world. It's God's creation, but we are only commanded in the Bible to love people. People are most important. Any philosophy that doesn't put people first is not from God.
  - Explore more: Learn about conservation and environmental efforts that are making an impact.

VI. Discussion
  - Think about how eagle's wings help them fly over long distances. They save energy by not flapping.
  - This Bible verse is about God raising up His people on eagle's wings and how they won't grow weary. How do you think eagle's wings relate to how God cares for His children? How do you think God lifts us up and carries us?

VII. Writing
  - Choose one of your writings from Days 2-4 to edit.
  - Read it out loud to look for things that don't make sense, don't flow or just don't sound right.
  - Look for spelling mistakes.
  - Check for correct capitalization and punctuation.
  - You can use an editing checklist to help you look for problems.
  - Have someone older than you check it over once you've fixed it. (You can fix it by just making marks on the page to note changes.)
  - Make your corrections and write a final draft. Rewrite it or type it.

Day 6

I.   Read Genesis 1:21-23.

II. Memory Verse
- o   Psalm 150:6
- o   Let everything that has breath praise the Lord. Praise the Lord!

III. Language
- o   Spelling/Handwriting
  - verse 23
  - words to know: fruitful, multiply, fifth, which
    - Spelling tips:
      - The word <u>fruitful</u> starts with the word fruit. The U sound is spelled with a U-I.
      - <u>Multiply</u> ends with a Y, even though it doesn't say E and it is a longer word. The word ply is spelled P-L-Y and that's how this ends.
      - The word <u>fifth</u> can be spelled just by carefully pronouncing it.
      - The word <u>which</u> has two H's.
- o   Vocabulary/Grammar
  - swarm (verse 21)
  - to abound, teem or be overrun (verb)
  - other definitions: to move about in great numbers, or a great number of things moving about (noun)
- o   Hebrew
  - baRA
  - created

IV. Science
- o   We talked about characteristics of birds. Now, let's talk about fish. What do you think makes something a fish? What do all fish have in common? What can you think of?
- o   Here's my list.
  - live in water, have fins, have scales
  - They are vertebrates. Do you remember what that means? They have a backbone.
  - They are cold blooded which means their body takes on the temperature of their surroundings.
  - They breathe, take in oxygen, through gills, slits that open on the sides of their bodies.
- o   What does the Bible tell us about fish?
  - They were important! Many of Jesus' closest disciples were fishermen. Catching fish was how they made their living and provided for their families. Find Israel on the Middle East map on Day 14. Can you guess why fish was a staple of their diet?
    - Being near water makes fishing accessible, practical and economical.

- Jesus probably ate lots and lots of fish! He cooks and probably eats some after He is raised from the dead (in John 21).
- Fish obey God's commands.
  - Jesus speaks and the fishermen who could catch nothing, suddenly have more fish in their nets than they can handle (in John 21).
  - There is also the story of how Peter finds the coin in the fish's mouth. Jesus tells him to get a fish and that there will be a coin in its mouth, enough to pay the taxes. It happens just like Jesus said. Can you imagine that fish swimming up to Peter to fulfill his calling as coin bearer? Or maybe God just put a coin into whatever fish Peter caught. ☺
  - Probably the most famous fish story in the Bible is found in the book of Jonah. ("For as Jonah was three days and three nights in the belly of a huge fish…" Matthew 12:40) We don't know what kind of fish it was, just that it was big and didn't chew Jonah up. We also know that it obeyed God. It either didn't normally eat people (but did on this occasion out of obedience) or it obeyed and didn't eat Jonah when it wanted to. It also took Jonah where he needed to go and spit him out. Because of the fish's obedience, over 100,000 people repented from their sins! You don't know how your little act of obedience might affect the big picture of God's plan!
  - Note: I'm not saying that the fish had any choice in obeying. The animals have to obey God's command. He has authority over all creation.
    - Some people think Jonah's fish was a kind of whale because they are so big and because there are whales with no teeth! They are enormous, but they eat these teeny creatures called krill. Their mouths have something that's more similar to hair than teeth. It's called baleen. However, whales are not fish. They do not breathe through gills. They have a blowhole on top of their heads and need to get to the surface to breathe air.
  - Let me tell you about one amazing fish, the salmon.
    - Salmon are born in a stream. They grow and then make a long journey to the Bering Strait, up near the Arctic Circle in the waters separating Russia from Alaska. They can swim for several years to get there.
    - When they arrive, they go back home to where they were born. That means that they have to swim upriver, going opposite of the way the river is flowing. They struggle; they jump up and over waterfalls; they fight their way back to their birthplace. They stop for nothing.
    - Why? Because fish obey God, remember? This is what they were created for. They obey their calling despite all the odds against them. They don't let their surroundings or the fact that fish don't swim upstream, against the current, stop them from doing what they are supposed to do.
  - Recall: What are some characteristics of fish?
    - live in water, fins, scales, gills, cold-blooded

34

○ Explore more: Learn fish anatomy and compare and contrast its body systems to those of humans. Or choose another fish to learn about.

V. Social Studies
- ○ One of our verses today says that God created the "great sea monsters." These are probably related to some of what we know of dinosaurs. Even today on rare occasion you can hear about someone seeing or finding a sea monster.
- ○ The most famous modern-day sea monster is the Loch Ness Monster which supposedly lives in Scotland but has never been scientifically documented.
- ○ Here's one image of sea monsters.

Provided by: http://www.strangescience.net
Originally published in: *Buffalo Land*
Now appears in: *Oceans of Kansas* by Michael J. Everhart

- ○ There has long been a fascination with sea monsters, and stories have been told in many cultures of fierce battles with them in the seas.
  - • While most of such stories are considered mythology, since there are so many of these stories, I believe they started somewhere. I believe that sea "monsters" were among the dinosaurs on the earth.
- ○ These animals are since extinct from hunting or changes in their environment. The stories of their impressive frames were passed down and probably changed, as stories tend to be, especially when the stories involve men capturing them or battling them.
  - • I will give more evidence for my belief in a future lesson.
- ○ We are still in "prehistory" in the Bible, before records were kept, but we have the Bible as the most accurate record of truth to guide us in knowledge.
- ○ One ancient record we do have is *fossils*. Fossils are the preserved remains of a once living thing.
- ○ Here are some fossil images: bones and a shell in a rock.

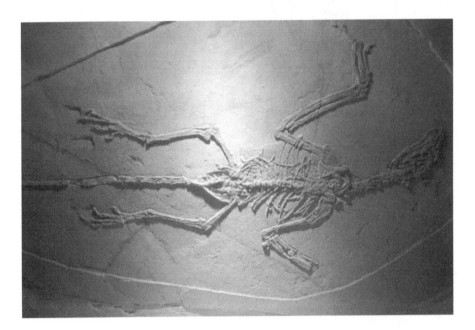

- A little farther into Genesis we'll get to the flood. It was an event that probably dramatically changed the landscape of the world. There have been fossils of marine (or water) animals found in the prairies of America, right in the middle of America, where it's flat and nowhere near water. Fossils have been found that show there used to be water there.
    - While some will say that shows the world has been around for millions of years and has shifted and changed, I say that it shows the earth was covered with water just like the Bible says!
- The record we have from fossils supports what the Bible says, that there was a Creator. There is no evidence, anywhere, that shows the slow development of animals over millions of years where one species ever changed into another, according to the hypothesis of evolution.
- Recall: What is a fossil?
    - It's the preserved remains of a once living thing.

o   Explore more: Learn more about the fossil record and what's been discovered and where. (One thing you won't find is a single fossil record that shows evidence of the evolution of one species to another. This should be unexplainable to those who believe we have millions and millions of years' worth of fossils!) You could alternatively find sea monster tales to read.

VI.   Discussion (2 Choices)
o   How can the salmon inspire you? OR
o   Do you think sea monsters existed? Do you think they exist today?

VII.   Writing
o   A sentence is made up of two parts, a subject and a predicate. The subject is who or what the sentence is about. The subject is a noun: a person, place or thing. The predicate tells us what the subject is or what the subject is doing. The predicate contains the verb.
- Rebecca ate dinner.
  - The subject is "Rebecca." The sentence is about Rebecca.
  - The predicate is everything else, the rest of the sentence. The predicate contains the verb. In this sentence the predicate is "ate dinner."
- The mountains are my favorite picnic spot.
  - What is the subject?
    - The subject is "the mountains."
  - What is the predicate?
    - The predicate is everything else, "are my favorite picnic spot." The verb is "are."
- I saw the cutest puppy ever on my way home.
  - What is the subject?
    - The subject is "I."
  - What is the predicate?
    - The predicate is "saw the cutest puppy ever on my way home."
- Try to identify some subjects and predicates in your writing. Every sentence must have both or it's not a sentence. (I'll tell you the exceptions another time!)
- Complete Writing Sentences 2 in your workbook.

Day 7

I. Read Genesis 1:24-25.

II. Memory Verse
   o Psalm 150:6
   o Let everything that has breath praise the Lord. Praise the Lord!

III. Language
   o Spelling/Handwriting
      • verse 24
      • words to know: creature, beast, ground, kind
      • spelling tips:
         ▪ <u>Creature</u> ends with T-U-R-E. It has the same vowel spelling pattern as breathe.
         ▪ <u>Beast</u> also has that same vowel spelling pattern.
         ▪ The word <u>ground</u> has the same vowel spelling pattern as out.
         ▪ I-N-D is a spelling pattern where the letter i says its name. <u>Kind</u>, bind, mind, find, rind, behind...
   o Vocabulary/Grammar
      • creep (vs. 24)
      • to move slowly and carefully, especially to avoid notice (verb)
      • Sometimes verbs have objects (just like prepositions).
         ▪ What question is answered by the object?
            • what
            • It's on the table. What is it on?
               ▪ the table
               ▪ The table is the objet of the preposition and answers the question on what.
         ▪ What did the earth bring forth?
            • living creatures, or just the noun, creatures
            • <u>Direct objects</u> follow some verbs and answer the question what.
            • Another example: He gave me the book.
               ▪ What is the verb in the sentence, "He gave me the book?"
                  • gave
               ▪ Gave what?
                  • the book
               ▪ In this case "book" is the noun, the object.
         ▪ We call these the direct object. We'll practice more another time.
   o Hebrew
      • Now we will put our words into a memory verse, Genesis 1:1.
         ▪ You can listen to it on our site. Go to the Online Support page and look under Helpful Links.

- Remember: the big letters mean that's where the emphasis is. Here are some English words with their emphasis marked to help you understand: beGIN, TRUMpet, anTICipate.
- In the beginning
  - be reSHEET
- God created
  - baRA eloHEEM
- in the beginning God created
- be reSHEET baRA eloHEEM
  - The "be" means "in" for this sentence.
  - Here, baRA is translated created.

IV. Science
  - Today we are going to learn about insects since our verse speaks of God creating creeping, crawling things. Insects are a type of animal, just like birds and fish. What is an insect? What characteristics are common to all insects? Make your list before you read mine.
  - My list:
    - Insects have three body parts: the head, the abdomen, and the thorax. The abdomen is the stomach. The thorax is where all of the insects' legs are attached.
    - Insects have three pairs of jointed legs. How many legs is that?
      - 6 legs
        - Bugs with more than six legs are not insects.
      - You have jointed legs. That means your legs can bend. Where do you have joints in your legs?
    - Insects can look like maybe they have eight legs, but the other two things you see are antennae. Insects have two antennae on their heads. *Antennae* are used to feel and to smell.
    - Insects have an *exoskeleton*. That means their skeleton, their bones, are on the outside of their body. Basically, they have a hard shell. Where is your skeleton?
      - Let's get sidetracked by the word "exoskeleton" for a minute. It has two parts "exo" and "skeleton." Our skeleton is our bones. What does "exo" mean? We know the word exit. Do you know the word exterior?
        - The exterior of your home is its outside. The exit takes you outside. The exo-skeleton is the skeleton on the outside.
    - Because insects don't have a skeleton like ours, they don't have a backbone. That means they are *invertebrate*, or they have no backbone.
    - Insects have compound eyes. *Compound* means made up of many parts. Compound eyes are sort of like many eyes in one. They have two compound eyes. Each eye has lots and lots of visual receptors, things that take in images. Insects don't see clearly, but they see a lot. It makes them good at detecting movement. Do you find it hard to catch a fly? Do they always see you coming?

- Use what you just learned about insects to figure out where the head of this ant is.

- (Hint: Where are the antennae and legs attached?)

- Recall: Insects have antennae, an exoskeleton, and are invertebrates. What are those things?
  - appendages used for feeling and smelling
  - hard shell—skeleton on the outside
  - no backbone
- Explore more: Learn insect anatomy and compare and contrast its body systems to those of humans. Or learn about a particular insect and its niche.

V. Social Studies
- What do you think?
  - Do you think people are naturally lazy or naturally hard working?
  - Do people in general tend to do what's easiest now or best in the long run?
  - Do people tend to wait until they have to do something to do it or do they plan ahead and get it done early?
- These things are what we call human nature, the way humans behave normally.
  - In the beginning people were perfect, but after Adam and Eve sinned, people weren't perfect any more. The Bible says we are all born sinners! We tend to be lazy if we can get away with it. We need God to save us from our sinful human nature and give us His holy nature by putting His Spirit in us when we are saved.
- In the Bible, the book of Proverbs is to teach us wisdom. God uses the ant to share wisdom with us.
- Proverbs 6:6-8
  Go to the ant, O sluggard,
  Observe her ways and be wise,
  Which, having no chief,
  Officer or ruler,
  Prepares her food in the summer
  And gathers her provision in the harvest.
- A sluggard is a lazy person.
- These verses are saying that the ants are *diligent*.
  - They are hard workers. They don't have anyone telling them to work, but they work anyway and prepare for winter, working ahead of the time to gather the food that is needed.

40

- Do you wait to work until you are told to work? Or do you see the work that needs to be done and take the *initiative* and get it done without being told?
- Diligence and initiative are character qualities that will serve you well in life if you learn them. We can study God's creation and His Word and learn His lessons to live wisely.
- Recall: It may be human nature to be lazy, but we don't have to obey the flesh like that. We can take initiative. What does that mean? What word describes a hard worker who will keep at a job and do their best without someone needing to make sure they are doing their work?
  - seeing work that needs to be done and just doing it
  - diligent
- Explore more: What character traits do you think are part of sinful human nature? What are the opposites of those and how can you cultivate them?

VI. Discussion
- What do you think would happen if God hadn't created insects?
  - Imagine the repercussions, the consequences.
  - Would it make the world a better place or a worse place? Why?

VII. Writing
- Use the discussion question as a writing prompt.
- Underline the verbs.
- Get a high five and/or hug for each one you find.

Day 8

I. Read Genesis 1:26.

II. Memory Verse
- o Psalm 150:6
- o Let everything that has breath praise the Lord. Praise the Lord!

III. Language
- o Spelling/Handwriting
  - • verse 26
  - • words to know: rule, image, likeness, over
  - • Spelling tips:
    - ▪ Rule has the vowel spelling with a silent E at the end of the word. U_E spelling pattern.
      - • Vowel consonant E is a familiar spelling pattern which makes the first vowel say its name.
    - ▪ Image ends with the word age. When a G is followed by an I or an E it has its soft sound. (J instead of G)
    - ▪ Likeness is the word like with the suffix, the ending -NESS.
    - ▪ The word over is spelled with the O_E spelling pattern.
- o Vocabulary/Grammar
  - • dimension (I chose this word for today.)
  - • measurement, or an aspect of something (noun)
- o Hebrew
  - • In the beginning God created the heavens and the earth.
  - • be reSHEET baRA eloHEEM et ha shaMAyim ve et ha Arets
  - • Today work on "In the beginning God created the heavens."
    - ▪ be reSHEET baRA eloHEEM et ha shaMAyim
  - • In the sentence, "ha" is "the".

IV. Science
- o Today we're going to learn about some other creeping things, arachnids. (You say that a-rack-nids.)
  - • What are those?
  - • The most commonly known arachnid is the spider. What do you know about spiders? What makes them different than insects?
    - ▪ My list:
      - • Different from insects
        - ▪ eight legs
        - ▪ no antennae
        - ▪ two body parts (head and body)
        - ▪ none have wings
        - ▪ Insects are mostly *herbivores*, meaning they eat plants.
        - ▪ Arachnids are mostly *carnivores*, meaning they eat animals.

- How do you think arachnids might be the same as insects?
  - Same as insects
    - exoskeleton
    - invertebrates
    - cold blooded
    - They do have appendages for sensing; they just aren't the same as antennae.
- Can you guess what else might be an arachnid, besides spiders?
- Here are some: ticks, mites, and scorpions.
  - Are arachnids in the Bible?
    - They are. Well, for one, the Israelites, under the Old Covenant are told not to eat them. Under the New Covenant, you can! Yuck!
    - A couple of times in the Bible you will read references to spider webs. Spiders build their webs with a strong, fine silk that comes from their abdomen. It is very strong for how thin it is, but you can just knock it down with one swipe.
    - Job 27:18 says, "He has built his house like the spider's web..." What do you think this verse might be saying?
      - In context the verse means that the godless think they have built a strong future for themselves and can protect and provide for themselves, but really it's all just as fragile as a spider's web.
  - Are there other arachnids in the Bible?
    - There are scorpions mentioned in several places. Mostly, it's about scorpions stinging! They have a venomous sting which means they put poison in your body when they sting you. It hurts and can even kill you.
      - They live in hot climates. We had two in our home in Istanbul. One we trapped. One was very small, maybe an inch and a half long, and I squashed it! Yuck again!
    - "He led you through the great and terrible wilderness, with its fiery serpents and scorpions and thirsty ground where there was no water; He brought water for you out of the rock of flint." Deuteronomy 8:15
      - Why do you think the serpents and scorpions are called "fiery?"
      - "Fiery" here I think refers to the fact that they are poisonous, not that they were on fire!
  - God gives Paul protection from a poisonous snake that doesn't harm him. (Acts 28)
  - Remember, we don't have to be afraid. Our God made the world and it's in His control. Even in the verse from Deuteronomy, we read that though it was a "terrible" place, God was able to take care of them there, even giving them water from a rock when there was no other way for them to get water.
  - Recall: What type of animal is a scorpion?
    - an arachnid
  - Explore more: Learn about a different type of arachnid.

V. Social Studies
  - I asked you on Day 7 what you thought were the repercussions, the consequences, of a world without insects. There would be repercussions because the world was created *interdependent*.
  - Interdependence is how things depend on each other. Let me give you an example.

- My family loves to eat pizza. It's a big treat. What are we dependent on for that pizza?
    - We are dependent on the store to have workers to make and sell us the pizza.
    - The store is dependent on their ingredient suppliers and their equipment suppliers.
    - They are dependent on the electric and water companies to supply them with electricity and water.
    - The ingredient suppliers are dependent on those who prepare the ingredients.
    - They are dependent on the farmers who are growing the tomatoes for the sauce and the wheat to make the flour for the crust and who are milking the cows that give us the cheese.
    - All of those people are dependent on trucks and truck drivers who carry these ingredients and supplies where they need to go.
    - And the plants are dependent on the sun and the rain or irrigation (watering) system.
    - I'm sure I didn't think of everything. Can you see how there is interdependence? How everything depends on other things?
  - Why don't you try an example? Look around your home. Choose something in your home that you or your family depends on. What is the "web of interdependence?" What are all the things and who are all the people that are dependent on each other to provide you what you depend on! How many things can you think of?
  - How are you dependent on members of your family? your community? your leaders?
  - Recall: What does interdependence mean? Things are dependent on each other.
  - Explore more: Learn what goes into the manufacturing and exporting/transporting of a product you rely on.

VI. Discussion
  - God likes it when we rely on Him. He wants us to depend on Him. We should never think that we are alone or need to do something alone. Jesus promises His people that He will always be with us. We are also told that angels are camped out around us. We are not alone.
    - When my daughter was two, she asked why these two men always came on the bus with her and my husband when they went to the Roma community where we would eventually start a church plant. When she asked, they were the only ones at the bus stop. We never saw what she saw. We knew they must be angels sent with them.
  - We are dependent on God to take care of us and to provide for us each and every day. That's why we need to be thankful every day.
  - Think of all the ways we are dependent on God and thank Him for each one.
    - Here are some ideas to get you started: the sun, day and night, your functioning body, eyes that know how to clean themselves, your family He placed you in...what are all the ways we are dependent on God just for the food we eat each day?

VII.   Writing
- o   Use the discussion question as a writing prompt.
- o   Can you find a prepositional phrase or direct object in what you wrote?
- o   Can you include a vocabulary or spelling word? Get a high five and/or hug for each one you include.

Day 9

I. Read Genesis 1:27-31.

II. Memory Verse
- o Psalm 150:6
- o Let everything that has breath praise the Lord. Praise the Lord!

III. Language
- o Spelling/Handwriting
  - verse 29
  - words to know: subdue, surface, earth, sky
  - The word <u>subdue</u> starts with sub and ends with due, like when a book is due at the library. The U sound is written U-E.
  - The word <u>surface</u> ends with the word face. Just like with G, when a C is followed by an I or an E, it has its soft sound. In face, the C says Ssss because it is followed by an E. The beginning of this word starts like surfboard. There are several ways to write the UR sound. This is spelled U-R.
  - The word <u>earth</u> starts with the word ear.
  - The word <u>sky</u> follows all the phonics rules.
- o Vocabulary
  - subdue (verse 28)
  - to bring under control (verb)
- o Hebrew
  - In the beginning God created the heavens and the earth. Practice the whole thing today.
  - be reSHEET baRA eloHEEM et ha shaMAyim ve et ha Arets
  - The "ve" is the "and" in the sentence.

IV. Science
- o We have another group of animals to learn about today. You belong to this one! Do you know what it's called?
  - mammals
- o What makes an animal a mammal? What are their characteristics? A dolphin is a mammal. What do you have in common with a dolphin?
- o My list:
  - We are vertebrates. We all have spines, backbones.
  - We are warm blooded. Our body temperatures are regulated by our bodies. We stay about the same temperature whether it's warm or cold outside.
  - We breathe with lungs.
  - We give birth to babies.
  - Mothers have milk for their babies. This sets up a different relationship between mother and child. The child spends more time with its mother and learns survival skills from the mother.
  - This one would be hard to guess from a dolphin, but mammals have hair or fur at some point in their life cycle.
- o There are more than 4,000 different species of mammals.

- The smallest is the hog-nosed bat, which weighs 0.05 ounces (1.42 grams).
  - That weighs about as much as one and a half paper clips!
- The largest is the blue whale, which can be 100 feet long (30.5 meters) and weigh 15 tons (300,000 pounds or 136,000 kilograms). (from http://kids.sandiegozoo.org/animals/mammals, conversions added)
  - That's about the same as seven and a half cars!
- As you can see, from a bat to a whale to humans, mammals are a very diverse group.
- What are some mammals in Scripture and what can we learn about them? Here are some mentioned: dogs, deer, pigs, bears, lions, goats, donkeys, sheep, horses, camels, leopards, antelope, rats and wolves.
- Let's look at sheep because the Bible compares us to sheep!
  - The Bible talks a lot about sheep either following or getting lost.
- Jesus says that His sheep know His voice and follow (John 10:27).
  - I've seen a flock following its shepherd. I didn't even hear him make a noise, but he might have. He just walked past the small flock, they were just standing around, and when he passed, they just turned and followed him. It was so amazing to me.
- Sheep have a very strong *instinct* to follow. They follow the sheep in front of them even if they are leading them into danger. Instinct is a natural reaction you have to do something; you do it with without thinking about it.
  - You blink instinctively when something comes near your eyes. You don't have to decide to blink.
  - Following the leader is instinctive in sheep.
- Here's an interesting sheep fact. Their peripheral vision is so great that they can see behind themselves.
- *Peripheral vision* is what you can see to the sides when you are looking directly forward.
  - How's your peripheral vision? Hold a finger up in front of your face. Stare straight ahead. Move your finger slowly to the side, around the side of your face. How long can you still see it? Make sure you keep looking forward.
- Recall: What are some of the characteristics of mammals? warm-blooded, vertebrates, live babies (as opposed to eggs), moms have milk for their babies, hair
- Explore more: Choose a mammal to learn all about.

V. Social Studies
  - There is actually a lot in the Bible about sheep.
  - They are a main animal sacrificed in the Old Testament. God required a one-year-old male sheep without blemish to be sacrificed. It had to be perfect.
  - Those blood sacrifices were for the forgiveness of sins. The Bible teaches that sin brings death. The only way to receive forgiveness is if there is death, the shedding of blood. God is holy. We have an awesome, holy God.
  - Let's look at sheep in the Bible.
    - All of us like sheep have gone astray, each of us has turned to his own way; but the Lord has caused the iniquity of us all to fall on Him. Isaiah 53:6
    - "I am the good shepherd; the good shepherd lays down His life for the sheep." John 10:11
  - What are these verses about?

- We call Jesus, the Lamb of God (John 1:29). He took our sins on Himself and died for us. He shed His blood so that we could have forgiveness of sins and live forever with Him.
  - Why?
    - Because He loves us!
- Ancient civilizations had sacrifices as part of their false religions. Some required humans to be sacrificed to appease their gods.
  - Of course, their gods were demons, and they did want humans to die because it's Satan's job description to steal, kill, and destroy (John 10:10).
- I want to point out that God doesn't desire us to sacrifice in this way. It was only required because it was necessary.
  - He says Himself that He desires love and obedience from us, not sacrifice. In 1 Samuel 15:22, Samuel says, ""Has the LORD as much delight in burnt offerings and sacrifices as in obeying the voice of the LORD? Behold, to obey is better than sacrifice..."
- Now, blood sacrifices are no longer necessary because Jesus was the final sacrifice. He was perfect and his death took the place of ours. We no longer have to die because He died for us. We can live forever with God in heaven.
- Explore more: What false gods are mentioned in the Bible? How did people view them? worship them? sacrifice to them? hope from them?

VI. Discussion (two choices)
  - How are humans like sheep and Jesus like a shepherd?   OR
  - God created a "good" earth. Do you think the earth is still "good"? Why or why not?

VII. Writing
  - Use the discussion question as a writing prompt.
  - Get a high five and/or hug if you write cheerfully.

Day 10

I. Read Genesis 2:1-3.

II. Memory Verse
- o Test yourselves on Psalm 150:6.
    - • Let everything that has breath praise the Lord. Praise the Lord!
- o Review Genesis 1:1.
    - • In the beginning God created the heavens and the earth.

III. Language
- o Spelling/Handwriting
    - • You can write your memory verse today.
    - • Test yourselves with words from Days 6-10.
        - ▪ fruitful, multiply, fifth, which
        - ▪ creature, beast, ground, kind
        - ▪ rule, image, likeness, over
        - ▪ subdue, surface, earth, sky
- o Vocabulary
    - • Test yourselves with words from Days 6-10.
        - ▪ swarm - to abound, teem, to be overrun
        - ▪ creep - to move slowly and carefully, especially to avoid notice
        - • dimension - measurement, or an aspect of something
        - • subdue - to bring under control
- o Hebrew
    - • Say Genesis 1:1 in Hebrew. What does it say?
        - ▪ be reSHEET baRA eloHEEM et ha shaMAyim ve et ha Arets
    - • The "et" shows that what follows is a direct object. We don't have the equivalent of this in English, though, it is found in some other languages. You don't have to fully understand this to be able to memorize the verse. (Direct object: God created what? heavens, earth)

IV. Science
- o We talked about the sun a little on Day 4, about how it lights our world and gives warmth and energy. Today let's talk about the other "light" in the sky; we call it the moon.
- o The moon is really no light at all. It reflects the light of the sun. The sun lights our days and our nights.
- o I think we need a demonstration. Gather three people or three balls or three other objects.
    - • One is the sun; one is the moon; one is the earth.
- o The sun stands still. We call the sun the center of the solar system. Everything revolves, or *orbits*, around the sun.
- o The moon orbits the earth, meaning it goes around the earth. It draws a circle around the earth. It takes a little less than a month to go around once.
- o The earth's daily spin gives us night and day. How many hours does it take for the earth to spin around one time?

- It takes 24 hours for it to turn around once which is why our days are 24 hours long.
- Who or whatever is playing earth, turn around once, slowly. When your front is to the sun, that's day. When your back is to the sun, that's night.
- Turn around again and look at the moon this time. Do you see how the moon would rise and set like the sun because of the earth's spin? Just like with the sun you are looking toward the moon or away from it. As the earth rotates, it comes into view and "rises."

  o From earth we only see one side of the moon.
  - Have your moon travel once around the earth. Go around one time making sure to always face the earth with your face (or with the same side).
  - Do you see how you turned yourself around in order to face the earth? The moon spins around one time as it makes its one-month orbit, keeping us from seeing what they call the "far side" of the moon.
  - Now can you put it all together? The sun stays still and the earth spins and orbits the sun and the moon orbits the earth. The earth orbits the sun one time a year. The moon orbits the earth about thirteen times a year. Don't get dizzy!

  o Now what about the different shapes of the moon? We have a new moon, a "thumbnail" moon, a crescent moon, a half moon, a three-quarters moon, and a full moon every month.
  - Can you draw a picture or act out the moon's orbit to figure out what makes us see the moon as these different shapes? Here's a hint. Remember that we see light. We can only see the part of the moon that the sun's light reflects off of.

  o Did you figure it out? The sun stays still. Only one side of the moon is getting hit with light from the sun.
  - Take your moon. Put the moon between the earth and the sun. (Moon, face the earth.)
    - Right now, the earth sees the new moon. It's all dark. The earth can't see the side of the moon facing the sun. Half of the moon is always lit up by the sun, but earth can't always see that side.
    - Let the moon start orbiting the earth. Stop and observe. What half of the moon is getting light from the sun? What can the earth see of the bright half of the moon? Earth can see part of it, and then finally all of it, and then it starts disappearing again.
    - Can you observe that?

  o Draw a picture of it too if that would help. I think it might.
  o Recall: What is called when the moon goes around the earth or the earth goes around the sun? orbit
  o Explore more: Learn the names of the phases of the moon. Learn the time lengths of the moon's and the earth's orbits. What do astronauts experience on the dark side of the moon?

V. Social Studies
  o In today's Scripture we read that God rested. He established a day of rest for His people, the Israelites or the Jews, where they could do no work. It was against the law to do any work that wasn't necessary for life. I had a Jewish friend who ripped off

toilet paper the day before the Sabbath, the day of rest, so she wouldn't have to work on the Sabbath! When Jesus began His ministry, He spent a lot of time defying Sabbath laws, showing that people are more important than rules. (Remember how God puts people first?)

- o What does it mean for Christians that God rested?
    - Hebrews 4:3 tells us that God's works were finished from the foundation of the world. He was done by the time it began!
    - On the cross Jesus says, "It is finished." His work was done. Our salvation was accomplished.
    - Paul talks about working to take hold of what we already have. Our salvation, our deliverance, our provision, our healing, everything we need, was accomplished for us. It was finished. We receive it on faith by the grace of God. When His kingdom is realized on earth, we will have perfected salvation and will have perfect rest in all these things.
- o Can I tell you a famous story about rest?
    - Christians used to call Sundays a day of rest and would not work on that day.
    - That's why things are more likely to be closed on Sundays. You don't see that much anymore, but back in 1924, there was an Olympic athlete, a runner named Eric Liddell. He was expected to win the 100-meter race, but he didn't run it. The race was on a Sunday and He wanted to honor God by not working. He went to church instead.
    - His country was upset! (He was British.) He was supposed to win them a gold medal. People didn't understand!
    - He ended up being placed in another race, the 400-meter race, a race four times as long and a race that he hadn't trained for. He won the gold. Someone reminded him that the Bible says God will honor those who honor Him.
    - No matter what you believe about physically resting on the Sabbath, Eric's heart was right before God and God blessed him for it.
    - The Jews' Sabbath is on Saturday, it goes from sundown on Friday to sundown on Saturday.
    - The Muslim Sabbath is on Friday. In Muslim countries businesses would be closed on Friday, not Sunday.
        - Even if shops aren't closed on Friday in Muslim countries, they are likely to be closed around noon, during the time for the midday prayer.
        - I've even seen whole grocery stores close for prayer time! Can you imagine seeing a grocery store close in America because all of the workers were praying?
        - In Islam there are five prayer times a day, but the Friday midday prayers are considered the most important, and so fewer skip those than at other times.
- o Recall: What do we call the day of rest? Sabbath
- o Explore more: What are the Jewish Sabbath laws established in the Old Testament? Or, study the Sabbath rest as it is taught in the book of Hebrews.

VI. Discussion
- o   What do you think God does when He rests? OR
- o   Read Hebrews 4. Here's a bit, verse 10. "For the one who has entered His rest has himself also rested from his works, as God did from His." What do you think it means that we can rest from our works? Do you think it's related to Ephesians 2:8? "For by grace you have been saved through faith; and that not of yourselves, it is the gift of God."

VII. Writing
- o   Use the discussion questions as a writing prompt.
- o   Can you include a prepositional phrase or direct object, a vocabulary or spelling word? Get a high five and/or hug for each one you include.

Day 11

I. Read Genesis 2:4-6.

*Genesis 2 is the story of man, beginning with his creation. It's not retelling the whole creation, just the events surrounding man's creation. In the next verses God creates man and the food that will feed them in the garden.

II. Memory Verse
- o Genesis 1:2
- o The earth was formless and void, and darkness was over the surface of the deep, and the Spirit of God was moving over the surface of the waters.

III. Language
- o Spelling/Handwriting:
  - • verse 4
  - • Words to know: shrub, sprouted, creation, mist
  - • Spelling tips:
    - ▪ The word <u>shrub</u> has one syllable, so it has one vowel sound.
    - ▪ You can hear the word "out" inside <u>sprouted</u>.
      - • Sprouted has the same OU spelling pattern as ground.
    - ▪ The word <u>creation</u> has the word eat in it.
      - • It ends with "ation," which you'll find in the word nation and station.
    - ▪ The word <u>mist</u> is spelled just like it sounds.
- o Vocabulary
  - • mist
  - • a cloud of tiny water droplets near the earth's surface (noun)
  - • What is a noun?
    - ▪ a person, place, or thing
    - ▪ could be the name of a person, place, or thing
- o Hebrew
  - • Say Genesis 1:1.
    - ▪ be reSHEET baRA eloHEEM et ha shaMAyim ve et ha Arets
  - • chaos
  - • TOhu va VOhu (long o and long u sounds – This is fun to say.)
  - • They can be translated together as chaos or you can take the words separately and translate them as formless and void.

V. Science
- o Today we're talking about water.
- o We learned the word mist. The definition says that mist is a cloud of tiny water droplets. In fact, that's what clouds are, water! Clouds are water in the air, in the form of tiny water droplets. We'll learn more about this in just a minute.
- o When there's a mist, you can walk through a cloud. It's kind of like damp air! When you are in fog, which is a heavy, thick mist, you are moving through a cloud.
- o The verse today says that there was no rain. How could that be?
- o What makes rain?

- Rain is part of a water recycling plan God created. Water was created. We cannot make water. All the water we will ever have was created in the beginning. We use the same water over and over again.
  - Water on the earth heats up in the sun which *evaporates* it, turns it into a vapor, a gas. The gas floats up. You see this when you heat up water on your stove. The water turns into steam and right above the pot is the water vapor. You can see it, but it's a gas at that point, not a liquid. It floats up away from the pot, right?
  - The water was heated up and turned into a gas. The gas, or water vapor, travels up. The higher you get in the atmosphere, the cooler it gets. The cool air cools the water vapor and turns it back into water droplets.
  - When you see a cloud, you are seeing billions of water droplets. They are so small at this point that there are more than 100 million water droplets in a cubic meter.
    - Stretch your arms out to the side. If you were carrying a box that big with a cloud inside, you would be carrying about 100 million water droplets.
  - The water droplets start joining together, getting bigger and bigger. These bigger droplets are easier to see and make the clouds look darker. Can you understand how that would happen?
    - The droplets at first are too small to even be seen by humans. But as the droplets join together, they get bigger and bigger until they become…? Did you guess what they become?
  - They join together to make bigger and bigger drops until they fall as rain. When it rains, that water returns to earth. It was water as a liquid, then as a gas, then as a liquid again. We call this the water cycle.
    - Can you draw a diagram of it?
      - water on earth evaporating
      - traveling up as a gas
      - cooling and condensing into water droplets
      - falling as rain
  - It takes really cold temperatures in the atmosphere to freeze the rain into ice because they are just so tiny, but the water droplets can become ice crystals in the sky. What do you think happens when ice crystals start forming together?
    - Snow!
  - You can make water vapor by boiling water. You can hold a plate (use an oven mitt) over the steam (water vapor) to catch some of the water in the air. If you have a pot with a glass lid, you can watch the water boil, and then watch as the water vapor rises up and condenses on the lid. That means you can watch it turn from liquid, to gas as steam, then turn back into water droplets on the lid of your pot.
  - Water vapor cooling and becoming a water droplet again is called *condensation*.
    - That's what you caught on the plate above the steam or on the lid over the pot. When the water rose, it cooled and turned into water droplets.
  - You can also observe *evaporation* by placing a plate out in the sun with a puddle of water on it. The water will disappear.
    - Of course we know it didn't disappear. It just changed. Where did the water go?
      - It traveled. Which direction?
        - Up!

- o The process of water changing through evaporation and condensation is called the *water cycle.*
- o Recall: What is the word that describes the process of water heating up and turning into vapor? evaporation   What happens during condensation? Water vapor cools until it becomes a liquid again.
- o Explore more: What are the different types of rains? What causes them? What different atmospheric conditions produce different types of precipitation?

V. Social Studies
- o For most of history, agriculture, or farming, was the main way of life for most people on earth. (Spelling note: agriculture is a word that uses the T-U-R-E spelling pattern.)
- o Things were perfect in the beginning. Adam still cultivated the land, but the land worked with Adam. Farming is hard work and nature can seem to be working against you. Bugs, too much rain, too little rain, weeds, even plant diseases can all ruin crops. The land was not yet cursed from sin, and so things worked perfectly.
- o We'll read a bit later that God walked with Adam and Eve in the garden. They had a Father talking to them, teaching them.
- o Non-biblical histories speak of cavemen who don't even use words to communicate and how it would take thousands of years to develop language and each advancement. But we know that Adam and Eve had a Father teaching them!

VI. Discussion
- o If you were the creator of the earth, what would you have created? What do you think would be the outcome of your new creation?

VII. Writing
- o Use the discussion question as a writing prompt.
- o Today you are going to be sentence spotting.
- o A sentence has a subject and predicate.
- o A fragment is just a fragment, a piece, of a sentence.
  - • According to you!
  - • That's something you might say, but it's not a sentence. It's just a piece of a sentence.
  - • That's true according to you. That's a complete sentence.
- o Don't forget what you've also learned about sentences. What do they begin and end with?
  - • capital letter
  - • ending punctuation (. ! ?)
- o Complete the Writing Sentences 3 page in your workbook.

Day 12

I.   Read Genesis 2:7-9.

II. Memory Verse
- o   Genesis 1:2
- o   The earth was formless and void, and darkness was over the surface of the deep, and the Spirit of God was moving over the surface of the waters.

III. Language
- o   Spelling/Handwriting
  - • verse 8
  - • words to know: breath, breathed, nostrils, being
  - • Spelling tip:
    - ▪ <u>Breath</u> has the same vowel spelling pattern as heaven. They have the short vowel sound.
    - ▪ Breath and <u>breathe</u> are very similar. The verb, breathe, ends with "the." It's spelled with the same vowel spelling pattern, but now it says E. This is like our word seas.
      - • The words read (reed) and read (red) are both spelled EA, but they are pronounced differently with both the short and long vowel sounds.
    - ▪ <u>Nostrils</u> has nothing fancy to it, no double letters. Just pronounce it like it is spelled – nos-trils – say that short I sound (like in hit).
    - ▪ <u>Being</u> is the word BE and the suffix ING.
- o   Vocabulary
  - • midst
  - • in the middle of (a noun)
  - • Look at this phrase from the verse: in the midst.
    - ▪ The word "in" is a preposition. It's a locator word, telling us where something is.
    - ▪ "In the midst" is a prepositional phrase.
    - ▪ What's the object of the preposition? In the what?
      - • midst
      - • Midst is the object of the preposition.
    - ▪ It's followed by another prepositional phrase, "of the garden."
    - ▪ The words *in* and *of* are the prepositions (others include on, by, around, beside…). They usually are telling us where something is.
    - ▪ What's the object of the preposition? Of the what?
      - • garden
      - • Garden is the object of the preposition.
- o   Hebrew
  - • Say Genesis 1:1.
    - ▪ be reSHEET baRA eloHEEM et ha shaMAyim ve et ha Arets
  - • darkness
  - • KHOshekh (Long o and short e sounds – The KH/kh is a sound that comes out sort of like you are clearing your throat. It is sort of like a k and h mixed

together. If you make a k sound on its own, you'll find it happens in your throat. Try to make a k sound deeper down in your throat. Now add a strong h sound along to that.)

IV. Science
- o Today we read about God breathing into Adam and giving him breath, life.
- o Let's start learning about our amazing bodies.
- o Today we are going to learn about breathing. In our body it's called the *respiratory system*. That's the system set up in our body that enables us to respire or breathe.
- o All of your body systems act instinctively. You don't have to think about. You just breathe.
- o You take your first breath after you are born. In your mother's womb your lungs were full of amniotic fluid, the liquid you were floating in. Once your body hit the air, you knew it was time to breathe. You just did it.
  - • Moms will be interested to learn that the labor process of contractions actually compresses the baby and helps squeeze the fluid out of the lungs so it's ready for that breath.
  - • Humans breathe oxygen which we get from the air, but a yet-unborn baby gets its oxygen from its blood. It has extra blood vessels that we don't have.
  - • All of these changes, to go from fluid to air in the lungs, happen at just the right time, all naturally.
- o I mentioned we breathe oxygen that we get from the air. How does that happen?
- o What is oxygen?
  - • We mentioned before that oxygen is an atom. It's the O in H_2O. There are aluminum atoms that together make up aluminum cans. They are a metal. Oxygen is a gas, like water vapor is a gas. It's in the air. You can't see air. You can't see the oxygen. You can capture it though. A blown-up balloon is full of gases. You can close a plastic zipper bag and trap air inside. You can't see it, but you can feel that there is something inside.
  - • Oxygen makes up about twenty percent of the earth's *atmosphere*, the layer of gases between the earth and space. That means if your hand was the earth and your fingers the atmosphere only one of your fingers would be oxygen. Most of the atmosphere, the air we breathe, is actually a gas called nitrogen, but it's only oxygen that our body needs. The rest gets breathed back out.
- o Where does the oxygen go?
  - • How do you take in oxygen?
  - • We take in oxygen through our noses and through our mouths. The air goes through your trachea or windpipe. If that gets blocked, that's when you choke.
  - • The air then goes into our lungs.
    - ▪ Can you fill your lungs? What do you feel expanding?
  - • Your diaphragm works to force air in and out of your lungs. Your diaphragm is a muscle that expands and contracts to pull in more air and then force it out of the lungs.
  - • There are 600 million alveoli (al – vee – oh – lie) in your lungs, little air sacs that fill with air when you breathe.

- From the alveoli the oxygen is taken into the blood stream and delivered to your heart where the oxygenated blood is pumped back out and then delivered all through your body.
  - What happens to the oxygen?
    - The oxygen is used in our bloodstream. When we breathe out, we aren't breathing out oxygen, but gases our bodies don't need.
  - Recall: What's the name of the body system that regulates our breathing?
    - respiratory system
  - Explore more: Learn more about lungs. What are alveoli and what is their job?

VI. Social Studies
  - Today we are going to learn about the compass rose.

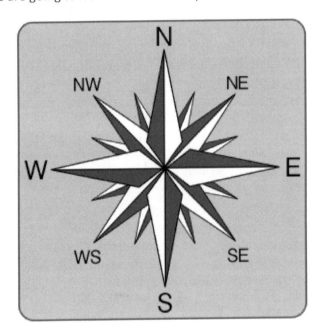

  - The compass rose is the marking on a map that shows which direction is north, south, east, and west. Typically maps are made with north pointing up.
    - What would a map look like if east was pointing up? south? west?
    - Pick a direction and draw a map of the world or your country with the new direction at the top (instead of north pointing up). That map would be just as correct, as long as your compass rose was accurate in telling you which direction was north.
  - We call countries that are part of the Orient, the Far East. Those are countries like China and Japan. Could they be called the Far West? How?
  - There is also a place known as the Middle East. Look at the map for Day 3. Can you find the Far East (look for China)? Where do you think is the Middle East?
    - Middle East countries include Saudi Arabia, Israel, Turkey, Iraq, Iran, Egypt, among others. You can look at the map for Day 14.
  - Recall: What does a compass rose tell us? which way on the map is north
  - Explore more: Learn the countries of the Middle East. What is that part of the world known for? What are the major religions, cultural attitudes, foods, exports, etc.?

VII. Discussion
- We talked about what makes something living and what makes a person different from an animal. Today's question is: when does a person become a person?
  - In our lesson we learned about a baby getting oxygen before it was born, the instinctive body systems at work.
  - When is a person a person?
    - A baby starts as just two cells.
    - A week later they are attached to the mother and the systems that protect the baby are being put in place.
    - A week later the brain, heart, and other organs start to form.
    - By the next week the heart is pumping and the very beginnings of the baby's form take shape.
    - By the next week (5 by how I'm counting, 7 by how they count in a 40- week gestation period) the baby's brain is rapidly growing and it starts getting facial features and little paddles where arms and hands are developing.
    - Two months later the baby can hear you.
- So, when is a person a person?

VIII. Writing
- Use the discussion question as a writing prompt.
- Underline the nouns in your writing.
  - A noun a person, place, or thing, but also the name of a person, place or thing.
- In your writing can you find a prepositional phrase such as "in the _____"?
- If you use a prepositional phrase, which noun is the object of the preposition?

Day 13

I.   Read Genesis 2:10-14.

II.   Memory Verse
    o   Genesis 1:2
        ● The earth was formless and void, and darkness was over the surface of the deep, and the Spirit of God was moving over the surface of the waters.

III. Language
    o   Spelling/Handwriting
        ● verse 14
        ● words to know: third, fourth, river, flows (adventurous kids could try--Tigris, Assyria, Euphrates)
        ● Spelling tip:
            ▪ Third is the ordinal number for three. The "er" sound is spelled with an I-R.
            ▪ Fourth is the ordinal number for four and begins with the word four, as in the number four, which ends with the word our, as in our house.
            ▪ River looks like it should say RIGH – ver.
            ▪ Flows has the same O sound as row and blow.
    o   Vocabulary
        ● divide (verse 10)
        ● separate into parts (used as a verb)
        ● other definition: disagree or cause to disagree
    o   Hebrew
        ● Say Genesis 1:1.
            ▪ be reSHEET baRA eloHEEM et ha shaMAyim ve et ha Arets
        ● face
        ● pnaa (Remember that I'm using double vowels to indicate the long vowel sound. That means this is pronounced, pnay, rhymes with day.)

IV.   Science
    o   We're not going to learn about rivers flowing today. We will do that another day, but I want to talk about another kind of flow. On Day 12 we learned that the blood in our body transports the oxygen to all of the places it's needed. Let's learn about how the heart works to supply our bodies with blood. This is called the *circulatory system*.
    o   The main *organ* that functioned in the respiratory system was your lungs.
    o   The main organ that functions in the circulatory system is your heart.
    o   Place your right hand on your chest. Can you feel your heart beating? If not, run around and then try again.
    o   You can also feel the blood moving through your body. Place two fingers across your wrist and press a little. Do you feel something? (You can also try with two fingers on the side of your neck.)
        ● What did you feel? It was a pulse. You didn't feel a constant rush. You felt it and then didn't, felt it, then didn't. We call this our pulse. ☺

- The smaller the animal (that's you) the faster the pulse.
    - When you felt your heart beating, it was pulsing. It doesn't just constantly push out. It sends out blood in bursts.
- With each pulse your heart is beating. What's happening when your heart beats? It's moving blood in and out.
- Your heart has four chambers: the right and left atrium and the right and left ventricle. You can take a look at the picture on the next page.
    - Blood enters into the right atrium and then ventricle and is pumped into the lungs where it picks up oxygen and gets rid of carbon dioxide.
    - Then it comes back into the heart through the left atrium and ventricle and the out through the aorta and into the body.
- Look at the inside of your wrist. Can you see blueish lines? Those are *veins.* Your veins carry the blood throughout your whole body. It's like a road system in your body. It starts with a large tube at the heart, an artery called the aorta, which sends out the blood with oxygen in it. It branches out to smaller arteries and then capillaries which deliver the blood. The blood then returns through our veins. There is lower blood pressure in our veins so that the blood is pushed in the right direction, moving it back to the heart to get re-oxygenated.
- I used a lot of new words there. *Arteries* are the main branches of the circulatory system. The aorta is like a highway and the other arteries are the exit ramps. The capillaries are the final destinations, and the veins bring it all back home.
- Do you know the word pressure? Press lightly on your leg with your finger. That is low pressure, just a little bit. Now press hard! That's high pressure.
- Imagine you put a straw in your mouth that was full of water and pointed it up to the sky so the water didn't fall out. If you blew very gently, how would the water go out of the straw? What if you blew really hard, with a lot of pressure?
    - Blowing with low pressure would make the water trickle out and blowing with high pressure would make the water shoot out.
    - Blood has pressure. It is pumped out of the heart and forced through the body. We want to have low blood pressure. We want our heart to not have to work too hard to do its job.
    - If we have high blood pressure, then our body has to work hard to do its job. That might mean that our arteries are clogged up.
    - We keep our arteries clear with good nutrition. That's for another day.
- Recall: What's the name of the system in our bodies that regulates our blood flow? circulatory system   What is the name of the main braches of our circulatory system? arteries
- Explore more: Learn what happens in the heart's four chambers. What affects blood pressure?

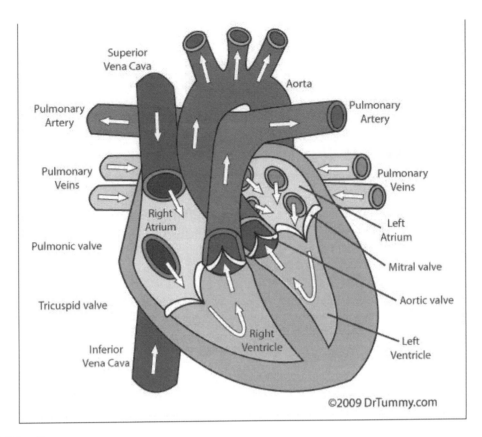

Superior Vena Cava

Aorta

Pulmonary Artery

Pulmonary Artery

Pulmonary Veins

Pulmonary Veins

Right Atrium

Left Atrium

Pulmonic valve

Mitral valve

Aortic valve

Tricuspid valve

Right Ventricle

Left Ventricle

Inferior Vena Cava

©2009 DrTummy.com

V. Social Studies
   o   You drew an upside down or sideways map on Day 12. Today make a map of your neighborhood.
   o   Draw streets. Put on at least some houses. Decide on a symbol for a house.
   o   You will draw on a compass rose. (Did you figure out the other day which way was north?)
   o   You will put a key on your map. A key is where you will draw your symbols and write what they mean.
   o   Do you have a playground or store in your neighborhood? firehouse? Make a symbol for anything you add to your map and add it to your key.
   o   If you live in the middle of "nowhere," you could have symbols for trees, creek, etc.
   o   Explore more: If you are feeling ambitious, you could measure some distances in your neighborhood, or even yard, and make your map to scale. It doesn't have to be precise. You could measure in steps.

VI. Discussion
   o   Do you think it's good or bad to have knowledge of evil? Why?

VII. Writing
   o   Use the discussion question as a writing prompt.
   o   Get a high five and/or hug if you started your sentences with a capital letter and finished them with proper punctuation.

Day 14

I. Read Genesis 2:15-17.

II. Memory Verse
- Genesis 1:2
  - The earth was formless and void, and darkness was over the surface of the deep, and the Spirit of God was moving over the surface of the waters.

III. Language
- Spelling/Handwriting
  - verse 15
  - words to know: cultivate, garden, Eden, continent
  - spelling tips:
    - <u>Cultivate</u> begins with the word cult and ends with the word ate.
    - <u>Garden</u> is spelled like car den, as in a den where a bear lives, like you had a room or cave where you parked your car.
    - <u>Eden</u> is a proper noun. It's the name of a place. What do all names begin with?
      - a capital letter
    - <u>Continent</u> is a word I just chose for today. Say it in syllables to spell it. con – tin – ent
- Vocabulary
  - cultivate (verse 15)
  - to prepare and use land for crops (verb)
  - other definition: to develop (ex. He cultivated a diligent attitude.)
  - When you cultivate something, that something is the direct object.
    - He cultivated the garden. He cultivated a positive attitude.
    - Which words are the direct objects?
    - Remember, the object answers the question, what.
    - What did he cultivate?
      - the garden, a positive attitude
- Hebrew
  - Say Genesis 1:1.
    - be reSHEET baRA eloHEEM et ha shaMAyim ve et ha Arets
  - deep
  - teHOM (short e, long o)

IV. Science
- We're going to look at what goes into cultivation. What does land need in order to produce crops? What do crops need to grow?
- You can probably answer that last question pretty well. What do you think?
  - Here's my answer:
    - sunlight: All living things need energy. Plants get theirs from the sun.
    - water: Living things need water.
    - nutrients: Nutrients will help them grow bigger and stronger.

- Nutrients are found in the soil. We get our nutrition from eating healthy foods full of vitamins and minerals. Plants eat minerals too. They need lots of nutrients just like us.
- Do you recognize the names calcium, potassium, and iron? They are all things you need and plants need them too.
  - Do you know where we get our calcium from?
    - It is found in dairy products such as milk.
  - Do you know where we get iron from?
    - It is found in protein products such as meats.
  - Do you know where we get potassium from?
    - It is found in fruits and veggies such as bananas and potatoes.
  - Do you remember what is the most common element in the air we breathe?
    - It's nitrogen. Guess the scientific symbol for the element, nitrogen.
      - This one was easy. It's N.
      - Find it on the Periodic Table chart in your Map Book. It's in the back. You also have a black and white version in your workbook. It's a list of all the different types of atoms.
        - Nitrogen is number 7.
        - Can you find oxygen?
          - It's right next to it at 8. Its symbol is O.
          - (Note: Keep out your Map Book.)
    - Nitrogen is a necessary nutrient for plants. Plants use nitrogen from the soil. The nitrogen gets in the soil from the atmosphere, from the waste products of animals, and from decaying plants.
    - It all works together in a cycle.
    - When farmers cultivate land, they plough (Note: read plow, rhymes with now) and till the soil. This turns over the soil, loosening it, and then smoothing it for planting. They also fertilize it, adding nutrients to the soil.
  - What does the Bible say about cultivation?
    - The Lord commands, in Leviticus 25:4, that the land be unused every seventh year, like the seventh day of rest. They were to let the ground lay *fallow*, which means unplanted.
    - The Israelites may not have realized this, but the Lord, of course, knew what He was talking about. Now we know that it's important to change what crops are grown in a certain place and to give soil rest, so that its nutrients can be replenished. Soil can be depleted of its nutrients and then crops won't grow well. A period of rest allows the nitrogen (and other nutrients) to get into the soil without the plants constantly draining it from the soil.
  - Recall: What's the most common gas found in air? nitrogen   What is it called when you leave farmland unplanted? fallow
  - Explore more: Learn about how nitrogen is made useable by bacteria in soil.

V. Social Studies
  - *Agriculture*, the practice of farming, was integral to early civilization. In fact, it was only since the mid 19th century that the world gradually started shifting to an industrialized society, one that produces in factories instead of on farms.

- o Early civilization relied on agriculture. Do you know what a civilization is? Try to define it.
  - • A civilization is a group of people that are organized in how they live and interact together.
- o Take a look in your Map Book for Day 14. The area between the two rivers, the Euphrates and the Tigris, is known as "the cradle of civilization."
  - • What do you think that term means? What's a cradle?
  - • A cradle is used for babies. This is where civilization was in its infancy. It's where the first cities were born.
- o Cities sprouted along rivers. Why do you think?
  - • Water is necessary for life, right?
  - • With water to support large numbers, large numbers of people could gather together in one place.
- o The area that we are talking about, between the rivers, is called Mesopotamia.
- o Mesopotamia was part of what is known as the Fertile Crescent.
  - • Look at the last map for Day 14 to find it. The Fertile Crescent is crescent shaped, though it looks more like a boomerang really. It stretches from the northern part of the Nile, across Israel, and over the area of Mesopotamia, and covering the land surrounding and between the Euphrates and the Tigris.
  - • You can look at the big map from Day 14 to find it on your own.
- o What do all those areas have in common?
  - • Water!
  - • Water is what makes that area *fertile*, or land that produces an abundance of vegetation. That means it's a great place to grow things, which was of high importance to an agricultural society.
- o Recall: Why is it called the Fertile Crescent? Fertile means land that produces an abundance of crops. The crescent-shaped area of land is around water which makes the ground ideal for growing crops. What is agriculture? farming
- o Explore more: Learn about early Mesopotamian society.

VI. Discussion
- o God made man to cultivate the land. Why does God make man work for a living? Why doesn't God just create the food ready to go?

VII. Writing
- o Use the discussion question as a writing prompt.
- o Did you use a direct object or prepositional phrase? Get high fives and hugs for what you included.

Day 15

I. Read Genesis 2:18-20.

II. Memory Verse
- o Test yourselves on Genesis 1:2.
  - The earth was formless and void, and darkness was over the surface of the deep, and the Spirit of God was moving over the surface of the waters.
- o Review Psalm 150:6.
  - Let everything that has breath praise the Lord. Praise the Lord!

III. Language
- o Spelling/Handwriting
  - Test yourselves on the spelling words from Days 11-14.
    - shrub, sprouted, creation, mist
    - breathed, nostrils, breath, being
    - third, fourth, flows, river (just for fun—Tigris, Assyria, Euphrates)
    - cultivate, garden, Eden, continent
- o Vocabulary
  - Test yourselves on your words from Days 11-14.
    - mist – a low lying cloud
    - midst – in the middle of
    - divide – to separate into parts
    - cultivate -- to prepare and use land for crops
- o Hebrew
  - Test yourselves with words from Days 11-15.
  - chaos, darkness, face, deep
  - TOhu va VOhu, KHOshekh, pnaa, teHOM
  - Say Genesis 1:1.
    - be reSHEET baRA eloHEEM et ha shaMAyim ve et ha Arets

IV. Science
- o In the verses we read today, Adam names all of the animals. We have names for all of the animals too.
- o To make it easy for scientists to know what they are talking about, a very specific pattern of classifying animals was developed. To *classify* is to arrange into categories.
- o We've actually been talking about animal *classes* when we were talking about mammals, reptiles, birds, etc.
- o Let me back up. Where do you live?
  - You could say your address, your street, your district/county, your state, your country, your continent, your hemisphere
  - That's what it's like with animal classification. The ranks are:
    - species (your address)
    - genus (your street)
    - family (your district/county)
    - order (your state)
    - class (your country)

- phylum (your continent)
- kingdom (your hemisphere)
    - Here's an example. You'll notice that the kingdom is animals. This classification system is not just for animals. We use it for all living things.
    - (Note: Read each category name and classification and then everyone can guess what the animal is based on the new information in each level. With each new level, they will receive more information and can change their guess.)

    Kingdom: Animal
    Phylum: Vertebrate
    Class: Mammal
    Order: Carnivore
    Family: Cat
    Genus: Panther
    Species: Tiger

- Based on what you know, what do you think human's classification is?
    - What kingdom do humans belong to?
        - kingdom: animal
    - What phylum? (Note: You can read the tiger example to remember what's at each level.)
        - vertebrate
    - What class? mammal
    - What order? primate (mammals with collar bones and grasping fingers)
    - family: hominids (primates with relatively flat faces and 3D vision)
    - genus: homo (hominids who stand upright and have large brains)
    - species: homo sapiens (homo with high forehead and thick skull)
- How did you do? Did you guess omnivore for order because humans eat meat and plants? The order of carnivore refers to an animal that eats meat.
- Here are some of the orders of mammals.
    - primates: includes monkeys
    - mammals with pouches: includes kangaroos
    - insect-eating mammals: includes shrews
    - flying mammals: just the bats
    - rodents, includes squirrels: there are about as many of these as the rest combined
    - carnivores: includes dogs, anything that eats meat
    - even-toed hoofed animals: includes the gazelle
- Recall: What does it mean to classify something? arrange it into categories
- Explore more: Learn more about how animals are classified. How are reptiles or birds divided into orders?

V. Social Studies
- We found the land of Mesopotamia, between the Euphrates and Tigris rivers, in the Fertile Crescent.

- o We are now in recorded history. The earlier we go, the less record we have, but we know some things, especially from *archeology*, the study of human history through digging up and researching artifacts.
- o People were settled in Mesopotamia in order to farm since about 4000 BC. This agricultural society relied on water from the river to *irrigate*, or water their crops. They got the water to their fields by digging ditches between them and the river.
- o A main crop would have been wheat and barley. What would those crops have been used for?
  - Those are grains and are used for making bread products. Their bread may not have been anything like we know it. It was likely flat.
  - Here is the work they put into eating a piece of bread.
    - Grain has to be cultivated, planted and tended.
    - When the grain is ready, ripe, it is harvested or cut down.
    - Grain is then bundled up. We call them shocks of grain, a bunch of grain tied together.
    - Grain is then threshed, beaten about. Nowadays threshing is done by machine, but then it wasn't. During threshing the grain falls off of the stalk.
    - Grain is gathered and then it is winnowed. To winnow grain, it is tossed up and the wind blows away the chaff, the little bits of straw. This is making the grain pure for consumption (that's eating!) Grain can be poured back and forth while the wind does its job. Jesus talks about a winnowing fork (Matthew 3:12). It was used to toss grain up into the wind. The kernels of wheat would fall back down and the chaff would be blown away.
    - Grain is then ground into flour on a flat rock using another rock as the grinding tool.
    - Then it's ready to use for cooking.
    - How important do you think grain was to their lives? How much of their lives do you think revolved around grain?
    - We'll learn later that the Egyptians used bread as currency (as money). Can you understand why it would be valuable?
- o During the period of early civilization, towns developed and so did their economy. They made pottery. They worked with leather, metal, and weaving.
- o Recall: What is the name for the study of history through digging up and observing artifacts? archeology   How did they irrigate their land? To irrigate the land means to water it, so that's when they dug ditches to carry water from the rivers to their land.
- o Explore more: What specific artifacts have archaeologists found from Mesopotamia? What can we learn from them?

VI.   Discussion
- o   Do you think you could name every animal? Rename an animal and tell why you chose the name.

VII.   Writing
- o   Choose one of your writings from Days 12-14 to edit.
- o   Read it out loud to look for things that don't make sense, don't flow, or just don't sound right.
- o   Look for spelling mistakes. Check for correct capitalization and punctuation.
- o   Check that your sentences have subjects and predicates.
- o   You can use an editing checklist to help you look for problems.
- o   Have someone older than you check it over once you've fixed it. (You can fix it by just making marks on the page to note changes.)
- o   Listen to their corrections and suggestions and make changes to your writing.
- o   Make a final draft. Rewrite it or type it.

Day 16

I. Read Genesis 2:21-25.

II. Memory Verse
- o Romans 3:23
- o For all have sinned and fall short of the glory of God.

III. Language
- o Spelling/Handwriting
  - • verse 24
  - • words to know: reason, join, slept, ashamed
  - • Spelling tips:
    - ▪ These both follow spelling patterns we've seen before.
      - • <u>Reason</u> is spelled with the same pattern as season.
      - • <u>Join</u> follows the same pattern as void.
    - ▪ <u>Slept</u> is spelled like it sounds. Say it slowly. There are four consonants.
    - ▪ <u>Ashamed</u> follows the rules. The A sound is made with a silent E.
- o Vocabulary
  - • fashion (verse 22)
  - • to take materials and make them into something (verb)
  - • In this example God takes the rib and fashions it into a woman.
  - • Examples of objects:
    - ▪ Direct object
      - • Phrase: caused a deep sleep
      - • Caused what?
        - o Direct Object: sleep, or a deep sleep
    - ▪ Object of a preposition
      - • prepositional phrase: out of Man
      - • What was she taken out of?
        - o Object of the preposition: man
- o Hebrew
  - • Here's your verse for the week. It's the first part of Genesis 1:2. The earth was formless and void, and darkness was over the surface of the deep...
  - • ve ha Arets (and the earth) haaTAH (was) TOhu va VOhu (chaos) ve (and) KHOshekh (darkness) al (upon) pnaa (face) teHOM (deep)
  - • You'll see the translation comes out a little differently from the Hebrew. Remember, I'm not using any capitalization or punctuation. The capital letters are where you put the stress on when you speak. The double aa is the long A sound. (I'm just reminding you.)
  - • You can learn haaTAH today. It translates here as "was."
    - ▪ Verbs change to show many things.
    - ▪ In English we can say "I was" and "You were." The verb changes form, but it keeps the same meaning.

- A couple of ways that verbs change in Hebrew is to show us the number and gender of the subject. Let me show you examples of what that means.
- We are here. They, a group of boys, are here. They, a group of girls, are here. You are here. All of these examples use the English verb "are", but in Hebrew each would have a different verb form. The verb would change based on how many people it was referring to and if it was referring to males or females.

IV. Science
- We're going to learn about the skeletal system. The skeletal system is all of your bones and how they fit together to hold you up! What bone did we read about in our Scriptures today?
- I'm sure you figured out that it was a rib.
  - Try to count how many ribs you have. Maybe lying down would make it easier. How many did you come up with?
  - People have 24 ribs, 12 on each side. (Men don't have one less rib; Adam lost one, but he had been created with a complete set and his kids of course were born complete.)
- Those rib bones are part of what we call the *rib cage*. Why do you think God created a cage inside of us? What is the cage guarding?
  - Your ribs are a protection for your heart and lungs.
- Place your hands on your rib cage and breathe deeply into your lungs. What happens to your rib cage?
  - It expands.
- Do bones bend?
  - No. So what's happening? How does your rib cage move when you breathe?
  - There are muscles (which we will discuss another day) attached to your rib cage that pull up on it when you breathe in.
- We learned about the jointed legs that insects have. A *joint* is where two bones connect. Those are the places where we can bend. Try to find as many of your joints as you can. How many can you come up with?
  - I can't even tell you how many joints you have. People disagree on what counts as a joint! You have 206 bones in you and they all have to connect, so you can see that you certainly have more than 100 joints.
- What couldn't you do if you didn't have joints?
  - You couldn't bend at all anywhere. You couldn't do much of anything except blink.
- I mentioned you have 206 bones. You have lots of small bones in your toes and fingers. In fact, you have 27 bones in your hand. How many is that in both hands?
  - The smallest bone is actually in your ear and measures just two and a half millimeters in length. How big is that?
  - The largest bone is called the *femur*. Can you guess which bone is that?
    - It's your thigh bone.
- Let me tell you something else interesting about bones. You were born with about 300 bones, nearly 100 more than you have today. Having more bones made you more

bendable because more bones means more joints. Being bendable was needed for growing inside your mother and for coming out.

- The biggest place this is necessary is in the skull. Do you know where your skull is?
- Baby's skulls aren't one solid piece like yours is now. It was in parts that grew together. In the womb the skull needed to be flexible. Outside the womb, it needs to be solid.
- Why do you think it's important to have a thick, solid skull?
  - Your skull protects your brain. Your skull has an important job!

- One last question...what would you look like without bones?
  - You would be nothing but a blob on the ground!
- Recall: What's the name of the biggest bone in your body and where is it? What's the name of the connectors between bones that enable you to bend?
  - femur, thigh bone
  - joints
- Explore more: Learn all the major bones of the skeletal system.

V. Social Studies
- Every culture has a marriage rite, or a ritual we do that somehow makes us married. What do two people do in your country in order to marry?
- In America we have a wedding ceremony. The bride dresses in a fancy white gown. The men wear tuxedos. Friends and family stand with us as we make vows to each other promising to love each other until we die.
  - We are officially married when someone with the proper authority signs a piece of paper saying we are married.
- There's a phrase, "jump the broom," referring to how slaves would marry. They would hold hands and jump over a broom together. Then they were official.
- In China, red is the color for the bride, not white.
- In Macedonia there are numerous traditions as part of the wedding ceremony.
  - Symbolic foods are prepared and everything is done by ritual.
  - There is a ritual haggling over the price of the bride.
  - There are superstitions over who the new couple's children will look like based on things that happen that day.
  - The bride's family can wail when she leaves the house, mourning the loss of their daughter.
- The Roma weddings in Macedonia last seven days.
  - The bride is "bought" with gifts from the husband's family. The groom's family buys everything, even the woman's wedding dress for her. (Girls, would you want someone else to pick out your dress for you?)
  - The last night of the celebration she is taken to her new husband's home. Runners go through the streets announcing the bride's purity. This is when they are officially considered married.
- In Turkey there are two days to a wedding, two parties.
  - The first party is for when the bride is decorated with henna; she gets a painted tattoo.
  - The second day is the wedding celebration. There is lots of dancing at both parties. On the second night the couple stands up front and everyone pins

money to their clothing. The bride is dressed in a fancy dress, but it does not have to be white.

- o Explore more: Choose a culture to learn what you can about their marriage rituals. How/when did your country's marriage ceremony originate?

VI. Discussion

- o Today's question. What is marriage?
  - (Parents: You can decide if you want to stop here or if you want to discuss the following verses with your children. I think this is interesting to think about and can be beneficial to have a firm belief about.)
- o Today we read in the Bible passage "the two will become one flesh." That's the Bible's first definition of marriage. It's the gift God gives a man and woman to be naked together and not ashamed. The only time that's possible is within God-ordained marriage because otherwise you are acting sinfully.
- o When Joseph takes Mary as his wife, marrying her, he does not become one flesh with her, but he is married to her. She is considered his wife.
- o When Jesus talks to the Samaritan woman at the well, He knows that the man she is living with (and presumably) sharing a bed with, is not her husband.
- o Is there a difference between being married in God's eyes and being married in man's eyes?

VII. Writing

- o I told you before about subjects and predicates. I said that every sentence needed them both.
  - There are exceptions to this rule. There can be a sentence without a subject. Well, it has a subject. We all know what the subject is; the sentence just doesn't repeat it.
  - We say that the subject is <u>understood</u>. Here's an example.
    - Come here!
    - The subject is understood as whomever the command is spoken to.
  - Another example is a reply such as, "Yes!" Or "No!" Those are still sentences even without a proper subject or verb. They are a complete thought and imply the rest of the sentence. When you say yes, it is <u>understood</u> that you mean, "Yes, I like that," or "Yes, it is," etc.
- o Sometimes a sentence can have too many subjects and predicates, and they should really be two sentences. One way to fix that is to add something called a semicolon (;) between the sentences. Here is an example.
  - Susan is my friend she and I like to sing together.
  - That shouldn't be all one sentence. You can fix it by adding a semicolon like this.
    - Susan is my friend; (semicolon) she and I like to sing together.
- o That's one way you can combine what should be two sentences into one. Each part of it has a subject and predicate.
- o Complete the Writing Sentences 4 page of your workbook. You are going to decide which sentences are correct sentences. If a sentence is not correct, you are going to fix it.

Day 17

I.   Read Genesis 3:1-7.

II. Memory Verse
   o   Romans 3:23
   o   For all have sinned and fall short of the glory of God.

III. Language
   o   Spelling/Handwriting
      •   verse 7
      •   words to know: sewed, themselves, touch, coverings
      •   Spelling tips:
         ▪   <u>Sewed</u> is a word that trips up many foreigners that I know. Sew is spelled like the word new, so they pronounce it sue. This is one of those words you just need to learn how it's spelled.
         ▪   <u>Themselves</u> is a combination of them and selves, the plural of self.
         ▪   <u>Touch</u> is spelled a little strangely. It's spelled like pouch or couch. It has an O-U for the short U sound.
         ▪   The word <u>coverings</u> is a plural noun. To cover is the verb. A covering is a noun. A plural noun means there is more than one.
   o   Vocabulary
      •   crafty (verse 1)
      •   clever at using deception to get what you want (used as an adjective)
         ▪   synonyms (words with similar meaning) shrewd, vulpine
         ▪   other definition: someone or something involved in making crafts by hand
      •   Adjectives describe nouns. What noun is described by the word, crafty?
         ▪   serpent
   o   Hebrew
      •   The first part of Genesis 1:2. The earth was formless and void, and darkness was over the surface of the deep.
      •   ve ha Arets (and the earth) haaTAH (was) TOhu va VOhu (chaos) ve (and) KHOshekh (darkness) al (upon) pnaa (face) teHOM (deep)
      •   Remember, I'm not using any capitalization or punctuation. The capital letters are where you put the stress on when you speak. The double AA is the long A sound. (I'm just reminding you.)
      •   You can learn *al* today. It means "upon."

IV. Science
   o   We've learned that water brings life. Sin brings death. Let's stick with life. We mentioned the Tigris and the Euphrates. Where are they?
      •   They are in the Fertile Crescent in what was known as Mesopotamia.
   o   What do you know about rivers?
      •   All rivers begin and end somewhere. Do you know where all rivers end?
         ▪   All rivers run into the seas and oceans.

- We use the term "sea level" when we talk about how high ground is. Mountain peaks are a certain number of miles (kilometers) above sea level. Why are there few land areas below sea level? (There are things below sea level, such as tunnels, but in general land is above sea level.)
    - The water would flow over it.
        - (Note: If they need help to visualize this, have them consider a bathtub with water in it. That's sea level, where the water comes up to. What happens to anything that goes below the water level?)
    - The height of the land is its *elevation*, how high it is. Can you think of another word that begins "elevat" that has to do with how high things are?
        - Did you think of elevator or even the word elevate?
            - These words all have the same, what we call, root. That means they will have related meanings.
- Why would elevation matter to rivers? What does elevation have to do with the fact that all rivers run to sea level?
    - *Gravity*, the force that pulls smaller objects towards larger ones, pulls everything on earth downward towards the earth (which is enormous compared to everything else on earth). Gravity, pulling everything downward, pulls the water downward as well. A river can only flow down.
    - Gravity is what makes things fall down when there's nothing to hold it up. It's also what holds you to the earth! Did you ever think about how you need to be held down so you wouldn't float away?
- Where does the water in rivers come from? All rivers have to have a beginning. How do they begin?
    - Rivers start very small and are technically called streams. The water is from runoff, rain water with nowhere to go.
        - When the ground is *saturated*, full to the brim, the extra water "runs off." It's got nowhere to go, and so gravity can get to work pulling the water to a localized point.
            - You can pour water on the ground or in a pot of soil until you saturate it. What will appear when it's saturated?
                - A puddle!
                - When the ground is saturated, no more water can go into the ground, so it just pools up on the surface.
    - Small streams get started in many areas.
    - Gravity keeps pulling water down to a lower point. As water joins together in one area streams form. The streams get pulled to the same location and join together into larger streams. This process keeps going until you have very large streams, or rivers.
    - And then where do they go?
        - They go towards sea level and end up in seas and oceans.
- Rivers are powerful. How do rivers show their power?
    - They cut through landscape. The rushing water tugs at the land it passes, causing *erosion*, the gradual wearing away of land.
    - Rivers can erode rocks as well. That's why you can find super smooth rocks. The water has worn away the rough edges.

- o Recall: Define elevation. Elevation is how high something is. Define gravity. Gravity is the force that pulls a smaller object towards a larger one (what pulls us down to earth and water down to sea level). How does water cause erosion? It wears away the land.
- o Explore more: Learn the major rivers of the world. Where do they originate? Where do they empty? What's unique about them?

V. Social Studies
- o We're going to look at rivers in geography. First find the two largest rivers in the world, the Nile and the Amazon. Look in Egypt in Africa using the Middle East map from Day 14. You can find the Amazon on the South America map for Day 17. Hint: Look for where they empty out into the sea and ocean.
  - • There's a dispute over which is longer. The Amazon is huge, though, draining the water from most of South America.
- o We've talked about how early civilizations relied on rivers for life. Check out the Cities and Rivers map for Day 17. The rivers are blue. The big cities are marked with black dots. Are the biggest cities still near rivers? Why or why not? What do you think?
  - • Now look at the map showing rivers in comparison to the state boundaries. Do you think rivers played a role in creating boundaries of territories?
- o There is also a *topographical* map of America for Day 17; that's a map that shows elevation. If you like, you could make a clay model of it. You would build up where the land has a higher elevation.
  - • The key is hard to read but the bottom is the lowest elevation and the top of the key shows the color for the highest elevation.
- o Recall: What's the name of the type of map that shows elevation? topographical
- o Explore more: Check out river maps and elevation/topographical maps of other countries/continents.
VI. Discussion
- o What would the world be like without gravity?

VI. Writing
- o Use the discussion question as a writing prompt.
- o Get a high five and/or hug if you use an "elevat" word.

Day 18

I. Read Genesis 3:8-21.

II. Memory Verse
    o   Romans 3:23
    o   For all have sinned and fall short of the glory of God.

III. Language
    o   Spelling/Handwriting
        •   second half of verse 8 (The man and his wife...)
        •   words to know: presence, enmity, bruise, whistle (thistle)
        •   Spelling tips:
            ▪   <u>Presence</u> is a homophone with the word presents, the gifts you get at a celebration. This kind of presence has to do with someone being there.
            ▪   <u>Enmity</u> is your vocabulary word today. Pronounce it slowly and carefully to spell it. What letter makes an E sound at the end of a longer word like this?
            ▪   <u>Bruise</u> ends with a silent E and has the same U spelling pattern as fruit.
            ▪   The word <u>whistle</u> has a silent t. I thought it was a little more useful of a word than thistle, which is in the verse. They are spelled the same except for the first letter. Think about how the word thistle would start.
    o   Vocabulary
        •   enmity (verse 15)
        •   hatred (noun)
        •   Is it used as an object? "And I will put enmity between you and the woman."
        •   The answer is yes. God will put what?
            ▪   enmity
            ▪   It's the direct object of the verb "put."
        •   There is a prepositional phrase; it's "between you and the woman."
        •   While we're looking at it, what are the objects of the preposition "between."
            ▪   you and the woman
        •   Between is the preposition and it tells us where something is.
    o   Hebrew
        •   Genesis 1:2 first part: The earth was formless and void, and darkness was over the surface of the deep.
        •   ve ha Arets (and the earth) haaTAH (was) TOhu va VOhu (chaos) ve (and) KHOshekh (darkness) al (upon) pnaa (face) teHOM (deep)
        •   Practice the verse.
        •   Do you remember that ve is "and" and ha is "the"?

IV. Science
- Today we're going to talk about serpents, but first, let's talk about reptiles.
- What is a reptile? What makes one animal a reptile and another animal not? Think about it. What's your list of reptile characteristics?
- Here's my list:
  - They are vertebrates. What does that mean?
    - It means they have a backbone.
  - They are cold-blooded. What does that mean?
    - They need to get their warmth from the sun. Their bodies take on the temperature of their environment.
  - They have dry, scaly skin. Scales are like small sections of skin put together. In some animals they overlap and in others they don't. Why do you think they have scaly skin?
    - There are two purposes for their skin. It is an armor for the animal, providing protection and it keeps moisture inside which is useful in regulating their body temperature.
  - They lay eggs on land. Their eggs have a soft shell. That's different than bird eggs. For instance, you know that chicken eggs have a hard shell that we have to crack to open.
- Now let's talk about snakes, the serpent from our story.
- How is the serpent cursed?
  - He's told that he will go on his belly from then on.
  - It's possible that what we know as serpents, or snakes, had legs before the fall, what we call the time when Adam and Eve sinned.
- There are in fact legless lizards, so I don't think the serpent was a lizard before becoming a snake. What's the difference between a legless lizard and a snake? Legless lizards have eyelids and ears that you can see.
- Let's stick with what we know of snakes today.
  - By the way, we use snake and serpent interchangeably; they mean the same thing. The common American name for them is snake. The scientific name of them is serpentes.
- Snakes are reptiles, so they are cold blooded and vertebrates. Their backbone is very bendable!
- They are carnivores. What does that mean?
  - They only eat animals, not plants. What animals do you think they eat?
    - Snakes consume a variety of items including termites, rodents, birds, frogs, small deer and other reptiles. Snakes eat their prey whole and are able to consume prey three times larger than the diameter of their head because their lower jaw can separate from the upper jaw. To keep prey from escaping, snakes have rear-facing teeth that hold their prey in their mouths.
    (from http://www.defenders.org/snakes/basic-facts)
  - Snakes range from tiny to huge, from just four inches to thirty feet long. That long snake is called a python. It can eat things like a small deer, but it only has to eat once a year. Snakes don't have to hunt daily.
- Snakes live in a variety of habitats. They can live in the desert, on the prairie, in forests, and even underwater.

- Most snakes, though, live in tropical weather, the hot humid forested areas of the world.
- Snakes are found in most countries, but not in icy regions. There are no snakes in Antarctica. More interesting, though, there are no snakes in Ireland or New Zealand.
- Do you know where those places are in the world? They are both island countries. How might that account for there being no snakes in those countries?
  - A *venomous* snake is a poisonous snake. It injects a poison into its prey when it bites.
  - How can you tell a venomous snake from a non-venomous snake?
    - There are a lot of ideas about this, but with so many exceptions, they aren't very helpful. In America, poisonous snakes are mostly very big and fat. If the snake has a rattle on its tail, it's venomous. The rattle shakes to warn you to back off. If you are bitten and there are fang marks, two closely set puncture wounds, then it was a poisonous snake. A ragged cut would be from a regular snake. Only venomous snakes have fangs. Venomous snakes also have broad heads.
  - Recall: What are some characteristics of reptiles? vertebrates, cold-blooded, dry and scaly skin, lay eggs on land
  - Explore more: You could learn more about snakes: varying habitats, defenses, etc. or choose another reptile to learn more about.

V. Social Studies
  - We talked a bit about human nature before. What shows of human nature in this story?
    - Adam and Eve blame others. Who do they blame?
      - Eve blames the snake.
      - Adam even blames God saying that God was the one who gave Eve to him.
    - It is human nature to not want to accept blame.
    - Like a lot of human nature, it's not good! In order to be forgiven for our sins, what do we need to do? Confess. We have to say that we did something wrong. If we won't take blame, then we can't receive forgiveness.
    - Also, we hold onto guilt when we lay blame elsewhere. We know deep down that we are guilty, even if we said it was someone else's fault. Guilt is a heavy burden to carry.
    - Jesus tells us to give him those burdens. He can take the guilt and shame from us and give us forgiveness and peace of mind.
  - What are some of the other parts to the curse that was the result of the fall, their sin?
  - I want to point out one part in particular. There is a prophecy about the future between the serpent (talking about Satan) and the "seed of Adam" talking about Jesus.
    - "He shall bruise you on the head, and you shall bruise him on the heel."
  - You could look at history through the lens of that verse. Satan doesn't want the seed of Eve, meaning a child of hers, to bruise him on the head.
    - What's more damaging, a heel wound or a head wound?

- Stomping on the head of snake seems a lot worse than getting bitten in the heel by a snake. But remember, this is a metaphor, a picture with words.
  - Satan has always been out to get Eve's children, God's children, especially the children of Israel.
- One last thing...Adam and Eve felt shame. There are some cultures in the world known as shame cultures. This is very common in the Orient, countries like China and Japan. Society is kept in order by a deep sense of honor and the need to maintain honor. Children are kept under control by instilling in them the severity of shaming their family. The biggest threat is *ostracism,* or shunning, telling someone they no longer belong, that they are no longer welcome. A parent could disown a child, saying you are no longer my child, if they bring shame onto the family.
  - This produces a lot of stress!
- What do other countries do? Some are fear cultures. People are kept in line by fear, by threats.
- Others are guilt cultures. There is a sense of guilt for wrong behaviors with the threat of punishment for the behavior.
- Which do you think is your country?
  - I think America is a guilt culture.
- By the way, what do you think is the church's way of ruling? How are Christians "kept in line"?
  - The church should be a love culture. Jesus says, "If you love me, obey my commandments." (John 14:15) We should obey out of our love for God. However, there is also a fear part to God's rule. Those who disobey should have a fear of God. His wrath, his extreme anger, is reserved for the unrighteous. Only those who are made righteous by Jesus Christ are free from the danger of wrath.
- Recall: What is human nature? how humans normally behave; In a shame culture there is a threat of ostracism. What is that? telling someone they no longer belong
- Explore more: What can you learn about shame cultures? Maybe you can find information on how to best share the gospel in a shame culture vs. a guilt culture. How does our culture affect our understanding of Christianity? of everything!?

VI. Discussion
- We (Eve's seed) and the devil are supposed to have enmity and be actively opposed to each other. The Bible says that Satan prowls around like a lion ready to destroy God's children (1 Peter 5:8). He's actively opposing us. Are we actively opposing him? Are you? How are you? How can you?

VII. Writing
- Use the discussion questions as a writing prompt.
- Get a high five or a hug for any spelling or vocabulary word you use.

Day 19

I. Read Genesis 3:22-24.

II. Memory Verse
   o Romans 3:23
   o For all have sinned and fall short of the glory of God.

III. Language
   o Spelling/Handwriting
      • verse 24
      • words to know: stationed, guard, direction, flaming
      • Spelling tip:
         ▪ Two words have the common spelling pattern T-I-O-N, <u>stationed</u> and <u>direction</u>.
         ▪ The word <u>guard</u> begins G-U.
         ▪ The word <u>flaming</u> uses the I in I-N-G to make the A say its name. It replaces the silent E at the end of flame and takes over its job.
   o Vocabulary
      • to station (verse 23)
      • to put someone in a position in a particular place for a particular purpose (verb)
      • Does the verb station have an object in verse 24?
         ▪ He stationed what? the cherubim and the flaming sword
         ▪ Sword is the noun, the object in the strictest sense. What is the adjective describing it?
            • flaming
   o Hebrew
      • First part of Genesis 1:2 The earth was formless and void, and darkness was over the surface of the deep.
      • ve ha Arets (and the earth) haaTAH (was) TOhu va VOhu (chaos) ve (and) KHOshekh (darkness) al (upon) pnaa (face) teHOM (deep)
      • Practice careful pronunciation of the emphasis and of the vowel sounds.

IV. Science
   o We've been learning about different types of animals. I want to also learn about where they live.
   o An animal's home environment is called its *habitat*. An animal habitat is the environment where it can get the food, water, and shelter it needs for survival.
   o When I say there are 10,000 species of a certain type of animal, that's not an exact number. The truth is that we can't count the number of animal species out there. There are probably more than 30 million insect species alone!
      • And each animal has its own habitat, its home.
      • These homes, however, intersect and overlap.
      • They can be grouped together into certain types of habitats. We call the broad characteristics of the habitats, *biomes*.
      • Here's a list of the world's major biomes.

- grasslands
- tundra, in polar regions
- deserts
- mountains
- salt water
- fresh water
- coral reefs
- rainforests
- deciduous forests
- coniferous forests
  - *Deciduous* trees are broadleaf trees, the kind that lose their leaves in winter.
  - *Coniferous* trees are pine trees. They have needles.
    - Maybe you could remember that needle trees are coniferous trees because fir trees have needles (sounds like the "fer" in coniferous). Also con is sort of like cone and pine trees have pine cones.
    - Why do we call coniferous trees evergreens?
      - They stay green in the winter unlike deciduous trees where the leaves change color when the weather cools.

o When we learned about animal classification, we compared it to saying where we live. We can describe where animals live in several ways as well.

o What about a squirrel? Where do they live?
- Did you say forests or trees? Right! Now what kind of forest or trees?
  - It depends on what kind of squirrel. The red squirrel lives in coniferous forests and the fox squirrel lives in deciduous forests.
- Where in the forest do they live?
  - They make their nests in holes in trees. Did you know there were hollow trees, empty on the inside? They make great animal homes.

o What is necessary in a habitat? Every animal has different requirements. The Monarch butterfly for instance, is a herbivore, but it only eats milkweed plants. That's a requirement for its habitat.
- Let me tell you something amazing about the Monarch. Those butterflies living in America, east of the Rocky Mountains, travel 3000 miles (over 4800 kilometers) to Mexico, to a specific region; other populations spend the winter elsewhere, many in California. This is similar to the salmon all knowing where to go in the Arctic Circle.
- Here's more amazing information. The Monarch will lay their eggs in Mexico over the winter. They will start heading back north in the spring and die. Their children continue the migration. The next generation knows exactly where to head to return "home" and following generations continue the cycle to the same spot in Mexico and then back home.
- They have a very specific habitat that sustains them, most notably the presence of the milkweed plant.

o When we look at different *biomes*, the characteristics of large habitats, remember that God made it all specifically as well. It all works together: the environment, the climate, the plants, the animals, etc. all work together and depend on each other. They are interdependent.

- o Each animal has its own *niche*, or role in the biome. Maybe its niche is eating flower nectar and spreading pollen.
- o But they all are part of the one *ecosystem,* all of the living things in an area all interacting with each other and their environment.
- o Recall: Can you give a definition or explain the following? niche, ecosystem, biome, habitat
- o Explore more: Choose a biome and learn about what very specific habitats are part of it.

V. Social Studies

- o Now that we've begun talking about official history, I want to explain how we talk about time.
- o We count years from before and after Jesus was born, sort of.
- o Actually, did you know that different countries use different calendars? In Ethiopia it's seven years earlier! Their new year begins in our September.
    - • When I asked my Ethiopian friend why, she answered, "We started counting the day we found out about Jesus."
    - • Do you remember the Bible story about the Ethiopian official who learns about Jesus and is baptized by Philip? (Acts 8) Maybe that was when their calendar started!
- o So what about the "normal" calendar. It's called the Gregorian calendar. It's also known as the Western calendar and the Christian calendar because it centers around the birth of Christ.
- o We use the symbols AD and BC next to year numbers.
    - • AD stands for the Latin, Anno Domini, or in the year of the Lord.
    - • BC stands for Before Christ. One is in Latin and the other English because BC came much later. When the division of the calendar was created, I guess maybe only the present and the future were considered important.
- o However, this dating system was created by Julius Cesar in 45 AD. His calendar was used until the Gregorian calendar corrected it slightly in the 1500s.
- o In this system there is no year zero. There is no bull's-eye zero date when Jesus was born.
- o Before Jesus was born we count down to His birth, like counting down to a rocket launch.
    - • Which is more recent the year 2000 BC or the year 500 BC?
        - ▪ 500 BC is more recent.
    - • Which is older? A civilization that was around 3000 BC or 2000 BC?
        - ▪ 3000 BC is older.
- o When you get to 1 BC, the next year is 1 AD. Then we start counting up.
    - • Which is older 7 AD or 500 AD?
        - ▪ 7 AD is older.
    - • Which is more recent 1700 AD or 2000 AD?
        - ▪ 2000 AD is more recent.
    - • We don't write AD after the year unless it's needed for clarity, to make sure it's understood.

- o   Recall: What do BC and AD stand for? Before Christ and Anno Domini (in the year of the Lord)
- o   Explore more: Learn about the Jewish and Muslim calendars.

VI.   Discussion
- o   How important is a calendar? Is it good that we have one? What would the world be like without one? What if every country had their own calendar, like Ethiopia does? or every state?

VII.   Writing
- o   Use the discussion questions as a writing prompt.
- o   Find prepositional phrases and direct objects in your writing. Get a high five and/or a hug for any you find. Hint: Look for nouns. Objects are nouns and every prepositional phrase ends in a noun. (This is true unless the noun has been replaced with a pronoun.)

Day 20

I. Read Genesis 4:1-7.
    (Note: This is called anthropomorphism. Sin is being talked about like it is a person. It's a descriptive writing technique. It gives a unique image of a black shadowy creature, crouch by the door, kind of peeking in and saying, "Psst, over here. Come with me."

II. Memory Verse
   o Test yourselves on Romans 3:23.
      • For all have sinned and fall short of the glory of God.
   o Review Genesis 1:2.
      • The earth was formless and void, and darkness was over the surface of the deep, and the Spirit of God was moving over the surface of the waters.

III. Language
   o Spelling/Handwriting
      • You can write your memory verse for today.
      • Test yourselves on your words from Days 16-19.
         ▪ reason, join, slept, ashamed
         ▪ sewed, themselves, loin, coverings
         ▪ presence, enmity, whistle, bruise
         ▪ stationed, guard, direction, flaming
   o Vocabulary
      • Test yourselves on your words from Days 16-19.
         ▪ fashion - to take materials and make them into something
         ▪ crafty, shrewd, vulpine -- clever at using deception to get what you want
         ▪ enmity – being actively opposed to someone or something, hatred
         ▪ station – to put someone in a position in a particular place for a particular purpose
   o Hebrew
      • Can you say the verse without looking?
      • ve ha Arets haaTAH TOhu va VOhu ve KHOshekh al pnaa teHOM
      • Now say it after Genesis 1:1. Can you put the two together?
      • In English, what did you just say?

IV. Science
   o We're going to look at one of the major biomes today, an area with common ecological characteristics. Let's learn about the frozen desert, the tundra.
   o The most famous tundra environment is Antarctica. It's a continent with no country. It's used only for scientific exploration and a little sightseeing.
      • Do you know what shape Antarctica is?
         ▪ It's located at the South Pole. On a map it's a strip of land across the bottom, but on a globe, and in real life, it's more like a circle covering the bottom of the earth. Take a look at the map for Day 20.
   o The opposite end of the earth, on top of the globe, is the Arctic. That's the location of the North Pole.

- The northern and southern hemisphere have opposite seasons, so when it is summer in the North Pole, it is winter in the South Pole.
  - When one of the poles is in summer, it is light all the time. At the same time, the opposite pole is experiencing winter and is dark all the time.
  - Why? The earth is tilted on its *axis*. If you have a globe, now's the time to look at it, otherwise, grab a ball. Mark the north and south poles or choose a marking on the ball to represent them.
    - Hold the ball so that the North Pole is pointing straight up.
    - Now imagine a line that runs through the earth from one pole to the other. That line is the axis. It's the line that the earth spins around; it's like the center post on a merry-go-round.
    - Now choose someone or something to be your sun.
    - Tilt your ball so that the North Pole gets the sun shining on it, not completely sideways, just tilted.
      - This is the position the earth is in, not directly up and down.
    - What happens on the poles? The way you are holding the ball now gives the North Pole light, day and night.
    - Spin the ball on its axis. That spinning is what gives us day and night, but the North Pole never leaves the sunlight. What does that mean for the South Pole?
      - It never sees the sunlight.
    - Now orbit the sun. Walk your ball around the sun while carefully holding it still so that the "north" stays pointing at the same point on the far wall. Can you see how the sun would start to peek out in the South Pole and then eventually things would switch, and it would be always light in the South Pole for their summer?
- In the dark of winter, the tundra can reach temperatures of -130 degrees Fahrenheit (90 degrees below zero in Celsius). The highest ever recorded temperature is 58 degrees Fahrenheit (14 degrees Celsius).
- Just like the hot deserts, the tundra has very little *precipitation*, or what falls from the sky, and of course what does come is snow.
- Is there plant life in Antarctica?
  - While most of the continent is solid ice, the coastal areas, which are the warmer areas, can sustain green life during the short summer. In Antarctica you can find moss and lichen mostly. You say lichen, liken.
  - When my family visited Finland, a cold-weather climate, the ground was very spongy to walk on in places because of moss and lichen (pictured).

- What animals do you think live in Antarctica?
  - There are several kinds of seals, whales, and penguins there as well as the albatross, a bird.
  - The most famous of the penguins is the emperor penguin, which is the largest of them all, standing at over three feet tall.
  - It's the only animal of Antarctica that has babies in winter. The father protects the penguin egg, holding it on top of his feet and covering it with the folds of his belly. He stands like that for two months to keep his baby alive.
  - The mother is off feeding during this time. Then the mother will return and take the egg and the father will get to go eat. This happens right around the time the egg hatches.
  - To survive the harsh winter, the dad penguins huddle together, all squeezed in. They don't do anything except keep their babies warm. They fast for months.
- Recall: What's the name of the invisible line that the earth spins around? axis
- Explore more: Learn more about Antarctica, the land, the animals, the plants. How do they survive?

V. Social Studies
  - Antarctica – I want to show you something about its name.
    - The Arctic Circle was known first. Antarctica was named for being opposite of the arctic.
    - Do you see "arctic" in there? Anti, as a prefix, can mean the opposite. So its name means the opposite Arctic.
    - Why is Antarctica the opposite of the Arctic?
      - It's on the South Pole while the Arctic is on the North Pole.
  - Most of the green on Antarctica is found on its *peninsula*.
    - Look at the map of Antarctica for Day 20.
    - The peninsula is the part that sticks out (on the upper left).
      - The definition of peninsula is that it has water on three sides.
      - That's different than an island which has water on all sides.
  - Look at the map of America on Day 17. Can you find another peninsula? What about on the world map on Day 2? (Note: Look on the maps before continuing.)
    - America has a sunny one in the southeast. Much of the state of Florida is a peninsula.
    - The country of Italy is another famous peninsula.
  - Another feature of the geography of Antarctica are its *fjords*.
    - The cold-climate country of Norway is probably most known for its fjords, but Antarctica has them too.
    - You can see all the bumps along the coast of Antarctica. Some of those are fjords.
      - They are all inlets, where water comes in between the land.
      - A fjord is an inlet with cliffs on either side.
  - Picture being in a narrow stream with high cliff rock faces on either side. To act out a fjord, two people could be the cliffs on either side and someone could lie down on the floor between them. That person is the water. Or maybe instead of a fort, you could build a pretend fjord today. ☺

- o Recall: What is the name of an area of land that has water on three sides? peninsula
- o Explore more: Learn about glaciers and other land features of Antarctica.

VI. Discussion
- o Look at verse 7 from today's Scripture reading. What should have Cain done?

VI. Writing
- o Choose one of your writings from Days 22-24 to edit.
- o Read it out loud to look for things that don't make sense, don't flow or just don't sound right.
- o Look for spelling mistakes. Check for correct capitalization and punctuation.
- o Make sure you are using complete sentences.
- o You can use an editing checklist to help you look for problems.
- o Have someone older than you check it over once you've fixed it. (You can fix it by just making marks on the page to note changes.)
- o Listen to their corrections and suggestions and make changes to your writing.
- o Make a final draft. Rewrite it or type it.

Day 21

I.   Read Genesis 4:8-12.

II. Memory Verse
   o   1 Corinthians 10:13
   o   No temptation has overtaken you but such as is common to man; and God is faithful, who will not allow you to be tempted beyond what you are able, but with the temptation will provide the way of escape also, so that you will be able to endure it.

III. Language
   o   Spelling/Handwriting
      •   verse 8
      •   Cain, wanderer, field, blood
      •   Spelling Tips:
         ▪   Cain is a name. We haven't had this word, but it has the same vowel spelling pattern as rain, where two vowels together make the first one say its name.
         ▪   Wanderer ends with the same sound repeated. It's spelled the same each time. Make sure each syllable has a vowel. How many syllables is it?
            •   3
            •   The first syllable ends with the word "and."
         ▪   The word field follows the spelling pattern, I before E except after C.
         ▪   The word blood has a double letter for its vowel sound. It looks like it could say – blue-d.
   o   Vocabulary
      •   my brother's keeper (verse 9)
      •   This is an expression. People use it to mean that we should look out for each other.
      •   The original meaning is more along the lines of being in charge of the other, controlling his coming and going (like keeping sheep).
   o   Hebrew
      •   We are going to finish the verse: Genesis 1:2b. …and the Spirit of God was moving over the surface of the waters
      •   Read this part of the verse and find what you already know.
      •   ve RUakh eloHEEM meraKHEfet al pnaa ha MAyim
      •   You know five of the words already!

IV. Science
   o   Today let's go to a different biome.
      •   First, let's learn another word, *ecology*. Ecology has a suffix, meaning it has a word part attached to the end of it. A word with –ology as a suffix means it is the study of something, so ecology is the study of whatever "eco" is related to.
      •   On Day 19 we learned the word, ecosystem, the system of how all living things in an area live together and relate to one another.

- So, ecology is the study of just that, how animals relate to one another and their environment, their surroundings.
  - The biome we'll look at today is the desert.
  - We've talked about the Fertile Crescent. That land is fertile because of its location along water, but it's really a desert region. That's why the whole region wasn't known as fertile.
  - What do you know about the desert?
  - Here are some things to know about the desert.
    - What defines a desert is that it has very little rain. We call cold weather deserts the tundra.
    - Today I'm talking about hot-weather deserts. They will usually have less than 10 inches (25 cm) of rain each year.
    - We usually consider deserts to be dry, sandy places. Did you know deserts grow?
      - *Desertification* is when arid, or dry, areas of the world become increasingly arid to the point where they begin to lose their bodies of water. When streams start to dry up then the vegetation dies. Without plants then animals leave the area. Life needs water.
        - Side note: Life needs water. Life needs light (energy). Jesus is the light of the world. Do you know who the Bible compares to water? The Holy Spirit (John 4) People need Jesus and the Holy Spirit to have life!
      - I remember reading about workers in Mauritania whose full-time job is sweeping back the desert. The sand is always encroaching on everything.
    - Is there life in the desert?
      - Yes. There are living things created to survive in what we would consider to be a harsh environment.
      - They still need water, but God has made a way. Many animals get water from plants. The most famous desert plant is the cactus.
        - Instead of leaves, it has spines, sort of like scales for a plant. These are close to the plant and reduce the exposure to wind and sun which lessens how much water is lost to evaporation.
        - A cactus stores water in its stem which is very large compared to other plants. Think of how a cactus stem compares to the stem of a flower!

      - One desert animal is the ostrich.
        - The ostrich is a very fast bird, on the ground. It cannot fly, but it can run as fast as a car on the highway.

90

- It has special air sacs connected to its lungs. Its lungs don't work the way mammals' lungs do. Air does not go in and out of its lungs; air can continuously flow through the lungs.
- The air sacs provide more room for more air, so it can breathe more slowly, taking in more air with each breath.
- Since ostriches can't fly, they are nomads, wandering from place to place to find food and water, not settling in one certain location.
  - Actually, a lot of their water comes from food. There is water inside all living things, and so the ostrich gets water from the things it eats.
- Recall: What makes something a desert? What happens during desertification?
  - very little rainfall
  - The water in an area dries up so that the living things die or move elsewhere.
- Explore more: Learn about other animals and plants unique to the desert. What characteristics do they have that enable them to survive there?

V. Social Studies
- Today's social studies lesson is on nomads, wanderers. In our Scripture today, who was told he would be a nomad?
  - Cain, it was part of his punishment for murdering his brother.
- In an agricultural society people have to stay put. Farming takes place in one location. Your farmland can't be packed up and taken with you! People settled where there was good land for farming, where it was fertile.
- When people settled, they set up homes, businesses, places of worship, etc.
- Nomads didn't. They wandered about without any permanent home. They traveled with tents for their shelters that could be taken down and carried along. They may have used camels to carry loads.
- Nomads often had herds. They would drive their animals on to find more food for them. When they'd cleared an area, they could move on.
- They could also have been involved in *trade*. Trade is buying and selling without money. They could take items gained in one area and take them to new places. They could trade one thing for another and in that way introduce new ideas, materials, foods, spices, fabrics, etc. to different areas.
- Recall: What is a nomad? How could they have helped develop civilization?
  - a wanderer
  - By enabling trade, they could introduce new ideas and materials into areas.
- Explore more: Learn about nomadic people. Maybe you'd like to learn more about the Bedouins.

VI. Discussion
- In what ways are we responsible to be our brother's keeper? In what ways are we not responsible?

VII. Writing
- Complete Writing Sentences 5 in your workbook.
- All you have to do is write the proper noun for each common noun.

- o Common nouns are common things, people, and places.
    - o A mountain, a man, and a cracker are all examples of common nouns.
- o Proper nouns are the names of people, places and things.
    - o Instead of a common mountain, a proper noun would be the Rocky Mountains.
    - o Instead of a common man, it's George Washington. Any name is proper. Each person is unique and is THE (insert name here). Every name is capitalized.
    - o Instead of a common cracker, it's a Ritz.
    - o The Rockies, George, and Ritz are all capitalized because they are names.
- o Give it a try on your worksheet.

Day 22

I. Read Genesis 4:13-15.

II. Memory Verse
- 1 Corinthians 10:13
- No temptation has overtaken you but such as is common to man; and God is faithful, who will not allow you to be tempted beyond what you are able, but with the temptation will provide the way of escape also, so that you will be able to endure it.

III. Language
- Spelling/Handwriting
  - verse 13
  - great, driven, vagrant, vengeance
  - Spelling Tips
    - The word great ends with the word eat. Think about having something great to eat.
    - The word driven is the word drive with one extra letter on the end.
    - The word vagrant is our vocabulary word today. It ends with the word ant. It only has two vowels.
    - The word vengeance is a harder one. There are two different vowels. One appears once and is silent. It is used just like in heaven. You'll also find in this word the rule that a C followed by an E or I makes its soft sound, S.
- Vocabulary
  - vagrant (verse 14)
  - a person who wanders from place to place, living by begging (noun)
- Hebrew
  - Genesis 1:2b …and the Spirit of God was moving over the surface of the waters
  - Read the whole thing.
  - ve RUakh eloHEEM meraKHEfet al pnaa ha MAyim
  - Today you can learn that RUakh eloHEEM means Spirit of God.

IV. Science
- Do you think Cain had anything else to fear besides man? Did humans have to fear wild animals back then? Do you think Cain ran into a dinosaur? We talked about reptiles before. Let's look at these largest of reptiles.
  - The largest reptiles we know of are the dinosaurs, which are *extinct*. That means none live any more. The stories that exist in cultures around the world of sea monsters and fire-breathing dragons, though possibly exaggerated, began with real encounters I believe.
  - Here are two excerpts from "The Existence of Fire Breathing Dragons" (http://www.creationworldview.org/articles_view.asp?id=50)

"God states in Job 41:15, 18-21: 'His strong scales are his pride, shut up as with a tight seal. . . . His sneezes [breathings] flash forth light, and his eyes are like the eyelids of the morning. Out of his mouth go burning torches; sparks of fire leap forth. Out of his nostrils smoke goes forth, as from a boiling pot and burning rushes. His breath kindles coals, and a flame goes forth from his mouth.'

 If you read all of Job 41 with some discernment and knowledge of fossil remains, you will come to the realization that the creature called Leviathan in Scripture is a species of Plesiosaur(idae) or Pliosaur(idae) . These were large aquatic reptiles. These creatures grew to lengths of 43 to 56 feet long. The Plesiosaurs had particularly long necks."

The author of the article believes a dragon could have burped a gas that ignited by some internal mechanism that God gave to it as a defense.

- And here's one more section of the article.

"There are various references to dinosaurs in the Bible. Leviathans are mentioned five times in Scripture; twice in Job, twice in Psalms and once in Isaiah. Isaiah lived about 700 BC. Behemoth in Job 40:15+ is clearly a land-dwelling dinosaur. An animal called a dragon is mentioned in the Book of Psalms. 'Flying reptiles' or 'flying serpents' are mentioned twice in Isaiah."

One interesting thing to note is that there are universal stories of giant reptiles. These stories have been told in different cultures, in different regions of the world, and through different centuries, yet all of these people have similar stories. Evolution scientists say that dinosaurs lived millions of years before humans and that they never had contact. If that were true, how did these stories begin? They didn't learn about dinosaurs from fossils. Fossils of dinosaurs were not found until hundreds of years after these stories were told.

- o Explore more: Learn about other types of dinosaurs. Specifically, you could see what you can learn about what the Bible calls "behemoth."

V. Social Studies
- o Since I'm talking about supposed dinosaur myths, let's talk about mythology in cultures. What is a myth?
  - a myth is a make-believe story
- o Some call the Bible mythology. I don't.
- o Some would call stories of fire-breathing dragons mythology. It's likely such stories have been changed and exaggerated as time goes on, which is what happens with oral histories, where new generations learn history through storytellers.
  - Have you ever played whisper down the lane?
    - The message changes as it's told over and over again.
  - There's a big difference between oral history and written history.
    - Oral history can change over time. Written history is preserved.
  - By the way, when the Dead Sea scrolls (ancient copies of the Bible) were found around 1950, it proved to skeptics that the stories of the Bible had not changed over time.

- The scrolls had been written around the time of Christ and showed that our modern Bible was accurate.
- Do you know any myths from your culture?
- In America we have the myth of Paul Bunyan.
  - Paul Bunyan is the tale of a frontiersman who was so big and strong he could do anything. He is told to have cleared much of western America for the pioneers.
  - One of the stories is about how he found Babe, his blue ox. It was blue because he found it in the blue snow. Why was the snow blue?
    - "Well now, one winter it was so cold that all the geese flew backward and all the fish moved south and even the snow turned blue. Late at night, it got so frigid that all spoken words froze solid afore they could be heard. People had to wait until sunup to find out what folks were talking about the night before."
    - (*Babe the Blue Ox* retold by Schlosser http://americanfolklore.net/folklore/2010/07/babe_the_blue_ox.html)
  - The most famous mythology comes from Greece. The stories revolve around a number of gods who had Zeus as their ruler. He was called the god of the sky and thunder and ruled from Mount Olympus (in Greece).
  - Let me tell you one of the Greek myths that is sometimes referenced in literature. The character is Achilles.
    - In the story, Achilles is the best Greek fighter among those fighting against the Trojans.
    - He could only be harmed in one area, his Achilles tendon.
      - Above your heel run your finger up. Do you feel a line going up from your heel? That's it.
    - The myth is that his mother dipped him in a special river that made him invincible, except she was holding him by the back of his heel.
    - In battle he was hit by an arrow, where?
    - When we say that something is our Achilles' heel, we are saying that it is our downfall. It's what caused us to fail.
- Do you know any other myths?
- Recall: What is a myth?
  - a made-up story
- Explore more: Learn another famous mythical Greek character, Icarus.

VI. Discussion
- Did Cain have the right to argue with God about his punishment? Was God wrong to protect Cain? What do you think it says about God that He does protect Cain?

VII. Writing
- Use the discussion question as a writing prompt.
- Get a high five and/or hug if you use any spelling or vocabulary word.

Day 23

I. Read Genesis 4:16-20.

    *Jabal, was he in agriculture or was he a nomad?

II. Memory Verse
- o 1 Corinthians 10:13
- o No temptation has overtaken you but such as is common to man; and God is faithful, who will not allow you to be tempted beyond what you are able, but with the temptation will provide the way of escape also, so that you will be able to endure it.

III. Language
- o Spelling/Handwriting
  - verse 20
  - father, dwell, tents, birth
  - Spelling Tips:
    - The word <u>father</u> does not have an O.
    - The word <u>dwell</u> is the word well with an extra letter in front.
    - <u>Tents</u> is a plural noun. Just make tent plural by adding one letter.
    - <u>Birth</u> has the same vowel spelling pattern as your word, third. Remember that every syllable has a vowel. That means every word must have a vowel.
- o Vocabulary
  - presence (verse 16)
  - being there, whether seen or not, or a group or people all together in a particular place for a particular reason, or an impact made by being there (noun)
- o Hebrew
  - Genesis 1:2b. …and the Spirit of God was moving over the surface of the waters
  - Read the whole thing together. Can you say parts of it from memory?
  - ve RUakh eloHEEM meraKHEfet al pnaa ha MAyim
  - Today learn that meraKHEfet means moving.

IV. Science
- o He was the father of those who cared for livestock. Livestock are farm animals, usually referring to things like horses and cows. What type of animals are those?
  - mammals
- o We're going to look at another mammal today, one that's mentioned in the Bible.
- o Do you remember the things that make an animal a mammal, that make you a mammal?
  - warm blooded (Their body temperature stays the same no matter what environment they are in.)
  - have hair
  - give birth to babies instead of laying eggs
  - moms give milk to their babies

- o The animal we're going to learn about today is the gazelle. Let's start with the Bible verses.
  - 2 Samuel 2:18 ...as fleet-footed as a wild gazelle...
  - 1 Chronicles 12:8 ...as agile as a gazelle on a mountain slope...
- o Maybe you need to know that fleet-footed means really fast and agile means that you can move quickly and easily in any direction. What do these verses tell us about gazelles?
  - They can go anywhere easily, even up a mountain slope, even escaping those after it.
- o So, what makes the gazelle move so easily? Let's see if we can find out. What can you observe about gazelles from these pictures?

Picture info: "תמונה 1108" by avishai teicherUser:Avi1111 - Own work. Licensed under Public domain via Wikimedia Commons - http://commons.wikimedia.org/wiki/File:%D7%AA%D7%9E%D7%95%D7%A0%D7%94_1108.jpg #mediaviewer/File:%D7%AA%D

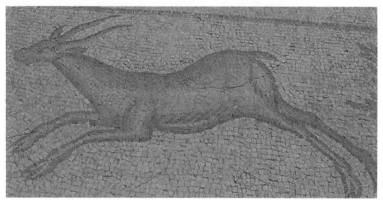

- The second picture is an ancient mosaic of a mountain gazelle. The picture was found in Israel.
- What did you observe about its body, legs, and feet? How do you think those things might help it be fast and agile?
- Let me tell you some things you can't observe.
  - There are 19 species of gazelle, most live in the plains of Africa and Asia, but there are gazelles that live in mountains. They are in the same family as sheep. They range in size from about two to five feet tall.

- They have smaller hearts and livers which need less oxygen which helps them with their endurance.
- Gazelles don't run. They pronk or stott. It's a leap where they spring from all four feet.
- Did you notice the hooves in the mosaic? Here's what I found out about those.
  - "Like claws, hooves are also made of keratin and are found on mammals such as pigs, deer, antelope, and horses. Hooves are usually found on herbivores or prey animals. They serve a very special purpose for most members of this group by offering protection from the impact of their feet striking the ground when running. Hoofed animals rely on being able to flee rapidly to avoid predators. Because more force is put on front hooves when the animal runs, they are often larger and can withstand greater force than the back hooves. Many mammals have hooves that are cloven with two parts. This structure allows the animal to walk easily in all sorts of habitats, from hard ground to soft, sandy soil. Hooves are also used for grooming, to dig for food, and for defense." (from Answers.com/Q/What_are_hooves_for)
  - All of this makes for speeds of up to 60 miles an hour. (That's nearly 100 km/hr.) That's about the speed of a car on a highway. But not only that, they can maintain a fast speed without having to stop. This means they can outrun fast predators who have to stop and catch their breath! Their coasting speed is half their sprinting speed, which is probably about as fast as your parents drive near your home.
  - Recall: What are some special things about the gazelle?
    - pronk, fast, hooves
  - Explore more: Choose another mammal to learn about. What are its unique features? How did God build in a defense, such as the gazelle's ability to make a getaway?

V. Social Studies
  - In Genesis 1 it says that man was to rule over the animals.
  - How has that happened? In what ways do people rule over animals?
    - Here are some I thought of:
      - pets
        - They have become man's friend, but live in their homes under their control. Pets are *domesticated;* they are tame, not wild. People use animals for companionship or entertainment.
      - working animals
        - Another type of domesticated animal are animals that work for humans. This includes animals such as horses, oxen, and camels that carry people or loads or pull wagons or carts. There are other working animals such as animals in shows. Have you ever seen a dog do tricks for money? People use animals for their profit.

- farm animals
  - These are also domesticated animals. While some farm animals work, others are for producing wool, milk, eggs or meat. People have the power to kill animals and eat them.
- Recall: What is the name for an animal that is tame, not wild?
  - domesticated
- Explore more: How are animals domesticated? How is a wild animal tamed and trained?

VI. Discussion
- What would you name your parents or describe them as, for instance, the father of those who dwell in tents and have livestock?

VII. Writing
- Use the discussion question as a writing prompt.
- Get a high five and/or hug if you use any spelling or vocabulary word.

Day 24

I. Read Genesis 4:21-24.
    *What kind of person is Lamech?

II. Memory Verse
    o 1 Corinthians 10:13
    o No temptation has overtaken you but such as is common to man; and God is faithful, who will not allow you to be tempted beyond what you are able, but with the temptation will provide the way of escape also, so that you will be able to endure it.

III. Language
    o Spelling/Handwriting
        • verse 21
        • lyre, implements, speech, striking
        • Spelling Tips:
            ▪ Lyre is a unique word. It is a homophone for liar, which is spelled L-I-A-R and means someone who told a lie. This is a musical instrument. It is spelled with two vowels, but neither one is in the other form of liar. What other letter can say I? The second vowel comes at the end.
            ▪ Implements is a plural noun. Pronounce it carefully to spell it correctly. (Say the short E sound where it belongs.)
            ▪ Speech has a double letter for its vowel sound.
            ▪ Striking follows the rules of grammar. Can you figure it out? Don't write strick – ing. There are two vowels, but they are the same.
    o Vocabulary
        • implement (verse 22)
        • tool made for a particular use (noun)
        • to put a plan into action (verb)
        • How is it used in verse 22? Is it a noun or a verb in that sentence?
    o Hebrew
        • We're finishing Genesis 1:2. ...and the Spirit of God was moving over the surface of the waters.
        • ve RUakh eloHEEM meraKHEfet al pnaa ha MAyim
        • Practice saying it from memory.
        • Do you remember VE and HA?
        • Can you say the whole verse?
            ▪ ve ha Arets haaTAH TOhu va VOhu ve KHOshekh al pnaa teHOM ve RUakh eloHEEM meraKHEfet al pnaa ha MAyim

IV. Science
    o The man today forged implements of iron and bronze. What does that mean?
        • It means that he made tools out of iron and bronze. That he forged them means that he used fire to do it. He heated up the metal to soften it and then hammered it into shape.
    o Are you able to find bronze and iron on the Periodic Table? You have a copy of it in your workbook and in your Map Book.

- You can only find Iron. Iron is a basic element. Everything on that chart under number 93 is what everything else in the world is made of. They are the elements our world is made of. (Note: #93 and above are synthetic, manmade, and useful for nothing. I talk about them in a lesson in Acts.)
- Bronze is made from other elements. It is made of copper and tin mixed together. Those you can go find on your Periodic Table.
  - Iron is Fe, number 26. The letters refer to the Latin names of the elements. The numbers are called their atomic weight and refer to how heavy they are. We'll talk more about what gives an atom its weight in another lesson.
  - Copper is Cu, number 29.
  - Tin is Sn, number 50.
- What do tin, copper, bronze, and iron all have in common?
  - They are metals.
- We know they are useful for tools, do you know what else bronze is used for?
  - Bronze and brass are both made from copper and are often used to mean the same or similar thing. There may be bronze or brass fixtures in your home. It's used in architecture.
  - It's a useful metal around things that can catch on fire because it doesn't cause sparks like some other metals.
  - It is used in sculptures and has been used in coins as well.
  - In ancient times bronze was used to make weapons.
- What is iron used for?
  - Iron is used to make other metals, similar to how bronze is made of copper and tin.
  - You may have an iron skillet in your home.
  - Iron is useful to plants. It's a nutrient that keeps them healthy.
  - Iron keeps you healthy too. Iron, in fact, is needed to carry oxygen through your blood.
- Do you remember what one type of food is that has iron?
  - Meats have a lot of iron. Some greens have a lot of iron, such as spinach.
- I also want to look at two types of minerals mentioned in Genesis 2: onyx and gold.
- I'm sure you've heard of one of those before. Let's start there.
  - Gold is a pure substance. It can be broken down to a single atom of gold. What do you think gold's symbol is?
    - It's Au. Not what you guessed? Au comes from the Latin word for gold, aurum, which means shining dawn.
  - Gold is considered a *precious metal*. What does it mean if we call something precious?
    - It means it has great value.
  - Gold is the only yellow metal. It's also very malleable, meaning it can be bent and stretched and hammered into different shapes (which is how we get our gold jewelry). Gold can even be made into threads for sewing and hammered so thin that it can be eaten!
    - I've never eaten gold, but if I did, it wouldn't taste like anything, but it's not toxic, meaning it's safe to put in your mouth.
- We can read about these uses in the Bible.

- "Then they hammered out gold sheets and cut them into threads." (Exodus 39:3a) This is from where directions are being given as to how to build the tabernacle.
- "He took the calf which they had made and burned it with fire, and ground it to powder, and scattered it over the surface of the water and made the sons of Israel drink it." (Exodus 32.20) This is about what Moses did after the Israelites made a golden calf to worship.

o Next let's learn about onyx.
- It's a semi-precious gem. What do you think that means?
  - Semi means partially, so it has value but only partial the value that a precious metal has.
- The onyx stone has light and dark layers, colored bands. Most traditionally the name is used for gems that are black or brown with white or light layers.
- This rock was used often for carvings and engravings.
- In the image on the next page, the white layer was carved and the black behind it is part of the same stone.

o Recall: What's the difference between precious and semi-precious metals or gems?
- Precious are more valuable.
o Explore more: What are the precious metals? What are considered precious stones? Learn their properties.

V. Social Studies
o There's a period in history known as the Bronze Age. It's considered to be around 3300 BC through 1200 BC.
o It's the period of history when people started making bronze tools instead of using stone tools.

- It happened at different points for different civilizations. It happened earliest in the part of the world we've looked at so far, in Mesopotamia.
  - The end of the Bronze Age came because people started making tools with another metal. Can guess which one?
    - Iron
  - The flood probably happened around 2300 BC, so that happens during this period. Abraham was around 2000 BC, so he was alive during this period.
  - It was a period of history where there were big new inventions.
    - It was the start of using written communication. Civilizations developed ways of writing.
    - It was when the wheel was invented.
    - But remember, all these developments took place at different times in different places.
      - For instance, the wheel wasn't invented in South America.
    - People in Asia, Europe, and Africa had an advantage over those in South America. Can you figure out what it was? (Hint: Look at the map of the world in the beginning of the Map Book.)
      - The people in Asia, Africa, and Europe were able to travel to each other. We mentioned how nomads traded. One thing they "traded" was ideas. The sharing of ideas was made possible as people traveled and explored to new lands.
      - The people in South America were isolated. They didn't have the same amount of contact with new ideas.
        - They also had different needs and resources, which leads to different inventions, each which meets the specific needs each group has with what they have available to them.
  - Recall: When was the Bronze Age? What marked its beginning and end?
    - 3300 BC – 1200 BC
    - the discovery of bronze, the discovery of iron as a use for tools
  - Explore More: Learn about the invention of the wheel.

VI. Discussion
  - What would be your saying you'd want to be known for?

VII. Writing
  - Use the discussion question as a writing prompt.
  - Get a high five and/or hug if you use any spelling or vocabulary word.

Day 25

I.   Read Genesis 4:25-26.

*Think about this time period. People are living a long time and having lots of children. Some are farmers (like Abel) and are establishing agricultural areas, and others are nomadic (like Cain) and are herders. God had not yet given permission to kill and eat animals, but we read of Lamech who killed men and children who messed with him. It seems likely someone like that might kill an animal! What do you think it was like then? Today we read how they began to call on God. What was happening before then? What happened after that? What do you think? What do you wish you knew about this time period?

II.   Memory Verse
- o   Test yourselves.
  - •   Say 1 Corinthians 10:13 from memory.
- o   Review Romans 3:23.
  - •   For all have sinned and fall short of the glory of God.

III.   Language
- o   Spelling/Handwriting
  - •   You can write your memory verse today.
  - •   Test yourselves on your words from Days 21-24.
    - ▪   Cain, wanderer, field, blood
    - ▪   great, driven, vagrant, vengeance
    - ▪   father, dwell, tents, birth
    - ▪   lyre, implements, speech, striking

- o   Vocabulary
  - •   Test yourselves on your words from Days 21-24.
    - ▪   my brother's keeper – to mind others
    - ▪   vagrant – a person who wanders from place to place, living by begging
    - ▪   presence – being there, whether seen or not, or a group or people all together in a particular place for a particular reason, or an impact made by being there
    - ▪   implement – tool made for a particular use, put a plan into action
- o   Hebrew
  - •   Test yourselves on this week's Hebrew words.
  - •   ...and the Spirit of God was moving over the surface of the waters
  - •   ve RUakh eloHEEM meraKHEfet al pnaa ha MAyim
  - •   Now say it all together, Genesis 1:1-2.
    - ▪   be reSHEET baRA eloHEEM et ha shaMAyim ve et ha Arets
    - ▪   ve ha Arets haaTAH TOhu va VOhu ve KHOshekh al pnaa teHOM ve RUakh eloHEEM meraKHEfet al pnaa ha MAyim

V. Social Studies
- People started to call on the name of the Lord. People throughout history have called on many different gods, including the sun and moon.
- When the moon goes around the earth one time, we call it a *lunar* month. When you see words like lunar or luna, it's talking about the moon.
- Why do you think ancient people worshiped the sun and the moon?
  - The sun and the moon seemed so powerful and magical to ancient people.
- A lunar eclipse is when the full moon goes into the shadow of the earth when the earth is directly between the sun and the moon. It only lasts a few hours. It's only happened a handful of times in thousands of years, but in 2014 and 2015 it happened four times. It can make the moon appear red, giving it the name, a blood moon.
- What do you think a total solar eclipse is?
  - A total solar eclipse is when the moon perfectly blocks out the sun's light from the earth, when it all lines up precisely.
  - Can you imagine how scared ancient people were, people who worshiped the sun, when it disappeared one day?
- Ancient peoples around the world had ceremonies to honor these celestial bodies and to scare away whatever might harm them.
  - It's extremely sad. The Bible talks about those who worship the creation instead of the Creator. How much greater is the one who made the creation!
  - Even more foolish are those who worship statues that they call gods. The statues are made with human hands, but they sacrifice to them and pray to them.
  - Satan takes advantage of these false religions and uses his demons to act among the worshipers. They may see supernatural things, but they aren't from God!
  - They are tormented by fear. Our God tells us to be free from fear!
    - Those caught in false religions feel the constant need to please or appease their false god.
  - They need to know that the one true God gives salvation as a free gift and desires us to love Him, not sacrifice to Him.
  - They need to know there is a God who loves them and wants to be with them and who will care for them as opposed to gods who don't care about human life.
- That's one way to tell true religion from false religion. True religion loves people. People are most important.
  - For instance, in Hinduism rats are sacred. Rats are not to be killed. The rats are allowed to multiply and eat your crops and cause you to go hungry, but it wouldn't be okay to kill the rats!
- Recall: What is an eclipse?
  - It's when the sun, moon and earth line up just right so that light is blocked from either the moon or the sun.
- Explore more: Learn more about eclipses and the signs people say they have shown, especially you could look into "blood" moons.

V. Science
- o Let's stay out in outer space for our science lesson.
- o In Genesis 2 we read that the heavens were completed. This is part of the reason why I think the heavens, that great expanse above us that we know as the universe, has an end, a boundary. There are other things like reading about the waters above the heavens. The heavens would have to have an upper boundary for something to be above it.
- o We talked about stars and the sun and moon which are all part of the heavens. Let's talk about what else is out there in the universe.
- o The Sun, Moon, and Earth are part of what is known as the Solar System. Earth is a planet. There are eight planets in our solar system with a couple of dwarf (smaller) planets as well. The Sun is at the center, meaning all of the planets orbit around the Sun. That's our solar system, the system of planets and moons that orbit our sun. Earth is the only planet that humans can live on. Any farther from the sun and it would be too cold, any closer, too hot. It perfectly rotates to give us day and night, and orbits to give us the seasons of the year.
- o I'm going to tell you the order of the planets. Pay attention and then name which planet is the closest and farthest. The order of the planets, from the closest to the farthest from the sun is: Mercury, Venus, Earth, Mars, Jupiter (the biggest), Saturn (known for the rings around it), Uranus, and Neptune. The most famous dwarf planet is Pluto because it comes next and used to be considered one of the planets.
  - • Did you catch which is closest to the sun?
    - ▪ Mercury is a mere 36 million miles from the sun (58 million kilometers.)
  - • Which planet is the farthest?
    - ▪ Neptune is the farthest from the sun. It's 2.8 billion miles away from the sun (4.5 billion kilometers). Pluto is even farther.
- o Earth isn't the only planet with a moon. What is a moon?
  - • It's a natural satellite, something that orbits a planet. The difference between a moon and a rock that's a planet is that a moon orbits a planet instead of a star.
- o Earth has one moon, but how many moons do you think there are in our whole solar system?
  - • Between all of the planets there are 146 moons in our solar system.
- o Do you think there other solar systems?
  - • Yes, there are! The word solar, refers to the sun. Remember, the sun is just a star. There are billions of stars. If a rock (that's what a planet is!) is orbiting the star, then it's a solar system.
- o There are also other rocks orbiting in solar systems. We know them as comets and asteroids. Comets are made of ice and dust and appear to have a tail, which is really just gases escaping. Asteroids are just rocks. Some are massive in size, 600 miles across (1000 km). 600 miles is about how far you would drive if you could just drive straight and fast on a highway for ten hours! While there are huge asteroids, there are also teeny, tiny asteroids; some are basically just dust.
- o What else is out there?

- Meteors are also rocks in space. When they enter into the atmosphere of our planet, they burn up. When we see these, we call them "falling stars." Have you ever seen one? Of course, they aren't stars at all, but rocks.
- Galaxies are even bigger than our solar system. A galaxy is a group of stars and each star could be a solar system!
- Our sun, which is a star, is part of the Milky Way galaxy; the Milky Way has over 200 billion stars in it. Astronomers, those who study the stars and planets, have observed 80 galaxies. It's hard to imagine just how big our universe is!
  - Think of it this way. It's like the room you are sitting in is a galaxy. A piece of dirt in the room is the Sun. How small would you be then?
  o Recall: What do you need to call something a solar system? Do you remember which planet is closest to the Sun? What are some of the rocks out there orbiting in our solar system?
    - rocks orbiting a star
    - mercury
    - asteroids, meteors, comets
  o Explore more: What else is in deep space?

VI. Discussion
  o When have you called upon the Lord?

VII. Writing
  o Choose one of your writings from Days 22-24 to edit.
  o Read it out loud to look for things that don't make sense, don't flow or just don't sound right.
  o Look for spelling mistakes. Check for correct capitalization and punctuation.
  o Make sure you are using complete sentences.
  o You can use an editing checklist to help you look for problems.
  o Have someone older than you check it over once you've fixed it. (You can fix it by just making marks on the page to note changes.)
  o Listen to their corrections and suggestions and make changes to your writing.
  o Make a final draft. Rewrite it or type it.

Day 26

I.   Read Genesis 5:1-2.

II.   Memory Verse
   o   Review Genesis 1:1. Can you say it from memory?
   o   Find it in the Bible. (This shouldn't be hard!)
   o   "In the beginning God created the heavens and the earth."

III. Language
   o   Spelling
       •   Complete Spelling Review 1 in your workbook.
   o   Hebrew
       •   Read or say from memory Genesis 1:1-2.
       •   Some reminders:
           ▪   I am not using capitalization or punctuation.
           ▪   You emphasize the capitalized part of the word. It is "stressed" when you say it.
           ▪   AA and EE make the long vowel sound. O and U always make the long vowel sound. A makes the sound of "ah" and E makes the sound "e" as in red.
           ▪   You can always refer to the Hebrew reference sheet to see everything that's been taught so far.
       •   1:1 be reSHEET baRA eloHEEM et ha shaMAyim ve et ha Arets
       •   1:2 ve ha Arets haaTAH TOhu va VOhu ve KHOshekh al pnaa teHOM ve RUakh eloHEEM meraKHEfet al pnaa ha MAyim

IV. Science/Social Studies
   o   Today go through the science terms for review. They are listed on the following page under "Science Review 1."
       •   What do you remember about each one? Ask someone to tell you what each one is. You can choose someone for each one or let them all call out or let them raise their hands. You could toss a ball to the person you want to answer, etc. You can do this for any of the reviews this week.

Science Review 1
The lesson number where the word was introduced is in parenthesis in case you want to look any up.

herbivores	animals that eat only plants (8)
carnivores	animals that eat only meat (8)
exoskeleton	hard external shell (7)
vertebrates	animals with backbones (5)
invertebrates	animals with no backbones (7)
gills	slits through which fish breathe (6)
antennae	used by insects for feeling and smelling (7)
sheep	mammals known for being followers (9)
reptiles	animals: cold-blooded, lay eggs, have scales, carnivores, vertebrates (18)
birds	animals: warm-blooded, lay eggs, two legs, feathers, vertebrates (5)
fish	animals that are vertebrates, lay eggs, gills, scales, cold-blooded (6)
mammals	animals: warm-blooded, give birth to live babies, vertebrates, hair (9)
insects	animals: invertebrates, have antennae and exoskeletons and six legs (7)
habitats	animal homes (19)
biome	broad characteristic of an animal habitat such as desert or mountain (19)
niche	each living thing's role in its biome (19)
ecosystem	an area where living things live and interact together (19)
ecology	the study of how living things live and interact together (21)
classify	organize by similarities (15)

V. Writing

- o Write for one minute. Start writing a story; it can be true or pretend. (That's called fiction, a not-true story.) Time yourselves. Just write and write and don't stop. I'll give you a word to start with to get your brain activated. Use that word in your first sentence to get you going. (You don't have to use the word if that word makes you think of another word that you want to use.) Just write!
- o Today's word is SWARM. (Note: I'm using vocabulary words for these. Make sure everyone knows what the word means. Also, they don't need to spell everything correctly. That's what editing is for. This week's writing assignments are for getting ideas down on paper. I don't recommend correcting these. Just encourage expression and creativity.)
- o You can share what you wrote by having everyone read out loud to each other.

Day 27

I.   Read Genesis 5:3-5.

II.   Memory Verse
- o   Review Psalm 150:6. Can you say it from memory?
- o   Find it in the Bible.
- o   "Let everything that has breath praise the Lord. Praise the Lord!"

III.   Language
- o   Spelling
  - •   Complete Spelling Review 2 in your workbook.
- o   Hebrew
  - •   Read or say from memory Genesis 1:1-2.
  - •   Review these words: reSHEET, baRA and eloHEEM. What does each mean?
  - •   Do you remember what "be" means in front of reSHEET?
  - •   Read or say from memory Genesis 1:1-2.
    - ▪   1:1 be reSHEET baRA eloHEEM et ha shaMAyim ve et ha Arets
    - ▪   1:2 ve ha Arets haaTAH TOhu va VOhu ve KHOshekh al pnaa teHOM ve RUakh eloHEEM meraKHEfet al pnaa ha MAyim

IV.   Science/Social Studies
- o   Today complete Science Review 2 in your workbook.

V.   Writing
- o   Write for two minutes. Time yourselves. Just write and write and don't stop. I'll give you a word to start with to get your brain activated. Use that word in your first sentence to get you going. Most importantly, just write!
- o   Today's word is MIST.
- o   You can share what you wrote with each other. Read it out loud.

Day 28

I. Read Genesis 5:6-7.

II. Memory Verse
- o Review Genesis 1:2. Can you say it from memory?
- o Find it in the Bible.
- o The earth was formless and void, and darkness was over the surface of the deep, and the Spirit of God was moving over the surface of the waters.

III. Language
- o Spelling
  - • Complete Spelling Review 3 in your workbook.
- o Hebrew
  - • Review these words: ha, ve, shaMAyim, Arets
  - • What does each mean?
  - • Say Genesis 1:1-2.
    - ▪ 1:1 be reSHEET baRA eloHEEM et ha shaMAyim ve et ha Arets
    - ▪ 1:2 ve ha Arets haaTAH TOhu va VOhu ve KHOshekh al pnaa teHOM ve RUakh eloHEEM meraKHEfet al pnaa ha MAyim

IV. Science/Social Studies Review
- • Go through the terms and ask questions. What do you remember?

Social Studies Review 1

The lesson number where the vocabulary word was found is in parenthesis.

continents: Africa, Asia, Europe, Antarctica, Australia, North and South America (2)

oceans: Indian, Pacific, Southern, Atlantic, Artic (2)

constellations: pictures made from connecting the stars (4)

hemispheres: the northern and southern hemispheres are two halves of the globe/earth (4)

equator: the dividing line that separates the northern and southern hemispheres (4)

lunar: having to do with the moon (25)

fossils: preserved remains of a once-living thing (6)

initiative: seeing what needs to be done and going and doing it (7)

interdependent: how things rely on each other (8)

map keys: show you the meaning of the symbols used on maps (13)

V. Writing

- o Write for three minutes. Tell a story. Time yourselves. Just write and write and don't stop. I'll give you a word to start with to get your brain activated. Use that word in your first sentence to get you going. (You don't have to use the word if that word makes you think of another word that you want to use.) Just write!
- o Today's word is CRAFTY.
- o You can share what you wrote. Read to each other.

Day 29

I.   Read Genesis 5:8-10.

II. Memory Verse
   o   Review Romans 3:23. Can you say it from memory?
   o   Find it in the Bible.
   o   For all have sinned and fall short of the glory of God.

III. Language
   o   Spelling
      •   Complete Spelling Review 4 in your workbook.
   o   Hebrew
      •   Review these words: ha, ve, shaMAyim, Arets
      •   Say Genesis 1:1-2.
         ▪   1:1 be reSHEET baRA eloHEEM et ha shaMAyim ve et ha Arets
         ▪   1:2 ve ha Arets haaTAH TOhu va VOhu ve KHOshekh al pnaa teHOM ve RUakh eloHEEM meraKHEfet al pnaa ha MAyim

VI. Science/Social Studies
   o   Complete the Social Studies Review 2 in your workbook.

V.   Writing
   o   Write for four minutes. Time yourselves. Just write and write and don't stop.
   o   Today's word is FASHION.

Day 30

I. Read Genesis 5:11-14.

II. Memory Verse
- o Review 1 Corinthians 10:13. Can you say it from memory?
- o Find it in the Bible.
- o No temptation has overtaken you but such as is common to man; and God is faithful, who will not allow you to be tempted beyond what you are able, but with the temptation will provide the way of escape also, so that you will be able to endure it.

III. Language
- o Spelling
  - Complete Spelling Review 5 in your workbook.
- o Hebrew
  - Do you remember what "et" means in front of shaMAyim and Arets?
    - It signals that a direct object follows.
    - God created what?
      - He created the heavens and He created the earth.
  - Say Genesis 1:1-2 from memory.
    - 1:1 be reSHEET baRA eloHEEM et ha shaMAyim ve et ha Arets
    - 1:2 ve ha Arets haaTAH TOhu va VOhu ve KHOshekh al pnaa teHOM ve RUakh eloHEEM meraKHEfet al pnaa ha MAyim

IV. Science/Social Studies
- o Go over these science terms. What do you remember?
  The lesson number where the vocabulary word was found is in parenthesis.

Science Review 3

energy	the ability to work (1)
decompose	become rotten, decay (3)
dispersal	seeds being moved around (3)
germination	the early growth of a seed plant (3)
atoms	the building blocks for all things (4)
molecules	atoms in combination (4)
refraction	the bending of light (2)
H_2O	name of a water molecule (4)
orbit	revolve around (5)
solar system	rocks orbiting a star (25)
evaporation	water turning into water vapor (11)
condensation	water vapor turning into water droplets (11)
atmosphere	the layer of gases between earth and space (12)
nitrogen	main gas found in the air (14)

VI. Writing
- o Write for five minutes. Tell a story. It can be fact or fiction, made up. Time yourselves. Just write and write and don't stop. I'll give you a word to start with to get your brain

activated. You can use that word in your first sentence to get you going. Don't plan what you are going to write about. Just write!

o   Today's word is CREEP.
o   Let anyone share who would enjoy doing so.

Day 31

I. Read Genesis 5:15-17.

II. Memory Verse
- We're going to learn Genesis 1:3.
- Then God said, "Let there be light"; and there was light.

III. Language
- Grammar
  - A noun is a person, place or thing.
  - An adjective describes a noun.
  - A verb is an action or a state of being (meaning verbs such as: am, is, are, was, were, will, be, has, would, could, etc.)
  - Play the grammar game.
    - Go on a parts-of-speech picnic today for your Grammar Review 1.
    - Go through the alphabet naming an adjective, noun, and verb, for each letter of the alphabet.
      - Here's an example.
        - I went on a picnic and I saw an angry ant acting.
        - I went on a picnic and I saw a big bear biting.
    - If you want, you can try to remember and repeat each phrase, but it's not necessary for the game.
- Hebrew
  - Review these words: haaTAH, TOhu va VOhu, KHOshekh
  - What does each mean?
  - Say Genesis 1:1-2 from memory.
    - 1:1 be reSHEET baRA eloHEEM et ha shaMAyim ve et ha Arets
    - 1:2 ve ha Arets haaTAH TOhu va VOhu ve KHOshekh al pnaa teHOM ve RUakh eloHEEM meraKHEfet al pnaa ha MAyim

IV. Science/Social Studies
- Go through these science terms for review. What do you remember?
  - You can grab a ball and toss it to the person who gets to answer next.
    - If you want to add a competition, let the person who is able to answer take a shot at a basket (improvise with anything) to earn a point, or an extra point.
  - As always, the day number of the lesson where you can find the word introduced is written in parenthesis.

Science Review 3 part 2

organ	the heart and lungs are examples of this (13)
vein	carry the blood back to the heart (13)
arteries	main branches of the circulatory system, carry blood away from the heart (13)
bronze	used for tools and weapons (24)
fallow	unplanted (14)
elevation	how high land is (17)
gravity	the force that pulls a smaller object towards a larger one (and us toward the earth) (17)
deciduous	trees with leaves that change color and fall in cold weather (19)
coniferous	trees with needles that stay green all winter (19)
tundra	a cold-weather area of little precipitation (20)
precipitation	rain and snow are examples of this (20)
desert	an area of the world known for little precipitation (21)
joint	where two bones connect (16)
femur	largest bone in the body (16)

V. Writing

- o Write for six minutes. Tell a story. Time yourselves. Just write and write and don't stop. I'll give you a word to start with to get your brain activated. Use that word in your first sentence to get you going. (You don't have to use the word if that word makes you think of another word that you want to use.) Just write!

- o Today's word is EXPANSE. (Note: The writing prompt words are vocabulary words. Make sure that everyone knows what it means. Also, they don't need to spell everything correctly. That's what editing is for. This week's writing assignments are for getting ideas down on paper. I don't recommend correcting these. Just encourage expression and creativity.)

Day 32

I. Read Genesis 5:18-20.

II. Memory Verse
   o Genesis 1:3.
   o Then God said, "Let there be light"; and there was light.

III. Language
   o Vocabulary
      • Complete Vocabulary Review 1 in your workbook.
   o Hebrew
      • Review these words: pnaa, teHOM, RUakh (spirit)
      • What does each mean?
      • Say Genesis 1:1-2 from memory.
         ▪ 1:1 be reSHEET baRA eloHEEM et ha shaMAyim ve et ha Arets
         ▪ 1:2 ve ha Arets haaTAH TOhu va VOhu ve KHOshekh al pnaa
            teHOM ve RUakh eloHEEM meraKHEfet al pnaa ha MAyim

IV. Science/Social Studies
   • Complete the Science Review 4 crossword puzzle in your workbook. If an answer has more than one word in it, you need to leave a space between the words.

V. Writing
   o Write for seven minutes. Tell a story. Time yourselves. Just write and write and don't stop. I'll give you a word to start with to get your brain activated. Use that word in your first sentence to get you going. (You don't have to use the word if that word makes you think of another word that you want to use.) Just write!
   o Today's word is SUBDUE.

Day 33

I. Read Genesis 5:20-24.

    *Enoch was one of two people in the Bible who never physically died before going to be with the Lord. The other was Elijah. God just took them. What's the Bible's description of Enoch?

II. Memory Verse
- Genesis 1:3.
- Then God said, "Let there be light"; and there was light.

III. Language
- Grammar
  - Complete Grammar Review 2 in your workbook.
- Hebrew
  - Review these words: meraKHEfet, MAyim
  - What does each mean?
  - Say Genesis 1:1-2 from memory.
    - 1:1 be reSHEET baRA eloHEEM et ha shaMAyim ve et ha Arets
    - 1:2 ve ha Arets haaTAH TOhu va VOhu ve KHOshekh al pnaa teHOM ve RUakh eloHEEM meraKHEfet al pnaa ha MAyim

IV. Science
- Today do Science Review 5 in your workbook.

V. Writing
- Write for eight minutes. Tell a story. Time yourselves. Just write and write and don't stop. I'll give you a word to start with to get your brain activated. Use that word in your first sentence to get you going. (You don't have to use the word if that word makes you think of another word that you want to use.) Just write!
- Today's word is DIMENSION.
- You can always share with each other what you wrote.

Day 34

I.   Read Genesis 5:25-29.

II.   Memory Verse
    o   Genesis 1:3.
    o   Then God said, "Let there be light"; and there was light.

III.   Language
    o   Vocabulary
        •   Complete Vocabulary Review 2 in your workbook.
    o   Hebrew
        •   Can you say Genesis 1:1-2 from memory?
            ■   1:1 be reSHEET baRA eloHEEM et ha shaMAyim ve et ha Arets
            ■   1:2 ve ha Arets haaTAH TOhu va VOhu ve KHOshekh al pnaa teHOM ve RUakh eloHEEM meraKHEfet al pnaa ha MAyim
        •   What does it say in English?

IV.   Science/Social Studies
    o   Go through these terms for review. What do you remember?
        •   You can grab a ball and toss it to the person who gets to answer next.
            ■   If you want to add a competition, let the person who is able to answer take a shot at a basket (improvise with anything) to earn a point, or an extra point.
    o   As before, the day number of the lesson where the term is introduced is written in parenthesis.

Social Studies Review 3

What area of the world is just west of the Far East? the Middle East (12)

agriculture: farming (14)

Mesopotamia: the land between the Tigris and Euphrates rivers (14)

Fertile Crescent: land from the Nile in Egypt, through Israel and into Mesopotamia,
where there was water creating fertile ground for farming (14)

archeology: the study of artifacts (15)

irrigate: to water the land, early farmers dug ditches from the river to their land (15)

societies and civilizations: people living together in an organized way (15)

erosion: the gradual wearing away of the landscape (17)

BC/AD: how we count years, from before and after Jesus was born (19)

peninsula: an area of land surrounded by water on three sides (20)

fjord: an inlet of water that's surrounded on three sides by high cliffs. (20)

nomads: people who wander and don't build permanent settlements (21)

Bronze Age: ended with the discovery of iron (24)

V. Writing
   o Write for nine minutes. Tell a story. Time yourselves. Just write and write and don't
      stop. I'll give you a word to start with to get your brain activated. Use that word in
      your first sentence to get you going. (You don't have to use the word if that word
      makes you think of another word that you want to use.) Just write!
   o Today's word is IMPLEMENT.

Day 35

I. Read Genesis 5:29-32.

> *I repeated verse 29. When was the ground cursed? Did you notice how old Noah was before he had children? Here are the other ages listed for when fathers had their first son: 130, 105, 90, 70, 65, 162, 65, 187, 182. Noah was 500. It reminded me of Abraham and Hannah as well as Zacharias and Elizabeth, all who had to wait for a child. It seems to be a pattern in the Bible. Why do you think God might choose to make His people wait?

II. Memory Verse
- Can you say Genesis 1:1-3 from memory?
  1. In the beginning God created the heavens and the earth.
  2. The earth was formless and void, and darkness was over the surface of the deep, and the Spirit of God was moving over the surface of the waters.
  3. Then God said, "Let there be light"; and there was light.

III. Language
- Grammar
  - Complete Grammar Review 3 in your workbook.
- Hebrew
  - Say from memory Genesis 1:1-2.
    - 1:1 be reSHEET baRA eloHEEM et ha shaMAyim ve et ha Arets
    - 1:2 ve ha Arets haaTAH TOhu va VOhu ve KHOshekh al pnaa teHOM ve RUakh eloHEEM meraKHEfet al pnaa ha MAyim

IV. Social Studies
- Complete Social Studies Review 4 in your workbook.

V. Writing
- Write for ten minutes. Tell a story. Time yourselves. Just write and write and don't stop. I'll give you a word to start with to get your brain activated. Use that word in your first sentence to get you going. (You don't have to use the word if that word makes you think of another word that you want to use.) Just write!
- Today's word is GOVERN.
- (Note: You might want to save this for your portfolio records.)

Day 36

I.   Read Genesis 6:1-4.

II.   Memory Verse
  o   1 John 1:9
  o   If we confess our sins, He is faithful and just to forgive us our sins and to cleanse us from all unrighteousness. (KJV)

III.   Language
  o   Spelling/Handwriting
    •   verse 1
    •   words to know: daughter, beautiful, whomever, forever
    •   spelling tips:
      ▪   <u>Daughter</u> and <u>beautiful</u> both have AU in them.
        •   Daughter has consonants that you can't hear. It has a G-H in the middle as part of the vowel sound.
        •   Beautiful has three vowels in a row.
      ▪   <u>Whomever</u> is whom and ever combined. Whom has four letters. There's a silent letter next to the W.
      ▪   <u>Forever</u> is for and ever put together, not the number four.
  o   Vocabulary
    •   strive (verse 3)
    •   struggle or fight vigorously (verb)
    •   other definition: to make great efforts to achieve or attain (verb)
  o   Hebrew
    •   We are going to do Genesis 1:3.
      ▪   Then God said, "Let there be light"; and there was light.
    •   va YOmer eloHEEM yeHEE or va yeHEE or
    •   Today try to read over the verse. What do you already know? What do you notice?
      ▪   You have three sets of repeating words. va, or, yeHEE
      ▪   **Or** is a new one for you.
      ▪   **Va** is translated "and", but you learned **ve** before. Hmmm…
      ▪   **yeHEE** is a form of the verb "to be" but it's translated two different ways – be and was. What's that about?
      ▪   We'll get to each of these this week.

IV.   Science
  o   Today we are going to talk about "mighty men" in social studies, men of supernatural strength, so today for science let's learn about strength. We've learned about several of our body's amazing systems. Today we'll learn about another, our *muscular system.*
  o   Our muscular system is all of our muscles and how they work to make our bodies move. Before even our muscles can do anything at all, what do they need?
    •   Energy because that's the ability to do work.
    •   How do muscles get the energy they need to work?

- Our bodies get energy from food. Muscles use energy created from our food by a chemical process.
    - The chemical process in us changes that food into the energy we need to move.
- Without muscles our skeletal system just sits there, our blood can't circulate, and our lungs can't take in air. None of those other body systems function unless we have muscles to make them work. Your heart is pumped by muscles. Muscles work to expand your lungs to let in air. Your bones walk, sit, jump, climb, and do everything else by muscles. You eat with muscles; you blink with muscles. You even have muscles in your forehead. That's how you can raise your eyebrows.
- We're going to back up because there's a lot going on to make your muscles move!
- What are the building blocks that everything on earth is made of?
    - Atoms are the building blocks of everything physical in the universe.
- Trillions and trillions of atoms make up just one cell in the human body. *Cells* are the building blocks of the body. You have brain cells, skin cells, blood cells, and all sorts of other kinds of cells that make up your body.
    - Each cell has about 100 trillion atoms in it and there are about 100 trillion cells in your body.
- What are muscles made up of? (Don't think too hard.)
    - Muscles are made up of cells just like everything in your body.
- Our muscle cells are long and thin. Many of these combined together make our muscle fibers.
    - A fiber is threadlike. Your clothing is made from fibers; maybe today you are wearing cotton fibers.
- These fibers are in bundles. The bigger the muscle, the more bundles.
    - Packed in with the muscles are blood vessels which carry to the muscles the energy they need. There are also nerve endings which we haven't talked about yet. They deliver messages from the brain.
- Let's revisit the energy needed to get those muscles moving. I told you that there was a chemical process that took our food and created the energy needed by muscles.
    - The energy is stored in something called ATP for short. Every cell has a little of it, but it's used up in just a few seconds.
    - Your body can make more ATP by taking glucose from your food. *Glucose* is a sugar found in our foods.
    - However, when the chemical process that creates ATP is complete, it also creates something called lactic acid, which can cause tight muscles.
- This process holds the muscles over with enough energy until more oxygen gets delivered to the muscle.
- What delivers oxygen to the muscle?
    - Your blood supply.
    - Do you remember how blood gets oxygen?
        - The heart pumps blood out to the lungs to get oxygen and then the oxygenated blood returns to the heart and is sent through your body. Some of that blood goes to your muscles and delivers the oxygen it needs to make more energy.
- The oxygen also works with glucose through a chemical process to make ATP, but without creating the acid that can hurt your muscles.

- o If you are working hard, you may find that you continue to breathe hard even when you are finished. Your body needs that extra oxygen to keep that lactic acid from building up. The oxygen combines with the acid to create water and carbon dioxide, which is a gas we breathe out.
- o We'll continue with the muscular system for our next science lesson because we haven't even gotten to how they move yet!
- o Recall: What's the name of the type of energy stored in cells to make muscles move? ATP   What are muscle fibers made of? cells (Everything else in our body is made of cells too.)
- o Explore more: aerobic and anaerobic respiration; What is ATP?

V.   Social Studies (Note to parents: Preview today's lesson please. You might want to read the first paragraph just below and then choose to skip to after the marked break.)
- o We have an unusual Bible passage today. I told you I thought that the stories of fire-breathing dragons were at least based on truth. Well, now I'm going to have to say that I believe there's some basis to the myths of god-like men. I believe there were some men of unusual strength and ability, but I believe a whole complex mythology of stories of where they came from was invented.
- o We hear the phrase "sons of God" in these verses. We read the same phrase when God calls the "sons of God" to come before Him and report in Job 2. Satan comes with the "sons of God" to report on what he's been up to. We read it one more time when the "sons of God" are rejoicing. It seems to solely refer to angels, the good and the bad, better known as demons.
- o Somehow (hey, I don't get this stuff anymore than you do, but we have to believe the Bible!) the "sons of God" come to earth and take wives for themselves. We do know that angels can appear as humans (Hebrews 13:2).
- o Their children were "mighty men" and "men of renown" meaning that they were strong and famous for it.
- o Maybe these men enticed the world to violence. Maybe God used them to bring the world to the point of needing to be washed clean by the flood. I said maybe. We don't know. But God is in control of everything and He uses all things to bring about His purposes.

   ****

- o The most famous strong man from Greek mythology is Hercules. It is said that his father is Zeus, the chief of the Greek gods that I mentioned before. He had supernatural strength, but a miserable existence. That reminds me of Samson. He also had supernatural strength but because he didn't live righteously according to God's laws, he ended up very miserable.
  - • In Greek mythology the gods are mostly miserable all the time because in the stories the gods are all bad guys, always seeking to harm each other. These are not characters to look up to in any way.
- o Hercules is a name you'll hear referenced sometimes. You might read about someone's "Herculean strength." Or you might hear something referred to as a "Herculean task."
  - • What do you think a Herculean task would be?
    - ▪ Something that's very difficult to do and requires great effort.
- o Wherever these stories come from, they seep into cultures. We still mention this name thousands of years later.

- o Recall: What does it mean if something's referred to as a Herculean task? very difficult
- o Explore more: Homer, *The Iliad,* Daedalus

VI. Discussion
- o If you were to create a mythical character, who would it be and what would the character be able to do?

VII. Writing
- o We've been learning about subjects and predicates. Now, we're going to combine them in a different way.
- o A simple sentence has one subject and one predicate. Here are some examples. What are the simple subjects and predicates?
  - We like to eat pizza. (we, like)
  - We ran through the park, over the bridge, down the road and up the stairs to get home. (We, ran)
  - Notice that a sentence doesn't have to be short to be simple.
- o Today we are going to combine two simple sentences into one. We saw that by using a semicolon we could make one sentence out of what could be two separate sentences.
  - Another way to combine two simple sentences into one is to use a *conjunction,* a word that connects two sentences.
    - The most common conjunctions are the words: and, but, or. Another conjunction is the word, so.
    - To combine the sentences you take away the period after the first and the capital letter beginning the second. You add in a comma and the conjunction that makes the most sense.
  - Try combining my simple sentences from above.
    - We like to eat pizza**, so** we ran through the park, over the bridge, down the road and up the stairs to get home.
  - How would you combine the following sentences?
    - Pizza is his favorite food.
    - He likes lentil soup too.
  - Pizza is his favorite food**, but h**e likes lentil soup too.
    - To combine the sentences we take away the period at the end of the first sentence and put in a comma instead. Then we add the conjunction that fits best. Finally, we connect the second sentence by changing the capital letter into a lowercase letter.
  - Complete Writing Sentences 6 in your workbook.

Day 37

I.   Read Genesis 6:5-12.

II.   Memory Verse
- 1 John 1:9
- If we confess our sins, He is faithful and just to forgive us our sins and to cleanse us from all unrighteousness. (KJV)

III.   Language
- Spelling/Handwriting
  - verse 6
  - words to know: inclination, regretted, faithfully, thoughts
  - spelling tips:
    - There is the spelling pattern, T-I-O-N, which is a suffix, or a word ending. The "shun" suffix turns a verb into a noun. Here it turned inclined into <u>inclination</u>.
    - In your spelling word <u>regretted</u> there is a set of double letters which keep the vowel sound short.
      - They keep <u>regretted</u> from saying regrEEted.
    - The word <u>faithfully</u> has the words faith and full in it.
    - The O-U-G-H in the word <u>thoughts</u> can have many sounds. The words tough, plough, dough and bought all sound differently but have the same spelling pattern. Bought has the same sound as in thought.
- Vocabulary
  - corrupt (verse 11)
  - being willing to do something wrong in order to get something for yourself (adjective)
- Hebrew
  - Genesis 1:3 Then God said, "Let there be light"; and there was light.
  - va YOmer eloHEEM yeHEE or va yeHEE or
  - Today learn that YOmer is a form of the verb to say.
    - In Hebrew there is no past, present, and future tense.
      - In English we can say, "I was or I am or I will be." Those talk about the past, the present, and the future.
    - In Hebrew the verbs aren't related to time. They have something similar to what we call the perfect and imperfect tenses.
      - The perfect tense refers to actions which have been completed.
      - The imperfect tense refers to actions which haven't been completed.
  - Here are some examples.
    - I came home. That's a completed action. That's the perfect tense.
    - I am coming home and I will come home. These are not completed yet because I haven't made it home yet. This is the imperfect tense.
  - Verbs have lots of forms and we won't go into it more today!

IV. Science
- We're going to continue with muscles. We've gotten energy to the muscles by using stored ATP and by using glucose and oxygen to create more. Now what does that energy enable the muscles to do?
- Muscles move by *contracting*. The fiber bundles slide together, stacking up.
  - Put your hands in front of you with your fingers pointing towards each other. Make your hands flat. Each finger is a bundle of muscle fibers. This is a relaxed muscle.
  - Now contract the muscle, pull it together, make it shorter. Your fingers are going to slide in between each other and stack up. That's a contracted muscle.
  - Now relax the muscle and slide your fingers back out, elongating the muscle.
  - Scrunch up your face. How many different muscles can you feel contracting?
  - Contract lots of different muscles in your body. How can you make the muscles at the base of your thumb contract?
- The opposite motion is when a muscle relaxes. Contract and relax different muscles in your body. Feel your muscles with your hands. What do you feel happening? Can you feel a muscle get shorter and longer?
- Maybe the easiest place to see your muscle stack up and then flatten again is in your biceps. That's the muscle you flex when you bend your elbow.

- Muscles move our bones, but they aren't attached to the bones. They are attached to something called *tendons*.
- Tendons are strong and flexible but they can't stretch. This combination allows them to be pulled by the muscle. It's attached to the muscle on one end and to the bone on the other end. When the muscle contracts and tugs on the tendon, it pulls the bone along with it.
  - This isn't an exact demonstration of how tendons work, but you could pretend your pen or pencil is a tendon. Two people can hold onto its two ends. One hand holding the pencil is the muscle and the other is the bone. The muscle contracts and pulls on the tendon. What happens to the bone?
  - Next time you are eating chicken drumsticks, look for bones, muscles and tendons. Tendons are the white strings you will find. The bone I'm sure you can find. What's the muscle?
    - The meat you are eating! The strings of meat are bundles of muscle fibers.
- Muscles don't have to be attached to bones. Can you find muscles in your body not attached to bones?
  - They can be attached to your skin which is how you can smile!
- You control the muscles we've been talking about, but you don't have control over all of your muscles. There are *involuntary muscles*, which are muscles that work instinctively, without your thinking about it. They work without you controlling them.

- o Your heart muscles squeeze and pump your blood through your body without you having to think about it. Your muscles expand your rib cage and let in air so that you can breathe, without your thinking about it. Those are involuntary muscles.
- o There are lots of involuntary muscles. Can you think of other things your body does without your thinking about it?
  - One way involuntary muscles work is to take the food you eat and get it through your body. Once you swallow your body takes over.
- o Another way your muscles work involuntarily is by your *reflexes*. You can close and open your eyes voluntarily, meaning you can choose when you want to open and close them. But the same muscles can work by reflex, which is what happens when you blink. Your body does it without your having to think about it. It's a reflex God gave us to protect us. It protects our eyes.
- o Can you think of any other reflexes you have?
  - Sneezing is a reflex.
  - You pull your hand away from something hot without having to decide you should.
  - What about your response to a tickle?
  - Shivering is also a reflex.
  - There are many reflexes, or involuntary movements, both in muscles that we can't control and in ones we can. These are just a few examples.
  - Another eye reflex is how your eye stays focused on what you are looking at, even when you move your head. That's an extremely fast reflex. It's also one of the reasons it is dangerous to drive after drinking alcohol. The alcohol slows your reflexes, and your eyes can't stay focused as well, making your sight blurry.
- o Recall: What are involuntary muscles? muscles that work without us controlling them; What attaches muscles to bones? tendons
- o Explore more: What are tendons made of? What causes muscles or tendons to tear? How do they heal themselves?

VI. Social Studies
- o Noah's generation was characterized by violence. The words violent and corrupt are its descriptors, neither good.
- o A generation can refer to generations within a family, as in you and your siblings are one generation and your parents are the previous generation and your grandparents are the generation before them.
- o We can also refer to generations more broadly. The next generation starts about every twenty years. Noah's generation was characterized by violence. There's something called "the greatest generation" which refers to those who were born in the first half of the 1900s and experienced and fought in World War II.
- o Modern generations include those called generations X, Y, and Z. What characterizes those generations?
  - Generation X is my generation. I was born toward the end of the twenty-year period from 1960 to 1980. We are supposed to be practical and accepting of people different from ourselves. We are supposed to be self-reliant because we were the first generation to have had two working parents. We are considered to be mistrusting of institutions. We were the first generation to

have video games and a computer at home. We're known for spending big and going into debt with credit cards. Do you think God sees my generation as greedy and selfish?

- Generation Y is from about 1980 to 2000. This generation is described as celebrating those different from them, optimistic, inventive, and individualistic. They assume technology will be used. They want to right what's wrong with the world. They aren't self-reliant and expect to be taken care of as the first generation of children raised by "helicopter parents" and who were given trophies just for participating.
- If you are born between 2000 and 2020, then you are probably part of Generation Z. How do you think your generation will be characterized?
  - o Recall: About how many years is a generation? 20
  - o Explore more: You can read more about generation descriptions and sub generations within those generations.

VI. Discussion
  - o How do you think God would describe your generation?

VII. Writing
  - o Use the discussion question as a writing prompt.
  - o Get a high five and/or hug if you include an adjective in each sentence.

Day 38

I. Read Genesis 6:13-22. FYI: a cubit is a form of measurement. Things like an inch and a meter are forms of measurement.

II. Memory Verse
- 1 John 1:9
- If we confess our sins, He is faithful and just to forgive us our sins and to cleanse us from all unrighteousness. (KJV)

III. Language
- Spelling/Handwriting
  - verse 19
  - words to know: violence, gopher, pitch, destroy
  - spelling tips:
    - The word <u>violence</u> ends the same way as the word presence that you had before. What letter can make an S sound when it's followed by an E? Violence ends with a silent E.
    - The word <u>gopher</u> has two letters to make the F sound. The letters are P-H. That's how you spell the F sound in telephone as well.
    - The word <u>pitch</u> has three letters making the CH sound.
    - The word <u>destroy</u> ends like the word boy.
- Vocabulary
  - establish (verse 18)
  - to create something intended to last (verb)
- Hebrew
  - Genesis 1:3 Then God said, "Let there be light"; and there was light.
  - Read it and say it all together: va YOmer eloHEEM yeHEE or va yeHEE or
  - VA is translated as "and;" this is the same word as VE. In front of a Y, the vowel sound changes, so VE becomes VA in front of YOmer and yeHEE.
  - VA actually has a lot of importance. For one, putting it in front of YOmer changes the vowel sound in the verb (from yomar to yomer). You are learning the words how they are in the verses.

IV. Science
- Today we are going to learn about how boats are made.
  - Noah was given measurements and some specific directions.
    - He was given measurements for the length, width, and height of the boat.
    - He was told that it should have three levels.
      - He was told that there should be one window close to the top and a door on its side.
      - He was told what materials to use: gopher wood and pitch.
- Thinking about these directions, I realized that I don't think I've ever seen a boat with a door. Have you?
  - We don't get into boats; we walk onto boats.
  - The ark was different. The animals went into the ark. We don't know a lot of specifics. How do you think all the animals got on the ark?

- Were the animals all kids? Were the heavy animals on the bottom deck and then the animals that could be carried moved upstairs by ladder? We don't know.
    - We do know that animals obey God. Remember the fish lesson?
    - We also know God has a way of letting animals know just where to go. Remember the salmon and the butterflies?
    - So we know that God could have directed the animals to the ark.
- Why don't boats have doors? What do you think?
  - It would seem water would get in. When we read just a little bit farther into Genesis, we'll read that God Himself closes the door of the ark. Maybe when He did that, He sealed the door to keep out the water.
- I'm off track. We're supposed to be talking about how to build a boat. Let's look at Noah's directions.
  - He was told to use gopher wood. This isn't the word gopher as we know it. It has nothing to do with the animal. It's the untranslated Hebrew word. It's the only place in the Bible that word is used, and we don't know what it is in modern language, so they leave it as the Hebrew word, gopher.
  - A good wood for building a boat is neither dry nor wet. Dried out wood would swell and expand too much when it got wet. If the wood was too wet, it would shrink during construction. Having no rain while building the ark was an asset to Noah.
  - A good wood is also *dense*, full of stuff. (Stuff isn't a very scientific term. ☺) A dense object doesn't float, so it's kind of funny that dense wood is best for boat building.
    - Things that don't float are dense. They don't have a lot of empty space, or air in them.
    - In a dense object the atoms and molecules are packed more tightly together.
    - If two objects are the same size (like two boards of wood), the heavier one is more dense.
    - If I gave you a golf ball and a ping pong ball which are similar in size, which do you think would float?
      - The ping pong ball would float because it's full of air.
      - So, which is denser, the ping pong ball or the golf ball?
        - The golf ball is denser because it has more weight for its size and because it has more "stuff" in it instead of being full of air.
      - A ping pong ball floats because it is less dense than water. A golf ball sinks because it is more dense than water.
  - Even though a dense wood is heavier, it's stronger and more stable. In general, most types of wood float, but there are types that are denser than water and therefore sink.
  - If a boat were one big block of dense wood, it might sink, but the wood is just the frame. There's a lot of air and empty space on the inside that makes the boat, as a whole, less dense.

- Besides the wood, Noah is told to use pitch which is a thick, sticky substance that would seal out water. You get it from trees. It can act like a glue. It would cover spaces between boards of wood and harden into place.
    - The rest of the directions are about measurements. You are going to measure out Noah's ark proportionally, meaning on a different scale. It will be the same exact shape, just a different size.
        - The measurements were 300 long, 50 wide, 30 high. There, of course, is not agreement over how big a "cubit" is, the measurement given in the Scripture today.
        - One approximation is 450 feet for the length of the ark and 75 feet for the width. (137 x 23 meters)
            - Those numbers are too big for us to measure out at home, so we need to find some proportions that will give us the same shape but different size. It's like when you click on the corner of a picture on the computer and drag it out or in to make it bigger or smaller. The measurements of the picture changes. Its width changes, but it stays the same shape. It grows and shrinks proportionally. When the width gets bigger, the height of the picture gets bigger.
        - We find proportions by dividing. How many times does 50 go into 300?
            - Hint: Counting by 50s is a lot like counting by 5s.
            - The width goes into the length six times. That means that if our width is one unit of measurement, our length will be six units of measurement.
        - Choose your measuring tool, something that will fit where you are six times in a row: a shoe, a book, or something like that. Mark the beginning and then measure six of your object, and then mark the end. That's the length of the ark.
        - Now the width is easy. It's just 1.
        - The height would be 3/5ths of your measuring tool, a little more than half.
        - You could also draw a diagram of the ark. You could draw it from the side. You could draw it from the outside view with a door and window, and/or from an inside view with the decks.
    - Recall: What is density?
        - the amount of stuff something has in it for its size, a dense object's molecules are more tightly packed in
    - Explore more: Learn about different boat designs. What is each type of design good for? What makes a good boat design? Learn the parts of a ship (eg. the hull) and what they are for.

V. Social Studies
    - We can also talk about density when we look at countries and their populations.
    - Let me give you an example before we look at a map of population density.
        - Right now in the room where you are sitting there are a certain number of people. You are probably a little spread out. You aren't too densely packed in. Now, if you all got up and sat on the same side of the room. Would you be a little more densely packed in? (Note: Go ahead and actually move and see.)
            - What if you all got up and sat on the same chair? (Go for it!)

- The number of people never changed. The population of your room didn't change. The population density changed. How much room each person had changed. That's what is described by the term *population density*.
- Take a look at the Day 38 population density map. The darker the spot on the map, the more people there are that live in that country compared to the size of the country. What does the map show?
- Do you know which countries are the darkest, meaning having the highest number of people per square kilometer (mile)?
  - The country with the highest *population density* is Bangladesh. Bangladesh is the small country to the right of India. India is the dark brown peninsula sticking into the Indian Ocean. There are nearly 3,000 people living in each square mile of Bangladesh. (That's more than 1,000 per square kilometer.)
- Why do you think Russia and other northern countries have a very low population density?
  - Their cold climates create areas of snow and ice where few people live. Russia, Canada, and Greenland have large areas of land where no one lives. Moscow is a very crowded city, but as a whole, the country of Russia has a low population density because of its frozen tundra.
- Why do you think Australia might have a low population density? You can look at the Australia map for an idea. It's in the Map Book for Day 38.
  - That brown land in Australia is arid or semi-arid land. That means it's really dry. Australia has a large desert. With a large desert, there is a large amount of land with few people living in it which lowers the population density for the whole country.
- On the other hand, all of those little dark dots on the population density map have a high population density not because there are so many people living there but because there is just not a lot of land to put them in.
  - Your family can practice population density by playing Sardines. ☺ That's hide and seek where one person hides and when you find that person you hide there with them.
- Other very dense countries include South Korea, India, Netherlands, Israel, Lebanon and Rwanda.
- Recall: What does population density refer to? how many people live in an area compared to the size of the area
- Explore more: What countries have the most people? (That's different than population density; that's just population.) What cities have the highest population densities? What problems might be created by densely populated areas? What problems might exist in very low population density areas?

VI. Discussion
- God gives Noah a task. He gives Noah responsibilities. He has to build a boat. He has to gather up food to bring. God sends the animals. God provided the plans for the boat. What is God responsible for and what are we responsible for in our lives? Where's the line between taking responsibility and trusting God to take care of things for us?
  - (Note: Here's one thought. Noah was to bring food on the ark for himself, his family, and his animals. He had no idea how long they would be on the ark.

He didn't have means of keep the food good all that time. There was no way he could have provided food for them all. He did what he was asked, as best as his humanness allowed, and God took care of the rest. God must have protected and preserved the food. And He must have multiplied it, never letting it run out.)

VII. Writing
- o Use the discussion question as a writing prompt.
- o Can you include an adjective in every sentence? Get a high five and/or hug if you can.

Day 39

I.   Read Genesis 7:1-16.

II.   Memory Verse
      o   1 John 1:9
      o   If we confess our sins, He is faithful and just to forgive us our sins and to cleanse us from all unrighteousness. (KJV)

III. Language
      o   Spelling/Handwriting
          •   verse 5
          •   words to know: seven, alive, wives, hundredth
          •   Spelling tips:
              ▪   The word <u>seven</u> ends with the word even.
              ▪   The word <u>alive</u> ends with the word live.
              ▪   The word <u>wives</u> has the same spelling pattern as the word alive.
                  •   It is the plural of wife. The F changed into a V to form the plural.
              ▪   The word <u>hundredth</u> has two letters added onto the end of the word hundred.

      o   Vocabulary
          •   righteous (verse 1)
          •   doing what is right (adjective)
      o   Hebrew
          •   Genesis 1:3 Then God said, "Let there be light"; and there was light.
          •   va YOmer eloHEEM yeHEE or va yeHEE or
          •   Today learn that yeHEE is a form of the verb "to be." The same word is translated in two different ways. One is commanding. The command form of the verb is the same as the form translated "there was."
              ▪   We command when we say, "Come here," or "Sit down." I tell my son to sit down and he sit**S** down. In talking about the same person, I use a different form of the verb. I use "sit" to command and he "sits" with an S on the end.
              ▪   In Hebrew there is not really a separate way to form the command.
              ▪   We have to tell by the context whether or not a command was being given.
              ▪   Translators have a tough job!

IV.   Science
      o   Today we read about them coming onto the ark by twos, male and female of all flesh. In order for animals to procreate, create new life, there needs to be a male and a female. That's why there's a mom and a dad for every child. If you have brothers and sisters in your family, you probably know about some of the differences between males and females. But there may be more differences than you realize.

- Let me tell you some differences in the male and female brain.
  - Males tend to be better able to think in three dimensions. Are you able to picture 3D objects? How about where roads go and how they connect? Can you picture how to get from your house to the store?
  - While males can visualize the road and the way to go, women can remember specific items better. This means they tend to navigate, or show the way to go, by landmarks. Your dad might say, "Go east about a mile," while your mom might say, "Turn right at the flower shop."
- Males and females don't only think differently, their brains actually work in different ways.
  - Women have less of a chemical called serotonin. The way their brain is set up makes it so that they worry more than men.
  - Male and female brains actually take different routes when taking in information. It makes males better at learning a single skill while it makes females better at reading others' emotions and understanding how others are feeling.
- Not only do male and female brains function differently, they are actually physically created differently.
  - Men tend to have more gray matter and women have more white matter.
  - What does that mean? Their physical brains are actually different from each other. That doesn't mean one is smarter than the other.
  - More gray matter means more cells in the brain, called *neurons*, but the white matter is what sends signals to the brain cells, making them useful!
  - So it kind of means that males have bigger brains but females are better at using the brains they have. And then again, every single one of us is different from each other!
- I said that there is no difference in males and females in who's smarter. Everyone can grow smarter. You exercise your brain just like you exercise muscles. That's why it's good to learn. You are exercising and growing your smart muscles. ☺ Every time you don't know something and then learn about it, you just got smarter. So, the next time you make a mistake, be thankful for the chance to get smarter. You have the chance to learn something from your mistake and make yourself that much smarter. This is for real. You really can and should exercise your brain.
- Recall: What are neurons? a type of cell in the brain
- Explore more: Learn about brains! Neurons, axons, and glial cells are things you could research.

V. Social Studies
- What do you think the first boats were like?
  - The first boat was maybe just a log.
  - Canoes, which were just hollowed out logs, and rafts, or logs tied together, probably were also early types of boats.
- We've learned that ancient civilizations grew up around water because life needs water. Their lives revolved around the rivers and seas, so we can be sure that water was used for transportation as well.
- Rivers were the first highways as roads had not been built yet. Water travel was an easier alternative for transporting goods, making rivers ideal for trade.

- o Early Mesopotamian boat design included a sail that was square in shape and fixed into place. If the wind changed direction, the sail couldn't be changed. Oars would be used to row back against the wind.
- o What can you observe about boats in Mesopotamia in this ancient artwork? How is it made? How was it used? etc.   From: http://www.egyptorigins.org/mesoboats.htm

- o The design was simple. They couldn't carry much. It looks like two workers were guiding the boat and taking the owner of the goods wherever he was headed.
- o Recall: What were some first types of boats? logs made into rafts or canoes
- o Explore more: You could search for more images of Mesopotamian water crafts. Make observations. Do you want to build a model?

VI. Discussion
- o Think about how you have been made unique. What qualities do you have that make you, you? How are you different from your siblings? Do you react differently in situations? Do you find different things funny? Do you like to be around people or to be alone? Do you like different types of subjects or games? Make observations about yourself and your family members.

VII. Writing
- o Use the discussion question as a writing prompt.
- o Underline the adjectives in your writing today. Did you use any?
- o Get a high five for any vocabulary or spelling word you included.

Day 40

I.   Read Genesis 7:17-24.

II.   Memory Verse
  o   Test yourself on 1 John 1:9.
    •   If we confess our sins, He is faithful and just to forgive us our sins and to cleanse us from all unrighteousness. (KJV)
  o   Review Genesis 1:3.
    •   Then God said, "Let there be light"; and there was light.
    •   Can you say verses 1-3?

III.   Language
  o   Spelling/Handwriting
    •   Review and test yourselves on these words.
      ▪   violence, gopher, pitch, destroy,
      ▪   daughter, beautiful, whomever, forever
      ▪   inclination, regretted, faithfully, thoughts
      ▪   seven, alive, wives, hundredth
  o   Vocabulary
    •   Review and test yourselves on these words.
      ▪   righteous – doing what is right
      ▪   corrupt - being willing to do something wrong in order to get something for yourself
      ▪   establish – to create something intended to last
      ▪   strive – to make a great effort to achieve something or to struggle
  o   Hebrew
    •   Genesis 1:3, Then God said, "Let there be light"; and there was light.
    •   va YOmer eloHEEM yeHEE or va yeHEE or
    •   You probably know this by now, but you can learn that "or" means light.
    •   Practice saying the whole verse.

IV.   Science
  o   Today we are going to learn about floods. Did you see this topic coming?
  o   What constitutes a flood? How would you define a flood?
    •   A flood is an overflowing of a large amount of water over what is normally dry land.
    •   There isn't a flood every time it rains. The water seeps into the ground or goes down drainage systems. What do you think might be some causes of floods?
      ▪   We talked before about the ground becoming saturated, completely filled up in an area so that it can't take in any more water. Any more water forms a puddle. If there's a whole lot of extra water, you've got a flood. This can happen from a lot of rain coming all at once, causing a flash flood, where a flood forms in under six hours, or it can happen by it raining steadily over days or even weeks.

- One flooding risk is clogged drains. Have you ever gotten a clogged drain in your home? Hopefully it didn't cause a flood, but what happens?
  - The sink or the tub starts filling with water.
  - That can happen with a clogged drain on a street. If too much trash or debris gets in the drain, it can clog it up so that water stops getting through or not much can get through. The water backs up and fills the street.
- Another flooding risk is a hot day melting a lot of snow cover. If a lot of snow melts all at once, it's like having a heavy rainfall in the area and can cause flooding.
- Another risk is a storm causing coastal flooding. In 2012 a hurricane flooded New York and other northeast locations. In 2011 an earthquake caused a tidal wave to rise up in the ocean and crash down over land causing a horrific flood. That event is called a *tsunami*, an earthquake triggering a large wave. The wave reached heights of over 130 feet (40 meters).
- One final flooding cause is the breakdown of a dam. A dam is constructed to hold back water. Many times these are made to harness water power to create electricity. Other times they are just walls for rivers or other bodies of water to keep them where we've decided we want them.
  - During a hurricane in 2005, the walls holding back water from New Orleans broke. Those walls are called levees. New Orleans is actually below sea level in many areas. Do you remember talking about why there's not a lot of land below sea level? What happens?
    - Those levees were supposed to keep back the water so that the area didn't get flooded. During a massive storm, the levees just couldn't do their job any more. Billions of gallons (liters) of water poured into the city streets, wiping out whole areas of the city.
- Floods can be sudden and destructive, but God is in control of the weather, and God can prepare you for it and get you out if need be. He's trustworthy, even if terrible things are happening. We never need to be afraid. We can know He's not forgotten about us and loves us and is taking care of us.
  - Recall: What is it called when a flood occurs rapidly, in under six hours? flash flood What's a tsunami? when an earthquake causes a huge wave
  - Explore more: What can you learn about different types of flooding? What's the elevation where you live? Can you find a local topographical map? What low lying areas are near you that might be flood zones? Learn about tsunamis and hurricanes.

V. Social Studies
  - Science and social studies are overlapping today. In science I mentioned some recent flood events in history. Now I'm going to give some scientific evidences of the ancient flood event we're reading about in the Genesis.

- We know the flood happened. We've talked about how myths from different cultures developed from somewhere. They grow into something outlandish and far-fetched, but there was an original experience that started the story.
  - The Bible's stories are different because the original stories were written down and preserved.
- Another one of such stories is that of the flood. There are stories of an ancient flood that wiped out the earth told all around the world. These myths involve many different features as cultures have sought to explain how an all-consuming flood could have happened. Many involve their gods.
  - How did a story of a great flood get to ancient cultures on six continents?
  - After the flood who's alive?
    - It's just Noah's family.
  - Their descendants cover the earth now. The remembrance of the flood remained as they told the story over and over through the generations, but the facts got lost along the way. Cultures added their own understanding of the gods and nature.
- Here's a little piece of the Mayan flood story.

  "This is not what I had in mind,"
  says Heart-of-Sky.
  And so it is decided to destroy
  these wooden people.

  Hurricane makes a great rain.
  It rains all day and rains all night.
  There is a terrible flood
  and the earth is blackened." (from http://www.jaguar-sun.com/maya.html)

- Another thing found around the world is geological evidences of a world-wide flood. We talked before about fossils.
  - In the Grand Canyon fossils of sea creatures have been found a mile above sea level.
  - *Sediment* is the material (such as sand) that is carried by water and deposited in a new location.
  - Also able to be seen in the Grand Canyon is a rock layer made of sediment that can be traced across America, into Canada, and even across the ocean to England. A rock layer can be traced across Europe and the Middle East. That shows that a layer of sediment was laid down across huge areas all at once. (info from answersingenesis.org)
    - That's what it would look like if there had been a world-wide flood.
- Explore more: Learn about the rock layers of the Grand Canyon.

VI. Discussion
- Why the flood? Why did God do it? Did He make a mistake in creating the earth? All of history is the story of God loving man. He creates him. Man sins, separating him from God. God redeems the situation so that man can be with Him because God is love. How does the flood move forward God's redemption plan and the story of

Christ? How does the flood show God's love for the world? "For God so loved the world…" (John 3:16)

VII. Writing

- o Choose one of your writings from Days 36-39 to edit.
- o Read it out loud to look for things that don't make sense, don't flow or just don't sound right.
- o Make sure you are using complete sentences with subjects and predicates. Are you starting every sentence with a capital letter and ending each sentence with a punctuation mark?
- o What adjectives did you include in your writing?
- o Look for spelling mistakes. Check for correct capitalization and punctuation.
- o You can use an editing checklist to help you look for problems.
- o Have someone older than you check it over once you've fixed it. (You can fix it by just making marks on the page to note changes.)
- o Listen to their corrections and suggestions and make changes to your writing.
- o Make a final draft. Rewrite it or type it.
- o (Note: You might want to save this for your portfolio. It's also a good time to put aside an example of math and to write down what books your child has been reading. You could also keep examples of anything else you've been working on apart from GC. You have examples of everything else in your workbook.)

Day 41 (check Materials List)

I. Read Genesis 8:1-5.

II. Memory Verse
- o Romans 6:23
- o For the wages of sin is death, but the free gift of God is eternal life in Christ Jesus our Lord.

III. Language
- o Spelling/Handwriting
  - • verse 4
  - • words to know: decreased, mountains, subsided, recede
  - • spelling tips:
    - ▪ The word <u>decreased</u> has four vowels and three are the letter E.
    - ▪ The word <u>mountains</u> has four vowels. The first two help spell the word mount which begins mountains. They are the two vowels in the word ground, sprout, and touch. The second pair of vowels are the same two as in the words Cain, and faith.
    - ▪ The word <u>subsided</u> has the words sub and side put together.
    - ▪ The word <u>recede</u> follows the rule that a C followed by an I or an E has an S sound.
- o Vocabulary
  - • recede (verse 3)
  - • to go back or gradually diminish (verb, action verb)
  - • synonyms: subsided, decreased (verses 1, 3)
- o Hebrew
  - • This week we're going to learn new vocabulary before learning the new verse.
  - • tov
  - • good
  - • Say Genesis 1:1-3.
    - ▪ 1:1 be reSHEET baRA eloHEEM et ha shaMAyim ve et ha Arets
    - ▪ 1:2 ve ha Arets haaTAH TOhu va VOhu ve KHOshekh al pnaa teHOM ve RUakh eloHEEM meraKHEfet al pnaa ha MAyim
    - ▪ 1:3 va YOmer eloHEEM yeHEE or va yeHEE or

IV. Science
- o In today's Scripture we read that God sends a wind over the earth which causes the water to start going down; it's receding, subsiding, and decreasing.
- o Wind is one thing that aids evaporation. Wind makes evaporation happen faster.
  - • What is evaporation?
    - ▪ Evaporation is when liquid turns into gas form. Water turns into water vapor when it becomes a gas. Where does water go once it turns into vapor?
  - • It travels up. What happens when it gets high?
  - • It cools off and condenses into water droplets which then combine together to make rain.

- If you want to set up an experiment and have a fan, you could set up two plates with a little puddle on each. Aim a fan at one of them and see which evaporates completely first.
  - Evaporation is occurring at all times. It's a continuous process. It never stops. The amount of rainfall and snowfall is equal to the amount of water that is evaporating from the earth. Why?
    - It's all the same water, right? It just goes round and round in a cycle. It's the same amount because it's the same water.
  - When we talked about the water cycle before, we learned that when water heated up it turned into water vapor and rose.
  - A liquid, like water, does need heat from a hot day to turn into a gas. That heat can come from the energy in the water molecules themselves. A tiny drop of water doesn't need a whole lot of energy to create the heat necessary to escape its liquid home and become a gas.
  - There are a few things at work in the process of evaporation.
    - We've already talked about heat and its role in evaporation.
    - Do you remember learning about how light warms the earth?
      - It excites the molecules and gets them moving. That movement creates the heat which warms the earth and us.
  - Moving molecules are what's happening during evaporation. Some of those molecules are colliding together. The crash creates heat, and that can be enough heat to transform one water molecule to escape as a gas.
    - You can act this out if you are careful not to hurt each other when you collide! Everyone is a water molecule and is moving around. When two of you collide, one escapes the bunch as water vapor.
  - Knowing this about collisions, how do you think wind aids evaporation?
    - The wind from your fan moves the molecules around causing more collisions. More collisions make the water evaporate more quickly.
  - Density is another factor in evaporation. Do you remember what density is?
    - It's the amount of stuff in something.
  - Well, when there is less water in the air, the air is less dense than the liquid and there's more room for water molecules to go up into the air. If the air is *saturated*, or full with water already, then there's little to no room for evaporation to occur. We call the amount of moisture in the air, *humidity*. When we reach 100% humidity, that means it's going to rain. The air is saturated with water.
  - Where do you think most water evaporates from?
    - Most water evaporates from the place with the most water.
    - Evaporation occurs mostly from the ocean, but it also occurs from water evaporating from the land as well, even from the water within plants. That type of evaporation is called *transpiration*, where the water from within plants enters the atmosphere. Transpiration accounts for about ten percent of the moisture in the atmosphere. So, how much does evaporation count for?
    - 100 percent minus 10 percent equals 90 percent. 90 percent of the moisture in the air comes from evaporation.

- o Recall: What are some things that affect how much and how fast water evaporates? What is the process of water entering the atmosphere from a plant called? What is humidity?
  - density, heat, wind
  - transpiration
  - the amount of water in the air
- o Explore more: Learn about dew point, pressure systems, and how humidity and dew point are related. How do we observe and measure these things?

V. Social Studies
- o In our Scripture reading today there was a specific location mentioned, where the ark came to rest. What's the location's name? (Note: If they don't know, read verse 4.)
  - Ararat
- o Ararat is located in Turkey. Find it on the map for Day 41. (Note: If you are having trouble, it's far to the east on the border with Iran.)
- o Many people have been looking for Noah's ark. Some think you can see the outline of it from above, that the ground, having covered it, shows its shape. Others claim to have found wood from the ark, but it's always suspicious because people use the area to make money off of tourists.
- o Do you have questions about Noah and his ark? What questions would you like to know the answers to?
  - Here are some of my questions. Where did Noah live before the flood? How far did he travel on the ark? When did this all happen? How long was he on the ark?
- o I'll try to answer these. First one's first. Where did Noah live before the flood if he ended up on Ararat?
  - He probably lived in the region of the world we've been talking about. Abraham later ends up in what's now Iraq. We don't know exactly, but on the map you see Turkey, Iraq, and the area of Mesopotamia.
- o When did all this happen?
  - Counting up the ages of the men known as the patriarchs, or fathers, we come to conclude that 1656 years after the earth was created the flood occurred. What year was that?
  - Well, it depends on when you think the earth was created. Christians believing in a literal six-day creation usually place the earth's age somewhere between 6000 and 7,000 years. I think it could even be a little less than 6000 years old.
    - You need to remember that even with an accurate Bible, it doesn't give us all the exact information. When it says that someone was 100 years old that could be 100 and 0 days or 100 plus 364 days old. Over all those generations it leaves us without exact numbers, but we can know in general.
    - In imprecise figures, there are 2000 years from Adam to Abraham (based on what the Bible tells us of ages). Then scholars place Abraham at around 2000 BC. Then it's been about 2000 since Christ. Those add up to 6000. You could write them on a timeline if that

helps you, but at the end of the year we will create a timeline together.

- So, maybe the flood happened between 2300-2400 BC.
o I know some kids like to ask about dinosaurs, if they were on the ark.
  - How big are reptiles when they are born?
    - They come from eggs, so pretty small.
  - Reptiles continue to grow their whole lives. Do humans?
    - No, little kids usually think that the older you get the bigger you are because it's true for kids, but by the time you are an adult, you are no longer growing taller.
  - Many young dinosaurs could have easily fit on the ark.
o My last question: how long was Noah in the ark?
  - Can you figure this one out? Here are the clues you need.
    - First, here are excerpts from Genesis 7:11 and 13. In the six hundredth year of Noah's life, in the second month, on the seventeenth day of the month, on the same day all the fountains of the great deep burst open. On the very same day Noah...entered the ark...
    - Now read excerpts of Genesis 8:13-16....it came about in the six hundred and first year, in the first month, on the first of the month, the water was dried up from the earth....In the second month, on the twenty-seventh day of the month, the earth was dry. Then God spoke to Noah, saying, "Go out of the ark..."
    - Once you've figured it out, you can read my answer.
  - He went in and out in the same month, the second month. He went in when he was 600 and out when he was 601. That's one year.
  - The rains started on the 17th day and he left the ark on the 27th day. That's ten days.
  - If they counted months by the moon, which completes an orbit every thirty days, that would make one year 360 days. 360 plus 10 makes 370 days on the ark. (12 months times 30 days equals 360 days.)
o One last interesting note: Enoch is the godly patriarch who never died. He was taken up to God. In the book of Jude we read one of his prophecies. It seems like naming his son Methuselah was another prophecy. That name can be translated, "when he is dead it will be sent." Methuselah died the year of the flood!
  - Methuselah was Noah's grandfather and the oldest person ever that we know of. He was 969 when he died. Noah's father died about five years before the flood.
o Recall: Where is Mount Ararat? Turkey
o Explore more: What is the physical geography of Iraq and Turkey?

VI. Discussion
  o Noah was on the ark for a year. Do you think he and his family wondered if the water would really ever go away?
  o Do you think you could trust God and patiently wait for something that long?
  o What do you think it was like waiting for the water to go down?

- o Do you think the waiting got easier or harder after it landed on the top of the mountain? (It landed in the 7th month, and they didn't get out until the 2nd month. They were not quite halfway through the wait yet.)

VII. Writing
- o Today we're going to practice compound sentences again.
  - Last week we learned the conjunctions, AND, BUT, OR.
- o I'm going to tell you some more. You can remember them with the crazy word FANBOYS. Each letter in the word is the first letter of a conjunction. That's called an anagram. Here we go.
  - The F stands for the word FOR. Here's an example. I was rushing, for I knew I was late. It sounds old fashioned to talk that way, but it is a conjunction.
  - The A stands for the word AND. We learned that one already. Can you give an example sentence using AND?
  - The N stands for the word NOR. Here's an example. I wasn't interested in going out, nor did I particularly want to stay home.
  - The B stands for the word BUT. We've learned that one too. Can you give an example?
  - The O stands for the word OR. You know that one. Can you give an example?
  - The Y stands for the word YET. Here's an example. I really like cake and cookies, yet they aren't the best thing for me to eat.
  - The S stands for the word SO. Here's an example. I was late, so I ran home as fast as I could.
- o Today you are going to write compound sentences with these conjunctions.
- o Complete Writing Sentences 7 in your workbook.

Day 42 (check Materials List)

I. Read Genesis 8:6-19.

II. Memory Verse
- o   Romans 6:23
- o   For the wages of sin is death, but the free gift of God is eternal life in Christ Jesus our Lord.

III. Language
- o   Spelling/Handwriting
  - •   Verse 14
  - •   words to know: abundantly, twenty-seventh, families, dried
  - •   spelling tips:
    - ▪   The word <u>abundantly</u> is what part of speech? It's an adverb, which gives away that its ending is probably spelled with an L-Y.
    - ▪   The number <u>twenty-seventh</u> is a hyphenated word. We always hyphenate numbers like that, twenty-seven, fifty-one, thirty-two.
    - ▪   The word <u>families</u> is the plural of family.
      - •   When a word ends in Y, sometimes you just add an S to make it plural.
      - •   Sometimes you change the Y into an I and add E-S.
      - •   How do you know when to do which?
        - ▪   If the Y comes after a vowel, leave it. Just add an S.
        - ▪   If the Y comes after a consonant, change it to I and add E-S.
      - •   In the word family, what letter does the Y come after?
        - ▪   Is it a vowel or a consonant?
        - ▪   What should happen to the Y?
    - ▪   You can ask the same questions to figure out how to spell <u>dry</u>. It ends with a consonant Y. Instead of adding E-S, you'll be adding E-D.
- o   Vocabulary
  - •   abate (verse 8)
  - •   to lessen, reduce, or remove (verb)
- o   Hebrew
  - •   form of the verb to see
  - •   yar (If you can, roll your R with a flicker of your tongue.)
  - •   va yar in the verse is translated "and saw"
  - •   Say Genesis 1:1-3.
    - ▪   1:1 be reSHEET baRA eloHEEM et ha shaMAyim ve et ha Arets
    - ▪   1:2 ve ha Arets haaTAH TOhu va VOhu ve KHOshekh al pnaa teHOM ve RUakh eloHEEM meraKHEfet al pnaa ha MAyim
    - ▪   1:3 va YOmer eloHEEM yeHEE or va yeHEE or

IV. Science
- o   We're going to continue with water today. When the water levels went down, where did the water go? We know that some of it evaporated and traveled up. But that's not

the only thing that happens to water. Where else do you think the water might have gone?

- Down!

o What pulls water down, just like everything else on earth?

- gravity

o Gravity pulls water down into the earth. It goes into the soil and fills in the spaces between rocks. What's it called with the something gets completely full?

- saturated

o When the ground is saturated with water, and it no longer has a place to go, it can puddle on top of the land, but what about the water under the ground? If it's already down underground but it can't go any farther, what do you think happens to it?

- It can pool up underground.

o We call the water that fills the soil and the spaces between the rocks, *groundwater*. Where it's completely saturated underground is called the *water table*.

o How do people get water from the ground?

- Wells are dug to reach the water table and to draw up water. The water we need for life, right?

o Life not only needs water, but it needs fresh water. We can't drink the salty water of the ocean.

o If salt water is found in the oceans and seas, where do you think fresh water is found?

- Fresh water is found in streams, lakes, and underground. The water gets replenished when it rains.

o Groundwater is an important part of the water cycle. The water underground is always moving, though sometimes very slowly. Do you remember what water is always moving toward?

- Water is always moving towards the lowest point. Water can get pulled in any direction but mostly it's joining streams and making its way to the oceans and seas.
- Water can move down by gravity and it can even flow up!

o The upwards flow of water is called *capillary action*.

- Water molecules stick together. They even cling to each other. This feature is what helps those tiny water droplets in the sky come together to make rain drops.
- Water molecules can also cling to things such as soil and since water likes to cling to itself, it pulls more water up along with it.
  - You can easily observe capillary action at work. Take a piece of paper and dip the end in water. Can you see water travel up the paper some?
  - My favorite way to see it is with sugar cubes. If you dip the end of a sugar cube in tea, you can watch it fill with tea because there are little spaces between each sugar grain that makes up the cube. That's like the soil in the earth.
  - And, maybe the best example is a sponge. If you place a sponge on a plate of water, does the water travel up, against gravity, into the sponge?

o You can also use a sponge or two to see how rain becomes ground water.

- Place one sponge on top of another.

- Pour water onto the top one. What happens over time?
  - The water will get pulled down into the bottom sponge. The top will dry out (like the dry ground that you walk on).
- Can you make the bottom sponge saturated?
  o Did you realize that even fish living in the salty ocean need fresh water to survive?
  - Think about this. If you put a plate of salt water out, what would happen? You can try it if you like, but it will take time because the water has to evaporate.
    - The water evaporates but the salt doesn't. The salt gets left behind.
    - What does that mean for the ocean? Can you figure it out?
      - I know because I make soup, and I add salt to the water. If I let the water boil down too much, then the soup gets really salty.
      - That's what would happen to the ocean. Water is evaporating from the oceans. If it wasn't replaced with fresh water, the oceans would get too salty to live in!
      - There's a sea called the Dead Sea. Why is it called that?
        - It's too salty for animals to live in. It's so dense you can sit in it and float!

      - You can experiment with salt water too if you like. Dissolve a spoonful of salt in a cup of water. Taste it. Try to float something in it. Keep adding salt. The more salt compared to the amount of water, the saltier the taste and the denser the water.
  o Recall: What is water called that is in the ground? groundwater, What is capillary action? when water is pulled upward against gravity,
  o Explore more: adhesive and cohesive properties of water, aquifers

V. Social Studies
  o Fresh water makes up only three percent of the earth's water. Look at the world map at the beginning of the map book. Most of the earth is covered in water. Those oceans are all full of salt water.
  o How much is three percent? If you had one hundred balloons and three were blue and ninety-seven were white, the three blue balloons would be the three percent. The ninety-seven white balloons would represent the salt water. The fresh water is what we drink, so it's very important!
    - You can see 100 balloons in the back of your workbook. (Note: If you'd like to color it in to represent the percentages, you can print out copies of that worksheet from our site. Look on the Online Support page.)
  o We build water towers to hold water. We build reservoirs to hold water. Do you have a water tower or a reservoir near where you live?

- o That's where we store water. Where does the earth store water? Where do you think fresh water is found?
  - The largest amount of fresh water is found in glaciers. It's frozen!
  - After that, most water is found underground.
  - Not quite one percent of fresh water is found on the surface. That's the water we see like streams and lakes. The rest of the fresh water is frozen or underground.
    - What's that in balloons? If you had 100 balloons representing the different places fresh water is found, 70 would be ice, 29 would be underground and 1 would be surface water.
- o So only a tiny bit of the earth's water is fresh water, and only a tiny bit of that water is surface water. If your fingers on one hand were the earth's surface water, one of them would be the Great Lakes in America, and one would be Lake Baikal in Asia. The other three fingers would be all the other lakes and rivers in the whole world!
- o Look at the topographical map of America on Day 17. The Great Lakes are in gray. They are in the north surrounding Michigan.
  - I had some extra room in the Map Book, so I included a view of the Great Lakes from space. Look for Day 42.
- o There's also a map of Asia in the map book for Day 42. Lake Baikal contains more water than any other lake, and as much as all five of the Great Lakes combined. You might first think it's the Caspian Sea, over on the left, above Iran. The largest lake actually looks very small on the map. Find it by going north from the O and L in Mongolia. Do you see it? Why does it seem so small?
  - Do you remember how we modeled the shape of the ark by using proportions? If we had measured with a foot ruler (instead of a book or something) our scale would have been 1 to 75.
  - What's the scale on the map of Asia?
    - You'd have to measure what's on the map and multiply it by forty-eight million to get the real size!
- o Recall: What's the name of the largest freshwater lake in the world? Lake Baikal
- o Explore more: Learn more of the physical geography of countries. Where are other major lakes and seas? What's the physical geography surrounding Lake Baikal? What makes it important? (Here's a word to help you with one answer to that question, endemic.)

VI. Discussion
  - o What do you think you would be feeling leaving the ark after a year? They were in a new place because the ark traveled. Their home was gone anyway. The world looked different. They were all alone. Everything must have been very green from all the water. What do you think it would have been like?

VII. Writing
  - o Use the discussion question as a writing prompt.
  - o Make sure you write with complete sentences. Get a high five and/or hug for every compound sentence that you use.
  - o Underline all of the verbs in your writing.

- Verbs can be action verbs, things that you do, but they don't have to be. Other verbs include: am, is, are, was, were, will, be, has, been, had, have, become and became. These are "state of being" verbs. They can also be called linking verbs or helping verbs. They can help action verbs by partnering with them. Here's an example. *You are learning so much today.* In this sentence ARE and LEARNING are both verbs. ARE is a helping verb in the sentence. It's helping out LEARNING, the action verb.

Day 43

I. Read Genesis 8:20-9:7.

II. Memory Verse
- o   Romans 6:23
- o   For the wages of sin is death, but the free gift of God is eternal life in Christ Jesus our Lord.

III. Language
- o   Spelling/Handwriting
  - •   verse 1
  - •   words to know: require, account, cease, aroma
    - ▪   The word <u>require</u> is spelled like it sounds and has a silent E.
    - ▪   The word <u>account</u> has a double letter and ends with the word count.
    - ▪   The word <u>cease</u> ends with an E, but it's not needed to make the vowel sound. There is only one letter S.
    - ▪   The word <u>aroma</u> has three vowels and starts and ends with the same letter.
- o   Vocabulary
  - •   intent (verse 21)
  - •   intention, purpose, what someone is determined to do (noun)
  - •   other definitions: resolved to do something, eager to show attention (verb)
- o   Hebrew
  - •   form of the verb to divide
  - •   yavDEL
  - •   va yavDEL is translated in the verse as "and separated"
  - •   Say Genesis 1:1-3.
    - ▪   1:1 be reSHEET baRA eloHEEM et ha shaMAyim ve et ha Arets
    - ▪   1:2 ve ha Arets haaTAH TOhu va VOhu ve KHOshekh al pnaa teHOM ve RUakh eloHEEM meraKHEfet al pnaa ha MAyim
    - ▪   1:3 va YOmer eloHEEM yeHEE or va yeHEE or

IV. Science
- o   We've learned that when we eat meat, we are eating muscle. In today's verses we read that they were told they can eat meat; before this they were only told they could eat plants. It's probably good that Noah's family didn't have the temptation to eat the animals that they were supposed to help be safe from the flood!
  - •   Did you notice that when the animals came on the ark that some came by twos and that others came in sevens? Those animals that were more numerous were probably the ones that Noah's family would be eating and offering as sacrifices.
  - •   While they are now given the animals as food, they are commanded to not eat blood. Reading that made me wonder, what happens to the blood when you cook it?

o When we cook a steak, we can make it rare, with it red inside, medium with pink in the middle, or well done with it brown all the way through. When I researched this, I learned that the red in meat doesn't have much to do with blood.

o When the animals are slaughtered, their blood runs out.

- There's a chemical called myoglobin that gives meat its pink color. When you cook it, the heat speeds up a chemical process where the myoglobin gains an oxygen atom.
  - *Oxidation* is when molecules gain oxygen atoms.
  - This is what's happening as you watch your meat turn brown.
    - What atoms combine to make water molecules?
      - Two hydrogen atoms and one oxygen atom makes H_2O, which is water.

o Heat is used in a lot of chemical reactions. Can you think of ways heat causes changes in food?

- Here's my list:
  - We use heat to boil water which changes water from a liquid to a gas.
  - Heat also changes liquids into a solid. Can you think of when that happens?
    - That's what happens when a cake batter turns into a cake.
    - It happens when eggs are cooked.

o Solids, liquids, and gases are what we call the stages of matter. Matter is the word we give to all the stuff in the world that takes up space.

- Water is one of the easiest things to think about when we talk about the stages of matter because it can pretty easily be in all three states.
- How does water become a solid?
  - It freezes into ice.
- We've already talked about water as a liquid and a gas.

o Water is still water in all three stages. It is still made up of water molecules. Water as a liquid, a gas, and a solid are all made up of H_2O molecules. The difference is how much those molecules are moving.

- When do you think the molecules are moving fastest: in a gas, a liquid, or a solid?
  - Molecules move fastest in a gas.
- When do you think the molecules are moving slowest?
  - Molecules move slowest in a solid. There is very little movement in solids, but there is movement in the molecules.
  - Are you surprised that the molecules are still moving in a solid?
  - In fact, water can evaporate from ice. It's much slower, but it does happen. Things are happening!
  - Whatever you are sitting on right now is moving under you! That's a strange thought!

o Recall: What are the three main stages of matter? What's something that happens during oxidation?

- gas, liquid, solid
- molecules gain oxygen atoms

o Explore more: There are two other states of matter. What are they? (There's an experiment involving a grape and a microwave to see one of them.) There are other things that can happen during oxidation, including losing electrons. Learn more about the chemical process. How is the chemical change shown in chemical equations?

V. Social Studies
- o In Genesis 8 we see animal sacrifices for the first time. The clean animals are sacrificed. We haven't read all of the instructions yet about clean and unclean animals, but Noah seems to have known the difference because more of each clean animal went onto the ark.
- o What's the significance of an animal being called clean?
  - When God gives the law to His people, He gives more instruction on sacrifices. One of the rules is that the animal is to be without blemish. It was to have no faults.
  - A clean, perfect sacrifice is an image of what Christ was to be for us.
  - Jesus was without sin.
  - We read in the verses how every man is intent on evil. Jesus, being born of God, was not like any other human. He was intent on being righteous and obeying His Father in heaven, even as a child.
  - He was the only human ever to have never sinned. He willingly gave himself up as a sacrifice for us. He didn't have to die. He could have saved Himself. He had the power, but He chose to lay down His life as a sacrifice.
  - His sacrifice was the final one.
  - The Bible says that God doesn't desire sacrifices and burnt offerings. His desire is that we do His will (1 Samuel 15:22). By the sacrifice of Jesus we can do His will because by His sacrifice our sins can be forgiven, making us holy, perfect like Christ so that we can receive His Holy Spirit which gives us the power to live sanctified lives.
    - Sanctified means holy, set apart for God.
- o The Old Testament points us to Jesus in many ways. The ark itself is a picture of Christ's salvation. Sinners will face the wrath of God. The only way to be saved from God's wrath is to enter through the door to salvation. The only way to be saved from the flood was to enter through the door of the ark. The only way to be saved from God's wrath against sinners is to enter into salvation through faith in Jesus Christ.
  - Jesus said, "I am the door; if anyone enters through Me, he will be saved." (John 10:9a)
- o Recall: What are two symbols of Jesus in Genesis? clean/perfect sacrifices and the ark
- o Explore more: You can read Hebrews 10 to read more about Jesus as the final sacrifice. What other symbolism can you find in what we've read of Genesis? What does the Bible say about God's wrath to come and how to be safe from it?

VI. Discussion
- o Are we saints or sinners?
- o Is God's wrath something to fear?

VII. Writing
- o Use the discussion question as a writing prompt.
- o Make sure you write with complete sentences.
- o Get a high five and/or hug for every compound sentence that you use.

o Underline all of the nouns in your writing. Nouns are people, places and things. A noun can start with a lowercase letter, or a noun can begin with an uppercase letter if it is the name of a person, place or thing.

Day 44

I. Read Genesis 9:8-17.

II. Memory Verse
- o Romans 6:23
- o For the wages of sin is death, but the free gift of God is eternal life in Christ Jesus our Lord.

III. Language
- o Spelling/Handwriting
  - • verse 14
  - • words to know: successive, generations, descendants, covenant
  - • spelling tips:
    - ▪ <u>Successive</u> has two sets of double letters.
    - ▪ <u>Generations</u> follows the rule that when a G is followed by an I or an E, it has its soft sound.
    - ▪ <u>Descendants</u> is spelled with the words descend and ants. The word descend has two different letters together making the S sound. Just like G, when a C is followed by an I or an E, it makes its soft sound.
    - ▪ <u>Covenant</u> is also spelled with the word ant. It starts with the word cove.
- o Vocabulary
  - • successive (verse 12)
  - • coming after another (adjective)
- o Hebrew
  - • ki
  - • that (but also can translate to because, when and if)
  - • Say Genesis 1:1-3.
    - ▪ 1:1 be reSHEET baRA eloHEEM et ha shaMAyim ve et ha Arets
    - ▪ 1:2 ve ha Arets haaTAH TOhu va VOhu ve KHOshekh al pnaa teHOM ve RUakh eloHEEM meraKHEfet al pnaa ha MAyim
    - ▪ 1:3 va YOmer eloHEEM yeHEE or va yeHEE or

IV. Science
- o I told you before about refraction. What is it?
  - • It's the bending of light.
- o When light hits something that it can travel through (a window as opposed to wall), it slows the light down.
- o Light is made up of seven colors mixed together, the colors of the rainbow, and when the light gets slowed down, the different colors get slowed down at different speeds.
  - • If the light is traveling straight through the material, we just see the normal white light because the colors are all still together. Normal light, or white light, is all of the colors mixed together.
  - • In the right circumstances, if the light is bent, then the colors get separated. This happens because they get slowed to different speeds causing them to refract at different angles. They bend and point in different directions

because of the differences in their speeds. That's when we see a rainbow because the colors are separated.

- If you don't know what an angle is, then clap your hands together and hold them together. Now keep your wrists together and open your hands. The space between your hands is the angle. In the case of the rainbow, it tells us which direction the light is going.

- It's like the diagram we drew in the first lesson. We demonstrated light by bouncing a ball. It goes down one direction and then up another direction. This time light goes through the surface instead of bouncing off of it because it's clear.

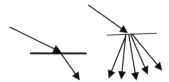

- The diagrams above show white light passing through a substance like glass or water. The lines below show the light is bent by passing through the substance.
  - On the first diagram see how the light changes direction. The different direction is described by the angle of refraction. The *angle of refraction* is the number that tells you how much the light bends.
  - The second diagram shows how the different colored light rays bend at different angles and head different directions. That separates the colors and we see a rainbow. (This isn't a precise diagram. It's just to show you the idea.)
- When the light separates into colors, we call that *dispersion*. The colors are dispersed.
  - Can you think of a word we learned that is similar to dispersion?
  - We learned about seed dispersal, when seeds were scattered. The seeds could travel anywhere. Light dispersal follows a particular pattern. It's dispersed in a precise way, not just randomly scattered about like seeds.
- o When light separates, we see the rainbow of colors that makes up light. Do you know what the colors of the rainbow are?
  - We remember them by the name, Roy G. Biv. It's an acronym. Each letter stands for a color.
  - The colors are: red, orange, yellow, green, blue, indigo, violet. Indigo is a dark blue.
  - You can make a rainbow by placing a glass of water by a window where the sun is shining through.
    - The light is being bent when it hits the water, slowing down the light rays. The different colors get slowed at different speeds and separate.
- o Isn't it fascinating that "white" light is actually all the colors mixed together?
  - Black isn't all the colors mixed together; black is the absence of light. That's why it's pitch black when there is no light.

- So, we know what makes a little rainbow. What makes a big rainbow in the sky? How does it get its shape?
  - What is the light hitting that is slowing it down and causing it to bend?
    - If you don't know, here's a hint. When does a rainbow occur?
    - Rainbows occur usually at the end of a rain. The light is hitting the water droplets in the air. We don't see a rainbow the whole time it's raining because it's cloudy. We need the clouds to break for the sun to shine light. The light hits the water droplets and bends.
  - But why the perfect rainbow shape?
    - When light hits the water, it bends at a predictable angle. If you stick your pencil in a cup of water, it will appear bent in the same way every time you do it.
    - When light hits the water drops in the sky, it bends in a predictable way.
  - Pay attention the next time you see a rainbow. The sun will be behind you. The light is flying over your head from the sun to the water droplets in the sky. Some of those light waves are hitting the water and bending in such a way as to reflect light back towards you for you to see the rainbow of colors. The red bends at a different speed than the blue and the colors separate, all bending at a different angle because they are traveling at different speeds.
  - What shape is a rainbow?
    - The rainbow you see is actually a circle. The refraction angles of the colors of light are just to make a perfect circle. God made the rainbow for us and He made it perfect.
    - What makes it so that we see an arch instead of a circle?
      - the horizon, the imaginary line that's the end of what we can see because the earth curves out of view
- Recall: What is it called when light bends? What is it called when light separates into colors?
  - refraction
  - dispersion
- Explore more: Learn more about optics: refraction, dispersion, angles, different surfaces, prisms, lenses.

V. Social Studies
  - In the Scripture reading today, we read about one of God's covenants with man. A covenant is an agreement, a pact. It's two people, or groups of people, coming together and making an agreement.
    - Usually there are terms. Each says what they promise to do. If you do these things, then I will do these things, and you sign the legal document and you've made a covenant.
    - In this passage God is making a pact with mankind, all of us.
  - God's covenants are very important. He can never break His covenant. The Bible says that if we are faithless, He is still faithful. (2 Tim. 2:13)
    - God's word is binding. He cannot lie. He is always faithful. We can trust His promises.
  - What's God's promise in today's reading?

- He says He will never again destroy the world with a flood. He gave us a sign of His promise. When it rains, we are reminded of His promise that He's been faithful to.
- What are the covenants in the Bible? Actually, the word testament, as in Old and New Testament is the Latin word for covenant. The whole Bible is God's promise to us. It's His word to us that He plans to keep!
- In the Bible there are promises to everyone and there are promises to certain people and there are promises to Israel. God's promise that the earth would never be flooded like that again was made to all people for all time.
- Here is one list of what is generally agreed upon as the seven covenants of the Bible. This is printed with permission from (www.gotquestions.org). I have edited it a little bit to make it easier to read.

1. **Adam Covenant.** Found in Genesis 1:26-30 and 2:16-17, this covenant is general [to all people]. It included the command not to eat from the tree of the knowledge of good and evil, pronounced a curse for sin, and spoke of a future provision for man's redemption (Genesis 3:15).

2. **Noah Covenant.** This general covenant was made between God and Noah following the departure of Noah, his family, and the animals from the ark. Found in Genesis 9:11, [this is the promise read today with the sign of] the rainbow.

3. **Abraham Covenant.** This unconditional covenant [meaning it can't be broken no matter what], first made to Abraham in Genesis 12:1-3, promised God's blessing upon Abraham, to make his name great and to make his progeny into a great nation. The covenant also promised blessing to those who blessed Abraham and cursing to those who cursed him. Further, God vowed to bless the entire world through Abraham's seed. Circumcision was the sign that Abraham believed the covenant (Romans 4:11). The fulfillment of this covenant is seen in the history of Abraham's descendants and in the creation of the nation of Israel. The worldwide blessing came through Jesus Christ, who was of Abraham's family line.

4. **Palestinian Covenant.** This unconditional covenant, found in Deuteronomy 30:1-10, noted God's promise to scatter Israel if they disobeyed God, then to restore them at a later time to their land.

5. **Moses Covenant.** This conditional covenant, found in Deuteronomy 11 and elsewhere, promised the Israelites a blessing for obedience and a curse for disobedience. Much of the Old Testament chronicles the fulfillment of this cycle of judgment for sin and later blessing when God's people repented and returned to God.

6. **David Covenant.** This unconditional covenant, found in 2 Samuel 7:8-16, promised to bless David's family line and assured an everlasting kingdom. Jesus is from the family line of David (Luke 1:32-33) and, as the Son of David (Mark 10:47), is the fulfillment of this covenant.

7. **New Covenant.** This covenant, found in Jeremiah 31:31-34, promised that God would forgive sin and have a close, unbroken relationship with His people. The

promise was first made to Israel and then extended to everyone who comes to Jesus Christ in faith (Matthew 26:28; Hebrews 9:15).

...

- o Recall: What is a covenant?
  - • a binding agreement between two people or groups of people
- o Explore more: Learn about one or more of the Bible's covenants. Use the verses listed above. There is another covenant mentioned in Daniel 9:27 as part of an end times prophesy. What's that about?

VI. Discussion

- o What promises has God made that you can believe in and wait for to see fulfilled?

VII. Writing

- o Use the discussion question as a writing prompt.
- o Make sure you write with complete sentences. Get a high five and/or hug for every compound sentence that you use.
- o Underline all of the adjectives in your writing.
  - • Adjectives describe nouns.
  - • Some call the words A, THE, and AN adjectives.
    - ▪ They are a special case called demonstratives.
    - ▪ You don't have to circle those.
  - • Don't forget tricky adjectives like numbers.
    - ▪ If I said "two kids," the two would describe kids.
  - • Other tricky adjectives are possessive adjectives.
    - ▪ My car, your car, our car... Those words describe car. They tell whose car it is.

Day 45

I. Read Genesis 9:18-10:32. (Note: Feel free to skip the genealogy.)

II. Memory Verse
- o Test yourselves on Romans 6:23.
  - For the wages of sin is death, but the free gift of God is eternal life in Christ Jesus our Lord.
- o Do you remember 1 John 1:9?
  - If we confess our sins, He is faithful and just to forgive us our sins and to cleanse us from all unrighteousness. (KJV)

III. Language
- o Spelling/Handwriting
  - Test yourselves on the words from Days 41-44.
    - decreased, mountains, subsided, recede
    - abundantly, twenty-seventh, families, dried
    - require, account, cease, aroma
    - successive, generations, descendants, covenant
- o Vocabulary
  - Test yourselves on the words from Days 41-44.
    - recede – to go back or gradually diminish
    - abate – to lessen, reduce, or remove
    - intent – intention, purpose, what someone is determined to do
    - successive – coming after another
- o Hebrew
  - Test yourselves on the words: tov, yavDEL, yar, ki
  - These are words for Genesis 1:4. God saw that the light was good; and God separated the light from the darkness.

IV. Science
- o Oh dear, Noah makes wine and gets drunk! I personally hate the smell of alcohol and never have it. Drunkenness is certainly considered a sin (Galatians 5:21) but alcohol is not forbidden (1 Timothy 5:23). In fact, Jesus' first miracle was making wine (John 2), so let's learn about making wine today.
- o What do you think wine is made from?
  - Wine is made from fruit, usually grapes, but any fruit can actually be used. In some places they make wine from rice. You mostly see red and white wines which are made from red and green grapes.
- o Choosing ripe fruit makes for tastier wine, as you might imagine. Then the fruit is cleaned and squished to get out the juice.
- o Sweetness can be added with sugars or honey.
- o Then yeast is added. That's what is added to bread to make it rise. This is the important ingredient in wine. It starts the process of *fermentation.*
  - Fermentation is the chemical process where the yeast is breaking down a substance. In this case the yeast is breaking down the sugars in the fruit which is changing them into alcohol.

- The yeast will make the juices bubble. You can see this when you make bread if you add yeast into warm liquid before adding all the flour.
  - The yeast will continue to ferment the wine as it is stirred and left to sit for several days.
  - Then the wine is strained to get out any solid pieces and then is left to sit and sit and sit. Some wines sit for years before they are drunk. A minimum is about a month.
    - That's why people talk about a wine's age. It's supposed to get better with age.
  - I mentioned bread rising. Fermentation also occurs when you make bread with yeast.
    - The same chemical process happens. Sugars, or *glucose*, are changed into alcohol. What's left over after that is carbon dioxide. That's the gas making the bubbles you see.
      - Do you remember hearing about carbon dioxide before?
        - Carbon dioxide is what we breathe out. We breathe in oxygen and other gases in the air. We breathe out what gases we don't use and carbon dioxide.
        - Our bodies take in oxygen and the chemical process of oxidation takes place. Carbon dioxide is one of the products of this process, meaning it's made by this process in our bodies. The carbon dioxide gets in our lungs and we breathe it out.
    - So carbon dioxide and alcohol are present in yeast bread dough. The bubbling you see is the carbon dioxide gas. That's what is making the dough rise when you let it sit. It's filling up with gas, a little like blowing up a balloon.
      - That's why you can punch dough down and it shrinks. The dough itself didn't get bigger, it was just filling up. When you punch it, you are releasing the carbon dioxide gases.
    - You might be surprised to learn that yeast is making alcohol in your bread dough.
      - Once, you put it in the oven, the alcohol evaporates.
      - There may be a miniscule amount left.
        - If you wanted to think of it in terms of balloons, you could take those 100 balloons and that would be the bread. To see the amount of alcohol in it, you'd take just one of those balloons and cut it up into a hundred pieces. One of those little pieces would be about the most you'd find in bread. There could be much less.
  - I told you that alcohol evaporates. Are you surprised that liquids besides water evaporate?
    - All liquids evaporate and water is among the slowest to do so because its molecules are strongly attracted to themselves, making it take more energy to break one loose and release it as water vapor.
  - Recall: What's the process called when sugars are changed into alcohol and gas? fermentation; What gas is created during fermentation? carbon dioxide
  - Explore more: Learn about the chemical changes during fermentation. What is its chemical equation?

V. Social Studies
- o   We read of many generations in today's reading. Do you know your family tree? How far back do you know your *ancestors*, those in your family who lived earlier? Has anyone in your family studied them?
- o   I have a relative who has researched my family.
  - •   I learned that the Sarchet family (Sar-shay, my mother's father's family) fled France because of religious persecution and founded the Isle of Guernsey.
  - •   There was also a Sarchet who was part of the Underground Railroad, helping runaway slaves get to freedom.
- o   Create a family tree.
  - •   You will be at the bottom along with your siblings.
  - •   You will connect above you to your parents. They will each connect to their siblings and above them to their parents.
  - •   Use your parents, grandparents and other relatives to make your family tree as big as possible. Learn some family history in the process.
- o   If you are American, can you learn when your family first arrived in America? Where did they come from?
- o   Almost every American is an *immigrant*, or someone who came from another country.
  - •   Why is America a country of immigrants?
  - •   We call Native Americans, Native Americans because they were native to the land. They were the first ones living there.
  - •   Europeans showed up on their boats and started claiming territory. Those first pilgrims were immigrants, just like all those who came after them.
- o   Recall: What is an ancestor? a person you are descended from What is an immigrant? someone who came from another country
- o   Explore more: Interview the oldest living members of your family. What can you learn about their childhood life? What can you learn of your family history? If you learn about when your family first came to America, learn about what was happening in the country where they came from and why they might have left.

VI. Discussion
- o   What's special about your family?

VII. Writing
- o   Choose something from Days 42-44 to edit.
- o   Read it out loud to check for things that don't sound right or that don't make sense.
- o   Use the editing checklist to check over your work. Mark corrections.
- o   Give it to someone older to do the same.
- o   Create a final draft (type or rewrite it).

Day 46

I. Read Genesis 11:1-28. (You can skip the genealogy.)

II. Memory Verse
- o Genesis 1:4
- o God saw that the light was good; and God separated the light from the darkness.

III. Language
- o Spelling/Handwriting
    - • verse 1
    - • words to know: journeyed, scattered, thoroughly, building
- o Vocabulary/Grammar
    - • mortar (vs. 3)
    - • a mixture used to bind bricks or stones together (noun)
    - • other definitions: a bowl for grinding something into a powder
    - • The noun, mortar, is an object of a preposition in verse three.
        - ▪ It says, "for mortar."
        - ▪ The word for is the preposition.
        - ▪ For what?
            - • for mortar
            - • Mortar is the object of the preposition.
- o Hebrew
    - • We have been working on words for Genesis 1:4. God saw that the light was good; and God separated the light from the darkness.
    - • between
        - ▪ This is a preposition.
    - • ben (This can also be "ven" in some cases.)
    - • A preposition with multiple objects is placed in front of each one.
        - ▪ "Between you and me" is a prepositional phrase. "You and me" are the objects of the preposition.
    - • We ask, "Between what?" We answer, "you and me."
        - ▪ In Hebrew we would say, "Between you and between me."
        - ▪ The preposition is said before each object.

IV. Science
- o Today we read about them trying to build a building to heaven. They wanted to "make a name" for themselves.
    - • People are still doing this today, wanting to make a name for themselves by having the tallest building.
    - • In Istanbul they advertise that they are building the world's tallest building in Europe. It gets them attention. (The funny thing is that they are building it in Asia.)
        - ▪ Part of the city of Istanbul is in Europe, and part is in Asia. Most of the country of Turkey is in Asia, but a corner of it is in Europe. When we lived in Istanbul, we could wake up in Europe and have breakfast in Asia. ☺

- You can find it on the Mt. Ararat map for Day 41. You can see a blue river line which divides Europe from Asia right at Istanbul (on the left).
- The earliest buildings that the world marveled at were the pyramids.
- Long after came the cathedrals of Europe with fancy spires that poked at the sky.
- It wasn't until the invention of steel and Andrew Carnegie creating a process to make it efficiently and to sell it cheaply that what we know as skyscrapers were built.
  - The Empire State Building in New York City has held the title of world's tallest building longer than any other. It was opened in 1931 and was 1,250 feet tall (381 meters).
  - The tallest buildings before the skyscrapers were around 500 feet (152 meters).
- The difference in skyscrapers was the steel. Before steel, buildings had strong exterior walls. But they could only support so much weight.
  - If your family stood around holding the edges of a bed sheet, you are all strong enough to support it to keep it off the ground.
  - But what's happening in the middle of the sheet?
    - Need to see it? Grab a sheet or blanket and hold it.
      - The middle sags down. It needs support.
  - The older buildings were made with bricks and stone that created strength on the outside of the building.
  - Steel gave interior support to a building; it put the strength on the inside.
- Steel is made from iron.
  - Iron is strong but it can break, which isn't good when it's holding you up in a tall building!
    - Maybe in your house you have iron and stainless-steel pots or pans and you can feel and see the difference.
- Iron is an element. It can't be broken down into other things. It's pure. Like gold is gold, and oxygen is oxygen. When you break down iron, you just get iron atoms.
  - The scientific symbol for iron comes from its Latin name, ferrum.
  - What do you think its scientific symbol is? (hint: It's from its Latin name.)
    - It's Fe.
    - You could try to spot it on the periodic table. What is its atomic number? (Hydrogen's atomic number is 1.)
      - 26
- Steel is made by two chemical processes. We've looked at both before. Want to guess what happens to make steel from iron?
  - First iron is heated. The heat produces carbon, another element.
  - Then oxygen is added which combines with the carbon to remove it. It turns the carbon into a gas. Which gas? What would a carbon atom and two oxygen atoms make? Can you figure it out?
    - Carbon dioxide is a carbon atom combined with two oxygen atoms.
    - We write it CO_2.
  - Where does gas go?
    - Up, up, and away!
  - What remains is steel. Steel is what we call an *alloy*, or a metal made from mixing two or more elements together. Steel is an alloy of iron and carbon.

- The amount of oxygen added controls the amount of carbon present. Steel is less than 2% carbon. (That's two of the hundred balloons.)
  - Steel is also combined with other metals. There are several different types. If you have what we call stainless steel in your kitchen, it's iron and carbon but also nickel and a couple other metals which keep it from rusting when it gets wet.
- Steel has a lot of properties making it perfect for building skyscrapers.
- What do you think are good qualities for a building material for a very tall building?
  - It's strong. It doesn't break.
  - It's durable which means it lasts a long time.
  - It's malleable which means it can be shaped in different ways, but it still needs to be sturdy.
- Steel can be made into wire, into sheets for the body of cars, and into the steel beams in buildings.
- What other metal have we learned about that was malleable?
  - gold
  - But we don't eat steel! Do you think it would break your teeth to try?
- Let me leave you with a picture of the 2014 tallest building in Dubai. Look at it compared to the tall buildings surrounding it. How does steel make it possible to build such a tall building?

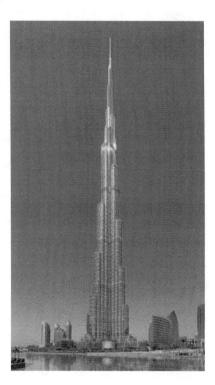

- Recall: What elements make up steel? What is a metal made up from a combination of elements called?
  - iron and carbon;
  - alloy
- Explore more: Learn about the properties of iron or the method of creating steel.

V. Social Studies

- o We learned a little about the history of the tallest buildings in the world. Genesis 11 not only marks the construction of a tall building, but the separating of people into language groups.
    - The largest language family is called Indo-European.
    - What languages do you think are in the Indo-European family?
        - This includes most European and Indian languages.
        - That means that English is also in this language family. Almost half of the people in the world speak a language in this family.
- o What makes languages related?
    - Languages in the same family came from the same language ancestors. At the tower of Babel, new languages were born. Those people separated from each other.
    - When those groups grew and split into other groups, each group's language would develop differently.
        - Languages are always changing. Our dictionaries add new words every year. Languages are always tending towards getting simpler over time.
        - American English is different from the British English that came over from England. Our language has changed, not only in how it is spoken, but in books as well, and in what is taught us as proper English.
    - When a language has no writing system, it changes more easily.
        - The changes happen more rapidly when a group is separated from others of the same language and intermingled with those of another language.
    - When our family lived in Macedonia, we had friends who were Roma. They don't have a written language. From living in Macedonia for hundreds of years, their language is made up of probably half Macedonian words. Exposure to another language and isolation from their "pure" language made it possible.
- o In English's language family there is also French, Spanish, Hindi, Greek, and Russian and lots and lots of others.
    - You may be thinking that these languages are really different from each other!
        - You'd be right.
        - Some languages like Spanish and German are easier for an English speaker to learn because of their common roots.
        - Russian is very hard for an English speaker to learn. Why?
            - Even though there is a common ancestor, for some languages, they were spilt so long ago and then isolated from others so that they developed much differently.
            - Languages that had a lot of contact with each other, grew more alike.
- o In each language family there are many subgroups. English is a Germanic language. French and Spanish, while in our big family, are in a different subgroup called the Romance languages. Russian is a Slavic language.

- Each of those groups have subgroups as well.
- There are thousands and thousands of languages in the world and they can be broken into hundreds and hundreds of families!
  - Recall: What's the largest language family? Name a Romance language.
    - Indo-European
    - French (Spanish)
  - Explore more: What's the second largest language family? What makes it different from European languages?

VI. Discussion

- I find it amazing that God says that man would be able to do anything they put their mind to.
- Do you think anything is possible? If you could put your mind to something and make it happen, what would it be?

VII. Writing

- We learned that we add a comma before the conjunction that we use to combine two sentences. Let's learn about a couple of other places to use commas.
- We use commas in lists. Here are examples. (Note: Read the commas out loud.)
  - I would like to have apples, bananas, pears, and mandarins in my salad.
  - I enjoy reading books, playing games, taking walks, and watching movies.
- Another time we use commas is in dates. Here are examples.
  - Monday, August 14th will be my birthday. (Not really ☺)
    - The comma comes between the two date words, the day name, and the month name.
    - If you skip the month, skip the comma.
      - Monday the 14th is my birthday.
  - I was born on July 25, 1988.
    - The comma separates the two date numbers, the day from the year.
    - If you skip the day, skip the comma.
      - I was born in July 1988.
- Complete the Writing Sentences 8 worksheet.

Day 47

I. Read Genesis 11:29-12:9.

*In verses 2 and 3 we read one of those covenants, where Abraham is told he will be blessed and will be a blessing and that he will be a great nation. In verse 7 Abraham is promised the land of Canaan for his descendants, but right now it's full of Canaanites. Canaanites are descendants of Canaan, Noah's cursed grandsons.

II. Memory Verse
- Genesis 1:4
- God saw that the light was good; and God separated the light from the darkness.

III. Language
- Spelling/Handwriting
  - verse 1
  - words to know: possessions, pitched, acquired, Lot
  - spelling tips:
    - The word <u>possessions</u> has two sets of the same double letter.
    - The word <u>pitched</u> has three letters making the CH sound.
    - The word <u>acquired</u> starts A-C-Q. What letter always comes after Q?
    - The word <u>Lot</u> is a name so what does it begin with?
      - a capital letter
- Vocabulary/Grammar
  - accumulate (verse 5)
  - gather or get more and more (verb)
- Hebrew
  - Genesis 1:4 God saw that the light was good; and God separated the light from the darkness.
  - and
  - u
  - This is pronounced OO. This is yet another form of the conjunction, and.
  - The last part of the verse, "the light from the darkness," literally translates to "between the light and between the darkness."
  - Can you figure out how to say that?
    - ben ha or u ven ha KHOshekh
  - Practice this part of the verse.

IV. Science
- We read yesterday about them trying to build a tower. Abram, whom I will call Abraham, doesn't have a big, strong home for his shelter. From what we read today, what kind of shelter is Abraham living in?
  - a tent
- What kind of life is Abraham living after God calls him to go, traveling instead of settling?
  - nomadic
- Why is a tent a good shelter for a nomad?

- His shelter needs to be portable, able to be carried and moved around. We read that he "pitched his tent." Do you know what it means to pitch a tent?
- It means to set it up and secure it. Tents use stakes to hold them in place. Stakes are sharp rods that can break down into the ground. They are kind of like big nails that hold your tent in place. Here's a cartoon picture with stakes.
- Tents also use poles, usually, to hold it up in the middle.

- ○ Why do you think it's important to have a tent? If it's a flimsy structure, what purpose does it serve?
  - Abraham is wandering in a desert area. Shelters protect from the sun, the wind, the heat. In other climates they protect from rain and snow and the cold. They're a refuge from the elements which can be more threatening than a lack of food or water.
  - Humans can live for forty days without food and three days without water, but they grow weak when they don't have them for long.
  - However, if the weather conditions are bad, a human might only survive for hours without shelter.
- ○ So how would you build a shelter if you needed to? First we need to decide why we're building a shelter. It needs to protect us from the elements. We want to shield ourselves from rain, wind, heat, and cold. What about the first, rain? What would protect us from rain?
  - We need something with a roof. If you had the equipment, a plastic tarp would work. If not, leaning branches together and then covering them with leaves is an alternative.
- ○ How would you defend against wind?
  - In this case you'd need something with walls. It seems like a similar thing would work if you could set it up against the wind. Leaves could blow away, so maybe leafy branches would work better or many twigs intertwined in the branches.
- ○ How would you defend against sun?
  - Mostly you need a roof, a covering to produce shade if you can't find shade where you are. It should also have space and be open so that air can blow through. It should also be near water.
- ○ How would you defend against cold?

- The shelter should be small to hold in your heat. It should be able to be closed so that your body heat can warm the space.
    - Did you ever get in bed and it was so cold and then after a little bit it warmed up?
    - The blankets don't have magical warming powers. Their job is to hold in your heat.
    - Do you know how hot you are?
        - Our body's internal temperature is about 98.6 degrees Fahrenheit and 37 degrees in Celsius.
        - Our bodies have a built in temperature control and we can use that to keep warm.
- The extra blanket or sweater you use to keep warm is an insulator, it holds in the heat. *Insulation* is a barrier that helps keep heat from escaping.
    - That's how animals like walruses and polar bears stay warm in frigid temperatures. They have good insulation. Their blubber holds in their body heat.
    - Your house probably has insulation. Ask your parents about what your home uses if they know. It's something that holds heat in your house. It helps keep heat from escaping.
- Recall: Why is it important to have shelter? What is insulation?
    - It protects from the elements.
    - It's a barrier that helps keep heat from escaping.
- Explore more: Learn about different types of natural and synthetic insulation. What kinds of insulation do animals have? people? homes?

V. Social Studies
- Can you follow Abraham's family tree? It sounds confusing, but there are two names you should know and how they are related to Abraham. Sarai, who was she? And Lot, who was he to Abraham?
    - Sarai was his wife and Lot was his nephew.
- Today we read about Abraham wandering. God told him to go and he went without knowing where he was headed. Let's trace his wanderings.
- Follow Abraham's route together using the Day 47 color map.
    - Here are the locations.
        - He begins in Ur. This is in Mesopotamia.
        - His family settles in Haran.
            - Abraham leaves from there but his father stays because we read that he dies there.
                - From there God calls him to leave. He's 75 years old at this point.
        - He goes through Shechem in Canaan.
            - What do you notice about this area of the map?
            - It's green! It's fertile land.
        - He builds an altar on a mountain between Bethel and Ai. (Bethel on the west and Ai on the east.)
            - This is just under Shechem on the map.

- By the way, Jerusalem is just south of that. They are all close together on the map.
  - Then he continues on to Negev.
  - Draw an estimate of his route on your workbook map on the Social Studies Review 5 page. Do the best you can.
    - He would have probably kept near water as he traveled.
      - Ur is on the Euphrates. Haran is between the Euphrates and the Tigris. Shechem is near the sea. The Negev region has two seas on its borders.
      - We also read that he traveled to Egypt, but don't know exactly where. We only know that he crosses the Negev region into Egypt but doesn't go farther than the Nile.
  - Recall: Where was Abraham when he first left to move toward the promised land of Canaan? Ur; What city did he pass through in Canaan, the promised land? Shechem
  - Explore more: Learn about any of the cities or regions mentioned. Look up Ur and Abraham and learn about Abraham's travels. Abraham is mentioned several times in the New Testament. What does it say about him?

VI. Discussion
  - Do you always like to know where you are going and what you are going to be doing? Would it be easy or hard for you to trust God to take you somewhere without telling you why or where or what? God asks us to trust Him that He's in control and always loving and good even when we don't understand what's going on or why things are happening. Can you think of a time your family has had to trust God even when you didn't understand?

VII. Writing
  - Use today's discussion for a writing prompt.
  - If you are writing about a time when your family trusted God, can you include a date? Does it need a comma?
  - Get a high five and/or hug if properly include a date.

Day 48

I. Read Genesis 12:10-20.

II. Memory Verse
   o Genesis 1:4
   o God saw that the light was good; and God separated the light from the darkness.

III. Language
   o Spelling/Handwriting
      • verse 14
      • words to know: donkeys, woman, Egypt, escorted
      • spelling tip:
         ▪ For <u>donkeys</u> you are spelling the plural form, meaning more than one donkey. You need to add an S. If a Y has a vowel before it, then the Y stays and you can just add an S, like in keys and donkeys.
         ▪ <u>Woman</u> is the singular noun, just one. It ends with the word man and the plural, women, ends with the plural of man, men.
         ▪ <u>Egypt</u> is the name of a place, so it needs to be treated like a name. The short I sound in the middle is made with a Y.
         ▪ <u>Escorted</u> has the word "or" in the middle of it.
   o Vocabulary/Grammar
      • severe (verse 10)
      • intense, extreme (adjective)
      • What does this adjective describe?
         ▪ the famine
   o Hebrew
      • Genesis 1:4 God saw that the light was good; and God separated the light from the darkness.
      • Today let's practice the first part of the verse.
      • Try to figure out how to say literally "and saw God the light that was good."
         ▪ va yar eloHEEM et ha or ki tov
      • Can you say Genesis 1:1-4a?
         ▪ be reSHEET baRA eloHEEM et ha shaMAyim ve et ha Arets
         ▪ ve ha Arets haaTAH TOhu va VOhu ve KHOshekh al pnaa teHOM ve RUakh eloHEEM meraKHEfet al pnaa ha MAyim
         ▪ va YOmer eloHEEM yeHEE or va yeHEE or
         ▪ va yar eloHEEM et ha or ki tov

IV. Science
   o Today's lesson is about famines. Do you know what a famine is?
      • A famine is when there is not enough food for everyone.
      • This doesn't mean if you run out of food at your party that you are experiencing a famine. A famine is a lack of food day after day.
   o The famine in our reading today was severe. What do you think a severe famine would be like compared to a regular famine?

- It probably means that a lot of people didn't have food or that it lasted a long time.
  - What do you think could be some causes of famines?
    - Famines are caused by either a lack of food or a lack of access to food, meaning you can't get the food that's there.
    - One cause of famine is poor, or basically evil, leadership who keep food or take food from the people they are supposed to serve and protect. We'll look at that in social studies.
    - Food comes first from the farm, so things that would hurt the crops could cause famines. What would hurt a farm?
      - Crops can be destroyed by the weather, by plant diseases, or by animals.
  - What weather conditions might destroy crops or keep them from growing?
    - Droughts are when there is little to no rain. Plants and animals need water to survive, so droughts can kill crops.
    - Floods are the opposite problem. Floods are too much water and can also kill plants.
    - If it gets too cold and the plants freeze, that will kill them.
      - Do you remember that there is water inside plants? Do you remember that water can evaporate from plants?
        - It's called transpiration.
      - Water expands when it freezes. If the water inside a plant freezes, it expands and bursts cells inside the plant, destroying them.
        - Do you remember that our body is made up of cells? Those are the building blocks of our bodies. Plant are built with cells too.
        - If too many cells burst and die, then the plant dies.
      - Can you design an experiment to see if water really expands when it freezes?
  - Did you know plants could get diseases? Have you ever heard of one?
    - I don't know much about plant diseases, but just like people can get sick from bacteria, plants can get sick from bacteria too.
    - There are more bacteria in your body than there are cells. Bacteria can be good for your body.
    - What we call "germs" refers to living things, too small for us to see. They are bacteria, viruses, and fungi that make us sick and make plants sick too.
    - When we are sick, we can often get others sick by spreading bacteria.
      - That's why we wash our hands, to wash off bacteria that might have gotten on them from touching others or other things that might have had germs.
      - When a plant gets sick, it can spread bacteria too. Farmers have to be on the lookout for sick plants and get them away from the others. If a disease spreads, it can destroy a whole crop. No crops means no food.
  - One final cause of famine that I mentioned is animals destroying crops.
    - One that I know about is the boll weevil. Cotton grows in what we call bolls, the protective covering that the cotton grows inside of. In America the bug

was feared in the southern states where cotton was the main crop produced and was how most people made their money.

- The boll weevil is in the animal kingdom and in the class of insect. It's just over half a centimeter long.   1 cm

- It's a tiny beetle.   (actual size)
- It devastated farms which solely produced cotton.
- In Exodus 10 there is the story about the plague of locusts God sends on Egypt when Pharaoh refuses to let God's people go. The locusts were sent to eat was what left of their plants, even trees. Hail had already destroyed a lot. That's another type of weather that can destroy crops.
  - Farming seems so fragile! You can see how reliant on God farmers are.
  - Recall: What are some causes of famine? when crops are destroyed on a wide scale
  - Explore more: Learn about different types of plant diseases or bugs that affect crops.

V. Social Studies
  - I mentioned that a cause of famine is bad leadership. When the communist party took over China in 1949, they promised to serve the people. It was led by Mao Zedong, known as Chairman Mao (like we would say President Lincoln).
  - Communism is based on the philosophy that one man is no better than another. Everyone is supposed to be equal. Part of that was forbidding religions not authorized by the government.
    - In reality their concern is only for the political party to stay in power and to have as much control as possible. They don't want people following God and not them. They got rid of anyone they saw as a threat; many highly educated people were killed or imprisoned.
  - During this time hundreds of thousands of Christians were killed who wouldn't deny their Savior.
    - When my family lived in Macedonia, we observed how their Christmas celebrations were kept when Communists ruled their area. They had Christmas trees and lights and presents, but it all happened for New Year's. The government knew the people wouldn't give up their favorite celebrations and holidays. They just changed the meaning. They don't have a Santa Claus based on a saint who gave gifts to the poor. They have Father Ice. (He looks almost the same but has a blue coat instead of red.)
    - There are some in Macedonia who remember Communism fondly. The Roma, better known as the Gypsies, were treated as equals. They were given jobs. Now, they are often refused jobs based on their ethnicity, just for being born Roma.
    - Others in Macedonia lost a lot. People had their businesses taken over by the Communists. Everything belonged to the government. Families lost everything they had worked for. Someone who was college educated and had a good job could be assigned by the government to work in a factory.
  - In Communism it's supposed to work that everyone gives to the central good. What happens is that the government takes everything for itself. The government then gives out jobs, land, etc. based on how it serves its own purposes. It controls people because it controls everything. If you don't like the government, don't expect a job or food, which brings us back to famine.

- o Ten years after the Communists took over China, 45 million people died of famine. The government demanded farmers' harvests and took everything they had.
  - • Sometimes the government demanded more than what the farmers had to offer and the farmers were killed for not meeting the demand.
- o It's a horrible thing. Let me tell you a good story now.
- o Remember the boll weevil?
  - • It was devastating the economy in the southern states in the 1920s. Many cotton farmers were newly freed slaves who had grown up working on cotton plantations. They only knew cotton.
  - • The boll weevil could destroy their lives if that cotton was all they were relying on in order to provide for their families.
- o A famous scientist and *botanist*, a person who studies plants, named George Washington Carver, taught the African American farmers to plant other crops, ones that could be eaten so that they could live off their land and not be reliant on cotton crops.
  - • He taught them to grow sweet potatoes, but most famously, he taught them to grow peanuts.
- o He was a Christian and sought the Lord for help.
  - • God blessed him with ideas. He came up with over 300 uses for peanuts.
  - • They could provide nutrition for the families who grew them, but by creating uses for peanuts, he created a market so that people would buy peanuts and the families could make money.
- o Recall: There were two names taught in this lesson. What were they and who were they? Mao and Carver (Mao Zedong and George Washington Carver) Mao was the leader of the Communist party in China when it took over. Carver was a scientist who helped African Americans survive and prosper on their family farms. What is a botanist? a person who studies plants
- o Explore more: Learn about Communism.

VI. Discussion
- o What do you think of the idea of Communism that everyone is equal and that everyone should give to the common cause?
- o What's wrong with the system? (A whole lot! But can you come up with a couple of ideas?)
- o Is there any way to make such a system work?

VII. Writing
- o Use the discussion question as a writing prompt.
- o Underline all of the adjectives in what you wrote. If there aren't any, then add some! Circle the nouns they describe.
- o Get a high five and/or hug if you didn't have to go back and add an adjective.

Day 49

I. Read Genesis 13.

II. Memory Verse
- Genesis 1:4
- God saw that the light was good; and God separated the light from the darkness.

III. Language
- Spelling/Handwriting
  - verse 2
  - words to know: formerly, belonged, number, exceedingly
    - The word <u>formerly</u> starts with the word form.
    - The word <u>belonged</u> has starts with the words be and then long.
    - The word <u>number</u> ends like the months September, November, and December.
    - The word <u>exceeding</u> has no S. It has a double letter making the middle vowel sound.
- Vocabulary/Grammar
  - sustain (verse 6)
  - support physically or mentally (verb)
  - Other definitions: suffer
    - You can sustain an injury.
  - What could the land not sustain?
    - "them" (talking about Lot and Abraham and their families and flocks)
    - The pronoun THEM is the direct object.
    - The verb is sustain.
    - Sustain what? them, which is the direct object
- Hebrew
  - Genesis 1:4 God saw that the light was good; and God separated the light from the darkness.
  - Here's the full verse that literally says "And saw God the light that was good and divided God from the light and from the darkness."
  - va yar eloHEEM et ha or ki tov va yavDEL eloHEEM ben ha or u ven ha KHOshekh

IV. Science
- What do you think it means that the land couldn't sustain Lot and Abraham and their families and livestock, which is all their animals?
  - It means that there wasn't enough of what they needed. They needed grass for their animals. The herdsmen were fighting, so they probably would have been fighting over grazing land or water, the two things their animals needed most. When Lot chooses land, he picks what appears "well-watered."
- We have a word that we use today to talk about something being able to support us for the indefinite future. The word is sustainability.
  - The suffix ABLE means to be able to do something. *Sustainability* is the ability to be sustained.

- o The land couldn't sustain Abraham and Lot. The way they were living was *unsustainable*.
- o Usually we use the term unsustainable and sustainable in relation to something we're doing. For instance, it's unsustainable to cut trees down faster than new ones can grow. Cutting down trees at a fast pace is an unsustainable practice. Eventually we'd be out of trees.
- o Can you think of things we, us humans, are doing that we couldn't possibly just keep doing forever and ever?
  - The biggest thing that comes to my mind is throwing away trash. It happens in many forms. Do you know where trash goes when it's taken away?
    - It goes to the trash dump. What would happen if we just keep piling up and piling up trash in the dump?
      - It would eventually (in a long time) fill the earth! It's unsustainable.
  - Some things decompose and break down into the ground. Other things, like plastics, just sit there in the ground. Still others, like batteries, leak poison into the ground. Can you think of why that would be dangerous?
    - Do you remember groundwater? That poison gets into the groundwater, which is water we drink and what plants and animals drink as well.
  - This is why we have recycling programs. It keeps trash out of the dumps. It reuses the materials. You can also reuse things instead of throwing them away.
  - In Macedonia I saw a dump truck dump a full load of trash into a river. Factories dump their waste into rivers around the world. In America there have been court cases against companies who have done this. They poison the water and local families get sick from it.
    - When they test our water, it shows traces of medicines in it! Everything that gets into the water gets spread around and not even water treatment plants can clean out everything people dump in. It's unsustainable to just keep dumping poisons into the water supply.
  - Another unsustainable practice is relying on non-renewable energy. Do you remember the word energy?
    - It's the ability to do work.
    - When people talk about energy, they are talking about the things we use to power our homes and cars.
    - When they talk about *renewable energy*, they are talking about sources of power that don't run out.
    - How do we make our cars go?
      - We use gas. Gas is made from petroleum oil which is non-renewable. It can't be renewed. Trees are renewable because they grow again. The oil used to make gas is found, not made. There's a limited supply. No more is being created. It's not renewing itself. There's a lot of it, but once it's used up. It will be all gone.
- o Let's look at the other side, what we call sustainable practices, doing things in a way that we'll be able to continue doing them in the future.

- Recycling is a sustainable practice. If we can use things and then recycle them, we can use them again and again.
  - How can you recycle at home? How can you reuse things?
- One source of sustainable energy is solar power. Have you ever seen solar power in use?
  - We use solar panels to convert, or change, the light's heat into electricity.
- o Recall: What is sustainability? What is renewable energy? What is an example of an unsustainable practice?
  - the ability to be sustained, to keep supplying what is needed
  - a source of power that won't run out
  - dumping trash in dumps
- o Explore more: Learn about renewable and non-renewable energies. You can find tutorials on how to make your own solar panels.

V. Social Studies
- o There were a lot of names in today's reading.
  - Names can be names of people, names of things, or names of places. All names are proper nouns and are capitalized!
- o Here are all the names I found: Negev, Bethel, Ai, Canaanite, Perizzite, Sodom, Gomorrah, Jordan, Mamre, Hebron. Most of these are names of places.
- o Let's start with the ones that aren't.
  - The Canaanites I already mentioned were the cursed descendants of Noah's grandson, Canaan. The land where Abraham has settled and God has said will belong to his family is in Canaan.
  - The Perizzites were descendants of Noah's son, Ham. They lived in southern Canaan near Bethel and Ai.
  - If you look on your map from Day 47, Shechem is just north of Bethel and Ai. All of these places are in Canaan. If you look a little south on the map from Shechem, there is a body of water. That's the Dead Sea where it's too salty for fish to live and people can float in the water without even trying because the water is so dense from all the salt in it.
- o Let's find on the map for Day 49 the new places mentioned.
  - We read that Lot saw that the Jordan valley was well watered and wanted to settle there.
    - The Jordan River is mentioned many times in the Bible. It flows into the Dead Sea.
    - God parts the Jordan River three times for the Israelites to cross it. It parts for Joshua, Elijah, and Elisha.
    - Find the Jordan River on the map.
  - Sodom and Gomorrah are cities famous for their sin. That's not something you want to be known for, but there is a modern-day city referred to as "Sin City." Do you know what city that is?
    - It's Las Vegas, Nevada, USA. It's known for its gambling. It's not a place I have any desire to visit. It sounds like a dangerous place to live.
  - The original "sin cities" of Sodom and Gomorrah were located southeast of the Dead Sea. Find the area on the map.

- The reading also mentions the oaks of Mamre in Hebron. Mamre is north of Hebron.
    - Hebron is to the southwest side of the Dead Sea.
    - Find the general locations on your map.
- We don't necessarily know pinpoint locations of everything in the Bible, but we do know some exact locations and how other locations were relative to those. Historians, archeologists, and cartographers use all the clues they have to try to recreate the past.
    - Do you know who all those people are: historians, archeologists, and cartographers?
        - Historians study history through primary sources, which is information directly from the source being studied, such as autobiographies, letters, diaries, and photographs. They also use resources as close to those primary sources as possible such as newspapers from the period.
        - Archeologists study history from artifacts they have dug up.
        - Cartographers are map makers.
    - Recall: What river did God part three times? Jordan River
    - Explore more: Learn more about the archeology involved in discovering the sites of Sodom and Gomorrah. You can go to http://www.biblearchaeology.org//.

VI. Discussion
- We talked today about sustainability. Do you think it's important? God created the earth and gave man rule over the land. Does that make us responsible? He's going to destroy the earth one day and we're going to have a new earth, so does it matter what happens to it before it's destroyed? What do you think?
    - My opinions! I think sustainability is a very good thing. There's no reason to be wasteful when it's not necessary. The earth is God's creation and He gave it to us. We should care for it, not destroy it. The biggest threat to the earth is sin. It's greed and selfishness, not pollution. That's just one ugly product that greed and selfishness produce. There are those who say we need fewer people so that there are fewer people hurting the earth. I've already warned you that any philosophy that puts anything before people is not from God. God loves us more than He loves the trees! When looking into sustainability, be careful to stay away from that which belittles the value of human life.

VII. Writing
- Use the discussion question for a writing prompt.
- Underline all the verbs in your writing from today. Don't forget verbs like IS and ARE.
- If you find any direct objects in your writing, get a high five and/or hug.

Day 50 (check Materials List)

I. Read Genesis 14:1-16.

II. Memory Verse
   o Genesis 1:4
   o God saw that the light was good; and God separated the light from the darkness.
   o Review Romans 6:23.

III. Language
   o Spelling/Handwriting
      • Test yourselves on the words from Days 46-49.
         ▪ journeyed, scattered, thoroughly, building
         ▪ possessions, pitched, acquired, Lot
         ▪ donkeys, woman, Egypt, escorted
         ▪ formerly, belonged, number, exceedingly
   o Vocabulary/Grammar
      • Test yourselves on the words from Days 46-49.
         ▪ mortar – a mixture used to bind bricks or stones together
         ▪ accumulate – gather or get more and more
         ▪ severe – intense, extreme
         ▪ sustain – support physically or mentally
   o Hebrew
      • Genesis 1:4 God saw that the light was good; and God separated the light from the darkness.
      • va yar eloHEEM et ha or ki tov va yavDEL eloHEEM ben ha or u ven ha KHOshekh
      • Practice the whole verse.
      • Can you say Genesis 1:1-4?
         ▪ be reSHEET baRA eloHEEM et ha shaMAyim ve et ha Arets
         ▪ ve ha Arets haaTAH TOhu va VOhu ve KHOshekh al pnaa teHOM ve RUakh eloHEEM meraKHEfet al pnaa ha MAyim
         ▪ va YOmer eloHEEM yeHEE or va yeHEE or
         ▪ va yar eloHEEM et ha or ki tov va yavDEL eloHEEM ben ha or u ven ha KHOshekh

IV. Science
   o There's a war going on in today's reading. There are allies and foes. There are kidnappings and rescues. Don't get bogged down in all of the names and miss the action!
      • Who was kidnapped and who was the rescuer?
         ▪ Lot and his family were kidnapped, and Abraham and his servants and their families were the rescuers.
   o We read in verse 10 that the kings of Sodom and Gomorrah fall into tar pits.
      • It sounds like they died in the tar pit because the rest of the verse says that those who survived fled.

o Reading about the tar pits made me curious about them. I knew what tar is, but I didn't know of anywhere in the world where you can just fall into something like a pit of tar.

o First things first, what is tar?

 • I don't really have a good definition of tar. It's black sticky stuff; often it's made from coal. We might use it to glue on roof tiles.

o However, when I started researching this, I learned that what people call tar pits are technically asphalt lakes. Do you know what asphalt is?

 • That's the hot black sticky stuff they pour to make roads. The lakes are just the black sticky stuff, not the gravel rocks mixed with it like our streets are made of.

o It turns out there are tar pits still around today. One is even in America, in Los Angeles, California. *Paleontologists*, those who study ancient fossils, have dug up many ancient animals from there. Why do you think there were so many animal bones found in the tar pit?

 • Animals would get stuck in the tar. They would get stuck and not be able to get out. If they got far enough in, they could sink into it.

 • Also, weak animals attract prey, so I would think when one animal got stuck, it would attack animals thinking they had found an animal in trouble that would make easy prey. Then those animals would get stuck too!

 • Here's a picture. From a distance it can just look like a body of water. But look at the thick sticky stuff clinging to the stick and stretching all the way to the ground.

o Have you ever heard of quicksand? Tar pits make me think of quicksand.

 • Quicksand is semi-liquefied sand. Do you remember how semi-precious stones are only partially as valuable as precious stones?

 ▪ Well, semi-liquefied sand is partially a liquid. It happens when solid ground of sand becomes overly saturated with water, so that the sand starts to float around in the water.

o Do you want to make quicksand? Maybe it would be a little like getting stuck in a tar pit.

- You'll mix a 16 oz. box of cornstarch (about 450 grams) with 1-2 cups of water. Start with a half cup of water and slowly add more until it has the consistency of honey.
- The faster you move in quicksand, the worse off you are. Try moving your hand fast in the quicksand you made. Is it harder to move quickly? Drop something in and try to rescue it. Does the quicksand/tar pit seem to hold onto it?
- When you are done, dump it into a plastic bag and throw it away. Don't goop up your drain.
- This experiment is from stevespanglerscience.com if you want to see a video of it.
  - Recall: What do paleontologists study? fossils, What is a tar pit full of? asphalt
  - Explore more: Learn the word viscosity. How does it relate to tar pits and quicksand and the science experiment?

V. Social Studies
  - We have lots more names in this lesson. We're not going to try to learn about them all. One place we should be able to find pretty easily. It's the valley of Siddim, which we are told is the Salt Sea. Why did they call it the Salt Sea?
    - It was so salty. The Salt Sea is what we know as the Dead Sea.
  - Look at the map of Israel from Day 49. It says that it is the topography of Israel. Do you remember seeing (or making) the topographical map of America? What does a topographical map show?
    - It shows the elevation of the land, how high the land is.
  - What do you see on the map to the west of the Salt Sea?
    - It's something called the highlands. What do you think are highlands? What do you think makes it different from mountains?
      - Highlands are a range of mountains, an area with many mountains. It doesn't have to have mountain peaks. There can be a *plateau* which is a flat area at a high elevation.
  - When you read that someone is "of" a place, that means that's where they live. The kings listed in today's reading were listed along with their cities and territories. Cities weren't like they are today. They weren't necessarily that far from each other.
    - They built walls around cities (like the one that fell around Jericho), so they couldn't have been very big. The cities had maybe thousands of people. Today cities have millions of people in them.
  - We're not going to look up all the king's cities, but let's try to find Elam and Zoar.
    - Elam is in today's Iran. Look at the map for Day 50 and then try to find that location on the Day 47 map and on the Day 2 world map.
    - Zoar was on the plains of the Dead Sea along with Sodom and Gomorrah. We don't know exactly where it was, but some would say it is on the east of the Dead Sea towards its southern tip.
  - Recall: What is the name for flat land at a high elevation? What are the highlands?
    - plateau

- a range of mountains or hills, where they are all right next to each other in an area
    - o Explore more: Research any of the other cities listed. Where are any those cities mentioned elsewhere in the Bible? What does it say about Elam?

VI. Discussion
    - o Do you think you could be brave enough to go on a rescue mission like Abraham?

VII. Writing
    - o Choose something from Days 46-49 to edit.
    - o Read it out loud to check for things that don't sound right or that don't make sense.
    - o Use the editing checklist to check over your work. Mark corrections.
    - o Give it to someone older to do the same.
    - o Create a final draft (type or rewrite it).

Day 51 (check Materials List)

I. Read Genesis 14:17-24. (When this begins, it's talking about Abraham returning from his rescue mission battle.)

II. Memory Verse
   o Genesis 26:4
   o I will multiply your descendants as the stars of the heaven, and will give your descendants all these lands; and by your descendants all the nations of the earth shall be blessed.

III. Language
   o Spelling/Handwriting
     • verse 21
     • words to know: priest, sandal, enemies, except; bonus word for the adventurous: Melchizedek
     • spelling tips:
       ▪ Priest follows the rule I before E except after C.
       ▪ Sandal starts with the word sand. There are two vowels in the word and they are both the same.
       ▪ The word enemies is the plural of enemy which ends in a Y. This follows the same spelling pattern as the word family. When the letter Y follows a consonant, the Y changes to an I and you add ES.
       ▪ The word except follows the rule that a C that is followed by an E has the soft sound.
   o Vocabulary/Grammar
     • array (Genesis 14:8, from Day 50)
     • dress someone in particular clothing (verb)
     • other definition: display and arrange items in a particular way
   o Hebrew
     • day
     • yom

IV. Science
   o Abraham doesn't want to take away any glory from God and doesn't want anyone else claiming they made "Abram" rich.
   o He takes nothing but the food they had eaten.
     • What is a share of food? How much does a man eat in a day or need to eat in a day? What about a kid? How much food do you think is enough? How much do you think is too much?
   o Why do we need food?
     • We know that our body gets its energy from food. It's an important part of how God made our bodies to work.
     • Growing bodies need more and more energy as they get bigger. Babies don't eat very much. They don't need as much energy.
   o We measure how much food energy we are taking in by something called calories. One calorie will produce one unit of energy in our bodies.

- Go look at a food package in your kitchen. What does it say is the number of calories in it?
- In other countries the word calories is sometimes translated as energy.
- o So how many units of energy do we need? Any guesses?
  - It's different for everyone because we use up different amounts of energy. If you run around all day, are you using more energy than someone watching TV or playing video games all day?
    - Yes! If you are running around, you would need more food than a kid just sitting around.
    - If we don't use up the energy we consume, that we eat, then the energy turns into fat. You gain fat by eating more food energy than you use up.
  - I will give you some general numbers of how many calories you need, but just remember these aren't exact numbers of how much you in particular need to eat.
    - Kids need about 1500 calories a day.
    - As they get to be about eleven years old, they need 2000 calories.
    - Teenage boys need 3000 calories a day.
  - Remember that your need for calories grows with you. It's not that when you turn eleven then all of a sudden you need more calories. When you are going through growth spurts, a time when you are growing quickly, you will eat more. You need the energy to grow!
- o Calories are good things for your body. Your body runs on their energy. Calories are only bad when you are taking in too many. Let me give you a few examples of how many calories are in your food. (Note: You may want to let them guess the number of calories for the food.)
  - 144   can of Coke
  - 108   homemade biscuit
  - 68   slice of bread
  - 110   Cheerios (1 ¼ cups)
  - 51   homemade chocolate chip cookies
  - 140   goldfish, 45 crackers
  - 377   one cup of soft vanilla ice cream
  - 188   one slice of cheese pizza, Dominos
  - 111   one scrambled egg with butter and milk
  - 80   apple
  - 71   orange
  - 117   one cup of apple juice
  - 406   extra-crispy chicken thigh from KFC
  - 520   quarter-pounder with cheese from McDonald's
  - 288   4 ounces of lean ground beef
  - 190   a serving of salted peanuts
- o One thing you shouldn't do from this list is think, I should drink soda instead of eating peanuts because peanuts have more calories!
  - That would be very wrong thinking. Soda provides calories but nothing else. We call them "empty calories."

- Your body needs more than calories; it needs nutrition, things like calcium which makes bones strong and vitamin A which helps our eyesight.
- Peanuts provide iron, among other nutrients, which helps get oxygen to where it's needed in our bodies.
  - o Recall: What is a calorie? a measurement of food energy
  - o Explore more: Learn about how our bodies use calories. How is food converted into energy in our bodies?

V. Social Studies
  - o We read today about Melchizedek. He's a king and a priest, or someone with authority in religious matters. He's the king of Salem which is early Jerusalem.
  - o It's kind of fascinating. Remember that there is no church. There is no religion called Judaism. People are worshipping all sorts of gods. God somehow revealed Himself to Abraham and Noah and Melchizedek because they have found the one, true God.
  - o We learn a little more about Melchizedek in Hebrews 7:1-4 which says: For this Melchizedek, king of Salem, priest of the Most High God, who met Abraham as he was returning from the slaughter of the kings and blessed him, to whom also Abraham apportioned a tenth part of all the spoils, was first of all, by the translation of his name, king of righteousness, and then also king of Salem, which is king of peace. Without father, without mother, without genealogy, having neither beginning of days nor end of life, but made like the Son of God, he remains a priest perpetually.
  - o Melchizedek is another symbol of Jesus in Genesis. Like Jesus he was a king and a priest. Like Jesus, he was a priest who didn't get appointed to the priesthood through his lineage, meaning the office wasn't passed down to him from his father or other ancestor. Also like Jesus, he is a priest forever. There was no end to the time he was to serve as priest. Jesus, likewise, is our high priest forever and ever.
  - o Melchizedek blesses Abraham and brings out bread and wine (verse 18). This is yet another symbol pointing us to Jesus.
  - o The bread and the wine are symbols of the body and blood of Jesus.
    - In 1 Corinthians 11:2-26 we read: For I received from the Lord that which I also delivered to you, that the Lord Jesus in the night in which He was betrayed took bread; and when He had given thanks, He broke it and said, "This is My body, which is for you; do this in remembrance of Me." In the same way He took the cup [of wine] also after supper, saying, "This cup is the new covenant in My blood; do this, as often as you drink it, in remembrance of Me." For as often as you eat this bread and drink the cup, you proclaim the Lord's death until He comes.
    - We call this *communion*, when we, as the church, share the bread and the cup, remembering Christ's sacrifice for us.
    - Do you see the similarity in the words communion and communism? What do they have in common?
    - The word common is related too. What is similar about their meanings?
      - The root of each word is the same. It means to have something in common, to share. That doesn't mean we both have brown eyes. It means you use the same things as me. On a college campus there

might be an area called "The Commons." It's a place for everyone. Everyone shares the space.

- In communion we are sharing in Christ's death, fellowshipping in his suffering. In remembering what He's done, we remember what we are called to do, to die to self, to no longer live but let Christ live in us, which is the gift He paid for on the cross.

- o Recall: What was the name of the priest of God? What is communion?
  - Melchizedek
  - when we share the bread and the cup and remember Christ's sacrifice for us
- o Explore more: You can research about Abraham paying a tithe to Melchizedek. Here's one site I used to research Melchizedek because I know some say that Melchizedek was Jesus Himself. I don't think he was, but either way, he points us to our Savior. https://www.christiancourier.com/articles/356-was-melchizedek-the-preincarnate-christ

VI. Discussion

- o Have you ever taken communion? What do you think of when you remember Jesus' sacrifice on the cross? Even before the cross Jesus sacrificed for us by giving up heaven to come to earth. What all did He give up or sacrifice for you?

VII. Writing

- o We practiced putting commas into dates, but now I want to make sure you are writing the date words correctly.
- o Date words are names, so we capitalize them.
  - The date words are the names of the days of the week and the names of the months of the year.
- o We always capitalize names. We capitalize people names and place names.
  - Place names include California and Russia and Pizza Hut and Long Beach.
- o We capitalize names of things too.
  - Here are some examples: Washington Monument, Statue of Liberty, Ark of the Covenant, London Bridge.
- o Complete Writing Sentences 9 in your workbook.

Day 52

I. Read Genesis 15.

II. Memory Verse
- o Genesis 26:4
- o I will multiply your descendants as the stars of the heaven, and will give your descendants all these lands; and by your descendants all the nations of the earth shall be blessed.

III. Language
- o Spelling/Handwriting
  - verse 15
  - words to know: heir, prey, pigeon, shield
  - spelling tips:
    - There are two homophones in our spelling list today. Make sure you know which word you are trying to spell.
      - You are spelling the <u>heir</u> to the throne not the air in the atmosphere. Hint: it starts with an H and there is no A in it.
      - You are spelling the <u>prey</u> that predators attack not the thing you do when you are talking to God.
      - The word <u>pigeon</u> starts with the word pig and ends with the word on. There is an E in the middle.
      - The word <u>shield</u> follows the rule that I comes before E except after C.
- o Vocabulary/Grammar
  - heir (verse 3)
  - the person who will inherit property, money, or position title after a person leaves a position or dies (noun)
- o Hebrew
  - night
  - LII-la (The hyphen is only for clarity between the Is and the L.)
  - Say Genesis 1:4.
    - be reSHEET baRA eloHEEM et ha shaMAyim ve et ha Arets
    - ve ha Arets haaTAH TOhu va VOhu ve KHOshekh al pnaa teHOM ve RUakh eloHEEM meraKHEfet al pnaa ha MAyim
    - va YOmer eloHEEM yeHEE or va yeHEE or
    - va yar eloHEEM et ha or ki tov va yavDEL eloHEEM ben ha or u ven ha KHOshekh

IV. Science
- o We're going to learn more about rivers today. Look at the Day 52 map of the Mississippi River. What do you notice?
  - It kind of looks like a tree, how it branches out, and then those branches can branch out as well.
- o Today we're going to learn about those different parts of a river and how they happen.

- A river begins with the *headwaters*. A river could begin with a spring bubbling up from underground. It could begin in a wet, marshy area with a large amount of snow melting. It could begin where thousands of streams all come together, or maybe it starts with just a trickle of water coming from a pond.
    - From what you've learned about elevation and sea level, where are the headwaters of the Mississippi River?
        - They are up in Minnesota.
- Can you think of any reason why the headwaters of a river are important?
    - Anything that happens to the water at the beginning will affect everything downstream.
- A *tributary* is a river whose water goes into another river. A large river is getting lots of its water from tributaries. Now look at the Mississippi River map again. Which rivers are the tributaries?
    - The large Mississippi River is getting its water from the rivers that connect to it. Some of those tributaries have tributaries that feed into them.
- The *channel* is the path the river takes. What do river channels look like?
    - A river can go straight through a valley with high rock cliff walls on each side of it. Some rivers curve back and forth. Some rivers even crisscross themselves like a braid. The channel can be wide or narrow. Each river is unique.
    - Where a river bends is called *meanders*. The river is meandering, or traveling a curvy path.
- How do you think a river's channel gets curvy? (Note: If they need a hint, ask them what erosion is and how erosion might change the shape of a river.)
    - Erosion wears away dirt and rocks and sand from one spot and that sediment is deposited, or dropped off, in another spot on the other side of the channel. Little by little a river can change its own shape.
        - Maybe you'd like to come up with a way to act that out, using people or props for the sediment, to show how the river changes shape.
    - In fact, rivers are always changing.
- Can you think of other ways a river could change, besides bending?
    - What might happen if the river developed because of a large amount of snow melting?
        - Maybe it would dry up in the summer.
        - There are such things as temporary rivers.
        - Parts of rivers can even be cut off from the rest through its own deposits of sediment, the materials carried along in the water such as small rocks.
- The riverbank is the land right next to the river.
- The mouth of the river, or the river *delta,* is where the river slows down and fans out as it empties into the sea or ocean or lake. Where's the mouth of the Mississippi?
    - If you look at the Day 17 map of America's wetlands (says Rivers and State Boundaries), you can see the fan-ish shape of the Mississippi's delta.
    - On the Day 47 map of the Middle East, you can see the green fan shape at the Nile's delta. Why is it green there?
        - It's fertile. Things grow easily there because of all the water.

o Recall: Draw a picture of a river. Label the headwaters, a tributary, the riverbank and the delta.

o Explore more: Why are river deltas important? What can you learn about them? habitat, sediment...

V. Social Studies

o In today's reading we get a history lesson before the history happens! It's called a prophecy. God knows the future. To Him it's as good as done. He tells Abraham many things that will happen. What are they?

- His descendants would be too many for him to even count.
- They will be given the land from the River Egypt to the Euphrates.
- They will be in a foreign land for 400 years where they will be oppressed.
- They will be brought out of the foreign land with a lot of possessions.
- The nation that enslaves them will be punished for it.
- Then it sounds like the fourth generation after they leave Egypt will come to the land of the Amorites and fight them, and God will use the Israelites to punish the Amorites for their sin.

o Almost all of these prophecies we see fulfilled in Genesis and Exodus. The last one we read about in Numbers 21.

o All of these have happened so far with the exception that I don't think Israel has ever yet been in possession of all of the land promised. If they had believed and obeyed, they would have. I do still think that the full land is theirs and will be theirs because God's promises cannot fail.

o Look at the three maps for social studies for Day 52 to see the two boundaries given here, the River Egypt and the Euphrates River, and how they compare to modern-day Israel's boundaries.

o The Bible tells us more about the boundaries of Israel in Numbers 34 and Ezekiel 47. A description from Wikipedia uses these references to place the northern boundary not at the Euphrates but near the modern-day northern border of Lebanon and then east some into Syria.

- The conclusion from Wikipedia is as follows: Hence, Numbers 34 and Ezekiel 47 define different but similar borders which include the whole of contemporary Lebanon, both the West Bank and the Gaza Strip and Israel, except for the South Negev and Eilat. Small parts of Syria are also included. (from http://en.wikipedia.org/wiki/Promised_Land)
- You can see these marked on the map showing Modern Israel's borders compared to ancient Israel's borders.
- This makes me wonder. I don't know why the Euphrates isn't included in the description of the Promised Land. Has the river moved? Was the river that's just north of the Lebanon border a branch of the Euphrates that got cut off over time? (I traced this in blue on the map of Syria in your map book for Day 52.) It's okay to have questions and not know the answers. We don't have to know everything in order to trust God's Word. I do know that God's promise was or will be fulfilled because God cannot lie!

o Recall: Between what two rivers did God tell Abraham his descendants would live? the River Egypt and the Euphrates

- o Explore more: Learn about the Gaza strip and the West Bank and when they were taken from Israel's control. You can see on the map of modern Israel that those areas are cut out of Israel.

VI. Discussion
- o Do you think Israel will ever live in the land described as being given to Israel? Do you think they should? When Jesus comes back to Israel to rule the world, who will live in Israel do you think? Would you want to be there?

VII. Writing
- o Use the discussion question as a writing prompt.
- o Get a high five and/or hug if you find a prepositional phrase in your writing today.
- o Circle the preposition and underline the object of the preposition.

Day 53

I. Read Genesis 16:1-6.

II. Memory Verse
   o Genesis 26:4
   o I will multiply your descendants as the stars of the heaven, and will give your descendants all these lands; and by your descendants all the nations of the earth shall be blessed.

III. Language
   o Spelling/Handwriting
     • verse 6
     • words to know: children, Egyptian, conceive, maid
     • spelling tips:
       ▪ <u>Children</u> begins with the word child.
       ▪ <u>Egyptian</u> is the name of an ethnicity, so as a name it is capitalized. It has some tricky spelling components. The "shun" ending is spelled T-I-A-N and the "jip" part is spelled with a G-Y.
       ▪ Do you remember the spelling rhyme to help you spell <u>conceive</u>?
       ▪ The word <u>maid</u> is a homophone. This is the kind of maid that cleans a house, not something you put together.
   o Vocabulary/Grammar
     • obtain (verse 2)
     • to get or acquire (verb)
     • You get something, so there must be a direct object in that verse. Here's the sentence. "Perhaps I will obtain children through her."
       ▪ Obtain is the verb.
       ▪ What was obtained? Find the direct object.
       ▪ The direct object is children.
   o Hebrew
     • There are two Ks today, one in each word. This is said more like a Q. Say Q words (like quiet and quick) and work on isolating the Q sound. It's like a K sound; it's just made farther back in your throat. Think about that as you say today's vocabulary words.
       ▪ called
       ▪ kaRA
       ▪ will call
       ▪ yikRA
     • When we add VA in front of it, we translate it in the past: va yikra, and called.
     • You don't have to understand all the ins and outs of this. Here's the explanation. The first is the perfected form of the verb. It's a completed action. He called. It's done. The second is the imperfect, the verb form for actions which haven't been completed.
     • Even though the second is in the imperfect form, where actions haven't been completed, we translate it in the past tense as if it is finished. We translate them with the English past tense because of that little VA in front of it.

- Using a different tense is a story telling technique. It doesn't match anything we use in English which makes it hard to understand. You have to accept that it's just the way it is. But learning the way other languages work can help you understand different cultures and can help you learn similar languages. Arabic is related to Hebrew and uses similar verb patterns. Learning how their languages work can help you understand the difference between time cultures, like in America and Europe, and event cultures in Asia.
  - For the interested: In a time culture if something happens at two o'clock and you get there at one, you are early. If you get there at three, you are late. In an event culture, there may be an event scheduled for two o'clock, but if you get there at three and it hasn't happened yet, you are early. If you get there at one and it already happened, you're late.

IV. Science
   o We read that Hagar conceives a child.
   o The word conceive means to become pregnant. It also means to dream up or to think up. Ideas are conceived. I think that's neat that the word has those two meanings. Each child is conceived by God. He has a bright idea. He forms the child and plans its future.
   o Psalm 139:13 says, "For You formed my inward parts; You wove me in my mother's womb."
     - The womb is where a baby grows. When a mommy's belly grows big it's not because her stomach is getting big. She didn't eat the baby!
   o The womb is lower on her belly than her stomach. Only women have a womb. God created them to carry babies and to care for them.
   o God makes every baby from a piece of the mother and a piece of the father. That's why children look like their parents. They are made from them.
   o Women have eggs in their bodies, but not like chicken eggs; they don't have shells. Each egg is actually a single cell, the biggest type of cell in a woman's body. The egg cells can barely be seen by the human eye, while all other cells are *microscopic*, meaning you need a microscope to see them. There are more than a million of these eggs in each woman.
     - Why so many? I don't know! I guess God wanted to be able to choose just the right one when the time comes. Actually, even a little girl has these eggs inside of her. Girls are born with them. A little girl can't have a baby because her body doesn't get ready to have a baby until she's a teenager and there has to be a father, but God prepared her for when the day comes.
   o When God chooses the right time, a piece of the father is joined with the egg cell and that is called conception. A new baby has been conceived in God's mind and in the woman's body.
   o In about nine months that baby grows from just an idea and a cell to a baby you can hold in your arms, a baby that was made in God's image. If you are in a hurry to get taller, just remember that every adult you see used to be almost microscopic!
   o Let me tell you one more thing about being in your mother's womb. Do you know why you have a belly button?
     - You were connected to a piece of your mother when you were in her womb. That's how you got your food and oxygen. You were connected by what's

called the umbilical cord. After you were born, it was cut to separate you and then what was left of it still attached to you fell off, leaving you with a cute button. Your belly button can remind you of how your mom took care of you even before you were born!

o Remember that God is the one who conceived you. You were God's bright idea. He made you on purpose! He says: "For I know the plans I have for you," says the LORD. "They are plans for good and not for disaster, to give you a future and a hope." (Jeremiah 29:11 NLT)

o Recall: What does it mean to conceive? What is microscopic?
    • to become pregnant or think up a plan or idea
    • can only be seen with a microscope

o Explore more: You could learn about a baby lives in the womb. Here are some words: uterus, placenta, amniotic fluid.

V. Social Studies

o Hagar is Sarah's maid. Her name is still Sarai, but I know her as Sarah, so we're going to call her that.

o Hagar's Egyptian, and it seems like maybe she was given to Abraham when they were in Egypt. We read that Pharaoh gave him animals and servants. Abraham didn't trust God to save his life and lied, saying Sarah was his sister. God prevented Pharaoh from truly taking Sarah as his wife, but it seems like suffering came out of Abraham's lie. It may have seemed good at first. He got Sarah back and all this stuff! When you sin, it may seem fun at the moment, or a lie might seem to keep you out of trouble, but sin only brings suffering. Sin ultimately leads to death, but it can also lead to a lot of pain and suffering on the way there. Happiness can never truly be found through sin. Abraham gets all of these gifts from Pharaoh, but now Hagar, one of those gifts, is in the way of God's plan for his family. She causes strife and arguing in their family.

o Today we read about the relationship between Hagar and Sarah.
    • Who is the master? Who is the servant?
        ▪ Sarah is the master. Hagar is the servant.
    • Hagar feels elevated in her position when she conceives a child. She looks down on Sarah who hasn't been given a child. She is sinning in that it's her job to submit to Sarah.
    • Sarah sins in return by treating Hagar so badly that she runs away.
    • I don't know much of the setup here, but I don't think that Hagar is getting paid. She's basically a slave. She probably is just taken care of by her mistress by being given a home and food and clothing.

o If Hagar worked for Pharaoh before, how do you think her life is different now among the Hebrews? How is it the same?
    • Hagar is Egyptian. She's a foreigner. She speaks a different language. Living in tents in the wilderness was not what she was used to. She was already a slave in Egypt, so she already had had a hard life. We don't know how she became a slave. If she was born Egyptian, then maybe her family owed money they couldn't pay to Pharaoh and she was taken to pay their debt. Some children were sold to get money. Other slaves in the Bible are captives taken during fighting. Someone could be born a slave as well by being born to a slave.

- o Up until the point of Sarah turning on her, life is okay. Hagar submits to Sarah's authority. Sarah is the one with authority over her, the power to order Hagar around.
  - Sarah treats her well enough.
- o Hagar becomes proud which can ruin any relationship. She thinks she's better than Sarah now. The Bible tells us that pride comes before the fall (Proverbs 16:18). She looks down on Sarah. To despise someone is to look at them with contempt, meaning you are looking down on them.
  - If Hagar was refusing to recognize Sarah's authority, Sarah, it seems, might have even beaten Hagar or had someone beat her to try to get her to submit. I don't know except that Sarah is treating her harshly enough to make her run away. The Hebrew word that is used to describe how Sarah, the Hebrew, is treating her Egyptian slave is also used in Genesis 15 to describe what the Egyptians will do to the Hebrew slaves.
- o The Bible doesn't forbid slavery specifically. The Bible does tell us we are to treat others how we would want to be treated. Do you think that commandment pretty much eliminates slavery? Jesus didn't come to change the laws and the political system of the day. He came to change hearts and minds. Paul writes to a slave owner in the book of Philemon and he encourages the slave owner to treat the slave as a brother.
- o Recall: What is Sarah's name at this point? Sarai; Who was her slave? Hagar
- o Explore more: Learn about the abolitionist movement in America.

VI. Discussion
- o In the end Jesus will come and rule. What kind of laws do you think Jesus will establish when He rules on earth?

VII. Writing
- o Use the discussion question as a writing prompt.
- o Get a high five and/or hug if you find any direct objects in your writing.
- o Circle the direct object. Underline the verb that comes before it.

Day 54 (check Materials List)

I. Read Genesis 16:7-14. Today's reading picks up after Hagar has run away from Sarah because she was being treated harshly. In the beginning it's talking about Hagar.

II. Memory Verse
- o   Genesis 26:4
- o   I will multiply your descendants as the stars of the heaven, and will give your descendants all these lands; and by your descendants all the nations of the earth shall be blessed.

III. Language
- o   Spelling/Handwriting
  - verse 10
  - words to know: authority, east, yourself, against
  - spelling tips:
    - The word <u>authority</u> starts with the word author, which ends with the word or. The first two letters are A-U.
    - The word <u>east</u> is only capitalized when it is naming an area, not when it's just a direction.
    - The word <u>yourself</u> is a compound of your and self.
    - The word <u>against</u> starts with the word again, which itself ends with the word gain.
- o   Vocabulary/Grammar
  - affliction (verse 11)
  - pain and suffering (noun)
  - other definition: something that causes pain and suffering (noun)
- o   Hebrew
  - to
  - le
  - to the
  - la (This is LE and HA smooshed together.)
  - Can you say from memory Genesis 1:1-4?
    - be reSHEET baRA eloHEEM et ha shaMAyim ve et ha Arets
    - ve ha Arets haaTAH TOhu va VOhu ve KHOshekh al pnaa teHOM ve RUakh eloHEEM meraKHEfet al pnaa ha MAyim
    - va YOmer eloHEEM yeHEE or va yeHEE or
    - va yar eloHEEM et ha or ki tov va yavDEL eloHEEM ben ha or u ven ha KHOshekh

IV. Science
- o   In our story today, Hagar is by a spring of water.
- o   Do you remember what the headwaters of a river are?
  - They are the beginning of a river.
- o   On Day 52 I told you that the headwaters of a river might begin by a spring bubbling up.
- o   Do you remember what groundwater is?

- It's the water stored and moving underground.
  - We use wells to get water from underground, but sometimes the water comes up to us in the form of a spring.
  - Can you demonstrate how to spring? (Note: I'm talking about the jumping up kind of springing.)
    - The water does something like that. It shoots up and then comes back down.
    - Springs are another part of the water cycle. Can you describe the water cycle?
      - Water goes in a cycle, a circle. It goes up through evaporation and transpiration from plants. It comes down as rain. That's the basic cycle.
      - Most evaporation occurs from the ocean which is where most water ends up as it is pulled by gravity down to sea level.
  - There are different types of springs. The most common are from groundwater finding its way to the surface through cracks in rocks. What happens to the rock as water keeps pushing its way through?
    - It erodes. The water opens its way, more and more, until you have water pouring out of a rock.
    - Growing up, my family used to take jugs and fill them up with water from a local spring.
    - These kinds of springs are the type that begin streams. Water can flow out regularly, or it could maybe just flow after a rainfall or after snow melts. How fast it comes out depends on how much pressure is behind it.
      - In the summer my kids make water squirters by poking a hole in the lid of a plastic bottle. Maybe your parents will let you try it. You can create a small stream by letting water flow out of your bottle-spring.
      - If you turned the bottle sideways and pointed it a little down, gravity would begin to pull water out of the hole. What happens when the bottle is squeezed?
        - It shoots out the water. When you are squeezing the bottle, you are applying pressure.
        - If you squeeze it gently, with low pressure, then the water comes out slowly. If you squeeze it hard, with high pressure, then what happens?
          - It shoots out farther.
  - There is water pressure in the ground and it regulates how forcefully the water flows. In fact, there is a type of spring that shoots water high up in the air because there is a lot of pressure.
    - There are two ways this happens. We'll look at one today.
    - One is called an artesian well. You can see a picture of one on the next page. At an artesian well, water shoots up from the ground. The force at work is gravity. How can gravity make something go up? Any ideas? Think about it a minute.
      - Need a hint? What does gravity do?
      - It pulls down, so think of water getting pushed down. How might that cause water to squirt up?
      - Do you need another hint? Think about how gravity makes one person on a seesaw go up.

- ○ Think of a balloon filled with water. If you pointed the opening up and held the water above the opening, could you get water to shoot up? (Note: If you have a balloon, you could try this.)
  - • That's what is happening at artesian wells.
  - • The groundwater is sealed off from traveling farther by rock that it can't break through. That's like the water being in the balloon.
  - • Then the water finds an opening at a lower elevation. Gravity is pulling down on the water. It's pushing the water toward that opening.
  - • A lot of water being pushed through a small opening makes a water spout.
- ○ When water is coming out of a hose, what happens if you cover part of the opening with your thumb?
  - • It shoots out farther. That's what happens with the artesian well. The water is being pushed out and the opening is small, so the water shoots out.
- ○ Recall: What force is at work in an artesian well?
  - • gravity
- ○ Explore more: Learn how siphoning works. How is that related to artesian springs?

V. Social Studies
- ○ Hagar is met by the angel of the Lord. I know I am familiar with all of the stories of where the Lord guides His people and helps them. I think of Abraham and Moses and Joshua and Gideon. But I don't think of Hagar. Here is someone in Scripture who has a

divine encounter. She obeys and goes back. Here is part of the prophecy she is given. I think the rest of it probably is talking just about Ishmael or his household, not his far-removed descendants. It says:

- God will multiply her descendants so that they will be too many to count.
- She will have a son to be named Ishmael which means God listens or God will hear.

o Ishmael is the father of the Ishmaelites. We will come across them later. He is the father of the Arabs.

o Isaac, Abraham's next son, is the father of the Jews.

- Both Jews and Arabs trace their lineage through Abraham.

o Look at the Day 54 map of Arab nations. Where's Israel?

- What else can you identify on the map? You should be able to find Egypt, Lebanon and Syria.

o There are well over 400 million Arabs in the world today. Half are under 25 years old which means their population is only getting bigger and bigger.

- There are over 21 million Jews. Abraham was told his descendants would be too great to count. Why the difference between the Arabs and the Jews?
- In Romans 11 we are told that believers are made part of Israel. Christians are God's people now too.
- How many Christians are in the world? I don't know. There are many who call themselves Christians who I think Jesus would say to them, "I never knew you."
- That said, here are the statistics.
  - 700 million Protestants, more than 2 billion Christians

o All of the numbers change daily (minute by minute), so in a way, they are too numerous to count!

o Something to remember is that not all Arabs are Muslims, though the majority are. Also, not all Muslims are Arab.

o How many Muslims are said to be in the world?

- There are over one and a half billion Muslims.
- Muslims say that their prophet, Mohammed, is a descendant of Ishmael.
- Study the maps for Day 54 showing religions worldwide.

o Recall: Are all Arabs Muslims? Are all Muslims Arabs?

- No
- No

o Explore more: Label all of the Arab nations on the map.

VI. Discussion

o What do you think of God blessing Ishmael and making his descendants even more numerous than Isaac's?

VII. Writing

o Use the discussion question as a writing prompt.

o Get a high five and/or hug if you use any of your spelling and/or vocabulary words.

Day 55

I.   Read Genesis 16:15-17:8 and verse 15.

II. Memory Verse
   o   Genesis 26:4
        •   I will multiply your descendants as the stars of the heaven, and will give your descendants all these lands; and by your descendants all the nations of the earth shall be blessed.
   o   Review Genesis 1:4.
        •   God saw that the light was good; and God separated the light from the darkness.

III. Language
   o   Spelling/Handwriting
        •   Test yourselves on the words from Days 51-54.
            ▪   priest, sandal, enemies, except
            ▪   heir, pigeon, prey, shield
            ▪   children, Egyptian, conceive, maid
            ▪   authority, east, yourself, against
   o   Vocabulary/Grammar
        •   Test yourselves on the words from Days 51-54.
            ▪   array – dress someone in particular clothing
            ▪   heir – the person who will inherit property, money, or position title after a person leaves a position or dies
            ▪   obtain – to get or acquire
            ▪   affliction – pain and suffering
   o   Hebrew
        •   We're going to put together the first part of Genesis 1:5 today. The NASB translation says, "God called the light day, and the darkness He called night."
        •   The Hebrew translates to: And calls God to the light day and to the darkness called night.
        •   Can you put the words together to say that sentence?
        •   va yikRA eloHEEM la or yom ve la KHOshekh kaRA LII-la
        •   Practice this part of the verse.

IV. Science
   o   We're going a little mathematical today for science. We're reading about the multitudes and the exceedingly great numbers of descendants that Abraham is going to have.
        •   We're going to learn about scientific notation. It may look like math, but it has science in its name. Math is an important part of science. Science is about observing the world and drawing conclusions. Part of that is measuring. Measuring not just sizes but speeds, angles, volume, all sorts of things.
   o   Scientific notation is a tool to help us write really big numbers. We've talked about some pretty big numbers in our different lessons, so we'll use those today.

o Let's start small with the number 10. The number 10 is the number 1 times 10, one time. We write it like this:

$$1 \times 10^1 = 10$$

o The number 100 is 1 times 10 times 10. We write it like this.

$$1 \times 10^2 = 100$$

o There's an easier way to think about this.
   - The number 10 has one zero, so we use the exponent 1, that's the little number at the top that tells us how many times to multiply by ten.
   - The number 100 has two zeros, so we write 2 for our exponent.
o Try one thousand. How would you write it in scientific notation?

$$1000 \quad 1 \times 10^3$$

o The number of zeros equals the number on the exponent. Now I'm going to show you a number in scientific notation and you write it as a number. Write the first number and then the number of zeros that the exponent tells you.

$$1 \times 10^6$$

o That's one million.

$$1{,}000{,}000$$

o To write five million we just multiply by five instead of 1.

$$5{,}000{,}000 \quad 5 \times 10^6$$

o Now let's look at some of the numbers from our lessons. Let's start small with the blue whale.
o The blue whale weighs about 300 hundred thousand pounds. How do you write that in scientific notation? (Note: You can cover up the answer and let them see the number if that helps.)

$$300{,}000 \quad 3 \times 10^5$$

o Did you figure it out?
o How about something bigger? The number of water molecules in a drop of water is about 400 quintillion. How would you write that in scientific notation?

$$400{,}000{,}000{,}000{,}000{,}000{,}000$$

$$4 \times 10^{20}$$

- ○ Are you starting to see how scientific notation could be useful in science?
- ○ Let's apply this to one of our science lessons. I told you that there are about 100 trillion cells in the human body. Write that as a number and as scientific notation.
  - • 100 trillion is the number one with fourteen zeros. It's written like this.

$$100,000,000,000,000$$
$$1 \times 10^{14}$$

- ○ If I had three coins in each hand, how many coins would I be holding?
  - • Six. I have two hands and each had three. I had three coins two times. The math is 3 times 2 equals 6. Apply that math to our next problem.
- ○ There are about 100 trillion cells in the human body. I also told you that there are about 100 trillion atoms in each cell. How would you find the number of atoms in the human body? (Each cell is holding 100 trillion atoms just like each hand was holding three coins.)
  - • You would multiple the number of cells times the number of atoms, 100 trillion times 100 trillion.
  - • Scientific notation makes it easy.
  - • To multiple the same number together you just add their exponents (those up-high numbers).

$$\text{100 trillion times 100 trillion is}$$
$$1 \times 10^{14+14}$$

  - • What's the answer?

$$1 \times 10^{28}$$

  - • That's 10 octillion. You have approximately 10 octillion atoms in your body!
- ○ Recall: How does scientific notation make things easier?
  - • It simplifies big numbers.
- ○ Explore more: If you know all about decimals, then you can learn more about using scientific notation. How would you turn numbers without zeros, such as 3,452, into scientific notation?

V. Social Studies
- ○ In our reading today Abram's name changes to Abraham. His wife Sarai will get her name changed to Sarah. What's in a name?
- ○ In the Old Testament we are often told the meanings of names.
  - • Ishmael was named for God listening.

- Abraham means father of a multitude.
- The name Sarah means princess.
- Abraham and Sarah will have a son named Isaac which means "he laughs." Abraham and Sarah both laugh when they are told they will have a son.
- One of the cities we have come across is Salem. It later becomes the city of Jerusalem, the capital city of Israel. It was named for the Canaanite god, Salem. In Hebrew, though, the same name translates to peace. Jerusalem means foundation of peace.
  o Here are some other biblical names and their meanings.
    - Samuel – heard of God
    - Peter – rock
    - Andrew – manly
    - Anna – grace
    - Nathaniel – gift of God
    - Ruth – friend
    - Rachel – ewe, which is a female sheep
  o Rachel doesn't seem to be this way, but in Nathaniel, Samuel and Ishmael, the EL at the end of their names is referring to God, like in eloHEEM. That made me think that the name Israel also ends in EL.
  o The nation of Israel also has a significant name. It means who prevails with God, or triumphant with God.
  o Maybe you'd like to look up the meanings of your names. Some can be weird! How are you like or not like your name's meaning?
  o Recall: What does Abraham mean? What does Sarah mean?
    - father of a multitude
    - princess
  o Explore more: Look into the names of other places we've already learned about. Where did they come from? What are their significances? What about where you live? Can you find about how it was named?

VI. Discussion
  o Abraham was 86 when Ishmael was born and 99 when God renewed the promise about his descendants. He will be 100 when Isaac is born, the child promised from the beginning. Do you understand Abraham thinking Ishmael was the answer to God's promise? Do you think he ever doubted if that's what God had intended? Do you think you could wait so many years and still believe it could happen?

VII. Writing
  o Choose something you wrote on Days 52-54 to edit.
  o Use your editing guidelines and check for correct spelling and punctuation.
  o Have someone else check your writing as well.
  o Make a final draft.

Day 56

I. Read Genesis 17:9-27.

II. Memory Verse
- 2 Corinthians 1:20
- For as many as are the promises of God, in Him they are yes; therefore also through Him is our Amen to the glory of God through us.

III. Language
- Spelling/Handwriting
  - verse 22
  - words to know: throughout, foreigner, twelve, ninety-nine
  - spelling tips:
    - The word <u>throughout</u> is a compound word putting together the words through and out.
    - The word <u>foreigner</u> breaks our I before E word. It has the word reign in the middle of it, like a king reigning over his kingdom. That has the vowel spelling pattern of the word eight, as in the number eight, if you can picture how that is spelled.
    - We have two other numbers we are spelling today. The first is <u>twelve</u>. It ends with a silent E. The E doesn't really do anything, but does it look really strange without it?
    - The number word <u>ninety-nine</u> is hyphenated.
- Vocabulary/Grammar
  - intercept (I just chose this for today.)
  - blocking something from getting to its intended destination (verb)
  - Today we read about the "sign of the covenant." What's the prepositional phrase in that?
    - of the covenant
  - What's the preposition?
    - of
  - What's the object, the noun?
    - covenant
  - What describes the noun in the phrase My covenant? What describes the word convenant? (Hint: What word comes before it?)
    - My
  - The word MY describes a noun. What type of word describes a noun?
    - adjective
  - The word MY is a possessive adjective. It's an adjective that tells who has the object, who possesses it. Can you list other possessive adjectives?
    - your (book), his, her, our, their
    - (Note: Don't confuse these with possessive pronouns. Those are words like: mine and yours.)
- Hebrew
  - We are working on Genesis 1:5. "God called the light day, and the darkness He called night. And there was evening and there was morning, one day."
  - evening

- Erev
- You can also practice the first half of Genesis 1:5 in Hebrew.
- va yikRA eloHEEM la or yom ve la KHOshekh kaRA LII-la va yeHEE

IV. Science
  o Today's lesson is on circumcision. It is an operation done on boys. It removes a small piece of skin. God chose it to mark them as His own.
    - Ancient civilizations did have surgical practices. We don't know much about them, but we do know some. This is sort of a history lesson instead of science, but medicine is a field of science, so let's go ahead with it and learn about surgical practices.
  o When you think about surgery, what images come to mind?
    - Maybe a doctor with gloves and face mask and gown, maybe a knife?
  o What do you think were some of the big problems faced by early surgical patients?
    - One big problem with surgery until the last century was that patients could die from infections. Being cut in surgery exposed a way for harmful bacteria to get into the body and multiply.
  o Why do doctors wear gloves and a face mask during surgery?
    - It protects the patient. The patient is vulnerable to germs getting into his body.
  o Some ancient remedies were to use tar and honey as *antiseptics*, or something that slows the growth of microorganisms, which is a living thing so small you need a microscope to see it, like the bad bacteria.
    - What's a microorganism?
    - What do antiseptics do?
  o The biggest breakthrough in controlling infection didn't come until the 1940s.
  o In 1928 penicillin, the first antibiotic, was discovered in London by Alexander Fleming.
    - It took more than a decade of work, though, by other scientists before it was introduced as a medicine available for widespread use.
  o Penicillin was an accidental discovery. It is made from a mold. Fleming came in his lab one day and found that some mold had grown in one of their experiment dishes and had killed the bacteria in it.
  o How does a mold kill bacteria and not other things in our bodies?
    - Penicillin works by preventing the building of cell walls. Bacteria have walls. The cells that make up our body systems, don't. Viruses also don't have walls, so they are not killed by *antibiotics*, or bacteria killers, such as penicillin.
  o Here are some pictures. The first is a bacteria cell. Notice the cell wall!

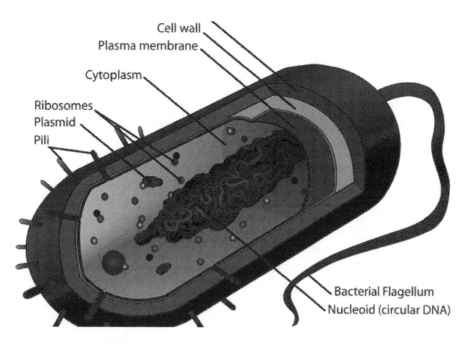

- The following image is what is described on Wikipedia as a "typical animal cell structure." Instead of a wall, its outer part is called a *membrane*. It's a thin layer that holds the form of the cell.
  - If you ever heat milk, maybe to make hot chocolate or pudding, the skin that develops on top as it cools is a *membrane*. Maybe you should make pudding today, for scientific purposes. ☺

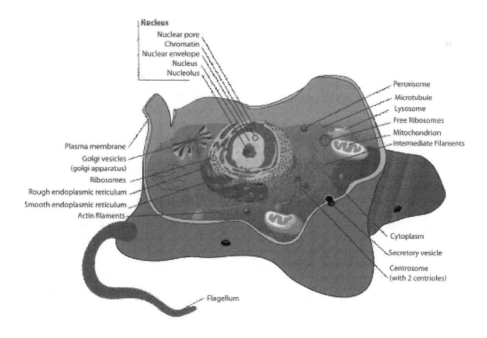

- Recall: What was the first antibiotic? What do antiseptics do? Why don't antibiotics kill the cells we need? What do our cells have instead of walls?
  - penicillin
  - slow the growth of bacteria

- They prevent cell walls from being built and the good cells don't have walls.
        - a membrane
    - Explore more: Learn more about how penicillin works or the structure of a cell.

V. Social Studies
    - In science we talked about a major breakthrough in medicine. It used to be that you could get a small cut and die from it because it got infected.
    - They think ancient Egyptians put moldy bread on wounds. Do you think they were onto something?
    - We know a little of ancient surgical practices. Read these laws from Babylon, the most famous city from Mesopotamia.
        - 215. If a physician makes a large incision with an operating knife and cures it, or if he opens a tumor (over the eye) with an operating knife, and saves the eye, he shall receive ten shekels in money.
        - 217. If he is the slave of someone, his owner shall give the physician two shekels.
        - 218. If a physician makes a large incision with the operating knife, and kills him, or opens a tumor with the operating knife, and cuts out the eye, his hands shall be cut off.
    - What can you learn from these laws?
        - Surgery was a risky business. It seems like ten shekels must have been a lot of money if they were willing to risk losing their hands! We can also see how a slave's life wasn't valued as much.
            - There's a sermon called "Ten Shekels and a Shirt" that's one of my favorites. You can find it on sermonindex.net. You can find its transcript online too. It's based on the Bible story about Micah being hired to be the priest to a false god. He received ten shekels of silver and food and clothing. That was his yearly wage, so maybe ten shekels for one surgery was a really good deal.
    - Those laws come from the *Hammurabi Code*. It was written by the ruler of Babylon in the 1700s BC.
        - God gives His law to Moses and Israel in the 1400s BC. Which came first?
            - Hammurabi's Code was written first.
        - There have been even older laws found. A tablet with laws written on them was found in an ancient Syrian city. It is said to date in the 2400s BC.
    - Some of the laws include:
        - A man's wife or children should be sold as slaves to work for three years to pay his debts. (BTW: This is still done today in places. Why isn't the man taken as a slave instead?)
        - If a woman doesn't do her work around the house, she is to be thrown into the Euphrates River. She may or may not make it back to the shore.
        - If a builder builds a house that collapses and kills the owner, the builder is put to death.
    - There is a strong sense of an "eye for an eye, and a tooth for a tooth" that is similar to the Old Testament law which makes some think that Moses copied the code.

- However, just from the laws I described above, I hope you can already see important differences. An eye for an eye is about justice. Where is the justice in selling your wife or child to pay for your debts?
- In every culture there were the same issues of lying, stealing, murder, etc. and every culture had to find a way to deal with it and bring about justice.
- The main difference with the law that God gave Moses and his people, is that it is the only one that was spiritual in nature. It wasn't just about how people should deal with other people in different situations. It was about the root cause of the problems, sin.
- The law of God was about sin and our need to live righteously. We are to worship one God only. We are not to make idols.
- And a big difference is that the Hammurabi Code offers no forgiveness. The law given by God provided means of receiving forgiveness and restoration, making things right with God.
- And what about selling your wife and children as slaves to work for three years to pay your debt? Not in the law of Moses. There is mention of selling yourself as a slave, and every 7th year debts were forgiven and slaves were set free. There are also other provisions to help the poor, so they wouldn't find themselves in such desperate situations.
  - Recall: What is the name of the code of law written in Babylon in the 1700s BC? Hammurabi's Code
  - Explore more: Read more of the code. What can you learn about Hammurabi?

VI. Discussion

- If you could make your own laws, what laws would you change? What laws would you create?

VII. Writing

- We've been working on adding commas and capitals to our writing to make it more proper. In fact, those capitalized names are called proper nouns. The lowercase nouns are called common nouns.
- Let's work on commas and capitals this week. Here's a review, with a little extra.
- Capitalize
  - the first letter in a sentence and
  - all types of names: names of people, names of places and names of things.
- We use commas in lists.
- We use commas to separate
  - date numbers and
  - date words.
  - Monday, March 14, 2011 (Note: read commas out loud!)
- We use commas when we're connecting two sentences with a conjunction.
- Here's a new one. Just like we use commas to separate date words, we use commas to separate place names, such as the city from the state or the state from the country.
  - Here are examples.
    - I visited Berlin, (comma) Germany.
    - I was born in Omaha, (comma) Nebraska.

- o That's a lot. Don't worry if you forget some. If you make a mistake, it's good for your brain because you'll get the chance to recognize what's wrong and decide what's right. When you fix your mistake, you will have learned something new and your neurons will get excited and connected, and you'll be that much smarter.
- o Complete Writing Sentences 10 in your workbook. At the top of the page, there is a reminder of the new rules.

Day 57 (check Materials List)

I. Read Genesis 18:1-8.

II. Memory Verse
- o 2 Corinthians 1:20
- o For as many as are the promises of God, in Him they are yes; therefore also through Him is our Amen to the glory of God through us.

III. Language
- o Spelling/Handwriting
  - • verse 4
  - • words to know: appeared, opposite, bowed, measure
  - • spelling tips:
    - ▪ Appeared and opposite have double letters to keep the vowels apart, so they don't have the long vowel sound. The long vowel sound is when a vowel says its name.
    - ▪ The word bow is a homograph, where a word is written the same way, but pronounced differently, bow rhymes with toe, or bow rhymes with now. This is talking about someone bowing down. He bowed before his visitors.
    - ▪ The word measure has the same beginning vowel sound and spelling as the word heaven.
- o Vocabulary/Grammar
  - • tender (verse 7)
  - • easy to cut or chew (adjective)
  - • other definition: showing gentleness (adjective)
    - ▪ (Note: In our family we tease that Mary was not too spicy and easy to chew…. Think *Silent Night*… tender and mild.)
- o Hebrew
  - • morning
  - • VOker (If you can, roll your R with a little flicker of your tongue.)
  - • You can also practice the first half of Genesis 1:5 in Hebrew.
  - • va yikRA eloHEEM la or yom ve la KHOshekh kaRA LII-la va yeHEE

IV. Science
- o We've talked about cooking meat and about making bread. It mentions that the honored guests were not just served those things but curds as well. Let's learn about making curds today, and you can try it.
- o Milk is a protein, like carrots are a vegetable and apples are a fruit.
  - • Milk is a liquid made up of microscopic protein particles. What does microscopic mean?
    - ▪ You can't see them with your eyes. You need a microscope.
- o What happens when you first put in a big spoonful of salt or sugar into a glass of water? (Right at first, before you stir it.)
  - • If you are debating, then why don't you try it to see.
  - • At first, it just sinks to the bottom.

- In a *suspension*, the stuff in the liquid settles to the bottom. Orange juice with pulp is a suspension. Why does the container say to shake before drinking?
  - The pulp settles down to the bottom. When you shake it, it mixes it back up.
- What happens when you stir the water with the sugar or salt in it?
  - The sugar or salt dissolves. It's mixed together, and whatever is in the water won't fall back down to the bottom.
  - The fancy name for that is colloid.
  - A *colloid* is a mixture that won't separate out over time.

o What is milk, a colloid or a suspension?
  - Milk is a colloid. It's made up of all these microscopic protein particles that don't settle over time. They stay mixed in. You only have to shake or stir your milk if you added chocolate powder to it!

o Curds are what you get when you separate the protein particles in the milk.
  - When an acid, such as vinegar or lemon juice, is added to the milk, it separates the proteins into two groups: the solids and the liquids.
  - The solids are the curds. The liquids are called whey.
  - Do you know the rhyme: Little Miss Muffet sat on her tuffet, eating her curds and whey?
  - She was basically eating cottage cheese.

o When the milk is separated, the curds are eaten or pressed into cheeses which are then eaten. The whey is sometimes used as a preservative, something that makes food last longer before it goes bad.
  - I actually learned that whey was a preservative from being overseas. They don't have a word for "whey," and in the local language what the containers say is "cheese bottom juice."

o So, whey is the juice on the bottom, or the liquid leftover once the curds are separated out of the milk.

o Here's how to separate the proteins in milk.
  - Add 2 tablespoons of white vinegar to ¼ cup of skim milk. (If you don't have measuring cups and spoons, that's just four big spoonfuls of milk and two of vinegar.) Stir. Strain off the liquid.
  - That's the experiment way. It's not for eating, too acidic. You can try it with different types of milk and different types of acids.
  - The simple cooking way to make curds (for eating) is to bring a two cups of milk to a boil. You are scalding it, bringing it just to the point of boiling and then turning it off. Stir in 4 teaspoons (NOT tablespoons) of vinegar, or you could even try orange juice for your acid. If nothing is happening, add another teaspoon or two of your acid.

o Recall: What happens to particles in suspensions? What's the difference between a colloid and a suspension?
  - They separate.
  - The particles in the colloid don't separate.

o Explore more: Learn more about cheese making. Learn about the chemical process taking place when acid is added to the colloid, milk.

V. Social Studies
- Whenever I read today's passage in the Bible, I always wonder how long it took them to prepare this meal for the guests. Did you think that must have taken a long time to get the meal ready?
  - The bread was probably a flat bread, which means the dough wasn't fermented. They didn't have to wait for it to rise!
- We get a little glimpse of hospitality in Abraham's culture. I think, in some ways, it's similar to cultural experiences I've had overseas among Muslims.
- First, what would you describe as the hospitality practices of America, or wherever you are from?
- What about if three strangers showed up at your door? What is the cultural expectation of hospitality?
  - I would say in America, we certainly wouldn't just invite three strangers in to sit and eat! We would stand at the door talking, being polite, hopefully.
  - Even if someone we know comes by, we find out at the door what's up, why they came, if they need something.
  - Guests would call before coming over. They would be offered something to drink or something to eat if there's food right there. Guests are free to turn it down. They wouldn't be expected to stay long and they would be given our attention while in our home.
  - Hospitality in America is making someone feel at home, that they should feel comfortable to help themselves to whatever.
- What are some differences between your culture and what we observe in this story of Abraham's culture?
  - Of course Abraham's guests couldn't have called ahead, but even today in Muslim cultures it can be considered rude to call before you visit someone. It's questioning their hospitality. Of course you would be welcome!
  - Abraham doesn't ask why they've come.
  - Abraham leaves his guests to rush around and organize a meal.
  - They are served instead of welcomed to "help themselves."
- I have literally been left sitting alone in a room for a long time while a meal was prepared for me. In one Muslim home in Istanbul, the kids and I were put into one room while my husband and the man of the house were taken into another room. I sat alone with my kids while she made dinner and served the men. I found out later they had chicken. The woman finally came and set up a small round table that stood just inches off the floor. We sat on the floor around the table and ate a pile of boiled whole potatoes.
  - There are a lot of cultural differences just in that one story. The men and women are treated differently. Which got more respect?
    - the men
  - What was the main point of the hospitality?
    - the food
    - to serve food is to show hospitality
- To reject food offered you is a major offense in many cultures.
- Some Muslims will say that they will invite you in, and you can stay three days before they will ask you why you came. That's certainly a different approach to hospitality.

It's not weird to end up spending the night at someone's house where you are visiting.

- Americans don't like to intrude or inconvenience others, but in a Muslim culture hospitality is expected.

o In a hospitality culture, there's a "fight" every time you try to leave someone's house. It's their duty to try to get you to stay. Even if they want you to go, they will insist you stay.

- They will also always invite you over even if they don't really want you to come. My friend taught me how to read peoples' eyes and smiles to see if it was a real offer to visit.
- This is part of their culture. Hospitality is so important in a Muslim culture that they have to offer it. It doesn't occur to them to not offer hospitality. It's built into them through the culture that they've been brought up in.

o They will also insist you eat, basically forcing food on you. It's polite to say no when offered something, so it means nothing to them when you turn down food because everyone says no when something is offered. They will give it to you anyway, and basically yell at you to eat it. They aren't being mean; they are being hospitable in their culture.

o There have been many a hungry and thirsty foreign exchange student in America who turned down food they wanted because they were following their own culture's rules for politeness.

- In America we tend to say what we mean and accept other's answers. If we offer and they say they don't want it, then we don't give it to them.

o Recall: How did Abraham show hospitality?

- He served a meal to his guests.

o Explore more: Choose a culture to learn about its hospitality rituals.

VI. Discussion

o What is hospitality? The Bible says to show hospitality without complaint (1 Peter 4:9). Romans 12:13 says to "practice" hospitality. How is your family practicing it? How can you do a better job of it?

VII. Writing

o Use the discussion question as a writing prompt.
o Get a high five and/or hug if you use any of the vocabulary or spelling words.
o Underline all of the adjectives in your writing today. Don't forget the possessive adjectives (your, my, our…).

Day 58

I. Read Genesis 18:9-15. (This continues the story of Abraham's three visitors.)

II. Memory Verse
- o 2 Corinthians 1:20
- o For as many as are the promises of God, in Him they are yes; therefore also through Him is our Amen to the glory of God through us.

III. Language
- o Spelling/Handwriting
  - • verse 14
  - • words to know: denied, advanced, appointed, difficult
  - • spelling tips:
    - ▪ <u>Denied</u> is the past tense of deny which ends in a Y. What letter comes before the Y in deny?
      - • N
      - • Is that a vowel or a consonant?
        - ▪ a consonant
      - • What happens to a Y that comes after a consonant when you need to add an E?
        - ▪ (Note: You don't need to tell them the answer now if you don't want to. The Y changes into an I.)
    - ▪ <u>Advanced</u> follows the rule that a C followed by an E has the S sound.
    - ▪ <u>Appointed</u> has a double letter to keep it from reading AY-point-ed.
    - ▪ <u>Difficult</u> also has a double letter.
- o Vocabulary/Grammar
  - • appointed (verse 14)
  - • designated, pre-arranged, scheduled (adjective)
  - • other definitions: assign a job to someone; set a time or place (verbs)
  - • I picked this word for two reasons.
    - ▪ The first thing I want you to notice is that if you don't know what a word means, you can see if know any similar words. Can you think of another word that also has "appoint" in it?
      - • How about appointment?
      - • If you know that an appointment is the set time you are supposed to be somewhere, then you can figure that maybe appointed has something to do with that.
    - ▪ The second thing I want you to notice is that appointed looks like a verb, but it is used as an adjective. What word does it describe? "appointed time"
      - • Sometimes we use verb forms as adjectives. Another example would be "the interested child."
      - • The noun is "child." What's the verb form used as an adjective to describe the child?
      - • interested

- Can you think of another? (Note: If they are stuck, how about "bored.")
  o Hebrew
    - one
    - eKHAD
    - Say Genesis 1:1-5a.
      - be reSHEET baRA eloHEEM et ha shaMAyim ve et ha Arets
      - ve ha Arets haaTAH TOhu va VOhu ve KHOshekh al pnaa teHOM ve RUakh eloHEEM meraKHEfet al pnaa ha MAyim
      - va YOmer eloHEEM yeHEE or va yeHEE or
      - va yar eloHEEM et ha or ki tov va yavDEL eloHEEM ben ha or u ven ha KHOshekh
      - va yikRA eloHEEM la or yom ve la KHOshekh kaRA LII-la

IV. Science
  o Today Sarah thinks she is too old.
  o What happens as we age? Name some things.
  o Let's see what you know about old age.
    - Based on what you learned about calories, do you think your grandparents need fewer calories than you? Do they need fewer calories than your parents?
    - They do need fewer calories than your parents, and maybe you, if you are pre-teen or a teenager.
    - Why?
      - They use less energy. Their bodies use calories more slowly. They also are probably less active.
  o Do you think that after the age of forty, a lot of people have trouble seeing small things that are very close to them?
    - They do. Have you ever seen people hold something farther away from themselves to be able to read it?
    - The scientific word for the eye condition is presbyopia. What happens is that the lenses in your eyes start having trouble focusing. Basically, the eye is losing its flexibility. Probably a lot of body parts start to lose their flexibility!
      - A little side note about the word presbyopia since we talked about this in vocabulary today. Can you find any related parts of words in there that you recognize?
        - Words related to sight have OP in them.
          - optics (the study of sight and light)
          - ophthalmologist (eye doctor)
        - Is the word Presbyterian familiar to you?
          - The root presby means old age.
          - So, presbyopia means something like old age sight.
          - Presbyterian is a church structure where the church is governed by elders. Elders, old age, get it?
  o Do you think your brain starts to shrink when you are in your twenties?
    - It does! Your brain will reach its maximum size in your early twenties.

- However, you can still actually improve your memory with age, even with a shrinking brain. The key is to keep your brain active, so never stop learning!
  o Do you think kids' voices are the hardest to hear when you get older?
    - Yes, little kid voices are higher pitched which makes them harder to hear as your hearing starts to decline.
    - You have hairs in your ears that vibrate and send the sound waves to your brain. They can become less sensitive with age.
  o Do you think that people shrink as they get older?
    - They do! Men can tend to lose an inch of height and women tend to lose two inches.
  o Do you think your nose keeps growing as you age?
    - No, it doesn't. But your ears do!
    - These questions and answers were chosen and rephrased from http://www.webmd.com/healthy-aging/rm-quiz-aging-body.
  o And what about Sarah? She thinks she is too old to have children. Age is the most important factor in whether or not a woman will have a baby. Those eggs I told you about start to get too old. Only 3% of the egg cells are still okay by the age of 40. Sarah's body told her she was long past being able to have a child. But God doesn't have to follow the laws of nature! By waiting, He made the birth miraculous instead of just unexpected.
  o Explore more: Learn about how hearing works.

V. Social Studies
  o Abraham gets a specific prophecy this time. It will be just one more year until it's fulfilled. What's the prophecy?
    - Sarah will have a son.
  o I told you before about the Dead Sea Scrolls. They were an ancient copy of the Bible that proved the Bible hadn't been changed over time. Today we're going to look at a few prophecies in the Bible that we know have come true.
  o How many prophecies do you think there are in the Bible and how many have been fulfilled?
    - According to the "Reasons to Believe" website, there are about 2500 prophecies in the Bible and about 2000 of those prophecies have been fulfilled.
    - Here are three quoted examples from their site about fulfilled prophecies. You can find more at: http://www.reasons.org/articles/articles/fulfilled-prophecy-evidence-for-the-reliability-of-the-bible.
  o In the fifth century B.C. a prophet named Zechariah declared that the Messiah would be betrayed for the price of a slave—thirty pieces of silver, according to Jewish law—and also that this money would be used to buy a burial ground for Jerusalem's poor foreigners (Zechariah 11:12-13). Bible writers and secular historians both record thirty pieces of silver as the sum paid to Judas Iscariot for betraying Jesus, and they indicate that the money went to purchase a "potter's field," used—just as predicted—for the burial of poor aliens (Matthew 27:3-10).
    - Probability of chance fulfillment = 1 in 10^{11}.
    - Note: What's that mean in balloons? That would be one balloon out of 100,000,000,000 (one hundred billion).

- Just a note: the author has come up with his own method of figuring probability. When all the fulfilled prophecies are taken together, they basically show the Bible to be as reliable as the laws of physics, you know, laws like when you drop something it falls down and that light will bend and make a rainbow when it passes through water.
  - Here are a couple more fulfilled prophecies.
- Mighty Babylon, 196 miles square, was enclosed not only by a moat, but also by a double wall 330 feet high, each part 90 feet thick. It was said by unanimous popular opinion to be indestructible, yet two Bible prophets declared its doom. These prophets further claimed that the ruins would be avoided by travelers, that the city would never again be inhabited, and that its stones would not even be moved for use as building material (Isaiah 13:17-22 and Jeremiah 51:26, 43). Their description is, in fact, the well-documented history of the famous citadel.
  - Probability of chance fulfillment = 1 in 10^9.
- The exact location and construction sequence of Jerusalem's nine suburbs was predicted by Jeremiah about 2600 years ago. He referred to the time of this building project as "the last days," that is, the time period of Israel's second rebirth as a nation in the land of Palestine (Jeremiah 31:38-40). This rebirth became history in 1948, and the construction of the nine suburbs has gone forward precisely in the locations and in the sequence predicted.
  - Probability of chance fulfillment = 1 in 10^{18}.
- Recall: About how many prophecies are there in the Bible and how many have been fulfilled? 2000 out of 2500
- Explore more: There are lots of prophecies out there. What has been fulfilled? What are we still watching for? I gave a link above if you want to read more of these descriptions of fulfilled prophecies.

VI. Discussion
- There are about 300 prophecies about Jesus in the Old Testament that were fulfilled in his lifetime. Some He purposed to do in order to fulfil the prophecy and others no human would have had control over such as what happened on the cross (pierced his side, no broken bones, casting lots for his clothes).
- There are still about 500 prophecies to be fulfilled. That means we are in the middle of the story! Every day we are getting closer to the end of the story, which is really the beginning of a whole other story when God creates a new heaven and a new earth where righteousness will dwell.
- Do you think of the Bible as something that happened long ago or do you ever think of yourself as being part of God's story? If there were chapters written about your life or about your family, what chapters of the Bible would they resemble? Would it be a story of God's faithfulness or of rebellion or of discovery?

VII. Writing
- Use the discussion question as a writing prompt. Can you use a verb form as an adjective? (fallen, broken, burnt...)
- Get a high five and/or hug if you use any of the vocabulary or spelling words.

Day 59

I. Read Genesis 18:16-33. (This continues the story of Abraham's three visitors.)

II. Memory Verse
- o 2 Corinthians 1:20
- o For as many as are the promises of God, in Him they are yes; therefore also through Him is our Amen to the glory of God through us.

III. Language
- o Spelling/Handwriting
  - verse 33
  - words to know: righteousness, command, judge, forty-five
  - spelling tips:
    - The word <u>righteousness</u> starts with the word right. That's followed by three vowels, all different.
    - The word <u>command</u> has a double letter. Why?
      - Double letters keep apart vowels to keep the first vowel from saying its name, or you could say to keep the first vowel short.
    - The word <u>judge</u> has five letters.
    - The word <u>forty-five</u> is one word and something you should be able to spell. Forty does not have the word for the number four in it.
- o Vocabulary/Grammar
  - venture (verse 31)
  - to undertake something risky or dangerous (verb)
  - other definition: a risky or dangerous undertaking (noun)
    - Can you see how this word is related to adventure?
- o Hebrew
  - Normally, you put the number before the noun it describes. There's one exception in Hebrew, one, the number one. In Hebrew you would say two apples and three days, but apple one and day one.
  - In our verse, "one day" will translate to yom eKHAD or "day one."
  - Try translating this part of the verse yourself.
    - Genesis 1:5b "And there was evening and there was morning, one day."
    - "And there was" will translate just like when we said "and there was light."
    - Also, the "and" used in this verse is VA.
    - va yeHEE Erev va yeHEE VOker yom eKHAD

IV. Science
- o It's happened. I couldn't find a science topic in here, but Abraham's countdown made me think that we could look a little more at scientific notation. We haven't only talked about really big numbers; we've also talked about some really small things. Let's learn to talk about their size, scientifically, instead of saying really, really tiny or even microscopic. What does microscopic mean?

- • can only been with a microscope
- ○ Let's review just a moment before we begin. Write the number 50,000 in scientific notation.

50,000

5×10^4

- ○ Hopefully you started with a five and then counted up the zeros.
- ○ We're going to do the opposite today.
- ○ How would you write the number, 0.0005? It's almost the same thing, but backwards. We use a negative exponent to show which way we're going. Do you want to try before you look?

- ○ It looks like this

0.0005

5×10^{-4}

0.0005
→ → → →

- ○ I've told you to count zeros. You could do that, but that's not exactly what's happening. We're really counting decimal places. We take the decimal point, the period, and move it until we have a nice number to work with. We're looking for a number from 1 to 9.
- ○ Because we are moving backwards, we use a negative number for our exponent (the up-high number). The exponent tells how many times to move the decimal point. The negative sign tells us to move backward, that we're making the number smaller.
- ○ The number 5 has a decimal point. You just can't see it. The number 5 could be written like this.

5.0 or like this

5.0000000000000000000000

- ○ That's still the number 5. There's no reason to write a decimal point and a zero after the five so we leave them off, but they still exist.
- ○ Try this one. What is the number 0.03 in scientific notation?

0.03

3×10^{-2}

- o Start with three. Multiply by 10. Count the zeros or the decimal places that you need to move over. Use a negative for moving backward and making the number smaller.
- o One more, try 0.00006.

0.00006
6×10^{-5}

- o How about something from our lessons? How small is a cell in the human body? Well, there are lots of different types of cells. The smallest are actually brain cells. There are different types of brain cells, but the kind you have the most of are the smallest. About three-quarters of your brain is made up of about 50 billion cerebellum granule cells (according to Wikipedia ☺). How big are they?

4×10^{-4} centimeters

- o Can you write that as a decimal?

0.0004 centimeters

- o I'm going to show you something about understanding what that number means.
  - One centimeter is about the width of a finger. If you divided that width up into ten thousand parts, four of those together would be the width of those brain cells. It is four ten-thousandths of a centimeter.
- o Recall: How do we show in scientific notation that we are making the number smaller?
  - with a negative exponent
- o Explore more: You could learn about the measurement μm. How big are red blood cells? (They are actually smaller than those brain cells, but they aren't complete cells because they have no nucleus.)

V. Social Studies
- o Today's reading seems to be about righteousness and justice.
  - Those are two character traits of God. He is righteous, meaning He does what is right. And He is just, meaning He acts fairly.
  - The Bible tells us that the punishment of sin is death. It would be just for us all to die. But God is more than just just. ☺ God is merciful and gracious and

compassionate. That's why we should always show gratitude because He saves us from our just punishment, one that we deserve.

- o Sodom and Gomorrah will soon receive a just punishment for their sins, but what stands out to me is verse 19. "For I have chosen [Abraham], so that he may command his children and his household after him to keep the way of the Lord by doing righteousness and justice, so that the Lord may bring upon Abraham what He has spoken about him."
- o God has made promises. He has to keep His promise. Here it says that Abraham needs to teach his children to do justice and to live righteously so that He can give him what is promised.
  - God can be very confusing to us. He doesn't have a brain like ours that aches when we try to understand how He works.
  - In order to fulfill His promises to His people, they have to live according to His ways. He has to fulfill His promises, so He has to ensure that there are always some of His people living according to His word.
- o We call this group, the remnant. There is always a remnant, a group that hasn't forgotten God and hasn't stopped living according to His ways.
- o Noah was a remnant. He was the one living righteously when everyone else was bent on violence and evil.
- o The remnant will always exist. Throughout Israel's history, we see the remnant shrink and then grow repeatedly. In Romans 11 we are told that believers are now part of Israel, God's people. There will always be believers, and I think there will always be a remnant of Jewish people as well.
- o A remnant is what is left over from something larger. You can have a remnant of fabric after you are done with a sewing project, some scraps that weren't used. Let's look at Romans 11 to see what we can learn about God's remnant. It's something we should always want to be part of.
  - Here's Romans 11:3-5. This is Paul writing. He starts by quoting Elijah from 1 Kings 19.
    - "Lord, they have killed Your prophets, they have torn down Your altars, and I alone am left, and they are seeking my life." But what is the divine response to him? "I have kept for Myself seven thousand men who have not bowed the knee to Baal." In the same way then, there has also come to be at the present time a remnant according to God's gracious choice.
  - What was happening here? What does Elijah say in his prayer?
    - Elijah thinks he's all alone, that he is the only one left who worships God and not idols.
    - What does God assure him?
      - There's a remnant. There are 7,000 men who haven't worshiped idols.
      - This, we are told, is by God's grace. We are all saved by God's grace. Justice says we should all die. By grace He made a way for us to receive forgiveness and the power to overcome sin.
- o So, although Abraham must teach his children to live righteously and justly, it's by God's grace that Abraham can, and it's by grace that Abraham even knew God, and

it's by grace that His promises will be fulfilled because His grace will ensure there will always be a remnant following Him.

- o Recall: What is the name for the people who remain faithful to God when everyone else falls away? the remnant
- o Explore more: What other stories about God's remnant can you find in the Bible? What does Revelations have to say about the remnant?

VI. Discussion

- o Are you part of the remnant today? How has God's grace made a way for you to be part of the remnant?
- o There are ways His grace has worked for all of us, but there are special ways He shows grace in each individual life. What are your family's stories of how God's grace brought you to Him and into the remnant, those left on earth who still live by faith in God and His Son Jesus Christ?

VII. Writing

- o Use the discussion question as a writing prompt.
- o Get a high five and/or hug if you use any of the vocabulary or spelling words.

Day 60 (check Materials List)

I. Read Genesis 19:1-2.

II. Memory Verse
- o Test yourselves on 2 Corinthians 1:20.
  - For as many as are the promises of God, in Him they are yes; therefore also through Him is our Amen to the glory of God through us.
- o Review Genesis 26:4.
  - I will multiply your descendants as the stars of the heaven, and will give your descendants all these lands; and by your descendants all the nations of the earth shall be blessed.

III. Language
- o Spelling/Handwriting
  - verse 9
  - Test yourselves on words from Days 56-59.
  - throughout, foreigner, twelve, ninety-nine
  - appeared, opposite, bowed, measure
  - denied, advanced, appointed, difficult
  - righteousness, command, judge, forty-five
- o Vocabulary/Grammar
  - Test yourselves on the words from Days 56-59.
    - intercept – blocking something from getting to its intended destination
    - tender – easy to cut or chew
    - appointed - designated, pre-arranged, scheduled
    - venture – to undertake something risky or dangerous
- o Hebrew
  - Here is Genesis 1:5. God called the light day, and the darkness He called night. And there was evening and there was morning, one day.
  - Literally you are saying: and called God to the light day and to the darkness called night and was evening and morning day one.
  - va yikRA eloHEEM la or yom ve la KHOshekh kaRA LII-la va yeHEE Erev va yeHEE VOker yom eKHAD

IV. Social Studies
- o Sodom was in ancient Mesopotamia. Another city there that we've read about but not studied is Babel. That's where they built the tower of Babel. We know it as the city of Babylon. It was mentioned in one of the fulfilled prophecies that we read about on Day 58.
- o Nimrod was the oldest son of Ham. Who was he a son of?
  - Noah
  - He becomes it seems, like an emperor. He conquers lands and builds cities, one of which is Babylon.

o The period we've been looking at in history right now is from about 2200 BC. (Abraham is around 2000 BC. Abraham comes along about 300 years after Noah. Noah was his great, great, great, great grandfather if I counted correctly.) There are many ideas of exact(ish) dates for things; however, they all disagree with each other! (I've done my best to calculate estimates based on research using the genealogies of the Bible as the basis.)

o Babylon has many references in Scripture, and they are all bad. It's not only the location of the tower of Babel, but it's where Daniel was thrown into the lion's den and where Shadrach, Meshach, and Abednego were thrown into the fiery furnace.

- Babylon was controlled by many different empires. One of its kings was Hammurabi who wrote the law code we looked at on Day 56. Do you remember any of Hammurabi's Code?

- While he was in charge, Babylon became the largest and most important city in Mesopotamia. Where's Mesopotamia? (Note: If they need a hint, it's between two rivers.)

 ▪ It's the area between the Tigris and the Euphrates.

- Hammurabi was a skilled leader and was able to unite all of Mesopotamia under Babylon's rule and named it Babylonia.

- You know where Mesopotamia is. Babylon is about 50 miles (80km) south of Baghdad, Iraq. You can find Baghdad on the Day 14 Middle East maps. It is along the Euphrates river.

o Babylon is known for being the location of one of the seven wonders of the ancient world, the hanging gardens. Here's one artist's image of it. We don't know exactly what it looked like.

o The gardens were said to have been built by King Nebuchadnezzar, the one who has the dream that Daniel interprets (Daniel 2). This puts the garden's creation at around 600 BC. Is that before or after Abraham's time?

- It's long after. We're just talking about Babylon today, not Abraham's time.

- o The hanging gardens weren't hanging down from somewhere. They were up high, though, instead of being in the ground. I think they were probably much higher than is shown in this picture.
    - The gardens are described as terrace after terrace going upward like steps. Pillars were hollow and filled with earth so that "trees of the largest size" could be planted (according to one ancient description, unmuseum.org/hangg.htm).
- o It was new and modern. No one had ever seen anything like it, a garden in the sky! I switched around social studies and science today so that you could learn about the garden and then learn about how they made it work.
- o Recall: What ancient city became the largest in Mesopotamia? In what modern country are Babylon's ruins found? What King is attributed with building the gardens?
    - Babylon
    - Iraq
    - King Nebuchadnezzar
- o Explore more: Learn about ancient Babylon or Nebuchadnezzar. There is disagreement over whether the gardens were in Babylon or in Nineveh.

V. Science
- o Why was the "hanging" garden such a marvel?
    - They had figured out new things. There was engineering at work.
- o What does a garden need?
    - It would need soil and water and sun.
- o There was plenty of sun. It was the desert. What would provide the water? (Look at a map if you aren't sure.)
    - the Euphrates River
- o But somehow the water would have to get from the river to the top terrace. Soil would also have to be transported to the different levels, but only once. Water would have to be delivered regularly, especially in a desert climate.
- o Here are pictures of a few of what we know as the simple machines, tools that make work easier. Which do you think might be useful in some way to deliver water to the gardens? How could they be used?
- o The first is a pulley. We'll look at the first two at other times as well. We're just imagining today how they might have watered their gardens.
    - The pulley is used for lifting. The top is fixed in place up high. Something is lifted onto the hook. The more rope that you use (the thin lines in the picture), the easier it is to lift the object. Can you think of a way this might be used in transporting water to the highest levels of the garden? (Note: We don't know how they watered the garden. There is no right or wrong answer. Let them imagine.)

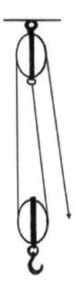

Cropped Image original by Welkinridge

o Another simple machine is the wheel and the axle. In this well picture, the wheel is the circle with spokes. The axle is the log looking thing that has the rope wrapped around it.
o How does this wheel and axle work to lift water?
  • You turn the wheel to raise and lower the bucket.
o How could this be used to get water way up high from a river?
  • We don't know for sure how they did it. Since they couldn't bring water straight up from the river, maybe an irrigation ditch brought water to outside the garden walls. Something like this could then lift water to each level. It would still need to be manned to carry and dump the water.

- One other simple machine that carries water is the screw. Do you have any screws in your home?
  - If you do, get it and run your finger along the groove. What do you notice?
    - It goes up and up and up.
  - That's how a screw can carry water. As it turns, the water is pushed up along the groove. Let's look at some pictures.
- The screw can be used in a number of ways. It can press down and lift up, but it's hard from this picture to figure out how it can be used to carry water.

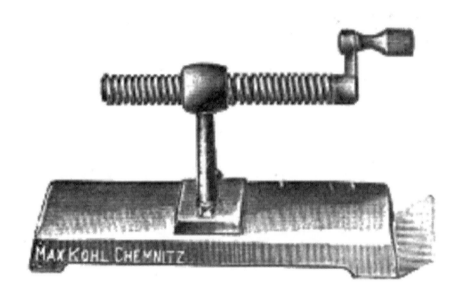

- I'm going to show you one more picture; this is of a screw. In order to carry water somewhere the screw needs a tube or trough to hold the water and the screw forces it upwards.

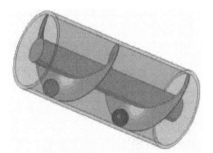

  - If you have a piece of hose or tube that you could try it with, you can wrap it around a stick and tape it into place. Stick one end in a bucket of water. Hold your stick at an angle and turn your screw.
- Recall: What simple machines might have been useful in carrying water to the gardens?
  - many of them in some way: pulley, wheel and axle, screw

      o   Explore more: What other uses are there for screws? Can you build a model? A working model?

VI. Discussion
      o   If you were hired to be the architect and engineer to design the newest wonder of the world, what would you make?

VII. Writing
      o   Choose something you wrote from Days 57-59 to edit.
      o   Read it out loud to check for things that don't sound right or that don't make sense.
      o   Use the editing checklist to check over your work. Mark corrections.
      o   Give it to someone older to do the same.
      o   Create a final draft (type or rewrite it).

Day 61

I. Read Genesis 19:3-4.

II. Memory Verse
- Review 1 John 1:9.
- If we confess our sins, He is faithful and just to forgive us our sins and to cleanse us from all unrighteousness. (KJV)

III. Language
- Spelling
  - Complete the Spelling Review 6 using your words from Day 40.
- Hebrew
  - Review: va YOmer
  - Translated: and said
  - YOmar is the imperfect form, used for incomplete actions
  - This could translate to: say, says, will say.
  - With the VA in front, we translate it in the past tense and change the vowel sound from YOmar to YOmer.
  - That little VA does a lot!
  - Say Genesis 1:5.
    - va yikRA eloHEEM la or yom ve la KHOshekh kaRA LII-la va yeHEE Erev va yeHEE VOker yom ekHAD

IV. Science
- Complete Science Review 6 which you'll find at the end of this lesson.

V. Writing
- Write for two minutes. Start writing a story; it can be true or pretend. Do you remember what we call a not-true story?
  - fiction
- Time yourselves. Just write and write and don't stop. I'll give you a word to start with to get your brain activated. Use that word in your first sentence to get you going.
- Today's word is SEVERE. (Note: I'm using vocabulary words for these. Make sure everyone knows what the word means.)
- You can share with each other what you wrote. Read it out loud for speech practice.

Science Review 6

Note: Review these terms and concepts. Then go back through and ask for them to be defined or explained. If they get the answer right, then they get to try to make a basket.

- You could use a trashcan, bucket, basket, or aim at a target if you don't have a "net." Use a ball, a crumpled up paper, whatever. Make it easy and simple.
- If you want to compete, they could get one point for getting it right and then throw for a bonus point. Handicap it for the varying ages (ie. make it closer for the younger ones).
- If someone gets it wrong, the question can go to the next person.

Lesson 37

muscular system	the body system that makes the other systems work
involuntary muscles	muscles that work without us controlling them
reflexes	reactionary movements that our bodies do by instinct
contract	how a muscle moves, stacking up muscle fiber bundles
bicep	the big muscle that contracts when you bend your arm up at the elbow

Lesson 36

cells	the body's building blocks
some types of cells	egg cells, muscle cells, brain cells
glucose	sugar used by our bodies that it gets from our food
ATP	where our bodies store energy

Lesson 39

neuron	a type of cell in the brain

Lesson 53

microscopic	needs a microscope in order to be seen

Lesson 51

calorie	a measurement of the energy found in food
Why are calories good?	They give your body the energy it needs.
Who needs the most?	teenage boys

Lesson 56

penicillin	the first antibiotic
antibiotic	bacteria killer
How does it work?	It prevents cell walls from forming.
antiseptic	slows the growth of microorganisms

Lesson 58

old age	What can you remember about some things that happen as you get older? brain and body shrinks, ears grow, eyes have trouble focusing up close, harder to hear higher pitched sounds/voices

Day 62

I. Read Genesis 19:5-7.

II. Memory Verse
- o Review Romans 6:23.
- o For the wages of sin is death, but the free gift of God is eternal life in Christ Jesus our Lord.

III. Language
- o Spelling
  - Complete Spelling Review 7 with words from Day 55.
- o Hebrew
  - Do you remember what OR means?
    - light
  - Review: yeHEE
  - Translated: let there be / there was
  - yeHEE is the imperfect form, an incomplete action
  - yeHEE could translate to: be, is, will be
  - "yeHEE or va yeHEE or" could literally translate to, "Light be and light is."
  - With the VA in front, we translate it in the past tense.
  - "And there was" is said "va yeHEE."
  - Say Genesis 1:4-5.
    - va yar eloHEEM et ha or ki tov va yavDEL eloHEEM ben ha or u ven ha KHOshekh
    - va yikRA eloHEEM la or yom ve la KHOshekh kaRA LIl-la va yeHEE Erev va yeHEE VOker yom ekHAD

IV. Science
- o Complete Science Review 7 which you'll find at the end of today's lesson.

V. Writing
- o Write for four minutes. Start writing a story; it can be true or pretend.
- o Time yourselves. Just write and write and don't stop. I'll give you a word to start with to get your brain activated. Use that word in your first sentence to get you going.
- o Today's word is STRIVE. (Note: I'm using vocabulary words for these. Make sure everyone knows what the word means.)

Science Review 7

Review the terms and concepts and then play Pictionary. Give each child in turn a term to draw and have the others guess based on their review. You can tell them before the review that they will be playing and that these terms will be what they need to guess to help them pay attention and remember the terms.

Lesson 40
floods	when there's water over land where there isn't normally
tsunami	a huge tidal wave caused by an earthquake
flash flood	a flood that occurs in under six hours

Lesson 41
evaporation	when a liquid becomes a gas
How?	liquid is heated; molecules can collide to create heat energy
saturated	full
humidity	how much water is in the air
transpiration	evaporation of the water from within plants (hint: related to evaporation)

Lesson 42
groundwater	water in the ground
water table	where water can't go any farther because of saturation
capillary action	when water travels against gravity, climbing up whatever it is clinging to

Lesson 48

What are some of the physical causes of famine?

natural disasters: floods, drought, severe weather; bugs that eat/destroy crops; plant diseases

Bonus: boll weevil was the name of the bug that destroyed cotton crops

Lesson 49
sustainable	something that can go on forever
name a sustainable practice	recycling
name an unsustainable practice	dumping trash into rivers or landfills
renewable energy	making our power (such as electricity or fuel) from a source that renews itself (ie. won't run out)
example of renewable energy	wind power, solar panels, etc.

Lesson 52
channel	the path of the river
headwaters	where a river begins
tributaries	a river that feeds into another river
delta	where the river ends and the water fans out making a fertile area

Lesson 54
springs	where groundwater comes out of the ground (or where the water table meets ground level)
artesian wells	where water shoots up out of the ground
	Bonus: caused by what force? gravity

Day 63 (check Materials List)

I. Read Genesis 19:8.

II. Memory Verse
- o Review Genesis 1:4.
- o God saw that the light was good; and God separated the light from the darkness.

III. Language
- o Spelling
    - • Complete Spelling Review 8 with words from Day 50.
    - • They will cut out the 42 word parts. Hide them for each other. Work alone, in pairs, or all together. Find the word parts and match them into words.
    - • There are 15 words: journeyed, scattered, thoroughly, building, possessions, pitched, acquired, donkeys, woman, Egypt, escorted, belonged, number, formerly, exceedingly (doesn't use Lot)
- o Hebrew
    - • Review Genesis 1:3 Then God said, "Let there be light"; and there was light.
    - • va YOmer eloHEEM yeHEE or va yeHEE or
        - ▪ What do those words say in English?
    - • Say Genesis 1:3-5.
        - ▪ va YOmer eloHEEM yeHEE or va yeHEE or
        - ▪ va yar eloHEEM et ha or ki tov va yavDEL eloHEEM ben ha or u ven ha KHOshekh
        - ▪ va yikRA eloHEEM la or yom ve la KHOshekh kaRA LII-la va yeHEE Erev va yeHEE VOker yom ekHAD

IV. Science
- o Complete Science Review 8 which you'll find at the end of today's lesson.

V. Writing
- o Write for six minutes. Start writing a story; it can be true or pretend.
- o Time yourselves. Just write and write and don't stop. I'll give you a word to start with to get your brain activated. Use that word in your first sentence to get you going.
- o Today's word is RECEDE. (Note: Make sure everyone knows what the word means.)

Science Review 8

You can just do questions and answers and fill in any information they are missing. Or you could toss a ball to the person whose turn it is to answer. They could pass it on to someone else, who will have to answer next.

Lesson 43
states of matter	solid, liquid, gas
what causes change in state	change in temperature
difference in molecules	molecules move least in a solid and move most in a gas
oxidation	chemical process where a molecule gains an oxygen atom

Lesson 44
shape of rainbow	circle
needed for a rainbow	light and water (or other object that will disperse the light)
dispersion	when light separates into colors
review: refraction	when light bends

Lesson 45
fermentation	the chemical process that breaks down a substance
yeast breaks down...	sugar (or glucose)
...into	alcohol and carbon dioxide
Bonus: scientific symbol	CO_2 for carbon dioxide

Lesson 46
steel, good building material	strong, durable (lasts), malleable (can mold it)
alloy	a metal made by mixing other elements
steel is an alloy of...	iron and carbon (can be mixed with other metals for different uses)

Lesson 47
basic shelter necessities	safe from elements (dry, warm, cool)
insulation	a barrier that holds in heat

Lesson 50
tar pit	asphalt lake
quicksand	where sand is saturated with water and then even more water is added so that the sand starts floating
paleontologist	studies fossils

Lesson 57
curds	protein solids separated out from milk
colloid	when a mixture doesn't separate
suspension	when a mixture separates over time
examples of each	milk is a colloid; OJ with pulp is a suspension

Lesson 59
    scientific notation   simplifies really big and really small numbers
    10,000 1×10^4 (count the zeros)
    0.0001 1×10^{-4} (count the zeros or the decimal places)

Lesson 60
    simple machines   make work easier
    help lift water   wheel and axle, screw, pulley

Lesson 38
    density   how much stuff is in a space
    density/floating   if more dense than water, sinks

Day 64

I.   Read Genesis 19:9-11.

II. Memory Verse
- Review Genesis 26:4.
- I will multiply your descendants as the stars of the heaven, and will give your descendants all these lands; and by your descendants all the nations of the earth shall be blessed.

III. Language
- Spelling
  - Play Sink the Spelling Ships. Use Spelling Review 9 in your workbook. This uses words from Day 45.
- Hebrew
  - Hebrew: tov
    - Translated: good
  - Hebrew: ki
    - Translated: that (can also be translated because, when, if)
  - Hebrew: va yar
    - Translated: and saw
    - It's "and" plus the imperfect form of the verb to see.
  - Practice the first part of Genesis 1:4 "God saw that the light was good."
  - va yar eloHEEM et ha or ki tov
    - What does that say in English?
  - Say Genesis 1:2-5.
    - ve ha Arets haaTAH TOhu va VOhu ve KHOshekh al pnaa teHOM ve RUakh eloHEEM meraKHEfet al pnaa ha MAyim
    - va YOmer eloHEEM yeHEE or va yeHEE or
    - va yar eloHEEM et ha or ki tov va yavDEL eloHEEM ben ha or u ven ha KHOshekh
    - va yikRA eloHEEM la or yom ve la KHOshekh kaRA LII-la va yeHEE Erev va yeHEE VOker yom ekHA

IV. Science
- Complete the multiple choice quiz. Do Science Review 9 in your workbook.

V.   Writing
- Write for eight minutes. Start writing a story; it can be true or pretend.
- Time yourselves. Just write and write and don't stop. I'll give you a word to start with to get your brain activated. Use that word in your first sentence to get you going.
- Today's word is CORRUPT. (Note: Make sure everyone knows what the word means.)

Day 65 (check Materials List)

I. Read Genesis 19:12-13.

II. Memory Verse
   o Review 2 Corinthians 1:20.
   o For as many as are the promises of God, in Him they are yes; therefore also through Him is our Amen to the glory of God through us.

III. Language
   o Spelling
      • Play spelling aerobics with Spelling Review 10.
      • You only need one set, but you could have everyone cut out their word strips and then alphabetize them. OR
      • After each person spells their word correctly that person can take the word and lay it on the floor in alphabetical order.
   o Hebrew
      • Review the first part of Genesis 1:4 together.
      • va yar eloHEEM et ha or ki tov
         ▪ What does that say in English?
      • Say Genesis 1:1-5.
         ▪ be reSHEET baRA eloHEEM et ha shaMAyim ve et ha Arets
         ▪ ve ha Arets haaTAH TOhu va VOhu ve KHOshekh al pnaa teHOM ve RUakh eloHEEM meraKHEfet al pnaa ha MAyim
         ▪ va YOmer eloHEEM yeHEE or va yeHEE or
         ▪ va yar eloHEEM et ha or ki tov va yavDEL eloHEEM ben ha or u ven ha KHOshekh
         ▪ va yikRA eloHEEM la or yom ve la KHOshekh kaRA LII-la va yeHEE Erev va yeHEE VOker yom ekHAD

IV. Science
   o Complete the Science Review 10 crossword puzzle in your workbook.

V. Writing
   o Write for ten minutes. Start writing a story; it can be true or pretend.
   o Time yourselves. Just write and write and don't stop. I'll give you a word to start with to get your brain activated. Use that word in your first sentence to get you going.
   o Today's word is SUSTAIN. (Note: Make sure everyone knows what the word means.)
   o As always, you can share with each other what you wrote.

Day 66

I. Read Genesis 19:14.

II. Memory Verse
- o Say 1 John 1:9 from memory.
  - • If we confess our sins, He is faithful and just to forgive us our sins and to cleanse us from all unrighteousness. (KJV)
- o Review Genesis 1:1.
  - • In the beginning God created the heavens and the earth.

III. Language
- o Vocabulary
  - • Play charades. In your workbook find Vocabulary Review 3. Take turns acting out and guessing. Guessers should have the word list in front of them.
- o Hebrew
  - • Review
    - ▪ ben/ven
      - ▪ from
    - ▪ va yavDEL
      - ▪ and separated (again, this is the imperfect form translated in the past)
  - • Say Genesis 1:1-5.
    - ▪ be reSHEET baRA eloHEEM et ha shaMAyim ve et ha Arets
    - ▪ ve ha Arets haaTAH TOhu va VOhu ve KHOshekh al pnaa teHOM ve RUakh eloHEEM meraKHEfet al pnaa ha MAyim
    - ▪ va YOmer eloHEEM yeHEE or va yeHEE or
    - ▪ va yar eloHEEM et ha or ki tov va yavDEL eloHEEM ben ha or u ven ha KHOshekh
    - ▪ va yikRA eloHEEM la or yom ve la KHOshekh kaRA LII-la va yeHEE Erev va yeHEE VOker yom ekHAD

IV. Social Studies
- o Complete Social Studies Review 6 which you'll find at the end of today's lesson.

V. Writing
- o Write for eleven minutes. Start writing a story; it can be true or pretend. Do you remember the name for a non-true story?
  - • fiction
- o Time yourselves. Just write and write and don't stop. I'll give you a word to start with to get your brain activated. Use that word in your first sentence to get you going.
- o Today's word is AFFLICTION. (Note: I'm using vocabulary words for these. Make sure everyone knows what the word means.)

Social Studies Review 6

Discuss to review and then pass the ball to whomever is going to answer the next question. Then that person tosses the ball on to someone else who will be the next person to answer. (Or you can do the basketball game like in Science Review 3.)

What were the original sin cities? (49)
> Sodom and Gomorrah

What river did the Lord part multiple times for Israel? (49)
> the Jordan River

What's the name of a flat area of land up high? (50)
> plateau

What's the name of a range of mountains and plateaus? (50)
> highlands

How were boats used in Mesopotamia? (38)
> as highway transportation, moved people and goods

Is there more fresh water or salt water in the world? (42)
> salt water

Where is most of the earth's fresh water? (42)
> It's frozen in the poles.

What city did Abraham leave to begin his sojournings? (47)
> Ur

Why is Mt. Ararat famous? In what modern country is it located? (41)
> It's where Noah's ark landed. Turkey

What's a generation? (37)
> all people of about the same age

What are ancestors? (45)
> those in your family who came before

What are some of the Romance languages? (46)
> French, Spanish (there are others)

What are some fulfilled prophecies? (58)
> Judas being paid 30 pieces of silver to betray Jesus, Potter's field
> (others: Jesus' death, his clothes taken by lot, his side pierced, no bones broken)

What are some of the covenants God has made with His people? (44)
> promise to never destroy the earth by a flood again, give the land of Canaan to Abraham's descendants, obedience brings blessings and sin brings a curse

What are some of the symbols of Jesus in what we've read of Genesis? (43, 51)
> Jesus is our ark of salvation, communion (Jesus' body and blood), Melchizedek was a king and priest not by lineage, perfect sacrifice

What biblical "law" does away with slavery? (53)
> love your neighbor as yourself

What's Hammurabi known for doing? (56, 60)
> writing Hammurabi's Code, a code of law for Babylonia, which he established by uniting Mesopotamia under his rule

What is the ideal idea behind communism? (48)
> that everyone has everything in common
> Here's something to read. It's another example of communism causing famine. This is described as socialism, but it's the same concept, what you work for goes to everyone, supposedly equally distributed as there is need.

Excerpt is from "The Great Thanksgiving Hoax" by Richard Maybury
[This is talking about how there was more at work at creating a bountiful Thanksgiving.
It's telling the story of the Pilgrims who came to Massachusetts on the Mayflower.]

After the poor harvest of 1622, writes Bradford, "They began to think how they might raise as much corn as they could, and obtain a better crop." They began to question their form of economic organization.

This had required that "all profits & benefits that are got by trade, working, fishing, or any other means" were to be placed in the common stock of the colony, and that, "all such persons as are of this colony, are to have their meat, drink, apparel, and all provisions out of the common stock." A person was to put into the common stock all he could, and take out only what he needed.

This "from each according to his ability, to each according to his need" was an early form of socialism, and it is why the Pilgrims were starving. Bradford writes that "young men that are most able and fit for labor and service" complained about being forced to "spend their time and strength to work for other men's wives and children." Also, "the strong, or man of parts, had no more in division of victuals and clothes, than he that was weak." So the young and strong refused to work and the total amount of food produced was never adequate.

To rectify this situation, in 1623 Bradford abolished socialism. He gave each household a parcel of land and told them they could keep what they produced, or trade it away as they saw fit. In other words, he replaced socialism with a free market, and that was the end of famines.

Day 67

I. Read Genesis 19:15-16.

II. Memory Verse
- o Say from memory Romans 6:23.
- o For the wages of sin is death, but the free gift of God is eternal life in Christ Jesus our Lord.
- o Review Psalm 150:6.
- o Let everything that has breath praise the Lord. Praise the Lord!

III. Language
- o Grammar
  - Complete Grammar Review 4 in your workbook.
- o Hebrew
  - Review
    - ben ha or u ven ha KHOshekh – What does this say?
    - from the light and from the darkness
    - The prepositions are repeated in front of each object.
  - Review Genesis 1:1-5.
    - be reSHEET baRA eloHEEM et ha shaMAyim ve et ha Arets
    - ve ha Arets haaTAH TOhu va VOhu ve KHOshekh al pnaa teHOM ve RUakh eloHEEM meraKHEfet al pnaa ha MAyim
    - va YOmer eloHEEM yeHEE or va yeHEE or
    - va yar eloHEEM et ha or ki tov va yavDEL eloHEEM ben ha or u ven ha KHOshekh
    - va yikRA eloHEEM la or yom ve la KHOshekh kaRA LII-la va yeHEE Erev va yeHEE VOker yom ekHAD

IV. Social Studies
- o Complete Social Studies Review 7 in your workbook.

V. Writing
- o Write for twelve minutes. Start writing a story; it can be true or pretend.
- o Time yourselves. Just write and write and don't stop. I'll give you a word to start with to get your brain activated. Use that word in your first sentence to get you going.
- o Today's word is VENTURE. (Note: I'm using vocabulary words for these. Make sure everyone knows what the word means.)

Day 68 (check Materials List)

I. Read Genesis 19:17-18.

II. Memory Verse
- o Say from memory Genesis 1:4.
- o God saw that the light was good; and God separated the light from the darkness.

III. Language
- o Vocabulary
  - • Complete Vocabulary Review 4 with words from Day 50.
  - • Students will cut out the word definitions on the second page. You'll also need one set of the words to define for this activity. Everyone else can cut out the words now and save them or cut them out on Day 69.
    - ▪ The definition cards will get mixed up. If they want to maintain ownership over the ones they personally cut out, they can put a color dot in each box or just draw a line down the boxes in that color.
    - ▪ If you want to get fancy, you can cut out the page, apply wide, clear tape over the words front and back and then cut them out. (That's cheap lamination.)
    - ▪ You'll use the word cards on Day 69 and the whole set on Day 70.
  - • Place the word cards around the room.
  - • The kids will place their definition cards next to the word it belongs to.
- o Hebrew
  - • Review
    - ▪ Erev
      - ▪ evening
    - ▪ VOker
      - ▪ morning
    - ▪ eKHAD
      - ▪ one
    - ▪ yom eKHAD
      - ▪ one day   (literally this says: day one)
  - • Review the last part of Genesis 1:5.
  - • va yeHEE Erev va yeHEE VOker yom ekHAD – What does this say?
  - • And there was evening and there was morning, one day.
  - • Say Genesis 1:1-5.
    - ▪ be reSHEET baRA eloHEEM et ha shaMAyim ve et ha Arets
    - ▪ ve ha Arets haaTAH TOhu va VOhu ve KHOshekh al pnaa teHOM ve RUakh eloHEEM meraKHEfet al pnaa ha MAyim
    - ▪ va YOmer eloHEEM yeHEE or va yeHEE or
    - ▪ va yar eloHEEM et ha or ki tov va yavDEL eloHEEM ben ha or u ven ha KHOshekh
    - ▪ va yikRA eloHEEM la or yom ve la KHOshekh kaRA LII-la va yeHEE Erev va yeHEE VOker yom ekHAD

IV. Social Studies
- o Complete Social Studies Review 8 in your workbook.
- o After you've checked the answers together, assign one side of the room to the Euphrates River and the other side to the Mediterranean Sea (or assign them to two couches). List the places they found on the map and have them go to the nearest body of water, either the Euphrates or the Mediterranean.
  - • Read them in this order: Egypt, Tigris River, Nile River, Mount Ararat, Negev, Red Sea, Ur, Israel
    - ▪ Euphrates: Ararat, Ur, Tigris
    - ▪ Mediterranean: Egypt, Red Sea, Negev, Israel, Nile

V. Writing
- o Write for thirteen minutes. Start writing a story; it can be true or pretend.
- o Time yourselves. Just write and write and don't stop. I'll give you a word to start with to get your brain activated. Use that word in your first sentence to get you going.
- o Today's word is APPOINTED. (Note: Make sure everyone knows what the word means.)
- o (Note: You might want to save this in your portfolio.)

Day 69

I. Read Genesis 19:19-20.

II. Memory Verse
  o Say from memory Genesis 26:4.
    • I will multiply your descendants as the stars of the heaven, and will give your descendants all these lands; and by your descendants all the nations of the earth shall be blessed.
  o Review 1 Corinthians 10:13.
    • No temptation has overtaken you but such as is common to man; and God is faithful, who will not allow you to be tempted beyond what you are able, but with the temptation will provide the way of escape also, so that you will be able to endure it.

III. Language
  o Grammar
    • Complete Grammar Review 5 by arranging your vocabulary word cards (the ones highlighted with a gray box) into three piles: nouns, adjectives and verbs.
    • Some of the words could go into more than one pile. It's okay whichever it is placed in. The possible arrangements are in the answer key.
  o Hebrew
    • Review
      ▪ LII-la (hyphen only for clarity between the Is and the L)
        ▪ night
      ▪ kaRA, va yikRA (the first is the perfect, completed form)
        ▪ called
      ▪ le, la
        ▪ to, to the
    • Review
      ▪ va yikRA eloHEEM la or yom ve la KHOshekh kaRA LII-la
      ▪ God called the light day, and the darkness He called night.
    • Say Genesis 1:1-5
      ▪ be reSHEET baRA eloHEEM et ha shaMAyim ve et ha Arets
      ▪ ve ha Arets haaTAH TOhu va VOhu ve KHOshekh al pnaa teHOM ve RUakh eloHEEM meraKHEfet al pnaa ha MAyim
      ▪ va YOmer eloHEEM yeHEE or va yeHEE or
      ▪ va yar eloHEEM et ha or ki tov va yavDEL eloHEEM ben ha or u ven ha KHOshekh
      ▪ va yikRA eloHEEM la or yom ve la KHOshekh kaRA LII-la va yeHEE Erev va yeHEE VOker yom ekHAD

IV. Social Studies
  o Complete Social Studies Review 9 in your workbook.

V. Writing

- o Write for fourteen minutes. Start writing a story; it can be true or pretend.
- o Time yourselves. Just write and write and don't stop. I'll give you a word to start with to get your brain activated. Use that word in your first sentence to get you going.
- o Today's word is INTENT. (Note: Make sure everyone knows what the word means.)

Day 70

I. Read Genesis 19:21-22.

II. Memory Verse
- Say from memory 2 Corinthians 1:20.
- For as many as are the promises of God, in Him they are yes; therefore also through Him is our Amen to the glory of God through us.
- Review Romans 3:23. For all have sinned and fall short of the glory of God.

III. Language
- Vocabulary
  - Play vocabulary concentration/memory with the vocabulary cards from Vocabulary Review 4 & 5.
  - Lay your cards with the words and definitions face down on the floor or table in front of you. Find all of the matches by turning over two cards at a time. If they match, remove them. If they don't match, turn them back over.
  - You can play alone or take turns with someone else choosing two cards to look at to see if they match. Or you could even play with two-person teams.
- Hebrew
  - On Day 71 we will start writing Hebrew. Today, one more time, practice Genesis 1:1-5.
  - In the beginning God created the heavens and the earth. [2] The earth was formless and void, and darkness was over the surface of the deep, and the Spirit of God was moving over the surface of the waters. [3] Then God said, "Let there be light"; and there was light. [4] God saw that the light was good; and God separated the light from the darkness. [5] God called the light day, and the darkness He called night. And there was evening and there was morning, one day.
    1. be reSHEET baRA eloHEEM et ha shaMAyim ve et ha Arets
    2. ve ha Arets haaTAH TOhu va VOhu ve KHOshekh al pnaa teHOM ve RUakh eloHEEM meraKHEfet al pnaa ha MAyim
    3. va YOmer eloHEEM yeHEE or va yeHEE or
    4. va yar eloHEEM et ha or ki tov va yavDEL eloHEEM ben ha or u ven ha KHOshekh
    5. va yikRA eloHEEM la or yom ve la KHOshekh kaRA LII-la va yeHEE Erev va yeHEE VOker yom ekHAD

IV. Social Studies
- Complete Social Studies Review 10 in your workbook.

V. Writing
- Write for fifteen minutes. Start writing a story; it can be true or pretend.
- Time yourselves. Just write and write and don't stop. I'll give you a word to start with to get your brain activated. Use that word in your first sentence to get you going.
- Today's word is OBTAIN. (Note: Make sure everyone knows what the word means.)

Day 71

I. Read Genesis 19:23-25.

II. Memory
- o Joshua 24:15
- o "[If it is disagreeable in your sight to serve the LORD,] choose for yourselves today whom you will serve: [whether the gods which your fathers served which were beyond the River, or the gods of the Amorites in whose land you are living;] but as for me and my house, we will serve the LORD."
- o I put brackets [] in the verse in case you want to leave that out. Everyone worships a god. When they say they don't believe in any god, they make themselves god, relying on themselves to make decisions, to provide for themselves and to take care of themselves. Everyone has to choose whom it is that they will serve.

III. Language
- o Spelling/Handwriting
  - • verse 10
  - • words to know: inhabitants, surrounded, rained, urged (surrounded and urged are from review day readings)
  - • spelling tips:
    - ▪ Inhabitants is spelled in, habit, ants.
    - ▪ Surrounded has the word round inside of it.
    - ▪ Rained is using rain as verb but it is spelled like the noun.
    - ▪ Urged starts with the city name of where Abraham began his journeying from.
- o Vocabulary/Grammar
  - • urge (verse 19:3 from a review reading)
  - • to strongly persuade someone to do something (verb)
    - ▪ He urged what?
      - • "them"
      - • What is them?
        - ▪ the direct object
      - • Them is called an object pronoun. They are pronouns that are used as objects, such as direct objects and as objects of prepositions.
      - • What are some of the other object pronouns? Let's use the word "for" to help us figure it out.
        - ▪ The gift is for…
          - • me, you, him, her, us, them
- o Hebrew
  - • Genesis 1:1 In the beginning God created the heavens and the earth.
  - • bereSHEET baRA eloHEEM et ha shaMAyim ve et ha Arets
  - • We're going to start learning to write Hebrew. We have Hebrew tracing pages generously made available to us from hebrew4christians.com. You can find copywork and coloring pages on their homeschool resources page.

You can find the link to those resources on the Online Support page of our site, genesiscurriculum.com.
- In Hebrew the vowels do not have their own alphabet letters.
    - Most vowel sounds are marked with little dots and lines over or under the letters. Hebrew is written without those markings. You just have to know what the word is from the letters there and from the context.
    - Their letter B with a little mark for a short vowel A sound would read BA.
    - If you wanted it to read, AB, you would need a letter in front of the B to attach the A sound to. We're going to learn that letter today, the one that helps out when you need a vowel in front.
- The first letter of the alphabet is the Aleph. That's its name. It is a silent letter. Sort of. It takes on the vowel sound attached to it. That's how a word can start with a vowel sound.
    - be reSHEET baRA eloHEEM et ha shaMAyim ve et ha Arets
    - eloHEEM, et, Arets
    - Each of those words has an Aleph.

IV. Science
- We read during the review week how a group of men were struck blind as a protection to Lot's family. (Genesis 19:11 They struck the men who were at the doorway of the house with blindness, both small and great, so that they wearied themselves trying to find the doorway.)
- Total blindness is the inability to perceive light.
- How do we see? (hint: Why can't we see when it's dark?)
    - We see light, not objects. What we see is actually the light bouncing off of objects. When there is no light, we don't see anything.
    - Total blindness is when your eyes can't take in any light, so the brain doesn't receive any input as to what it's seeing.
    - Your *pupil* is what takes in light. That black dot in the center of everyone's eye is really a hole that lets in light. Your pupil grows bigger when the light is dim to let in more light. It gets smaller when the light is bright. The muscles that control the dilating, the open and closing of our pupils, are involuntary muscles. Our eyes know what to do all by themselves.
        - You can look into each other's eyes and go in and out of the light to see the pupils change size.
- The technical definition of blindness is eyesight rated at less than 20/400 in your best eye with the best correction possible with glasses.
- What does that mean? Have you had your eyes checked and been told your eyesight was 20/20? Any guess what that means? What if I told you that when you take the eye test, you stand 20 feet away?
    - It means that from 20 feet away you can see the same thing that most others can see at 20 feet away.
    - A legally blind person can see something 20 feet away that most people could see from 400 feet away.

- So a legally blind person might be able to see things that are right in front of them or at least be able to perceive what's around them in a general sense, if not at all clearly.
  o How do glasses help?
    - Do you remember the word refraction?
      - Refraction is the bending of light.
    - Another part of our eyes is called the *retina*. It's responsible for recording the image of what we see. If it's recording a blurry image, then the light is refracting wrong.
    - The part of our eye responsible for focusing those light rays through refraction is the *cornea*. If there is any problem of unevenness with the cornea, then the light bends in the wrong direction.
    - Glasses correct that by refracting light onto the right spot on the retina.
      - Glasses are not magnifying lenses. Glasses that help one person can make things blurry to someone else because it's changing how the light bends and how the light is taken in by your eyes.
  o Do you understand how amazing our eyes are? We don't have to wait for pictures to load. We can look anywhere and instantly light from every direction hits our eyes and is refracted and projected onto the back or our eye which sends the signals to our brain which tell us what we are seeing, all instantaneously.
  o Take a look at the eye diagram on the next page and find the pupil, cornea, and retina. What is each part responsible for?
  o Also look at the iris in the picture, especially in relation to the pupil. What part of your eye do you think it is?

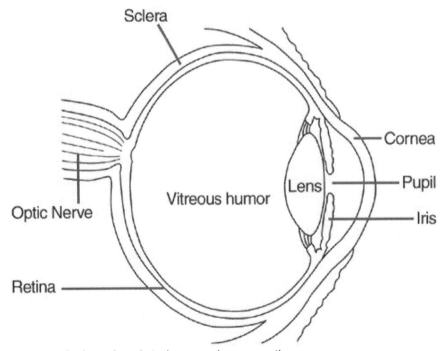

- It's the colored circle around your pupil.

V. Social Studies

- o We saw some more culture at work in the story of Lot that we've been reading. Why was Lot sitting at the gate? He bows to the men entering the city, enables them to wash their feet, and protects them even more than family.
- o Have you heard the story of the US soldier in Afghanistan being taken in by an Afghan family? The Afghan family faced death threats, had their business burned and were forced from their home for taking in an American.
  - • What did they do? They showed hospitality. The Afghan man said, "By rescuing and keeping him safe for five nights in our home we were only doing our cultural obligation." (http://www.thedailybeast.com/articles/2013/11/08/the-afghan-village-that-saved-navy-seal-marcus-luttrell.html)
  - • The father risked the lives of his family in order to protect the one he had taken into his home. Does this sound familiar to the story of Lot?
- o Lot offers water to his guests so that they can wash their feet.
  - • Walking through desert areas in sandals makes for dirty feet. It can also lead to cracked and bleeding feet and washing them can protect them and bring relief.
  - • In the New Testament we read about Jesus washing the disciples' feet (John 13). Jesus also points out when He's not offered water to wash his feet (Luke 7:44).
- o When Lot first greets the angels, he bows to them. Not just any bow, he puts his face to the ground. We would see that as worship, but Lot is not reprimanded for doing so as the angel reprimands John for bowing down to worship before him (Revelation 19:10).
  - • Lot's bow wasn't one of worship. He did not know they were angels. Abraham didn't send a text message letting Lot know they were coming.
- o We call this kind of bow a kowtow. (Note: Kow is said cow, and tow rhymes with cow.)
- o It involves kneeling and putting your forehead to the ground. It was used in ancient Asian cultures. It is not really used today apart from martial arts and formal, traditional ceremonies.
  - • There is still bowing in Asian cultures. Japan especially is known for bowing. People greet each other with bows and how far you bow shows your respect. Anyone older than you is shown more respect, so try bowing to your parents today. They can return the bow with a head nod forward since you are beneath them!
  - • Learning about bowing makes me wonder how the church in Japan treats it. Do they all bow the same to each other and see each other as equals?
- o We don't know why Lot was "sitting in the gate." This wasn't a little fence gate. Cities had huge thick walls. The gates had a gatehouse that was a meeting place and often a courthouse. We don't know if Lot was just looking to see who was coming or if he was on duty watching those coming to learn their business in the city.
- o Recall: What's the name of the bow that involves kneeling and putting your head to the floor? kowtow
- o Explore more: Learn about Afghan culture.

VI. Discussion
- o Did you notice that the men in the Bible story are still trying to get into the house even after they've been struck blind? The Bible talks about people being "given over" to their sin. It becomes an addiction. You have to have it. Is there anything in your life that has a hold on you? It could be television or internet or talking back or getting angry. We shouldn't be addicted to anything. The way free is through Jesus and repentance.
  - What has ever had a hold on you where you felt like you had to do it?
  - What has it caused you to do wrong in order to do it?
  - What are you going to do about it?

VII. Writing
- o Today we learned about object pronouns. We are going to practice these today because they can trip us up, especially in certain circumstances.
- o When we use a name along with a pronoun, it can confuse us as to which pronoun to use. Here are two examples.
  - Matthew and me played soccer all afternoon.
  - The new Frisbee is for my brother and I.
- o Are those sentences correct? There's an easy way to check. Just take out the other person and see if it sounds right.
  - Me played soccer all afternoon.
    - Is that right?
    - No! You would say, "I played soccer all afternoon," so the correct sentence is: Matthew and I played soccer all afternoon.
- o What about the next one? Let's take out the other person and check.
  - The new Frisbee is for I.
    - Is that right?
    - No! You would say, "The new Frisbee is for me." The correct sentence is: The new Frisbee is for my brother and me.
- o Complete Writing Sentences 11.
  - Choose the correct pronoun to fill in the blank. If the pronoun is the object of a verb or preposition, then you need to use an object pronoun. You can also check by taking out the other person to see what sounds right.

Day 72

I. Read Genesis 19:24-26.

II. Memory Verse
- o Joshua 24:15
- o "[If it is disagreeable in your sight to serve the LORD,] choose for yourselves today whom you will serve: [whether the gods which your fathers served which were beyond the River, or the gods of the Amorites in whose land you are living;] but as for me and my house, we will serve the LORD."

III. Language
- o Spelling/Handwriting
  - • verse 21
  - • words to know: escape, punishment, dawn, seize (words are from Genesis 19 from over the review weeks)
  - • spelling tips:
    - ▪ The word <u>escape</u> is spelled like it sounds and ends with a silent E.
    - ▪ The word <u>punishment</u> is spelled like it sounds. Say each syllable.
    - ▪ The word <u>dawn</u> has the word AW in the middle, like what you say when we see a cute puppy.
    - ▪ Remember i before e? Well, not today in the word <u>seize</u>.
- o Vocabulary/Grammar
  - • jest (verse 14)
  - • to speak or act jokingly (action verb)
- o Hebrew
  - • Genesis 1:2 The earth was formless and void, and darkness was over the surface of the deep, and the Spirit of God was moving over the surface of the waters.
  - • ve ha Arets haaTAH TOhu vaVOhu ve KHOshekh al pnaa teHOM ve RUakh eloHEEM meraKHEfet al pnaa ha MAyim
  - • Practice writing the Aleph in your workbook with Hebrew Writing 1.

IV. Science
- o Lot was told to flee to the mountains because nothing can be done to destroy Sodom until Lot reaches a safe place. Lot has little choice in the matter of staying safe! The angels take him by the hand to get him out of the city and won't do anything until they know he is safe.
- o Today let's learn about mountains.
  - • A mountain is an area of land that stretches up to a peak at a high elevation, usually above 2000 feet (600 meters).
- o To talk more about mountains we really have to talk about what's inside the earth.
  - • The earth is in layers. It's not just dirt, rock, and water under our feet. Let's go deeper.
- o The layer of the earth that we see and dig into is known as the earth's *crust*. Guess how deep it goes?
  - • The crust is about 20 miles deep (35 kilometers), though it can vary.

- The crust is all of the earth that you can see: the mountains and the beaches, all of it. Even the land under the water.
- The water table is part of the earth's crust.
- No one has been deeper than the earth's crust.

o The earth's crust is the outer ring of the earth, but it isn't one solid ring. It's made up of pieces, huge areas of rock. We call them *plates*, *tectonic plates* to be exact.

- The word tectonic refers to building or constructing. Tectonic plates are how the earth, the part we can see, is constructed.
- When these rocks, these plates move away from each other, what do you think happens?
  - It leaves a gap needing to be filled.
- When these rocks, these tectonic plates, move toward each other, what do you think happens?
  - They collide and pile up rock.

o Both of those things can create mountains.

- When plates collide, they push rock upward. The rock has to go somewhere. The scientific descriptive word for this is "uplift."
- The other is called *sea-floor spreading*, and it's when plates under the sea pull apart and the hot, liquid rock underneath the crust rushes into the gap.
  - This hot, liquid rock is what lava is. The sea water cools it and it solidifies back into solid rock. When that happens, new crust is formed.
- Creationists believe that both of these things happened during the flood. When we read that God opened the "floodgates of the deep," maybe the sea floor spread and opened the way for hot, liquid rock to rush in heating the water and creating a massive spray of steam up into the air.
  - What happens to steam in the air?
    - It cools and then rains down.
- It's also believed that the massive flooding aided the quick shifting of the plates to create mountains or to push hills higher.
- This is also related to how volcanic mountains form. Lava is the hot, liquid rock that is under the earth's crust. When there is an opening in the crust that lets pressure push this rock up to the surface, it spills out as what we know as lava.
  - When liquid cools what does it become?
    - a solid
    - The lava forms solid rock when it cools and as more and more rock is placed around this opening, it builds itself into a volcanic mountain.
- This leads us to another mountain fact. Mountains grow. They are not standing still. They are growing. Plates continue to shift and lava continues to flow (sometimes).

o Recall: What is the outer part of the earth's surface called? What is the rock called that the earth's crust is constructed with? What is happening when the sea floor spreads? Then what happens?

- the crust
- tectonic plates

- Tectonic plates are shifting apart from each other.
- The gap opens a way for hot, liquid rock to rush into the opening. The rock shoots upwards, cools, and forms new rock which becomes part of the crust.
  - Explore more: Find a map of tectonic plates. Think of how plates shift and compare that map to a map that shows mountains, volcanoes and earthquakes.

V. Social Studies

- Lot asks to flee to a small town that is then called, Zoar, meaning, small. It is close enough that he's just going to walk there, quickly.
  - Lot and his daughters are refugees after they leave their home.
- A *refugee* is someone who is forced to leave their country due to life endangerment. This is the technical definition, though there are many considered refugees in their own countries like Lot was. They have lost their homes and are reliant on others to protect and provide for them until they can do so for themselves.
- Many refugees are known as war refugees, though there is often more at work.
  - In recent years millions of Christians have fled Middle Eastern countries because while the country was at war, they were a particular target of one side or the other. Those against Christianity were taking advantage of the war as an excuse to kill Christians. Many fled for their lives, leaving their homes, businesses, and most of their belongings.
- I know many refugees with sad stories.
  - One woman's whole family was killed before she decided to leave her home. She walked from Ethiopia to Lebanon and then was basically made a slave when she tried to work as a housekeeper. She eventually made it to Turkey where she was put in prison and treated horribly.
  - When one family fled Syria in 2013, they said goodbye to each other before they walked the final stretch to the border, even though they were all together. They knew that they would be shot at as they tried to get across the border and didn't know if they would all survive. (They did.)
  - Another family left Pakistan because they were targets of religious persecution. They had an uncle killed and one of their teenagers was beaten to the point of needing hospitalization.
    - They flew to Turkey, had their passports confiscated, and were trapped. They could not travel without passports so they couldn't leave; their new country, though, won't accept them as citizens. They thought the United Nations would help them, but the UN was slow to recognize them as refugees, so they received no help.
      - After seven years they were recognized as refugees and after nine years were moved to America!
    - I know several people who have been waiting over a decade for the UN to place them in a country accepting refugees.
- The UN's job is hard because there is a constant flow of refugees. In 2014 the reported number was over 50 million refugees. Half of those are reportedly children. Guess what continent produces the most refugees?
  - The majority come from Africa.
  - Many refugees are placed in camps. Refugees are sort of like prisons with more freedom to move around, but only within the camp. They are supposed

to be cared for there and protected. They are given food and shelter, but there is a lack of any family space, education, or job opportunities. They are stuck. Refugees are often trapped where they fled to.

- o One famous story of refugees is that of The Lost Boys of the Sudan. Muslim militias attacked Christian villages, slaughtering everyone. Children were left alone and walked on foot across two countries to get to Kenya. They grew up in camps. Eventually the US took in a few thousand of them and settled them into American life.
  - I know someone who was a volunteer to help a few of them learn how to live in America. She talks of how they were overwhelmed by the choices offered and confused about what kind of work the dogs did since in America they were fed so well. (A whole aisle at the grocery store with food just for dogs???)
- o At the time of writing this, I have neighbors who are refugees from Syria. They have started a school for Syrian children. Because of the war in their country, many young children had never even started school. They lost three years of education. Adult refugees are the teachers, the cooks, the cleaners, and the helpers, and child refugees are the students. It's a little piece of hope in a grim situation.
- o Recall: What is a refugee? someone who has to flee their home country to save their lives (technically Lot didn't flee his country, but they had to leave everything and flee their home town—It's much harder when you are in a new country with a different language!)
- o Explore more: Learn about the refugee situation in the world. Can you chart where they are and where they came from?

VI. Discussion
- o If someone told you that an angel said you had to abandon your home and belongings and flee, would you be willing to go?
- o How hard do you think it would be to leave your home and go to another country?
- o The Bible actually says a lot about foreigners. They are easily oppressed and taken advantage of, so they have a special place in God's heart. Just like we are admonished to care for widows and orphans, we are told to love the "strangers" in our midst. Here's one verse, Leviticus 19:34. "The stranger who resides with you shall be to you as the native among you, and you shall love him as yourself, for you were aliens in the land of Egypt; I am the LORD your God."

VII. Writing
- o Use the discussion question as a writing prompt.
- o Get a high five and/or hug if you use any of the vocabulary or spelling words.

Day 73

I.   Read Genesis 19:27-29.

II. Memory Verse
- o Joshua 24:15
- o "[If it is disagreeable in your sight to serve the LORD,] choose for yourselves today whom you will serve: [whether the gods which your fathers served which were beyond the River, or the gods of the Amorites in whose land you are living;] but as for me and my house, we will serve the LORD."

III. Language
- o Spelling/Handwriting
  - verse 26
  - words to know: pillar, toward, smoke, technique (Pillar is from verse 26 and technique I just chose for today.)
  - spelling tips:
    - Pronounce the word, pillar, "pill" "LAR" to remind you of how to spell the ending.
    - The word toward has the words TO and WAR as part of it. To as in go to bed.
    - The word smoke is spelled like it sounds and ends with a silent E.
    - Technique starts with the word TECH which has four letters and no K. The second "K" sound is made with a Q.
- o Vocabulary/Grammar
  - inhabitant (verse 25)
  - someone who lives in a place (noun)
- o Hebrew
  - Genesis 1:3 Then God said, "Let there be light"; and there was light.
  - va YOmer eloHEEM yeHEE or va yeHEE or
  - Here is this verse in Hebrew script. That's a period over on the left. You read Hebrew right to left.

  וַיֹּאמֶר אֱלֹהִים, יְהִי אוֹר; וַיְהִי אוֹר.

  - Find the Aleph in the verse. There are four. This is in the workbook on the Hebrew Writing 1 page. Go find and circle the Aleph wherever you see it in the verse. (Hebrew Bible verse pictures are used with permission from: http://www.mechon-mamre.org/p/pt/pt0101.htm)

IV. Science
- o Fire and brimstone destroyed the cities and inhabitants of the valley for their sin against God.
- o Today let's talk about the brimstone which rained out of heaven with fire and caused the smoke rising from the cities.
  - Brimstone is an ancient word for sulfur. Sulfur is another element, like gold, oxygen, iron, hydrogen, and carbon. They aren't made up of different types of atoms. Sulfur is made up of only sulfur atoms.

- ○ While we're talking about elements and atoms, this would be a good time to look at what makes the atoms different from one another.
- ○ What are atoms?
    - They are the building blocks of everything physical in the universe. What in the room you are in is made up of atoms?
        - Everything you can see and even some of what they can't see, like the air.
    - Everything is made up of atoms in different combinations.
    - When atoms join together, what is it called that they make?
        - molecules
    - What atoms make up a water molecule?
        - H_2O (Two hydrogen atoms and one oxygen atom make up one water molecule.)
- ○ What we call the *elements* are the atoms, the atoms that build together into different molecules. Each element is different from the others and cannot be broken down into anything else. Gold is only made of gold atoms. Oxygen is only oxygen atoms. Carbon is only carbon atoms. They are elements.
- ○ Is water an element?
    - No, it's a made of molecules, hydrogen and oxygen atoms together.
- ○ Is steel an element?
    - No, it's an alloy, a mixture. It's iron and carbon (and can be mixed with other metals as well).
- ○ In the back of your map book I put a chart of the elements. It's called the periodic table. There is another one in the back of your workbook.
    - Before we look at it, guess the scientific symbol for sulfur.
        - It's just the letter S.
- ○ Find on the periodic table the elements: oxygen, sulfur, carbon, nitrogen, iron, gold, and hydrogen.
    - Which of those do you remember the symbol for?
        - oxygen, O
        - sulfur, S
        - carbon, C
        - nitrogen, N
        - iron, Fe
        - gold, Au
        - hydrogen, H
- ○ What do you notice on the chart along with the symbols and the names of the elements?
    - There are numbers too. Lots of different numbers. On the color chart at the back of your map book, there is a box in the middle that tells about some of those numbers.
    - The main number at the top of each box (on our charts) is its *atomic number*. What do you notice about those?
        - They go in order. That's how the elements are placed, in order of their atomic number.
            - So, what is it? It's the number of protons in the atom.

- Protons are positively charged particles and electrons are negatively charged particles.
  - That's positive and negative like the two sides of a magnet. Two positive sides of a magnet push each other away, but a positive and negative side attract each other and hold themselves together.
- Protons and electrons are the energy in the atoms. Having an equal number of positive and negative particles means they all attract to each other and hold themselves together creating the element.
- So, basically the difference between the elements is how many of these positive and negative particles are inside of the atom!
  - That's pretty crazy isn't it? Think about it. The difference between oxygen and chlorine is that one has 9 more electrons and protons than the other!

o Use the periodic table to answer the following questions.
  - How many protons and electrons are in hydrogen? (Hint: Find its atomic #.)
    - Hydrogen has one proton and one electron.
  - How many protons and electrons are in one atom of oxygen?
    - Oxygen has 8 protons and 8 electrons.
  - How many protons and electrons are in an atom of gold?
    - One gold atom has 79 protons and 79 electrons.

o There is another number in each box. What do you notice about it?
  - It goes up with the number of protons and electrons (for the most part), but it goes up unevenly and more quickly.

o That number is the atomic mass. *Mass* is basically what we know as weight.
  - When you step on a scale, how does it know how much you weigh?
    - It measures how much the scale goes down when you step on it.
    - What pulls you down?
      - gravity
    - Weight is gravity pulling down on your mass.

o The mass is the number of protons (positive particles) and the number of neutrons. What are neutrons?
  - Neutrons are neutral. See the connection?
  - They are not positive nor negative. They are just there, bound into the center of the atom. The center of an atom is the *nucleus*.
    - The mass of an atom is determined by how many particles are in its nucleus. What types of particles are in the nucleus?
      - Protons and neutrons
    - Bonus question for older students: Why is the mass a decimal if it's just the number of protons plus the number of neutrons?
      - The atom is defined by the number of protons. The number of neutrons can vary slightly without changing what the element essentially is. The mass shown on the chart uses an average of the number of neutrons found in the element.
  - Protons and neutrons are in the nucleus.

- The electrons orbit around the nucleus. Their existence holds the atom together, in balance.
- Take a look at the diagram of Carbon with an atomic number of 6.
  - Recall: Draw a picture of an atom. Pick an element from the periodic table.
    - Draw a circle. That's your nucleus.
    - Draw plus signs in it. Each plus sign is one proton. The number of protons equals your atom's atomic number, its position on the periodic table.
    - Then draw the same number of minus signs outside of your nucleus circle. Those are your electrons.
    - Draw a little zero inside your nucleus circle for each neutron.
    - Electrons don't travel in perfect circles around the nucleus, but there are rules about where they travel which we will not go into today.
    - Show your drawing to someone and tell them what each thing represents and what atom you drew.
  - Explore more: Learn what the columns mean on the periodic table.

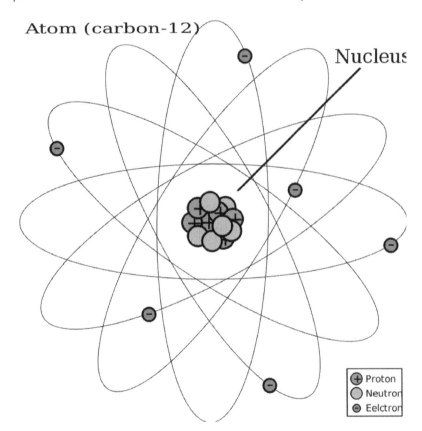

Atom (carbon-12)

Nucleus

Proton
Neutron
Eelctron

V. Social Studies
  - Science took up all our time today. Today would be a good day to ask your parents about your state's history. Do they know when it became a state? Famous people? Landmarks? Historical events? You can talk about this now or maybe it could be dinner conversation.

VI. Discussion
- In verse 29 in today's reading it seems to say that Lot and his daughters (could have been his whole family) were saved because of Abraham. Did you ever think that your prayers could save a family! God's love for you can reach to those you love.
- Thinking of that, who should you be praying for?
  - People you know and people you don't know.
  - What about those in prison for their faith?
  - Who can you reach with God's love through prayer?
- What could you pray for them?
  - How do you think your prayers could change their lives?

VII. Writing
- Use the discussion question as a writing prompt.
- Get a high five or a hug for completing your writing cheerfully.

Day 74

I. Read Genesis 20:1-2.

II. Memory Verse
- Joshua 24:15
- "[If it is disagreeable in your sight to serve the LORD,] choose for yourselves today whom you will serve: [whether the gods which your fathers served which were beyond the River, or the gods of the Amorites in whose land you are living;] but as for me and my house, we will serve the LORD."

III. Language
- Spelling/Handwriting
  - verse 27
  - words to know: ascend, preserve, remember, between (first three words are from Genesis 19)
  - spelling tips:
    - The word <u>ascend</u> has two different letters making the "S" sound.
    - The word <u>preserve</u> has the word, serve, inside of it.
    - The word <u>remember</u> has how many syllables? Each syllable has one vowel and it's the same in each syllable.
    - The word <u>between</u> is the words be and tween together.
- Vocabulary/Grammar
  - ascend (verse 28)
  - to go up (verb)
- Hebrew
  - Genesis 1:4 God saw that the light was good; and God separated the light from the darkness.
  - va yar eloHEEM et ha or ki tov va yavDEL eloHEEM ben ha or u ven ha KHOshekh
  - Practice writing Aleph with the Hebrew Writing 2 worksheet.
    - The top line can be skipped. I included that for the artists in the family who want to try calligraphy. They can use a felt tip marker or a calligraphy pen to practice, anything with an angled tip.
    - Everyone else can use the second line and just trace the letters within the lines and then write their own on the lines provided.

IV. Science
- We didn't get too far on Day 73 about sulfur. Sulfur is a solid, but it's not a metal or a rock. It's bright yellow, but when it's burned, it lets off a suffocating odor and turns "blood red." (Wikipedia)
- We also read about Abraham's wife being taken away. We don't really know what happened to Lot's wife who turns into a pillar of salt.
  - Was there a lot of salt around the area where this happened? Take a look at your maps if you need to. Where were Sodom and Gomorrah?
    - They were near the Dead Sea which is full of salt.

- We don't know for sure what happened to his wife, exactly. It says she was "behind" the others. She could have been lagging far behind in reluctance to leave and have been covered with volcanic ash later to be covered with salt from the surroundings, or maybe salt just piled down on her, burying her in place, or maybe God literally changed her into a pillar of salt.
- While we're looking at chemical elements, let's look at salt.
  - Salt is not an element. You can't break it down into salt atoms. There is no such thing as a salt atom. Salt is made up of two different kinds of atoms.
  - Salt's chemical name is sodium chloride. The symbol for it is NaCl. Find those two elements on the periodic table.
    - Did you notice that Cl is the element chlorine?
    - Salt is made up of equal parts sodium and chlorine.
- Can you observe what shape salt is? (Note: if you can, look at some salt.)
  - Salt is square shaped. All salt crystals are square and white. Here's a picture of a grain of salt taken from a microscope.

- What do you know about salt in water?
  - We know that salt dissolves in water. Is salt water a solution or a colloid?
    - If you need a hint, a solution is when the solids separate out from the liquid over time.
    - It's a colloid; the salt won't separate out over time. (Note: if you want to make sure, make some salt water and set it out.)
- Later I'll show you a picture of Lot's wife's salt statue, but now let's use salt to review about the periodic table.
  - What's the scientific name for salt?
    - Sodium Chloride
  - What two elements is salt made from?
    - sodium and chlorine
  - What are the symbols for sodium and chlorine?
    - Na and Cl
    - The first letter of each is capitalized and the second is lower case.
  - What is the atomic number of sodium?
    - 11
  - How many protons are in an atom of sodium?
    - 11
  - Are protons positively or negatively charged?
    - positively

- Just put your thumb up, like you are "pro" something. If you are for it, you are positive towards it. Does that help?
  - Where are protons located in the atom?
    - They are in the nucleus.
  - How many electrons are in an atom of sodium?
    - 11
  - Are electrons positively or negatively charged?
    - negatively
  - What else is in the nucleus besides protons?
    - neutrons
  - How do you find out how many neutrons are in the nucleus of an atom?
    - Atomic mass – atomic number = number of neutrons
  - About how many neutrons are in a sodium atom?
    - 22 – 11 = 11 (If you know rounding, then 23 – 11 is a closer estimate.)
- Explore More: How do the sodium atoms join to the chlorine atoms? Learn how atoms bond.

V. Social Studies
   - I told you I would show you a picture. Here it is. This is known as "Lot's Wife" pillar. It is made of rock salt, the mineral form of sodium chloride (NaCl). It's located on what's called Mount Sodom.
     (Photo By Wilson44691 (Own work) [Public domain], via Wikimedia Commons)

   - Look at the Day 49 map. Mount Sodom is located to the west of the Dead Sea. The sea and the cities were in the valley. The cities were on the plain, the low, level ground. What is to the west of the Dead Sea valley?
     - the highlands

- • Mount Sodom is part of the highlands.
- o The whole mountain is made of sodium chloride. What's that?
  - • salt
  - • It is a mountain of rock salt. That's the stuff they put on the ground to melt ice in the winter.
- o Mount Sodom has caves. In one of them Lot hid with his daughters.
  - • In the next picture is someone's photograph of a salt cave in Mount Sodom.
    (By Wilson44691 (Own work) [CC BY-SA 3.0 http://creativecommons.org/licenses/by-sa/3.0)], via Wikimedia Commons)

- o There are other stories in the Bible involving caves. What do you think are some ways they were used?
  - • to hide (Joshua 10:17, 1 Samuel 13:6)
  - • as a prison (Joshua 10:18)
  - • to live in to be protected (Judges 6:2)
  - • as a bathroom (1 Samuel 24:3)
  - • Caves were also used as graves. Abraham will bury Sarah in a cave.
- o Caves are part of our history. Maybe you've visited famous caves near where you live. They are considered landmarks in some areas.
- o Recall: What is Mount Sodom made of? rock salt; Where is it located? west of the Dead Sea; Name a few ways caves have been used. living, hiding, prison, bathroom, grave
- o Explore more: What are the most famous caves? You could research Petra.

VI. Discussion
- o Like Lot's daughters, Abraham sins in a kind of desperation. Don't make decisions when you are feeling desperate! Call out to God and wait for His peace so that you can see your situation more clearly.
- o Has there ever been a time you felt desperate? Did you take action? What was the result?

VII. Writing
- o Use the discussion question as a writing prompt.
- o Get a high five and/or hug if you use any of the vocabulary or spelling words.

Day 75

I. Read Genesis 20:3-5.

II. Memory Verse
- o Joshua 24:15
- o "[If it is disagreeable in your sight to serve the LORD,] choose for yourselves today whom you will serve: [whether the gods which your fathers served which were beyond the River, or the gods of the Amorites in whose land you are living;] but as for me and my house, we will serve the LORD."

III. Language
- o Spelling/Handwriting
  - • Test yourselves on words from Day 71 to Day 74.
    - ▪ inhabitants, surrounded, rained, urged
    - ▪ escape, punishment, dawn, seize
    - ▪ pillar, toward, smoke, technique
    - ▪ ascend, preserve, remember, between
- o Vocabulary/Grammar
  - • Test yourselves on words from Day 71 to Day 74.
    - ▪ urge – to strongly persuade someone to do something
    - ▪ jest – to speak or act jokingly
    - ▪ inhabitant – someone who lives in a place
    - ▪ ascend – to go up
- o Hebrew
  - • Genesis 1:5 God called the light day, and the darkness He called night. And there was evening and there was morning, one day.
  - • va yikRA eloHEEM la or yom ve la KHOshekh kaRA LII-la va yeHEE Erev va yeHEE VOker yom ekHAD
  - • LII-la is pronounced LIE-lah. I'm going to use the regular font from now on.
  - • What words in Genesis 1:5 do you think have an Aleph?
  - • Find them. You can circle them in your workbook on the Hebrew Writing 2 page. (Note: I found five in Genesis 1:5.)
  - • You will see all sorts of extra dots and marks above and below the Aleph and other letters. Those are the vowels. You don't have to write the vowels when you write a word. They only have to be added if it's needed for clarity.

IV. Science
- o Complete the Periodic Table Science Review 11 worksheet.
- o Explore More: What are the groups of the periodic table. Learn about the common characteristics of the elements of one or more of the groups.

V. Social Studies
- o God was going to punish Abimelech. He punished Sodom and Gomorrah. Here are some other stories of how God punishes.

o Achan and his whole family are swallowed whole in a sinkhole because Achan disobeyed and stole gold and silver from Israel's enemies which God commanded to be destroyed.

- Because of his sin, all of Israel was punished. Their covenant was broken and they no longer had His blessing because of Achan's sin. Israel lost their next battle and tens of thousands of Israelites died in battle.
- Israel partners with God to get rid of the sin in their midst. Achan and his family are killed and God's blessing is restored.

o God uses enemy armies to conquer Israel when they need disciplining to cause them to repent. Then God punishes the foreign armies for what they did to the Israelites.

o In Revelation it talks about Mystery Babylon being destroyed by God for her many sins.

o We have already seen God destroy the whole earth. That was a punishment on everyone except Noah.

o What observations can you make from all we've learned? Who is punished? How are they punished? Who is saved from punishment?

- Those who sin against God are punished. Many are killed giving them no chance of repentance. God saves those who are righteous and those closest to them. Lot is saved for his own righteousness and for Abraham's sake. Lot's daughters are saved for Lot's sake.

o How do discipline and punishment differ?

- Sometimes they can look the same, like being conquered in battle. But when your life is spared, you have the chance to repent.

o How does this next verse relate to discipline and punishment? First you should know that pruning is cutting branches, trimming them down which actually encourages them to grow more. With that in mind, how is this verse related to discipline and punishment? "He cuts off every branch in me that bears no fruit, while every branch that does bear fruit he prunes so that it will be even more fruitful." John 15:2 (NIV)

- The cutting and pruning are like punishment and discipline.
- Which is which?

o Cutting off a branch is like punishment. It's basically killed. The branch can't grow any more if it's not attached to a tree. It's dead wood. Pruning is like discipline. Part of the branch is cut off, but the branch still lives and having been cut will enable it to grow more.

o Did you notice that pruning and cutting both look the same? They both involve cutting off much of the branch. They look almost the same, but they have a different purpose.

- Why should we want to avoid God's punishment?
- Why should we want God's discipline?

o Explore More: What are other Bible stories of God's punishment? What about Acts 5? Why do you think God punishes instead of disciplines?

VI. Discussion

o God is patient and loving, but He does punish those who sin against Him and against His people. It may be instantly, it may be on earth, it may be after death, but it will happen. We also see how whole groups of people are punished. Families are punished. Cities are punished. Countries are punished. It's important who you are united with! When we become Christians, we become citizens of heaven and members of the body of Christ. That's who we should stand with.

- o Who are you "aligned" with? Does that protect or endanger you?
- o God is still just and can work it out for the individual among the group (as He does with Lot and Noah, but they still lost their homes and their lives as they knew them because of the sins of those around them.)
- o Do you ever look at the wars in the world and consider that God is using them as punishment and discipline?

VII. Writing
- o Choose something you wrote from Days 72-74 to edit.
- o Use your editing guidelines and ask someone else to check it too.
- o Create a final draft.

Day 76 (check Materials List)

I.   Read Genesis 20:6-8.

II. Memory Verse
   - 2 Peter 3:9
   - The Lord is not slow about His promise, as some count slowness, but is patient toward you, not wishing for any to perish but for all to come to repentance.

III. Language
   - Spelling/Handwriting
     - verse 7 (first sentence)
     - words to know: frightened, innocence, prophet, nation
     - spelling tips:
       - The word <u>frightened</u> uses the I-G-H spelling pattern.
       - A hint for the word <u>innocence</u>: it has two Cs.
       - The sound of F in the word <u>prophet</u> is spelled with P-H.
       - The ending T-I-O-N on the word <u>nation</u> is a common one.
   - Vocabulary/Grammar
     - integrity (verse 5)
     - the character quality of holding to strong moral principles (noun)
     - Name two prepositions and two objects in this phrase from today's reading.
       - in the integrity of my heart
       - Answers: in, of; integrity, heart
     - What is the possessive adjective in the phrase? (in the integrity of my heart)
       - my
   - Hebrew
     - Genesis 1:1 In the beginning God created the heavens and the earth.
     - be reSHEET baRA eloHEEM et ha shaMAyim ve et ha Arets
     - Today we will start learning the next letter of the Hebrew alphabet, Bet. This makes the B sound.
     - This letter uses a dot inside of it. You must include that dot. It's not a vowel sound. Without the dot it makes a different letter sound.
     - Do you know what Abba means? Galatians 4:6 says the Spirit in us cries out, "Abba, Father!" Abba is the Hebrew word for father. Years ago I had a Jewish friend over and she had to call home. When her dad answered the phone she said, "Abba?" I thought it was sooooo cool to hear someone actually say that.
     - I'm talking about the word Abba because it not only uses the letter Bet, but the Aleph as well. Remember to read it right to left (even though it's a palindrome, the same backwards and forwards).

     - What words in Genesis 1:1 do you think will have bet?

- Just an interesting note: Do you notice anything about the first two letters of the alphabet? aleph-bet, alpha-bet? There is a connection, but it pre-dates the Hebrew alphabet. Arabic's first letter is also the "Aleph." They both come from the Phoenician alphabet.

IV. Science
  o Abimelech rises early in the morning. In an earlier lesson we acted out the phases of the moon and saw how orbits changed what we saw of the moon.
  o Today, let's look at how the earth's rotation causes the sun to rise each morning and how the earth's orbit causes that time to change every single day.
    - Where my family lived in Turkey, during the Muslim holiday of Ramadan a cannon is shot off at sunset each night. The people are supposed to fast from food and drink all day between sunrise and sunset. The booming of the cannon means you get to eat. (It's a neat cultural experience. The roads are empty. Everything is quiet. Everyone is at home waiting to eat. If it's summer, then the windows are open and you only hear the clink-clink of silverware coming from all sides once they are allowed to eat.)
    - The interesting thing, though, is that every day the cannon goes off about a minute later or earlier, depending on the time of year. Their fast is at least a half hour shorter or longer by the end of the month than when they began.
  o Have someone shine a flashlight at you as you turn in a circle. That's sunrise and sunset. When the light is in your face, that's day. When you can't see the light, that's night. As you turn around, when you first see some light, that's sunrise. In 24 hours the earth turns around one time giving everyone day and night.
  o The change in time each day is caused by the earth's orbit, the path it travels around the sun. Look at the picture. (By following Duoduoduo's advice, vector image: Gothika. ([1]) [GFDL (http://www.gnu.org/copyleft/fdl.html) or CC-BY-SA-3.0 (http://creativecommons.org/licenses/by-sa/3.0/)], via Wikimedia Commons)

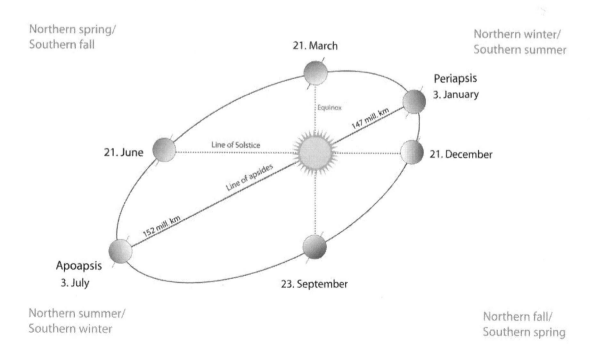

- o Make observations about the earth's orbit around the sun.
  - Its shape is an ellipse. That makes the earth closer at some points in the orbits. That doesn't really affect the earth's temperature. Once you're 150 million kilometers away from something, a couple more million doesn't change much.
- o Let's act out the earth's orbit. Do you remember what the imaginary line through the earth is called?
  - the axis
  - The axis is the key to the changes in sunrise and sunset times.
- o What is the earth doing on its axis?
  - It's rotating on its axis. It spins like a top and the axis is the handle.
- o You'll notice in the picture that the axis isn't up and down; it's not vertical.
  - Choose a pencil or pen to be your earth's axis.
  - Hold it upright. We'll call the top of the eraser (or flat end) the North Pole. We'll call the point the South Pole.
- o The earth spins at a pretty constant speed. When the earth turns around once, that's a full day, 24 hours. Since that part just stays the same, you don't really need to act that out. We need to figure out what causes the changes we notice as the seasons change. The days are longer in summer and shorter in the winter. Let's observe why.
  - Use your flashlight. Tilt the top end of your axis stick toward the sun. Now don't change the position of your hand. Stay just like that!
  - Which pole is getting all the light?
    - The North Pole
  - Which pole is getting no light?
    - The South Pole
  - Which pole is having summer?
    - The North Pole
  - Which pole is having winter?
    - The South Pole
  - When the North Pole is having summer, is it warm or cold in the northern hemisphere?
    - warm
  - When the South Pole is having winter, is it warm or cold in the southern hemisphere?
    - cold
- o Now start your orbit. Keep facing the same wall of the room, but walk in an ellipse around the sun. Stop when neither end of your axis is pointing towards the sun at all.
  - What seasons are the two hemispheres experiencing?
    - spring and fall
- o Continue your orbit. Stop when the South Pole (bottom of your stick) is pointing in the direction of the sun.
  - What season is the southern hemisphere experiencing?
    - summer
  - What season is the northern hemisphere experiencing?
    - winter
  - Where is there no light or hardly any?

- - the North Pole
  - o Can you see that the North Pole went from having all the light to no light?
    - It's most dramatic on the poles where in summer the sun doesn't set and in winter the sun doesn't rise, but we all experience the changing daylight hours to varying degrees depending on where in the world we live.
  - o Recall: What's the imaginary line that the earth rotates around? axis; What does the earth orbit? Sun; What shape is the earth's orbit around our sun? ellipse; What about the earth's axis causes the sun to set earlier or later (same thing that causes the seasons)? It's tilted so that parts of the earth are either pointing towards or away from the sun.
  - o Explore more: Learn why the poles are colder than the equator. Here's a website that might help. (http://www.hko.gov.hk/education/edu06nature/ele_srad_e.htm)

V. Social Studies
  - o God says to Abimelech that he will "surely die" if he does not give Sarah back to Abraham. We would call this the *death penalty* or *capital punishment*, when people are killed as the punishment for their crime.
    - We've already learned the memory verse that the wages of sin is death, meaning that all sin earns us the death penalty.
  - o When Jesus is before Pilate, Pilate says "I have found in Him no guilt demanding death; therefore I will punish Him and release Him." (Luke 23:22b) He believes there are crimes that "demand" death but that Jesus didn't commit them.
  - o We learned before about Hammurabi's Code and a little about the Mosaic law. Both included capital punishment. Hammurabi's Code had crimes that were punishable by execution, the killing of someone as punishment. In fact a rebellious child could be killed under the Mosaic law. Deuteronomy 21:18-21 explains that the whole community has to be in agreement and that the sin had to be serious and continuous over a long time even though the parents had disciplined the child repeatedly.
    - The Mosaic Law seems to have about 10 crimes punishable by death and Hammurabi's code, 25, including that wife who wasn't a good housekeeper.
  - o There is a long horrible history of ways people have been put to death for crimes they presumably committed. Some rulers softened the rules and saved execution for war criminals, while others seemed to kill just about anyone.
    - Henry VIII (Henry the 8th) of England was a king famous, or maybe I should say infamous, for executing people. Anyone who disagreed with him or whom he considered a threat was banished or killed. He reigned in the first half of the 16th century AD. About what years do you think that would have been?
      - The first half of the 16th century is from 1501 to 1550.
      - Centuries refer to the previous hundred years. The 16th century refers to the years 1501 through 1600.
  - o A time period famous for its executions even has a name. It's called the "Reign of Terror." It was just after the start of the French Revolution. There was a revolt against the government and anyone associated with the ruling classes was killed, often by being beheaded in a guillotine. About 40,000 people were executed in less than one year.

- The Reign of Terror was from September 1793 to July 1794. That was towards the end of what century?
  - 18th century
- When the colonies were first established in America, they followed the laws of the places they had come from. Pennsylvania was the first to change their death penalty laws. They created more definitions of crimes and then only first degree murder received such a punishment. That's when someone plans to murder someone before they do it.
- Nearly a hundred years later Rhode Island and Wisconsin abolished the death penalty and Michigan called for it only in cases of *treason*, when someone betrays their country, like someone spying for another country.
- In the last half of the 20th century, the number of countries that have abolished (completely done away with) the death penalty has more than doubled.
  - In the United States there is still support for capital punishment; although in the last forty years, well over 100 people have been freed while awaiting execution because it was later discovered that they were innocent.
  - It actually even costs more to execute someone than it does to keep them in prison for life. I know it doesn't seem to make sense, but at least in America, it's true. (Some of the history of the death penalty information comes from http://www.deathpenaltyinfo.org/part-ii-history-death-penalty.)
- Recall: What years would make up the last half of the 20th century? 1951-2000; What crime is treason? betraying your country; What's another phrase for the death penalty? capital punishment
- Explore more: I don't really want to send you to learn about capital punishment. There are many supreme court cases about it, if that's an interest to you. You could also learn more about the uprising that led to the Reign of Terror and who was ruling at the time in France.

VI. Discussion

- What do you think about the death penalty? When do you think it is called for? Should there be protections for people accused of crimes punishable by death? (For instance, should it be required that there be more witnesses to the crime than for other punishments?)

VII. Writing

- Let's continue with practicing pronouns. Fill in the correct pronoun.
  - It could be a subject pronoun: I, you, he, she, it, we, you, they
  - It could be an object pronoun: me, you, him, her, it, us, you, them
- Fill in the missing pronouns on Writing Sentences 12 in your workbook.

Day 77

I. Read Genesis 20:9-18. This is the continuation of the story of Abimelech taking Sarah.

II. Memory Verse
- o 2 Peter 3:9
- o The Lord is not slow about His promise, as some count slowness, but is patient toward you, not wishing for any to perish but for all to come to repentance.

III. Language
- o Spelling/Handwriting
  - verse 10
  - words to know: womb, wander, thousand, pieces
  - spelling tips:
    - There is a silent B on the end of the word <u>womb</u>, like in comb and lamb.
    - The word <u>wander</u> has the word AND inside of it.
    - The word <u>thousand</u> has the word sand at the end of it.
    - In the word <u>pieces</u>, I comes before E this time before C.
- o Vocabulary/Grammar
  - vindication (verse 16)
  - being shown innocent of an accusation of wrongdoing (noun)
  - What word describes vindication?
    - your
    - What kind of word is your?
      - possessive adjective
      - It tells whose vindication it is. It's Abraham's vindication. It's his. His, that's another possessive adjective.
- o Hebrew
  - Trace the letter Bet on your Hebrew Writing 3 page.

IV. Science
- o Today we're going to learn about one of the animal gifts Abraham received, oxen.
  - The first thing that comes to mind when I think of oxen is the Oregon Trail! When my kids would act out the Oregon Trail, some kids would always have to be the oxen.
  - Do you remember that oxen is the plural of the word ox? (It was one of your spelling words.)
- o Oxen are related to cows; they are kind of like cousins.
- o We don't eat oxen the way we eat cows (where we get all of our hamburgers from). Oxen are mainly used for their muscle. They are trained to pull loads.
  - They are used in farming in other countries around the world. The oxen pull the plow which turns up the ground before planting.
  - Here are some images. (first image: By Yann (Own work) [GFDL (http://www.gnu.org/copyleft/fdl.html) or CC BY-SA 4.0-3.0-2.5-2.0-1.0 (http://creativecommons.org/licenses/by-sa/4.0-3.0-2.5-2.0-1.0)], via Wikimedia Commons)

- Do you think they used oxen for plowing their fields in ancient Mesopotamia?
  - It's likely, isn't it? What kind of society would use oxen for plowing?
    - agricultural
- The first picture is of a paddy. Rice is grown in paddies instead of fields. Can you see in the picture how wet the ground is?
  - Rice is mostly grown in Asia and it's grown on flooded land.

- Oxen are trained and bred specifically to work in the wet environment.
- The wooden bars around their necks that connect them to the plow is called the *yoke*.
  - Oxen are used to pull carts and wagons as well. By far most travelers on the Oregon Trail used oxen to pull their wagons as they made their way west across America.
  - There are more pictures on the following page. The first is from Australia.

  - Below is a picture from India. What do you observe in these pictures?

  (By Antônio Milena/ABr. [CC BY 3.0 br (http://creativecommons.org/licenses/by/3.0/br/deed.en)], via Wikimedia Commons)

- o In the old picture from Australia, there is a "train" of oxen. Can you count how many pairs are working together?
  - • There are ten pairs. How many oxen is that?
    - ▪ 20 oxen
- o Recall: Are oxen cows? no; What makes them valuable? They are used to pull heavy loads.
- o Explore more: You could learn more about growing rice.

V. Social Studies
- o This isn't from our reading today but from our science lesson on oxen. Since I mentioned it, let's learn a little about the Oregon Trail.
- o In the first half of the 19th century, the US government was interested in opening up the western part of the country. About a third of what we know as America had just been bought from France in a trade known as the Louisiana Purchase. The new land covering the entire center of the country needed to be explored and settled. The western part of what we know as America wasn't part of America at this time.
  - • Take a look at the map showing America at the time of the Louisiana Purchase. It's in the map book for Day 77. The original colonies along the east coast were states. Other areas east of the Mississippi River were considered "territories." Florida and much of the southwest belonged to Spain.
  - • It was hoped that a water route to the Pacific Ocean could be found.
  - • In 1804, Thomas Jefferson, the then president of America, sent Louis and Clark on an exploration. They couldn't find any rivers that would carry them across the country. They had to go much of the way on foot.
- o Three and a half decades later…how many years is that? (Hint: a decade is ten years)
  - • thirty-five
- o Three and a half decades later the US government sent out a team to establish a colony in what was known as Oregon country. Oregon became a state twenty years later in 1859.
  - • It was a long road in between, literally.
  - • The Oregon Trail from Independence, Missouri to Willamette Valley, Oregon covered about 2000 miles (3200 km).
    - ▪ Take a look at the Oregon Trail map for Day 77 in the map book.
    - ▪ Independence, Missouri is known as a jumping off point, or where people joined others to head off on the trail.
  - • Consider that most people had to walk that distance; they walked halfway across America.
  - • The oxen pulled their wagons full of supplies. They didn't carry people for the most part.
- o The Oregon Trail was the path taken by those wanting to *migrate* west. Can you hear the connection between the words migrate and immigration? It's easier to see it than to hear it. To migrate means to move from one place to another, especially traveling a far distance and often to find work.
  - • Early migrants to Oregon had to clear the path for others, again, literally. They chopped down what was in their way and made roads for the wagons.
- o It wasn't only hard physically; it was a dangerous trip. Can you think of dangers they might have faced on the way?

- About ten percent of all migrants on the Oregon Trail died along the way. If those hundred balloons were travelers, ten of them would die before reaching Oregon.
- The most common cause of death was disease.
  - *Cholera* (collar-a) was the disease that claimed the most lives on the trail.
    - It caused dehydration because it made people vomit and have diarrhea.
    - People contracted cholera by drinking unclean water.
- Another common cause of death was accidents, especially gun accidents. People were accidently shot or their guns malfunctioned.
  - Those travelling west were afraid of Native Americans, even though for the most part they didn't need to be. They bought and brought guns even if they weren't experienced in using them. Inexperience isn't the best idea around weapons.
- But even with all that, the most dangerous part of the trip was crossing rivers. Can you guess why?
  - There were no bridges yet.
  - They would have to walk across the rivers or float across. Walking across could work if it wasn't too deep and if the water wasn't flowing to quickly. People could get swept away.
  - To float across they balanced their wagons on rafts or canoes. It was difficult and not uncommon for a wagon to tip over and fall into the water.
  - Native Americans were hired to help with the crossings of either kind.
  - Oxen had to walk or swim to the other side. Sometimes Native Americans would help by pulling the front animals by reigns so that the others would follow and they could help pull the load across.
    - This was dangerous for oxen as well and it was also possible for them to drown if the waters were too rough.
  - o Recall: Where was the jumping off point for the Oregon Trail? Independence, Missouri; What was the name of the disease that killed the most people on the trail? cholera; What does it mean to migrate? relocate from one area to another
  - o Explore more: Learn more about the Oregon Trail. There are lots of stories. Why were they going west?

VI. Discussion
- o Abraham made an assumption about Abimelech that proved to be false. Abraham decided that Abimelech didn't have the fear of God, but we read about Abimelech's integrity before God. The problem with assumptions is that we often don't know they are wrong, or we don't find out they are wrong until later.
- o Can you remember a time when you made an assumption? You probably make them all the time! Can you remember a time when you made a false assumption? What happened?
- o How can you keep from making false assumptions?
- o (Note: Another discussion topic is how God opens and closes wombs.)

VII. Writing
- o Use the discussion question as a writing prompt.
- o Get a high five and/or hug if you include a possessive adjective. (my, your, his, her, its, our, their)

Day 78

I. Read Genesis 21:1-8.

II. Memory Verse
   o   2 Peter 3:9
   o   The Lord is not slow about His promise, as some count slowness, but is patient toward you, not wishing for any to perish but for all to come to repentance.

III. Language
   o   Spelling/Handwriting
      •   verse 1
      •   words to know: laughter, Isaac, weaned, bore
      •   spelling tips:
         ▪   The F sound in <u>laughter</u> is spelled with a G-H.
         ▪   The name <u>Isaac</u> has a double letter.
         ▪   The word <u>weaned</u> is the past tense of a verb. Wean has the same vowel spelling pattern as your spelling words season and reason.
         ▪   The word <u>bore</u> is a homonym and a homophone. "Sarah bore a son" and "She is such a bore" and "The termites bore a hole in our roof" are all spelled the same way even though they have different meanings. Those are homonyms. Boar, the wild animal, is spelled differently, but sounds the same. That's a homophone.
   o   Vocabulary/Grammar
      •   wean (verse 8)
      •   to gradually get used to not having something you've become dependent on
   o   Hebrew
      •   Genesis 1:1 In the beginning God created the heavens and the earth.
      •   bereSHEET baRA eloHEEM et ha shaMAyim ve et ha Arets
      •   Find the Bet and Aleph in Genesis 1:1. You can find and circle them on the Hebrew Writing 3 in your workbook.
         ▪   I found 2 Bet and 6 Aleph.

IV. Science
   o   Today we have a fun topic, laughter. Go ahead, tickle someone.
   o   Did you get someone to laugh? Did everyone else laugh too? That's because laughter is contagious.
   o   What body systems do you think are involved in laughing?
      •   The respiratory system is involved. Our diaphragm contracts and forces out the air causing the noises of laughter. Do you remember where your diaphragm is?
         ▪   It's under your lungs. Laugh and feel your belly move. That's your diaphragm at work.
         ▪   It can be hard to laugh on command, but faking it can lead to real laughter. Or, just keep tickling each other.
      •   The muscular system is what is contracting your diaphragm.

- Go ahead and laugh again. What other muscles do you feel contracting when you laugh?
    - A whole lot! Arms, legs, your whole body can get involved. (Tickling has actually been used as a form of torture because it forces sustained muscle contraction.)
- Are the muscles involved in laughing working voluntarily or involuntarily?
    - Involuntarily; They just do it. It can even be hard to not laugh when you want to.
- The other body system at work is the nervous system, which we haven't done a whole lesson on yet. That's your brain and the system of nerves that delivers the messages to and from your brain.

o What are things that make you laugh?

o Laughter isn't about humor. People laugh when they are just happy or feeling joyful or accepted, but people can also laugh because they are nervous or embarrassed.
- Babies laugh long before they can talk. We don't learn to laugh. It's just part of being human.
- Laughter is a social activity; it's something we do with others. We're more likely to talk to ourselves then laugh by ourselves.

o Laughter begins in the brain. Scientists don't know much about it. There is no laugh part of the brain. Different types of laughter can originate in different parts of the brain. Tickling, being embarrassed, and hearing a joke all send different signals to the brain but can all invoke laughter.

o How many times a day do you think you laugh? I'm not talking about big belly laughs, just any little laugh.
- You might be surprised. A baby can laugh hundreds of times a day. An adult more like a dozen or two. You're probably in between.
- Maybe you'd like to conduct a study today on how often you or your family members laugh. You can hang a tally sheet somewhere and try to keep track.
- Laughter is associated with playing, so the more you play, the more you laugh.

o Do you like to laugh? Does it feel good?
- You feel good because it's good for you! It's beneficial, meaning helpful, to your nervous system, circulatory system, muscular system, and your immune system, the system that fights sickness in your body.
    - Laughter helps your circulatory system by opening up your blood vessels more, increasing your blood flow.
    - Laughter helps your immune system by producing more cells which fight bad bacteria and viruses.
    - Laughter helps your nervous system by releasing *endorphins*, a chemical that stops pain signals, so people can feel less or no pain when laughing. Some doctors prescribe laughter to help people who can't sleep because of pain!
    - And as for your muscular system, it gives them a workout, increasing strength and tone. You can laugh a lot today and count it for PE. ☺

- o Recall: What are some of the ways laughter is good for you? (Directly above) What does your nervous system control? brain and its signals; What does the immune system do? fights sickness and disease
- o Explore more: There's lots to explore here. What are you interested in? How about the nervous system? How do nerves send pain signals to the brain?

V. Social Studies
- o We have another joyous topic, feasting. Abraham throws a feast to celebrate Isaac's first step in growing up. What is America's famous feast day?
  - Thanksgiving
  - Do you know when Thanksgiving is?
    - It's the fourth Thursday of November.
- o Do you know when Thanksgiving became a holiday in America?
  - That was a trick question.
  - What we know as the first Thanksgiving was in 1621 when the early pilgrims in America celebrated finally having an abundant harvest along with Native Americans who had helped them along the way.
  - In October of 1777 all thirteen of the original American colonies celebrated a Thanksgiving feast.
  - George Washington had a day of Thanksgiving on the last Thursday of November of 1789 as a day of prayer and thanksgiving.
  - In 1863 Abraham Lincoln established Thanksgiving as an annual, national holiday, setting it on the last Thursday of November, like Washington.
  - In 1939 President Franklin Delano Roosevelt changed the date of Thanksgiving to the fourth Thursday in the month. That year the last Thursday was on the last day of the month. Businesses wanted more shopping days before Christmas. That year everything was confused. Some states celebrated the original Thanksgiving, some the new Thanksgiving, some both. School calendars were wrong, football schedules were off. Families had off on different days and couldn't celebrate together. In 1941 Congress passed into law that the fourth Thursday of November be declared Thanksgiving.
- o I thought it would be neat to read a historical document. I've included Abraham Lincoln's proclamation, establishing the holiday of Thanksgiving. America was in the middle of the Civil War, when southern states had withdrawn from the United States. The North was fighting to put America back together. The South was fighting to keep the North from changing its way of life. Slavery was legal in the South and brought in a lot of money for the South. Abraham Lincoln also wrote a proclamation declaring slaves free the same year he wrote this proclamation establishing Thanksgiving. It is a smart thing to give thanks in the midst of adversity.

"The year that is drawing toward its close has been filled with the blessings of fruitful fields and healthful skies. To these bounties, which are so constantly enjoyed that we are prone to forget the source from which they come, others have been added which are of so extraordinary a nature that they cannot fail to penetrate and soften even the heart which is habitually insensible to the ever-watchful providence of Almighty God.

In the midst of a civil war of unequaled magnitude and severity, which has sometimes seemed to foreign states to invite and to provoke their aggression, peace has been preserved with all nations, order has been maintained, the laws have been respected and obeyed, and harmony has prevailed everywhere, except in the theater of military conflict, while that theater has been greatly contracted by the advancing armies and navies of the Union.

Needful diversions of wealth and of strength from the fields of peaceful industry to the national defense have not arrested the plow, the shuttle, or the ship; the ax has enlarged the borders of our settlements, and the mines, as well as the iron and coal as of our precious metals, have yielded even more abundantly than heretofore. Population has steadily increased notwithstanding the waste that has been made in the camp, the siege, and the battlefield, and the country, rejoicing in the consciousness of augmented strength and vigor, is permitted to expect continuance of years with large increase of freedom.

No human counsel hath devised nor hath any mortal hand worked out these great things. They are the gracious gifts of the Most High God, who, while dealing with us in anger for our sins, hath nevertheless remembered mercy.

It has seemed to me fit and proper that they should be solemnly, reverently, and gratefully acknowledged, as with one heart and one voice, by the whole American people. I do therefore invite my fellow-citizens in every part of the United States, and also those who are in foreign lands, to set apart and observe the last Thursday of November next as a day of thanksgiving and praise to our beneficent Father who dwelleth in the heavens. And I recommend to them that while offering up the ascriptions justly due to Him for such singular deliverances and blessings they do also, with humble penitence for our national perverseness and disobedience, commend to His tender care all those who have become widows, orphans, mourners, or sufferers in the lamentable civil strife in which we are unavoidably engaged, and fervently implore the imposition of the Almighty hand to heal the wounds of the nation and to restore it, as soon as may be consistent with the divine purpose, to the full enjoyment of peace, harmony, tranquility, and union.

In testimony whereof I have hereunto set my hand and caused the seal of the United States to be affixed.

Done at the city of Washington, this 3d day of October, A.D. 1863, and of the Independence of the United States the eighty-eighth.

Abraham Lincoln"

- o Recall: Who established Thanksgiving as an annual, national holiday? What year? What was happening in America at that time?
  - President Abraham Lincoln
  - 1863
  - the Civil War
- o Explore more: Find the Emancipation Proclamation online and read it. What was its significance? Impact?

VI. Discussion
- o Has God ever made you laugh? Has He ever done a miracle or arranged circumstances for your family that just made you laugh?

o One of our laughing stories was when the phone repair man showed up at our house. Our phone hadn't worked for three days. We were in a foreign country and the government controlled the phones. To get it fixed meant spending the day at the government building to request to be put on the list for someone to come fix it. My husband was putting off taking care of it because who wants to spend the day like that when there's so much else to do? We were surprised by the repairman, who just showed up at our apartment, and asked him why he was at our house. He was just as surprised by our question and asked if our phone wasn't working. He thought it was very odd that our phone wouldn't be working and we'd be surprised that the repairman was there to fix it. Somehow the Lord got us on his fix-it list and our phone was working again. It made me laugh and it made the repair man laugh because I kept asking him why he had come.

VII. Writing
   o Use the discussion question as a writing prompt.
   o Get a high five and/or hug if you include a possessive adjective. (my, your, his, her, its, our, their)

Day 79

I. Read Genesis 21:9-16.

II. Memory Verse
   o 2 Peter 3:9
   o The Lord is not slow about His promise, as some count slowness, but is patient toward you, not wishing for any to perish but for all to come to repentance.

III. Language
   o Spelling/Handwriting
      • verse 11
      • words to know: Sarah, listen, die, angel
      • spelling tips:
         ▪ <u>Sarah</u> is a name. Make sure it begins like all proper nouns should. It ends with a silent letter.
         ▪ The word <u>listen</u> has a silent letter.
         ▪ The word <u>die</u> is a homophone. You can dye your clothes with the letter Y, or you can roll a die or drop dead. That's the kind you are going to spell, again, with the letter I.
         ▪ Finally, the word <u>angel</u> is only tricky because it's spelled so closely to the word angle, the measurement that tells us which way a line is going. The word angel has the word gel in it.
   o Vocabulary/Grammar
      • distress (verse 11)
      • extreme sorrow or worry (noun); or to cause extreme sorrow or worry (verb)
      • Read verse 11. Is distress used as a verb or a noun in this verse?
         ▪ verb
   o Hebrew
      • Trace and write the letter Bet. Use Hebrew Writing 4 in your workbook.

IV. Science
   o Today we read that Hagar sat a bowshot away from Ishmael. On Day 80 we'll learn that Ishmael becomes an archer. So, how far is a bowshot away? What causes the arrow to go farther or shorter distances? Let's learn a little about the physics of the bow and arrow.
      • *Physics* is the branch of science that studies energy and how it interacts with matter, which is everything in the physical universe.
      • What subject have we studied that is part of physics? What have we studied that has to do with energy?
         ▪ light (Note: They can have other answers too.)
         ▪ What is light?
            • moving energy
            • What is energy?
               ▪ Energy is the ability to do work.
   o Today it's the physics of archery.

- There is more to it than we can learn about today, but we can learn some basics of what makes things move.
- If energy is the ability to work, what is work? Any guesses?
  - *Work* is when a force moves an object, even if it's as small as an electron.
  - Here we go again. What is force?
    - *Force* is something that affects the motion of an object.
- Let's go through each of these.
  - Let's start with force. What is force?
    - something that affects the motion of an object
    - We've already learned about one force. What happens when you throw a ball up in the air?
  - Something changes its upward motion and pulls it back down. What force is that?
    - gravity
  - There was also a force that pushed the ball upward. That's called an applied force. You applied force to the ball to push it upward.
- Was work done when you threw the ball upward?
  - Yes, work is when a force moves an object. When you threw the ball upward, what was the object being moved?
    - the ball
  - What was the force?
    - You tossing the ball up was the applied force.
- Was work done when the ball fell back down after getting as high as it could go?
  - Yes! Work doesn't have to make you sweat. Work is a when a force moves an object. What is the force that moves the ball back down?
    - gravity
- See if you can answer this correctly. Think before you answer: work is a force moving matter. If you push against the wall, is work being done?
  - No, the wall doesn't move. It doesn't matter how hard you are working at pushing it.
- Pretend to shoot a bow and arrow. When is work being done?
  - Work is done when you pull back on the bowstring. You are applying a force that moves the arrow and bowstring back.
  - Then work is done when the string boings forward and moves the arrow forward. That force is a spring force. The bow string has to return to normal, just like if you pushed down on a spring, it has to return to normal when you let go.
- There are other forces at work when you shoot a bow and arrow, but we're going to stop there today.
- By the way, how far is a bowshot away? We don't know for sure. 200 yards (meters) was about the range of a medieval archer. The distance would have been less than that in Abraham's day because distances get farther as the bow improves. There are bows today that can shoot well over 1,000 yards (meters).
- Recall: What is energy? What is work? What is force?
  - the ability to do work
  - force moving an object

- something that affects the motion of an object
    - Explore more: What other forces would affect the flight of an arrow? (gravity, air resistance, friction) Learn more about the physics of a bow and arrow.

V. Social Studies
  - I can understand Ishmael's mocking Isaac and his feast, and I can understand Sarah being upset and wanting Ishmael and Hagar out.
    - For thirteen years Ishmael was Abraham's *heir*, the one who was going to inherit Abraham's wealth and status as the head of the clan.
      - That was to be his *inheritance*, what you receive as an heir to someone who has died.
    - Ishmael was the next *patriarch* in line. Do you know what a patriarch is?
      - the male head of a family or tribe
      - What do you think they call the female head of the family or tribe?
        - That's the *matriarch*.
        - This is off topic, but there are tribes in Africa where women are the rulers. They are matriarchal societies.
  - But not Israel, they are ruled by the patriarchs, and Ishmael was next in line to receive the money, position, and power, and then another baby came along.
    - The guy who was going to be over him was being celebrated because he wasn't a baby any more. (That was the feast we read about yesterday.)
    - What do you think Ishmael was feeling?
      - He was probably jealous at least.
  - The customs of the time were that the rights of the heir went to the firstborn son, no matter who the mother was. Who was Abraham's firstborn son?
    - Ishmael
  - God made it clear to Abraham that the covenant promise He made with Abraham to give him a child was concerning Isaac. God's promise to bless the world through Abraham's descendants was a promise about Isaac.
  - Why do you think Sarah wanted Hagar and Ishmael to leave?
    - Even though she knew God's promise, she also knew the customs of the land and the rights of the firstborn. She wanted Isaac to be firstborn.
    - For thirteen years everyone in the clan saw Ishmael as the heir. It's possible she was worried that they wouldn't change their minds and respect Isaac as the rightful heir.
  - All of this happens before God establishes His law with Moses and the Israelites. There are no official Israelites yet. Later the law becomes that the firstborn son gets a double portion of the others.
    - We will see the rights of the heir play out other times in Genesis. We also see other firstborn sons lose their birthright due to their sin and foolishness.
  - God also often uses the youngest, or who's considered "the least," in His plans. What do you think God might be showing when He chooses someone like David to be king, when he was the youngest of all his brothers?
    - Maybe God's point is that He is the one who "made the man." David became a great king only because God decided it would be so and placed him there.

- The first king of Israel is Saul. He questions why he would be chosen asking, "Am I not a Benjamite, of the smallest of the tribes of Israel, and my family the least of all the families of the tribe of Benjamin?" (1 Samuel 9:21)
    - God doesn't mind defying expectations. I think He enjoys it. But He established laws of the firstborn, and they are important too. We'll see it more as we read Genesis.
    - Recall: What is the person called who is to receive an inheritance? Who is the patriarch in your family? Who is the matriarch?
        - heir
        - probably mom and dad)
    - Explore more: There is a lot in history about heirs. Many heirs have been killed so that others could take the inheritance. You could alternatively learn about patriarchal and matriarchal societies/tribes.

VI. Discussion
    - Ishmael makes fun of Isaac, and Sarah kicks him out of the clan. When have you been made fun of and how did you handle it? How should you handle it?

VII. Writing
    - Use the discussion question as a writing prompt.
    - Get a high five and/or hug if you include a possessive adjective. (my, your, his, her, its, our, their)

Day 80 (Check Materials List)

I. Read Genesis 21:14-21. This begins with the end of yesterday's reading.

II. Memory Verse
   o 2 Peter 3:9
   o The Lord is not slow about His promise, as some count slowness, but is patient toward you, not wishing for any to perish but for all to come to repentance.

III. Language
   o Spelling/Handwriting
      • Test yourselves with the words from Day 76-79.
         ▪ frighten, innocence, prophet, nation
         ▪ womb, wander, thousand, pieces
         ▪ laughter, Isaac, weaned, borne
         ▪ Sarah, listen, die, angel
   o Vocabulary/Grammar
      • Test yourselves with the words from Day 76-79.
         ▪ integrity – the character quality of holding to strong moral principles
         ▪ vindication – being shown innocent of an accusation of wrong doing
         ▪ wean – to gradually get used to not having something you've become dependent on
         ▪ distress – to cause extreme sorrow or worry
   o Hebrew
      • Genesis 1:4 va yar eloHEEM et ha or ki tov va yavDEL eloHEEM ben ha or u ven ha KHOshekh
      • Find the Bets and Alephs in Genesis 1:4. You can find and circle them on the Hebrew Writing 4 page in your workbook.

IV. Science
   o Today we are going to keep learning about force and work. Hagar gets water from a well.
      • What is a force?
         ▪ something that affects the motion of an object
      • What is work?
         ▪ when a force moves an object
   o Wells are made by digging down to the water table underground. A bucket is lowered and lifted back up. When is work done in the process of getting water from a well?
      • Work is done when gravity pulls the bucket down to the water.
      • Work is done when a person uses an applied force to the rope to pull it up.
   o Turn the page and look at the picture of the well. It uses a simple machine to make lifting the bucket easier. Do you remember what simple machine it uses?
      • It uses the wheel and axle. Can you find the wheel and axle in the picture?
         ▪ The axle is the rod across. What happens when you turn the wheel?
            • The rope gets wound around the axle, pulling up the bucket.

- You can make a little well by tying a thread onto a pencil and paper clip, laying it across a cup, and turning the pencil to pull up the paper clip.
  o Simple machines can make work easier by reducing the amount of force needed to move an object.
    - Work is when a force moves an object.
    - We decide how much work was done by figuring how much force is used over how much distance.
    - Pushing a pencil across a table is less work than pushing a desk across the room. Pushing a desk takes more force and the force is being used over a greater distance.

> Pushing a pencil a short distance is less work than pushing a desk a farther distance. It's less force over a smaller distance.

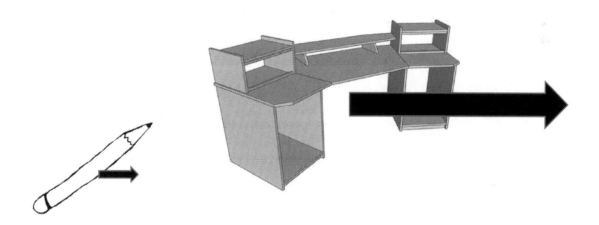

- o The same amount of work can be done when more force is applied over a short distance as when less force is applied over a greater distance.
    - As an inexact example, it could take the same amount of work to push a desk a few centimeters as it takes to push a pencil part way down a street.
    - The math for this is Work = Distance times Force.
    - For instance, if the force was 2 and the distance was 100 for the pencil, work would equal 200.
      - 2 x 100 = 200
    - The same amount of work would be accomplished if the force to move the desk equaled 100 and the distance moved was 2.
      - 100 x 2 = 200
    - The amount of work is equal. Which uses less force?
      - pushing the pencil
      - So you can get the same amount of work down with less force (using less muscle), if you use that force over a longer distance.

using a little force over a big distance ▬▬ the same amount of work as using a big force over a small distance

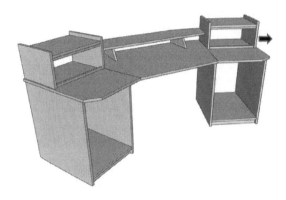

- Now, let's apply that lesson to the well.

o In order to use a well, we have to lift the heavy bucket of water up. If we want to use less force (and make it easier for ourselves), then we have to apply the force over a greater distance. That's where the wheel and axle come in to help.

- o In using a well, if you were just turning the axle by hand, it would be hard. We have to create a greater distance in order to use less force (less muscle). We spread the force out over a greater distance by making a large wheel attached the axle.
  - The larger the wheel, the less force is needed to turn it in order to lift the bucket.
  - If the wheel is six times larger than the axle, it will be six times easier to lift the bucket.
- o Recall: Did you ever notice that truck and bus steering wheels are much bigger than car steering wheels? Why do you think that is?
  - Without understanding it all, you can know that the bigger the wheel, the less force is needed, so the big steering wheel makes it easier for them to turn their large vehicle. (Note to parents: In the age of power steering, this isn't an issue, but they still just make one size steering wheel to fit the vehicle whether it has power steering or not.)
- o Explore more: Learn the formulas for finding force and work. Use them.

V. Social Studies
- o We learned about how being first born gave someone the rights of an heir, but the order we are born can affect more than that.
- o Birth order and its effect on us is a very interesting thing.
  - What's your birth order in the family? What's your birth order among just the other boys or girls among your siblings?
  - Before I begin, this is, in part, just for fun. I call this section of lessons social studies and this information today is truly a study of social behavior, but don't let this lesson define who you are. You can defy expectations, just like God likes to do.
- o How do you think your experience growing up has differed from your siblings?
- o Do you think you are treated differently than you siblings?
  - Let's see why those things might be.
- o How do you think a firstborn's experience is different than a second born or sixth born?
  - First borns get all the attention because there is only one kid. That's not the fault of the parents. It's just the way it is.
  - They might be treated more strictly as parents figure out how to parent.
  - They might have more expectations to speak early, walk early, etc. because the parent has no one else to focus on and is more hyper about making sure their kid is doing well.
- o How do you think that affects the firstborn?
  - They have high expectations put on them and feel responsible for meeting those expectations.
- o What changes when more kids come along?
  - Attention has to be shared. Again, that's not the parents' fault. It's just a fact.
  - Parents might be more relaxed and accept that kids will learn and develop and that they don't need to push to make it happen.
- o Some things to note before you read the birth order descriptions.

- Being born five years or more after a sibling can put you back to being more like a firstborn, though I would think this would be more so if your older sibling were at school and you got the full attention during the day.
  - Also, being the first girl or first boy, even if not the firstborn, is also considered to put you in firstborn position in terms of how it affects you.
  - Being a blended family, having adopted kids, etc., all changes things.
  - Plus, every family is different! These are generalizations. See how they fit you.
- Here are birth order descriptions.
  - First born
    - want to please people
    - leaders (since they were always looked up to by siblings)
    - responsible
    - achievers
    - cautious
  - Middle kids
    - adaptable
    - mediators
    - unique talents (wanting to be different from older siblings)
    - friendly
  - Youngest kids
    - outgoing
    - charmers
    - develop unique skills (wanting to be different from older siblings)
    - uncomplicated
    - fun-loving
  - Only children
    - responsible
    - organized
    - comfortable as the center of attention
    - mature
    - leaders
- Recall: What social study topic did we study today?
  - birth order
- Explore more: I tried to focus on the positive side of birth order. You can look at what struggles each group has. How do you see that in your life? What can you do about it? (You always have a choice. Being born in a certain position in a family doesn't define who you are.)

VI. Discussion
- How do you think birth order has affected you? Do you think the birth order descriptions match you and your family? Why or why not?

VII. Writing
- Choose one of your writings from Days 77-79 to edit.
- Use the editing guidelines and ask someone to edit it as well.
- Create a final draft.
- Save this in your portfolio. Add some math. Write down the books you are reading.

Day 81

I.   Read Genesis 21:22-24.

II. Memory
- Job 19:25
- As for me, I know that my Redeemer lives,
  And at the last He will take His stand on the earth.

III. Language
- Spelling/Handwriting
    - verse 22 (You could substitute "they" for "Abim…army.")
    - words to know: swear, therefore, falsely, army
    - spelling tips:
        - The word <u>swear</u> ends with the word ear.
        - The word <u>therefore</u> ends with an E.
        - The word <u>falsely</u> is what part of speech?
            - adverb
        - How would you write the plural of <u>army</u>?
            - The Y comes after a consonant, so you change the Y into an I and add E-S.
- Vocabulary/Grammar
    - posterity (verse 23)
    - descendants of a person, or all future generations (noun)
        - What adjective describes posterity in the verse?
            - my
        - What type of adjective is the word my?
            - possessive adjective
        - There is a preposition repeated three times in the part of the verse written below. What is it?
            - "that you will not deal falsely with me or with my offspring or with my posterity"
                - with
            - What are the three objects of the preposition with?
                - me, offspring, posterity
            - What part of speech is the word is me?
                - object pronoun
                    - A pronoun replaces a noun. Instead of with Lee, I would say, "With me."
- Hebrew
    - The next letter of the Hebrew alphabet is the Gimmel. (When you say it, gimm begins like "give." The -el is just like in ELoheem.
    - It is the letter for the sound for G. This is what it looks like.

ג ג ג ג ג ג ג ג ג

גאל

The word to the left, "goel," is the kinsman redeemer, as in the story of Ruth. We don't know that last letter (the L sound), but what are the first two letters? (answers: Gimmel, Aleph)

IV. Science
  o Abimelech mentions his offspring, his children. What makes his children uniquely his?
  o Science can tell us what child belongs to which parent. They can look at a child's DNA and can compare it to parent DNA.
  o Have you heard of DNA? Have you seen a picture like this before?

  o This picture shows the shape of DNA. The shape is called a *double helix*. DNA is long strands that look like a twisting ladder.
    • It is found in every cell of our body.
    • If you took all of the DNA in your body and put it end to end, it would reach to the sun and back several times!
  o So what does DNA do?
    • DNA tells each cell what to do. It's the boss. There are over 200 types of cells in our bodies, like the cells that make our skin, and the cells that enable us to see, and the cells in our blood. Each has the same DNA code inside.
    • The DNA copies the right piece of information from itself, making RNA. The RNA delivers itself, the instructions, to the ribosome.
    • The ribosome follows the instructions to build the right kind of protein.
    • The protein has to be built in the right shape with the right chemicals at the right time in order to do its job.
    • The proteins then fulfill their calling, whatever they were designed to do, like maybe grow a new skin cell where you got cut.
    • Let's go over this again.

- The DNA is the boss. It knows what to do.
- The RNA is the messenger. It tells what to do.
- A ribosome is the builder. It builds the workers.
- Proteins are the robot workers; they do the job they were created to do.

- Act out the process or draw a picture of it. The DNA knows what to do and has the information needed. (I need a new skin cell, done just like this.) The RNA takes that message to the ribosome. (Here's the kind of worker we need to build a skin cell.) The ribosome builds the worker. The worker produces the cell.

o DNA is in each and every cell in your body. It's found in the cell's nucleus. What else has a nucleus?
- atoms

o Do you remember how many cells are in your body?
- trillions
- If each cell in your body were as big as a grain of salt, you'd be as big as a tractor trailer!

o Each of those cells has DNA inside. And each of the over 200 types of cells do different jobs in our bodies.

o Humans mostly are the same, so our DNA is about 99.9% the same. Our bodies need to follow the same instructions to live.
- What do you think the .1% of DNA that is different controls in our bodies?
- That's the DNA that tells how we look: the color of our skin, our eyes, our hair, etc.
- That's the part of the DNA that is shared with our parents.

o Each set of instructions from the DNA is called a *gene*. We get the "how we look" genes from our parents.
- The DNA instructions in those first two cells that come together in a mother's womb give the instructions for new cells to be made with that same DNA, so those genes are built into us from the very beginning.
- That DNA instructed more and more cells to be built, in the right place, at the right time, in the right way, to form the perfect you.

o Recall: What shape is DNA? double helix; Where is DNA located? in the nucleus of every cell; What does DNA do? It gives the instructions for what needs to be done in your body.

o Explore more: What do DNA and RNA stand for? What are nucleotides? What do amino acids have to do with ribosomes and proteins?

V. Social Studies

o Along with Abimelech there is Phicol, the commander of his army. What does that mean?
- It basically means that he's in charge.

o Let's start at the top and work our way down. I'm going to do this based on the US Military.

o The army is a branch of the US military. (We won't go into the others today.) What does the army do?

- The army is the branch of the military that fights on land. They fight in wars, but they also do peace-keeping missions, protecting areas of the world.
  - The army has two parts.
    - The regular army, which is all of those who are full-time army workers. At times of war they can be *deployed*, or sent out either to fight or for some other mission.
    - The *army reserves* makes up the rest of the army. These soldiers live at home and work at normal jobs. One weekend a month they have training and a couple of weeks a year they have training. This keeps them prepared in case they are needed in fighting or peacekeeping anywhere in the world.
  - The army is divided into 10 Commands (Unified Combatant Commands).
    - These are areas such as transportation or special operations.
    - They are also areas of the world, such as North and South America.
  - There is a general in charge of each command area.
    - These generals are over a field army, the soldiers assigned to their command area.
  - The field army is divided into corps. Each corps is made up of divisions. Those divisions can have 10,000 soldiers in them! You need at least two divisions to have a corps and at least two corps to have a field army.
    - The divisions are then divided into brigades.
    - And then brigades are separated into battalions of 1,000 soldiers and battalions are separated into companies of 100 soldiers, and companies are separated into platoons of 50 soldiers, and platoons can divided into squads of eight soldiers.
  - Each of those groups has to have a leader.
    - There are 29 ranks in the army, the top rank is the general. Everyone has to listen to him. The bottom rank is a private.
    - The term commander isn't a normal ranking in the US Army today, but in some countries the commander is like the head general over the whole army.
  - In the US, involvement in the army is voluntary; you don't have to do it. The only time that isn't true is when there is a draft, when the government can force the people it chooses to join the military, basically young men. This happens sometimes during times of war. Some people even left America to not get drafted. In many countries there is mandatory military service of six months to two years that men must complete as young adults, and people are always looking for ways to get out of it.
  - Recall: Where does the army fight? What's the top-ranking officer in the army? What are the army reserves? What does it mean to be deployed?
    - on land
    - general
    - People who have normal jobs but train to be ready to fight if needed.
    - sent to fight
  - Explore more: What are you interested to learn?

VI. Discussion
  - Do you think you would ever want to join the army? Why or why not?

VII. Writing
- o Today we are going to practice two possessive adjectives. What are possessive adjectives?
  - They tell us who something belongs to.
- o They are its and their.
  - These are often spelled wrong, so we are going to work on them.
- o Its is spelled wrong often because it sounds like it's, with an apostrophe S.
  - The apostrophe tells us that it's a contraction, that it's short for something. Do you know what I-T-'-S is short for?
    - it is
  - If you are ever unsure of which "its" to use, say the sentence with "it is" to see if that's what you are really trying to say.
  - There are example sentences in your workbook to help you.
- o The word their is often spelled wrong because there are several different ways to spell words that sound like it.
  - T-H-E-I-R is the possessive adjective. That is their house. That is their dog.
  - T-H-E-R-E is the word when you are showing where something is. It's over there. Go hide over there.
  - T-H-E-Y-'-R-E means they are. It's a contraction. They're is short for they are. They're the ones who are going to help us today.
- o Use Writing Sentences 13. Today you are going to fill in the proper form of the words its and their.

Day 82

I.   Read Genesis 21:25-34. Abraham and Abimelech have made an agreement, but...

II.   Memory Verse
- o   Job 19:25
- o   As for me, I know that my Redeemer lives,
     And at the last He will take His stand on the earth.

III.   Language
- o   Spelling/Handwriting
  - •   verse 28
  - •   words to know: ewe (pronounced: yoo), complain, oath, Philistine
  - •   spelling tips:
    - ▪   The word <u>ewe</u> is a palindrome, meaning it's written the same forward and backward.
    - ▪   <u>Complain</u> ends with the word plain as in not fancy. It has the same vowel spelling pattern as rain.
    - ▪   <u>Oath</u> starts with the word oat which has the same vowel spelling pattern as boat.
    - ▪   The word <u>Philistine</u> is a name, so it begins like all names do. The F sound is made with two letters like your spelling words gopher and prophet. The word ends with a silent E like it should say Phil-i-stINE.
- o   Vocabulary/Grammar
  - •   seize (verse 25)
  - •   to take hold of suddenly and forcibly (verb, action verb)
- o   Hebrew
  - •   Can you say Genesis 1:1-2?
    - ▪   be reSHEET baRA eloHEEM et ha shaMAyim ve et ha Arets
    - ▪   ve ha Arets haaTAH TOhu va VOhu ve KHOshekh al pnaa teHOM ve RUakh eloHEEM meraKHEfet al pnaa ha MAyim
  - •   Practice writing the Gimmel in your workbook with Hebrew Writing 5.

IV.   Science
- o   Abraham sets aside seven ewe lambs. What are ewe lambs?
  - •   female baby sheep
  - •   And why do sheep have lambs for babies and not walruses?
- o   The DNA from the parents is in the first two cells that begin the process of forming a baby in the womb. The DNA is replicated in the new baby that forms, giving the baby the appearance of its parents.
- o   So what makes the new baby a ewe instead of a ram, a male sheep. The answer is in the DNA, so let's look at it some more today.
  - •   What does DNA do?
    - ▪   It has the instructions.
    - ▪   What takes the instructions and delivers them?
      - •   RNA, the messenger
      - •   What does the RNA deliver the message to?

- ▪ ribosome, the builder
- ▪ What does the ribosome build?
  - ▪ protein, the worker that builds the cell that's needed
- ○ One of those proteins wraps a piece of DNA around itself. The structure is called a *chromosome*.
- ○ The DNA in the thread of chromosome has hundreds to thousands of sections. Those sections are the instructions. Each complete instruction from the DNA is called a *gene*. The chromosomes carry this gene information and use it to create new cells that are uniquely yours.
  - When new blood cells are formed, your genes (which are a piece of a chromosome which are a piece of DNA) make sure the new cells are of the right blood type for you.
  - When you grow new skin, which you do all the time, the genetic information in the chromosomes make sure it's the right kind and color of skin for you.
- ○ Chromosomes are found in the nucleus of every cell. There are 23 pairs of them, how many chromosomes in all?
  - 46
- ○ So, what makes a lamb a ewe instead of a ram?
  - 22 of the chromosomes are identical to its pair.
  - But there are 23 pairs of chromosomes.
  - One pair can be different. If the chromosomes making up the 23rd pair are identical to each other, then it's a female. (If you are a girl, all of your chromosomes are in identical pairs.)
  - If that last pair is made up of two different types of chromosomes (we call them X and Y), then it's a boy. That one little difference, makes a big difference.
- ○ Speaking of identical, identical twins look identical because they have identical DNA. The original cell split into two, so they were literally created equal. One interesting note, though, they do not have identical fingerprints. Every single human in the world, ever, has a unique fingerprint. So God made a way for even identical twins to be their own unique person.
- ○ Recap: Chromosomes are found in the nucleus of a cell. They are proteins that carry our genetic information, our genes, the information that makes our cells uniquely ours.
- ○ Recall: How many pairs of chromosomes are in humans? What makes a lamb a ewe? What are genes? Where are genes? Where are the chromosomes?
  - 23 (Down Syndrome is when there is an extra chromosome.)
  - All 23 pairs of chromosomes are in identical sets.
  - Each set of instructions from the DNA.
  - They are sections of the chromosomes.
  - in the nucleus of each cell
- ○ Sheep, by the way, have 54 pairs of chromosomes. Peas have 2; hermit crabs have 254.
- ○ Explore more: How do cells replicate? What is the chromosome's part in it?

V. Social Studies
- We read about the commander of the army again. Where does the army fight?
  - on land
- Do you know what the other branches of the military are?
  - air force
  - navy
  - marines
- Here's an easy one. Where does the air force fight?
  - They fly planes and fight from the sky.
  - While planes were used in World War I, their main job was reconnaissance, or spying, looking at what the enemy was doing. They could observe the movements of the troops, the groups of soldiers.
  - In WWII airplanes were very significant in battle. Planes were used for many strategic bombings, carefully planned attacks on specific targets such as factories that built weapons. One bombing raid was carried out by the Doolittle Raiders, a team of planes, led by a man named Doolittle, that hit specific targets in Japan.
    - (Note: Your family might enjoy the missionary biography of Jacob Deshazer, one of the Doolittle Raiders.)
  - The most well known is that the US used planes to drop atomic bombs on Hiroshima and Nagasaki, Japan. Those bombs caused such large-scale death and destruction that the Japanese surrendered and WWII ended.
- Where does the navy fight?
  - in the water
  - The navy uses ships.
  - Naval warfare precedes air warfare simply because boats have been around much longer than airplanes.
    - You can probably picture an old-time sailing ship, with cannons pointing out of the sides.
  - In WWII, one of the most significant naval battles happened as a result of the Doolittle raid. The Japanese retaliated by attacking at Midway, an island in the Pacific Ocean.
    - The Battle at Midway was the first time the Japanese navy had been defeated in nearly 100 years.
    - It occurred between June 4th and 7th in the year 1942.
    - Military historian John Keegan called it "the most stunning and decisive blow in the history of naval warfare." (from Wikipedia, http://en.wikipedia.org/wiki/Battle_of_Midway)
    - US codebreakers, were able to decipher the Japanese plans for attack and US forces were able to set up an ambush.
      - Militaries use codes to sends messages, so the enemy can't get its information and plans.
      - The codebreakers had the job of figuring out what those plans were, and many times they were successful.
    - Having the plans of the Japanese, enabled the US to make a surprise plan of attack.

- The US sunk four the six aircraft carriers used by the Japanese in the Battle of Midway.
  - Aircraft carriers are huge boats that carry planes and have a runway for planes to take off. In this way, the Battle of Midway was fought in the air too.
- Recall: What is one way airplanes were used in WWII? Why are the cities of Hiroshima and Nagasaki significant? What was one of the most significant naval battles of WWII?
  - strategic bombing
  - The US dropped atomic bombs on them, ending WWII.
  - the Battle of Midway
- Explore more: Learn more about Hiroshima and Nagasaki and what happened there.

VI. Discussion
- What's unique about you? What information do you think is in your genes? There are stories about identical twins, separated at birth, who came together as adults and found they had so much in common, not just in how they looked, but in the music and foods they liked, little silly things they both did, etc. So, what do you think your genes say about you? How well do you know yourself? How would you describe yourself (not just in how you look)?

VII. Writing
- Use the discussion question as a writing prompt.
- Get a high five and/or hug if you use any of the vocabulary or spelling words.

Day 83

I. Read Genesis 21:33 - 22:4.

II. Memory Verse
- o Job 19:25
- o As for me, I know that my Redeemer lives,
  And at the last He will take His stand on the earth.

III. Language
- o Spelling/Handwriting
  - • verse 1
  - • words to know: son, said, there, planted
  - • spelling tips:
    - ▪ We have two homophones again today. Make sure you know what word you are spelling when you hear it.
    - ▪ <u>Son</u> is a male child.
    - ▪ <u>Said</u> is a word you just have to memorize. It looks like s-AY-d.
    - ▪ <u>There</u> is over there, talking about a location.
    - ▪ <u>Planted</u> is using plant as a verb in the past tense.
- o Vocabulary/Grammar
  - • offering (verse 3)
  - • a gift, something offered (noun)
    - ▪ What is the adjective describing the noun, offering?
      - • burnt
- o Hebrew
  - • Can you say Genesis 1:3?
    - ▪ va YOmer eloHEEM yeHEE or va yeHEE or
  - • Find and circle the Gimmels on the Hebrew Writing 5 page in your workbook. The verse is Genesis 1:16.
  - • (Note: There are two.)

IV. Science
- o Abraham plants a tamarisk tree.
  - • It's a deciduous tree. What does that mean?
    - ▪ It has leaves; the leaves shed in the fall.
  - • The tamarisk is a tree that God designed to live in desert regions.
- o Do you remember any of the ways the cactus was built for the desert?
  - • It was mostly about water. It had a large stem and scales for holding in more water.
  - • The tamarisk tree also has leaves. Its leaves are very small scales.
  - • Do you remember how scales help desert plants?
    - ▪ They slow evaporation. When you want clothing to dry, you stretch it out in the sun. Scales are folded in to avoid having the sun hit the leaf.
- o Another name for it is the "salt cedar." The tamarisk thrives in *saline* soil, or salt-water soil.

- Its leaves take in salt water and evaporation leaves behind salt on the leaves.
- Thinking about what you know of the area of Israel we've been learning about, why do you think this was a good tree for Abraham to plant?
  - We know that Mount Sodom is a mountain of salt. Probably a lot of the surrounding areas had saline soil.
- How does the salt water get into the leaves?
  - The water and salt are in the soil. It's the tree's roots that first take in the salty water from the soil.
  - Roots mostly grow horizontally, because the top part of the soil has the most oxygen.
    - The system of roots under the soil can be as big as the system of branches in the tree's crown.
    - It needs to be in order to support the tree, and all the kids that climb in it!
  - The water goes up from the roots into the tree trunk which has inside of it a system of tubes that carry the water and minerals from the soil up into the branches and finally to the leaves.
    - The tubes are kind of like drinking straws for the leaves.
  - Back down through the tubes goes sugar from the leaves.
- Where did the sugar come from? That's for another day. But do you know where maple syrup comes from?
  - It comes from the sap of a maple tree. What do you think that sap is?
    - It's the sugar water traveling from the leaves down through the tubes in the tree trunk.
- The tamarisk tree has very small pinkish or white flowers.
  - Since the flowers are so small, there are many of them and they produce lots of seeds, up to 500,000.
  - The seeds in the flowers have a small tuft of hair on the end of them, so they can float far distances through the air or on water.
    - Do you remember what it's called when seeds are scattered?
      - seed dispersal
- Tamarisk seeds germinate very quickly. Do you remember what germination is?
  - It's the early growth of a seed plant.
  - The roots and shoot of a tamarisk tree can poke out within 24 hours, even if it's still floating along on the water and hasn't found a soil home yet.
- Recall: What is saline? What takes the salt water in from the ground? Is a tamarisk tree deciduous or coniferous?
  - salt water
  - the tree's roots
  - deciduous, meaning it has leaves
- Explore more: Learn about the insides of tree trunks.

V. Social Studies
- Abraham planted the tamarisk tree in Beersheba and then was told to go to the land of Moriah. Let's find those places on the map.
- What do you see labeled in white on the Day 73 map?
  - Beersheeba

- Jerusalem - Why Jerusalem? We'll get to that.
  - Again, I didn't place specific dot locations because different maps seem to have it in slightly different locations.
- Both Beersheeba and Jerusalem were in the highlands. What are highlands?
  - an area made up of mountain ranges and plateaus
  - What are plateaus?
    - a flat area at a high elevation
- What is a valley?
  - the low land between highlands (or hills or mountains), typically with a river running through it
- What is in the valley next to the Highlands in Israel?
  - the Dead Sea (the Salt Sea)
- What river runs through the valley and into the Dead Sea?
  - the Jordan River

o Modern day Beersheeba is sometimes known as the capital of the Negev. Where is the Negev?
  - The Negev is a desert area in southern Israel. Abraham traveled there.

o There is, of course, debate over where exactly Abraham went to sacrifice his son. I'll share my favorite.

o God tells Abraham to go to the land of Moriah.

o We know that it takes three days to get there and that he takes servants with him, not something needed if it wasn't a lot of work.
  - Tradition calls the specific place where Abraham bound his son to sacrifice him, Mount Moriah.

o Here's an excerpt describing the history and future of Mount Moriah.

About a thousand years later at this very location, King David bought the threshing floor of Araunah the Jebusite and built an altar to the Lord so that a "plague may be held back from the people" (2 Samuel 24:18, 21). After David's death, his son King Solomon built a glorious temple on the same site. Solomon's temple lasted for over four hundred years until it was destroyed by King Nebuchadnezzar's armies in 587/586 B.C.

Seventy years later the temple was rebuilt on the same site by the Jews who returned to Jerusalem following their Babylon captivity. Around the first century, King Herod made a significant addition to this structure, which then became known as Herod's Temple. It was this temple that Jesus cleansed (John 2:15).

However, in A.D. 70, the Roman armies led by Titus, son of the Emperor Vespasian, once again destroyed the temple. All that remains of the Temple Mount of that era is a portion of a retaining wall known as the "Western Wall" or the "Wailing Wall." It has been a destination for pilgrims and a site of prayer for Jews for many centuries.

The God who first called Abraham to Mount Moriah still has plans for that place. The Bible indicates that a third temple will be built on or near the site of

Solomon's temple (Daniel 9:27). This would seem to present a problem given the political obstacles that stand in the way: the religious activities on the Temple Mount are currently controlled by the Supreme Muslim Council (the Waqf). Yet nothing can put a wrinkle in God's sovereign plans. Thus, Muslim control of this area simply fulfills the prophecy of Luke 21:24 that "Jerusalem will be trampled on by the Gentiles until the times of the Gentiles are fulfilled." (used with permission from http://www.gotquestions.org/mount-Moriah.html#ixzz3OuKPpKkO)

- o Recall: Put it together. Why is Jerusalem on the map?
  - The Bible doesn't give us an exact location for Mount Moriah but some believe that it is the same location that later was used to build the temple in Jerusalem.
- o Explore more: Learn about the Temple Mount and its history.

VI. Discussion
- o Is there anything in your life you feel like you couldn't give up if God asked you to?

VII. Writing
- o Use the discussion question as a writing prompt.
- o Get a high five for any possessive adjectives you can find in your writing today.

Day 84

I. Read Genesis 22:1-5. This is the same story from yesterday with another verse added.

II. Memory Verse
- Job 19:25
- As for me, I know that my Redeemer lives,
And at the last He will take His stand on the earth.

III. Language
- Spelling/Handwriting
  - verse 4
  - words to know: lamb, burnt, worship, knife
  - spelling tips:
    - <u>Lamb</u> has a silent letter at the end of the word, just like the word womb.
    - <u>Burnt</u> does not end in a D.
    - <u>Worship</u> has the word OR inside of it.
    - <u>Knife</u> has a silent letter at the beginning of the word, like the verb, to know.
- Vocabulary/Grammar
  - arose (verse 3)
  - stood up, emerged (action verb)
    - Arose is the past tense of the verb, to arise. We use the past tense when the action happed in the past.
    - What's the past tense of run?
      - ran; Yesterday, I ran home.
    - What's the past tense of eat?
      - ate; We ate chicken noodle soup yesterday.
- Hebrew
  - Can you say Genesis 1:4?
    - va yar eloHEEM et ha or ki tov va yavDEL eloHEEM ben ha or u ven ha KHOshekh
  - Practice writing Gimmel with the Hebrew Writing 6 worksheet. The top line can be skipped. That's for the artists in the family who want to try calligraphy. They can use a felt tip pen or a calligraphy pen to practice. Anything with an angled tip. But again, that's just for the artists who would enjoy such a thing. Everyone else can use the second line and just trace the letters within the lines and then write their own.

IV. Science
- There is a simple machine in today's reading. It's the wedge. Here's a picture.

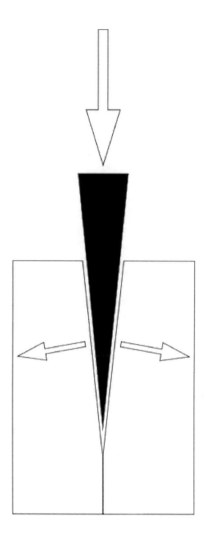

- Can you figure out when a wedge is used in today's reading? It's in verse 3.
  - Abraham splits wood. How do you think he did that?
    - probably with some kind of ax
    - Looking at the picture of the wedge, can you picture that as an ax splitting a log?
- What is a simple machine?
  - It's a tool that makes work easier?
  - What is work?
    - It's when a force moves an object.
    - What's a force?
      - It's something that affects the motion of an object.
- What's one way simple machines make work easier?
  - One way is to lessen the force needed to accomplish the work.
- How does the wedge make work easier? Any ideas?

- The wedge helps us by changing the direction of the force. We apply a downward force with the ax, and the shape of the wedge pushes outward. The direction of the force is changed, pushing the wood out and splitting it.
  - If we just grabbed hold of a log and pulled out on both sides, could we split it?
    - Unlikely! It takes a lot of force.
- What about the sharp edge of the ax? How does that help?
  - Its shape concentrates the force at a point, making it very strong on impact because the force hits in one place instead of being spread out.
- Can you think of what in your home might be a wedge?
  - Some examples are: knives, sewing needles, scissors, doorstops, nails, forks.
  - Are any of those surprising to you? Can you see how they are all wedges?
  - What do they have in common?
    - They all have a point or an edge.
- Recall: How do wedges make work easier? Do you remember how wheels and axles make work easier?
  - The wedge focuses the force in one spot and changes the direction of the force.
  - They spread work needed over a longer distance so less force is required.
- Explore more: Learn about vectors (related to the direction and strength of a force).

V. Social Studies
- Abraham says that they are going to worship on the mountain.
- What was his act of worship going to be?
  - sacrificing his son
  - Actually, the whole thing was an act of worship because he was obeying God's command.
- What do you do to worship God?
  - When we talk about worshiping God today, we mostly mean singing. Let's look at some of the ways people worshiped God in the Bible.
- First, what is worship?
  - It's showing honor and love to God.
  - By that definition how is obedience worship?
    - Jesus said repeatedly that if we loved Him, we would obey Him. Obedience is showing our love for God.
    - It is honoring to obey without arguing or complaining.
- Can you think of other ways people worshiped God in the Bible?
  - There is certainly singing. The biggest book in the Bible is a book of songs that honor God and speak of our love for Him.
  - People bowed down in worship.
  - King David, who wrote most of the songs in the Bible, also danced before the Lord (2 Samuel 6).
  - In the Old Testament there are offerings and sacrifices commanded by God that show honor to God.
    - But one offering was voluntary. It was the offering of thanksgiving.
    - What does it mean that it was voluntary?

- It means that it wasn't required. People only did it when they chose to do it.
- Why do you think it's important that giving thanks is voluntary?
  - It shows that your heart is really thankful if you do it just because you want to.
  - The Bible says that one day everyone will show honor to Jesus and bow before Him, but we can't truly love God unless it's our choice to love Him. You can't be forced to love someone.
- Just like in the Old Testament, giving in the New Testament also shows love to God.
  - Here's a verse from Philippians. This verse is Paul writing to the church in Philippi about the money and gifts they had collected for him.
    - But I have received everything in full and have an abundance; I am amply supplied, having received from Epaphroditus what you have sent, a fragrant aroma, an acceptable sacrifice, well-pleasing to God (Philippians 4:18).
  - Here's another verse. Paul was writing to the church in Corinth about giving.
    - For the ministry of this service is not only fully supplying the needs of the saints, but is also overflowing through many thanksgivings to God (2 Corinthians 9:12).
  - What do these verses say about giving?
    - It's a way to give thanks to God, to sacrifice to God, and to please God.
- Recall: What is worship? What are some ways that God is worshiped in the Bible?
  - showing honor and love to God
  - obedience, singing, dancing, giving
- Explore more: Learn about the different types of offerings in the Old Testament.

VI. Discussion
  - By this definition, do you worship God?
    - *Worship is to honor with extravagant love and extreme submission* (Webster's Dictionary, 1828).

VII. Writing
  - Use the discussion question as a writing prompt.
  - Get a high five and/or hug if you use any of the vocabulary or spelling words.

Day 85

I. Read Genesis 22:5-9. (This is a continuation of the same story. You'll have to stay tuned for the exciting conclusion.)

II. Memory Verse
- o Job 19:25
  - As for me, I know that my Redeemer lives,
    And at the last He will take His stand on the earth.
- o Review last week's memory verse.
  - 2 Peter 3:9 The Lord is not slow about His promise, as some count slowness, but is patient toward you, not wishing for any to perish but for all to come to repentance.

III. Language
- o Spelling/Handwriting
  - Today you can write your memory verse.
  - Test yourselves on the words from Days 81-84.
    - swear, therefore, falsely, army
    - ewe, complain, oath, Philistine
    - son, said, there, planted
    - lamb, burnt, worship, knife
- o Vocabulary/Grammar
  - Test yourselves on the words from Days 81-84.
    - posterity – descendants of a person, or all future generations
    - seize – to take hold of suddenly and forcibly
    - offering – a gift, something offered
    - arose – stood up or emerged
- o Hebrew
  - Can you say Genesis 1:5?
    - va yikRA eloHEEM la or yom ve la KHOshekh kaRA LII-la va yeHEE Erev va yeHEE VOker yom ekHAD
  - Complete Hebrew Writing 7 in your workbook. It's the letters Aleph, Bet and Gimmel.

IV. Science
- o Can you find the wedge in today's reading?
  - Hint: It's in verse 6.
  - knife
- o Isaac says that they have brought along fire. Did they really have a torch with them? I'm not sure, but it sounds like it.
  - Where I lived in Turkey, people do carry around fire. People will get hot coals from someone else to use to get their own fire going. It saves a lot of work and consumes less fuel.
  - Today, we're going to learn about fire and starting a fire.
- o What do you think fire is?
  - Fire is an exothermic reaction between oxygen and a source of fuel.

314

- Let's figure out what exothermic means.
- Do you have thermal underwear, a thermos, or a thermometer in your house? What do those things have in common?
  - The have to do with temperature. The first two keep things warm. Something with "therm" in it has to do with heat.
- Do you remember the word, exoskeleton? What is an exoskeleton?
  - It's when an animal's skeleton is on the outside; it has a hard outer shell.
  - What does exo mean?
    - out or outside
    - What are other "ex" words that have to do with outside?
      - exit, exterior, extraordinary (outside the ordinary)
  - An *exothermic reaction* is one that produces heat; it gives out heat.
- Do you remember what the chemical process of oxidation does?
  - It combines oxygen with other atoms, like hydrogen combining with oxygen to make H_2O. What's that?
    - water
  - Oxidation is what is happening during a fire as well.
- Fires need three things. What are they?
  - Oxygen, energy (which is usually heat), and some source of fuel (what you are going to burn, like wood)
- Abraham arranges the wood for the fire. Why does wood have to be arranged? What should you try to do when you arrange wood for a fire?
  - You need to make sure there is a flow of air so the fire is getting oxygen. If the wood is piled too tightly, there won't be airflow.
- Stacking wood and allowing for oxygen to get in there takes care of two of the ingredients for fire. The hardest to come by is the heat. That's why some people carry fire with them. Once the fire is burning, it produces its own heat to keep the process going.
- What are some ways that fire gets heat to start burning? In other words, how do you light a fire?
  - Matches or flint rocks create an instant burst of heat.
  - They need to be used on fuels that have a lower *combustion* temperature, the temperature that it will start burning at.
    - Combust means burn.
- Usually things like matches are used on small areas. For instance, you light a wick, not the fat candle; you light thin paper or a thin twig, not a log. Why, do you think?
  - Hint: Think about how a wedge helps.
  - It focuses all of the heat energy into one place to get that one place really hot, hot enough to start burning.
- Once combustion takes place, you have a fire. What's combustion?
  - burning
  - Let's look more closely at what's happening when a fire is started.
- When heat, oxygen, and fuel are present, the first thing that needs to happen is to wait for the heat to get hot enough to start the chemical reaction. It can seem like

hard work sometimes to start a fire, if you don't have the right tools, but what would happen if you didn't need a lot of heat to start a fire?

- The world would be on fire all the time! Woods could just catch on fire because there is plenty of wood and oxygen present in the woods.

o Once there is oxygen, fuel, and enough heat, the heat begins to decompose, or break down, the fuel source. That releases gases such as hydrogen, carbon dioxide, oxygen, and nitrogen. What do you think you see those gases as?

- They are in the smoke rising from the fire.
- This is interesting. Two of the gases are hydrogen and oxygen. What happens when they are together? They form water vapor, so water is created by fire! Weird, huh?

o When it gets hot enough to break apart the molecules in the fuel, those molecules combine with the oxygen which causes combustion, burning. What's that process called?

- oxidation

o Why would molecules break apart because of heat?

- The heat energy excites the molecules and gets them moving really fast.

o After wood has burned, what's left?

- You are left with charcoal which is the wood with its gases removed (they've been burned off.) Charcoal is carbon.
- You also have ash. That's what wasn't combustible, the stuff in the wood that wasn't able to be burned.

o Recall: To put out a fire you only have to remove one of the three ingredients. What are they and what are some examples of how you could remove them?

- heat (blowing on the wick of a candle lowers the heat, throwing water on a fire cools it and removes the heat), oxygen (stomping on a fire, covering it, stop/drop/and roll), fuel (turning off the gas on the stove)

o Explore more: Learn and understand the chemical formulas for combustion.

V. Social Studies

o We've talked about some symbols of Jesus in Genesis. Can you remember any of them?

- the ark that saves us from God's wrath
- Melchizedek the high priest
- the bread and the wine as symbols of Jesus' body and blood broken and spilled out for us

o The story that we are in the middle of reading now has many symbols of Jesus.

- Do you recognize any similarities between Isaac and Jesus?
- Here are some:
  - Abraham is offering his only son as a sacrifice.
    - God offered His only son as a sacrifice.
  - Abraham laid the wood that was going to burn Isaac on his back.
    - Jesus was made to carry his own cross to his crucifixion.
  - Abraham says that God will provide the sacrificial lamb.
    - Jesus was the Lamb of God. He was the lamb sacrificed on our behalf. He took the punishment for our sin, which was the death penalty.

- o The Bible isn't made up of isolated stories. The whole thing is the story of God's love for His people and how He is working it out so that they can be with Him forever.
- o Right now we are in the middle of the story. What major events are happening in the world? How do you think God is using those in His grand plan?
- o Explore more: Read the Passion, the story of Christ's crucifixion with the story of Abraham and Isaac in mind.

VI. Discussion
- o God doesn't just work on a large scale. He knows each of us individually.
- o How is God working in your life to bring you to Him or to make you more and more like Jesus?

VII. Writing
- o Choose something you wrote from Days 82-84 to edit.
- o Use your editing guidelines and ask someone else to check it too.
- o Create a final draft.

Day 86

I. Read Genesis 22:9-12.

II. Memory Verse
- o Hebrews 11:1
- o Now faith is the assurance of things hoped for, the conviction of things not seen.

III. Language
- o Spelling
  - • verse 10
  - • words to know: two, wood, stretch, technology (I just chose this one for today.)
  - • spelling tips:
    - ▪ There are two homophones in our spelling list.
      - • The word <u>two</u> is the number two. It's spelled differently than the word you use to go *to* the store. And they are both spelled differently than when you want to go *too.* Today, make sure you can spell all three and know the difference.
      - • The word <u>wood</u> here is the kind we get from trees. It's spelled differently than when we ask, "Would you like to go too?"
    - ▪ The word <u>stretch</u> has three letters making the "CH" sound.
    - ▪ The word <u>technology</u> has a C-H for the "K" sound.
- o Vocabulary
  - • altar (verse 9)
  - • an elevated surface where religious rites are performed, especially the offering of sacrifices (noun)
  - • The word altar has a homophone that's a verb. To alter something is spelled with an E-R and means to change something.
- o Hebrew
  - • Review Genesis 1:1.
    - ▪ be reSHEET baRA eloHEEM et ha shaMAyim ve et ha Arets
  - • The next letter of the alphabet is the Dalet.
  - • It makes the sound of our D. This is what it looks like.

ㄒ ㄒ ㄒ ㄱ ㄱ ㄱ ㄱ ㄱ

  - • What two letters can you recognize in the word below?
    - ▪ The first letter (on the right) is the D, Dalet. The second letter is the V sound, Bet without the dot. The last we haven't learned yet, the R.
    - ▪ The word is devar and it means word.

IV. Science

- ○ We talked before about shelter and its importance for survival. We can look at another survival skill today, how to start a fire.
    - • What are the three things necessary for a fire?
        - ▪ heat (energy), fuel, oxygen
    - • If you were in the woods, what types of things would you look for for fuel?
    - • When you start a fire, you usually use different kinds of fuel. It's good to choose different sizes of things. A log is good for burning for a longer time, but it's not easy to get burning. A leaf or thin twig is easier to get burning, but it won't burn for long.
        - ▪ It's also good to look for dry things, otherwise the heat energy will be used in evaporation before it can be used to start a fire.
        - ▪ If you are stuck in a wet area, you can look around for drier parts of trees. Start with a very, very small fire and keep your next size small pieces nearby to be dried out from the heat. You can a build a fire this way, little by little, adding on small pieces at a time until you have a fire going.
    - • That's fuel. To ensure oxygen you need to lightly pack your fuel. Start with the smallest and driest materials. Build a nest-like bundle of dried grasses, leaves and small twigs. Above it build a teepee of kindling, small branches. Once your fire is going, you can add on bigger kindling and then logs that will keep your fire going for a longer time.

    - • Now the hard part, the heat source. If you have matches or a lighter, you're good to go. Another tool is a flint and steel set. Flint creates a spark when struck by metal.
    - • Here are some methods you could use to start a fire in an emergency, an emergency, not for fun. A fire is not a toy to play with.
        - ▪ The most primitive method would be to spin a stick in a piece of wood. The rubbing produces heat which can start your fire. You make

a notch in a piece of wood and put a small piece of twig in the hole. Over it place your stick which you spin between your hands to make it rub fast enough.

- This is a hard method to use.

- Another method involves metal and batteries. The easiest metal to use would be steel wool, but you can use metal paper clips and even a metallic gum wrapper.
  - The metal is rubbed against a battery (the part that makes the connection). A 9-volt battery is a good kind to use, and you could use your cell phone battery.
- A final method involves sun light. The sun's energy warms us, right? Focusing that energy produces enough heat energy to start a fire.
  - You just need the sun and something that will focus the light. Some things that can be used are glasses, magnifying lenses, mirrors, cans, and water.
  - The goal for all of them is to direct the sunlight to a small point. Just like the wedge focuses all of the force on an edge making it more effective, a lens or mirror focuses all of the heat energy from the sun into one small point. All the heat concentrates in one spot, and it gets hotter and hotter, making it effective for starting a fire.
  - Prepare a small nest of *tinder* (small, dry things that will easily combust or burn).
  - Aim the sunlight at the tinder using your lens or mirror. You'll have to move to find the best distance.
    - The bottom of a can can be used as a mirror by shining it. You can shine it with things like sand or toothpaste, even chocolate can work.
    - Water can be used in something like a clear plastic bag. Fill the bag with some water. Tie it off into a ball.
    - In frozen conditions, you could even use ice as your water in a clear container to focus the sun's rays.
- What are some things that you think you should be careful of when starting a fire?
  - Be careful not to burn yourself. Work away from yourself, such as when you are striking a flint.
  - Be sure to have a contained area to build your fire. You can build a wall of rocks around your fire to contain it in one area. A strong wind can spread your fire to nearby combustible materials, things that can burn easily. It's wrong to build a fire outside on a windy day in hot, dry weather. Why?
    - Dry things catch fire more easily and the wind can spread a spark, the heat needed to start a fire going.
  - Gasoline is highly combustible and is dangerous around any kind of fire.
  - And make sure you know how you would put it out before you light it.

- o Recall: What are good choices for tinder? Why is stacking kindling like a teepee a good idea? What are some ways to produce heat? What are some fire safety tips?
  - dry, small (leaves, grass, twigs)
  - It allows for oxygen flow.
  - rubbing, metal and batteries, sunlight
  - Know how to put out a fire. Keep fire away from materials that catch fire easily (especially gas). Make sure your fire is contained.
- o Explore more: Can you describe how a lens works to concentrate the light? Learn more about lenses if not. You can also explore why batteries can produce heat.

V. Social Studies
- o The angel of the Lord says to Abraham that he knows that Abraham fears God, Abraham proved it by his willingness to sacrifice his only son.
- o What is the fear of the Lord?
  - Here are some verses about the fear of the Lord.
    - The fear of the Lord is the beginning of wisdom (Psalm 111:10a).
    - The fear of the LORD is the beginning of knowledge; Fools despise wisdom and instruction (Proverbs 1:7a).
    - The fear of the LORD is to hate evil (Proverbs 8:13a).
    - Let all the earth fear the LORD; Let all the inhabitants of the world stand in awe of Him (Psalm 33:8).
    - The fear of the LORD is a fountain of life, that one may avoid the snares of death (Proverbs 14:27).
  - What is the fear of the Lord?
    - It's to be in awe of God; it's hating evil; it's life; it's the beginning of knowledge and wisdom.
      - You can't even begin to have true knowledge and wisdom without the fear of the Lord.
    - What should you do in order to fear God?
      - Recognize how great God.
      - Recognize we must say no to evil in our lives.
      - Recognize God is holy and perfect and commands us to be perfect (Matthew 5:48).
      - Recognize we can't be perfect without God's help.
  - What are advantages of fearing God?
    - We've already read that life, knowledge, and wisdom are benefits. What do these verses say about it?
    - Do not fear those who kill the body but are unable to kill the soul; but rather fear Him who is able to destroy both soul and body in hell (Matthew 10:28).
    - The secret of the LORD is for those who fear Him, and He will make them know His covenant (Psalm 25:14).
    - His mercy extends to those who fear him, from generation to generation (Luke 1:50 NIV).
    - These verses all say that life is ours through the fear of the Lord. We can be shown mercy and saved from hell and also receive God's

friendship. He will reveal Himself to those who fear Him. If you want to know God, fearing Him is the first step.

- o Recall: What is the fear of the Lord? Why is it important?
  - Maybe a definition could be: understanding how great and perfect God is and how not great and not perfect you are.
  - It saves us from sin, death, and hell.
- o Explore more: Where in the Bible do people show the fear of the Lord? (eg. Moses, Joshua...) What are the consequences? Where in the Bible do people not show the fear of the Lord? (eg. Achan, Pharaoh...) What are the consequences?

VI. Discussion

- o Do you have the fear of the Lord? Why or why not? How is it demonstrated in your life? Or how does your life demonstrate your lack of the fear of the Lord?

VII. Writing

- o Genesis 22:9 Then they came to the place of which God had told him; and Abraham built the altar there and arranged the wood, and bound his son Isaac and <u>laid</u> him on the altar, on top of the wood.
- o Today we're going to look at the correct use of lay and lie.
  - You lie down to go to sleep, but you lay a book on the table.
    - There are a couple of ways to tell which one to use.
    - One is by their definitions.
      - To lie means to recline.
      - To lay means to put or place.
    - Another difference between the two is that to lay takes an object. You lay something down; you put something down. That something is the direct object.
- o Try these examples.
  - I'm going to go lie/lay down.
    - LIE
    - You could say, "I'm going to recline."
  - I'll lie/lay the keys here for when you need them.
    - LAY
    - You could say, "I'll put the keys here."
- o Complete Writing Sentences 14 in your workbook.
  - Think: Does it mean recline or put? Try to use the word "put" in the sentence.
  - Get a high five and/or hug if you underline the direct objects in the "lay" sentences. Ask, "Lay what?"

Day 87

I. Read Genesis 22:13-14.

II. Memory Verse
- o Hebrews 11:1
- o Now faith is the assurance of things hoped for, the conviction of things not seen.

III. Language
- o Spelling/Handwriting
  - verse 14
  - words to know: thicket, caught, provide, mount
  - spelling tips:
    - The word <u>thicket</u> starts with the word thick and ends like your spelling word prophet.
    - The word <u>caught</u> rhymes with bought, but it is spelled with an A instead of an O.
    - The word <u>provide</u> ends with a silent E. Say and spell the syllables.
    - The word <u>mount</u> has the same spelling pattern as your spelling words mountains and account.
- o Vocabulary/Grammar
  - thicket (verse 13)
  - a dense group of shrubs, bushes or small trees (noun)
  - What does dense mean? Remember what density is?
    - Density is how much stuff is in a place.
    - If something is dense, then there is a lot of "stuff" in it.
  - There are three prepositions and prepositional phrases in this part of verse 13 shown below.
    - "behind him a ram caught in the thicket by his horns"
    - What are the three prepositional phrases?
      - behind him, in the thicket, by his horns
    - What are the three prepositions?
      - behind, in, by
    - What are the three objects of the prepositions?
      - him, thicket, horns
- o Hebrew
  - Review Genesis 1:2.
    - ve ha Arets haaTAH TOhu va VOhu ve KHOshekh al pnaa teHOM ve RUakh eloHEEM meraKHEfet al pnaa ha MAyim
  - Trace the Dalet on the Hebrew Writing 8 page in your workbook.

IV. Science
- o In today's story we have a ram caught in a thicket.
- o What is a ram?
  - It's a male sheep.
- o What do you remember about sheep?
  - They are mammals.

- They follow each other blindly, meaning without thinking. They will just go with the flock wherever, even if it's into danger.
- They have terrific peripheral vision. What does that mean?
  - Peripheral vision is all that you can see to the side without turning your head. In fact, sheep's peripheral vision is so great that they can see behind them.
- What do you remember about mammals?
  - warm blooded (Their body temperature stays the same no matter what environment they are in.)
  - have hair
  - give birth to babies instead of laying eggs
  - moms give milk to their babies
- What else do you know about sheep? What about their hair?
  - Their hair is wool. Those who raise sheep cut off the wool once a year in the spring. Cutting off a sheep's hair is called *shearing*.
- Let's learn a little about wool. Do you know how wool gets from a sheep's back to your back in the form of a sweater?
  - After shearing, the wool is washed and washed and then picked over to clean out sticks and leaves and seeds that might be stuck in the sheep's wool. What is that an example of, a seed getting caught in an animal's hair and getting carried around?
    - seed dispersal
  - Wool is then carded, kind of like being combed. It can be done by hand or by machine. Here is a picture of a carding machine.

  - Some of the rollers have combs that clean and fluff the wool. It enters on the left and is received into a trough on the right, which you can't really see.
  - What simple machine is at work in the carding machine picture, over and over again?

- You can see the wheel and axle at work. The wheels are the rollers. The axles are the poles that stick out on the end.
  - Can you find at least a dozen?
- After the carding, you have fluffy wool to be spun.
  - Wool fibers are basically spun into what you know as yarn. It can be done by just hanging a weight from the fibers and giving it a spin, but here is a machine that does the job much faster, the spinning wheel.
  - Looking at the picture, how do you think it might work? What simple machine do you see?

- This uses a wheel and axle. It looks like she is using her feet to push that log which spins the wheel. The strip around the wheel reaches up and over the small axles, the rods coming out to the right in the picture at the top of the wheel. She's holding the fibers in her left hand. The fibers are attached to those rods and are being spun tightly around the rods.
  - How much of the fiber is "fed" to the spinning wheel at once will determine how thick your yarn will be.
    - Thread is also spun in this way.

- If you have yarn at home, pick it apart to see how it's really fibers spun together.
  - Before we stop for today, what inside the sheep determines whether it is a ram or a ewe?
    - The chromosomes make the determination. (In females all the chromosomes are the same.)
    - What do the chromosomes carry?
      - They carry our genes, the DNA instructions, the genetic information that makes each of us unique.
  - Recall: What's it called when sheep's wool is cut off? What simple machine is used in processing wool into yarn?
    - shearing
    - wheel and axle
  - Explore more: Learn more about the process of processing wool, or build your own spinning machine with a weighted spool.

V. Social Studies
  - Today we're going to talk about some history involving spinning thread, in particular the Lowell Mills of Massachusetts.
    - It is believed the first spinning wheels were in use in the 11th century AD. What years would that have been?
      - 1001-1100
    - While the spinning wheel got more refined over the decades, the biggest change to the process was the Industrial Revolution.
  - The *Industrial Revolution* was a change in the function of society as technology changed the way people lived. This took place first in England and then spread throughout Europe and North America during the last half of the 18th century and the first half of the 19th century. What years are those?
    - 1751 – 1850
    - New machines allowed large-scale production of products. People moved from their farmland to the cities to get jobs in the newly built factories.
    - Employers no longer needed skilled workers that had mastered their trade. They just needed people who could perform a small simple task, over and over again. Because of this, children were often employed because they could be paid less than a man. Women also could be paid less than men.
  - One place this change was seen was in Boston, Massachusetts where a man named Francis Lowell built a *textile*, or fabric, factory. By 1850 Lowell had 10 textile factories that employed 10,000 people, a third of Boston's population. (If those 100 balloons were everyone living in Boston, 33 of them would have worked for the mill.)
    - They were called Lowell Mills. They spun cotton into thread. Their machines were fed by cotton picked by slaves in the south.
    - Many argued that the workers at the mill were not better off.
      - Children were given school in the evenings, but after working twelve hours they were too tired to stay awake for lessons.
      - At least seventy-five percent of the workers were women and were called the Lowell Mill Girls. They were paid half the wages of a man.

326

- As factories grew and grew and grew, technology advanced. The workers were expected to work faster and at more machines. It could be dangerous work, working too quickly near the fast spinning machines, especially when you were exhausted from fourteen hours of work. If your hair got caught in a spinning spool of thread, you could be scalped!
- The workers got fed up with the life they were forced into by the rich bosses who controlled their lives.
    - The women formed a *union*, an organized group of workers that fights for their rights.
    - It was the first women's union.
    - The Lowell Mill Girls' union worked to fight long hours and low wages.
        - One thing they did was to organize *strikes*, where they got as many people as possible to stop working until the bosses met their demands.
- The children of Lowell didn't have a union that I know of, but they had others fighting for them.
    - A photographer named Lewis Hine took pictures of child workers to expose the harsh conditions they lived under.
    - In the 19th century, new laws were introduced to limit the number of hours factory employees could work and restrictions on child labor were put into place.
- Here is one of Lewis Hine's Lowell Mill Girls picture. The girl in the picture is twelve.

- Recall: What was the industrial revolution? When was the industrial revolution? How were the Lowell Mills a part of creating laws to protect workers? What was one technique they used to fight unfair treatment?
    - a time when technology changed society, moving people from an agricultural existence, to living and working in cities because factories were being built and employed a lot of people

- around the turn of the 19th century (last half of the 18th century and the first half of the 19th century)
- The Lowell Mill Girls formed the first women's union to fight how they were treated and the children were photographed to expose how they were being used by their profiteering bosses.
  - strikes
  - Explore more: Read about labor laws in the early part of the 19th century. How were they changing because of the Industrial Revolution?

VI. Discussion

- What part would you have played if you lived during the Industrial Revolution? Big boss and factory owner, mill worker, inventor of the new machinery, union director planning strikes, would you still be a farmer?

VII. Writing

- Use the discussion question as a writing prompt.
- Get a high five or a hug for every prepositional phrase you find in your writing.

Day 88

I. Read Genesis 22:15-19.

II. Memory Verse
- o Hebrews 11:1
- o Now faith is the assurance of things hoped for, the conviction of things not seen.

III. Language
- o Spelling/handwriting
  - verse 15
  - words to know: declare, Abraham, second, seashore
  - spelling tips:
    - Declare ends with a silent E to make the A sound.
    - Abraham is a name so it begins with a capital letter.
    - Second ends like pond.
    - Seashore is a compound word, which means it's two words put together into one. What two words is it made up of?
- o Vocabulary
  - declare (verse 16)
  - to state clearly, to make known publicly (verb)
- o Hebrew
  - Review Genesis 1:3.
    - va YOmer eloHEEM yeHEE or va yeHEE or
  - Find the Dalet in Genesis 1:4-5 on the Hebrew Writing 8 page. Start with verse five. Which word would have a D sound in it? Find it and then look for the same letter in verse four. There is one in each verse, but there are other similar looking letters.
    - Genesis 1:4 va yar eloHEEM et ha or ki tov va yavDEL eloHEEM ben ha or u ven ha KHOshekh
    - Genesis 1:5 va yikRA eloHEEM la or yom ve la KHOshekh kaRA LII-la va yeHEE Erev va yeHEE VOker yom ekHAD

IV. Science
- o Abraham's descendants are going to number as the stars and as the sand. That's what we're going to talk about today, stars and sand.
- o What do you remember about stars?
  - The sun is a star and it gives us light and heat.
  - They don't move.
  - They form constellations.
- o Do you have an idea about what stars are made of?
  - They are burning balls of gas. They don't just sit there. The gases heat and rise and cool and fall. There are constant explosions on the stars. (That's what gas and heat do together, produce explosions.)
  - Stars are made up of the elements, just like everything else in the physical world.

- They are about seventy-five percent hydrogen and twenty-five percent helium. If you held up four fingers, that would be three fingers of hydrogen and one finger of helium. Which gas is there more of?
  - hydrogen
  - There can be a small mix of other gases and materials present in the star as well.
- Find hydrogen and helium on the periodic table. What do you notice?
  - They are numbers 1 and 2. What does that mean?
  - They are the two lightest elements. They have the fewest protons and electrons.
- How many protons does helium have?
  - two
- How many electrons does helium have?
  - two
- How many neutrons does helium have?
  - $4 - 2 = 2$
- Where are the protons and neutrons in the atom?
  - in its nucleus
- Where are the electrons?
  - They orbit around the nucleus.
- Are electrons or protons the positively charged particles?
  - Protons are positive. (If you are "pro" something, you are positive about it. ☺)

o Now what about sand. How would you describe sand? What do you think it is?
- Sand is mostly rocks. Here's a picture of some sand under a microscope.

- Actually, sand can have lots of shapes and colors because it's made from lots of different types of rocks and other materials, such as small pieces of shells.

o So if sand is really small rocks, where do you think it comes from?
- Sand is created by erosion. Do you remember what erosion is?
  - Erosion is the gradual wearing away of land.
  - Rivers erode river banks and carry along little pieces of rock in them. Rocks are rolled along and worn down and deposited along the way. That's why riverbanks can be sandy.

- Ocean waves wear away at rocks and carry along bits that break off and deposit them elsewhere.
- Water in the ocean is always moving, and so it's always wearing away at the rock on the ocean floor.
- The sand on beaches and on riverbanks doesn't stay put. It gets moved around by the water in its environment.
- If rivers and oceans cause erosion that produces sand, why are deserts full of sand?
  - Of course, the first answer is because God made it so, but the second answer is erosion.
  - Water isn't the only way erosion occurs. Can you think of anything else that might cause erosion?
    - What happens to an eraser when you use it?
      - You rub and rub and pieces of it come off. It's being eroded in its own way.
    - What might cause rubbing in the desert?
  - Wind causes erosion in the desert. The rock is slowly worn away.
    - Wind carries off rocks that are small enough to be moved by wind.
    - Those rocks land and bang into rocks that stayed in place, chipping away at them.
    - Any tiny bits that break off can then be carried by the wind to chip away at other rocks.
- Recall: What are stars? balls of burning gas; What are stars made of? mostly hydrogen and then helium; What creates sand? God ☺ and erosion; What are two ways that erosion occurs? water and wind
- Explore more: What interests you stars or sand? Learn about how the hydrogen and helium interact in stars or more about what's in sand and where it comes from.

V. Social Studies
- Abraham is told that all of the nations of the earth will be blessed because of his obedience. What are all the nations of the earth?
  - The number of official countries changes, so I couldn't even tell them all to you if I wanted to.
- Today you are going to learn some of the nations of the world. Learn the names and locations of the countries marked on the map for Day 88.
- On Day 90 you will have to locate these in on a map along with the Middle East countries we've talked about before.
- Explore more: If these countries are too easy for you, you can add more to your map to learn. The same goes for Day 89.

VI. Discussion
- Abraham is told that all the nations of the earth will be blessed because of his obedience.
- Did you ever think your obedience could make world-wide impact? It can! How does knowing that change your thoughts towards obedience in the little things?
  - This reminds me of a story of a teenager who was kind to Japanese prisoners of war. Her parents had been missionaries who were killed by Japanese

soldiers in WWII. She visited the prisoners and brought them gifts to show them love. She knew her parents would have wanted her to forgive them and to love them.

- A famous Japanese war hero found out about her and what she had done and it set him off investigating Christianity. He became an evangelist in Japan, leading thousands to Christ. It started with a teenager's obedience to love and forgive.
- This story is from the biography of Jacob Deshazer that I mentioned before. He was one of the Doolittle Raiders.

VII. Writing
- o Use your discussion question as a writing prompt.
- o Get a high five and/or hug if you use the word declare in your writing today.

Day 89

I. Read Genesis 22:20-24.

II. Memory Verse
- Hebrews 11:1
- Now faith is the assurance of things hoped for, the conviction of things not seen.

III. Language
- Spelling/handwriting
  - verse 20
  - words to know: eight, child/children, sensational, tremendous (I just chose these last two.)
  - spelling tips:
    - The word <u>eight</u> is another homophone. What are the two kinds of "eights?"
      - eight the number
      - ate, like eating
      - Today you are spelling the number eight, with an I-G-H in the middle.
    - The word <u>children</u> is an irregular plural. Plurals are words that indicate more than one.
      - A regular plural is when the word follows the rules, like just add an S or ES.
      - I'll give you some words with irregular plurals and you see if you know what they are.
        - man (men)
        - goose (geese)
        - mouse (mice)
        - sheep (sheep)
        - deer (deer)
        - person (people)
        - knife (knives)
        - loaf (loaves)
        - cactus (cacti)
        - That last one was kind of a trick.
      - The word <u>sensational</u> should be spelled by syllables. The "shun" is spelled in the most common way.
      - The word <u>tremendous</u> starts like tree with its first three letters and its last three letters are just like in righteous.
- Vocabulary/Grammar
  - omniscient
  - all knowing

- o Hebrew
  - Review Genesis 1:4.
    - va yar eloHEEM et ha or ki tov va yavDEL eloHEEM ben ha or u ven ha KHOshekh
  - Trace and write Dalet on the Hebrew Writing 9 page.

IV. Science

- o We have another list of family today.
- o We're going to talk about DNA some more and genetics, those genes carried around in our chromosomes that make each of us uniquely us.
  - Today we're going to talk about my favorite part of genetics. On Day 90 we'll practice it.
  - We get our genes, our genetic makeup, from our parents. But why then aren't you identical to your siblings? Let's find out.
- o We've learned that a person's genes come from their parents. You get genes from your mom and from your dad. Their genes came from their parents, and so you are also getting parts of your grandparents' genes.
  - You couldn't have all of your dad's genes and all of your mom's genes. You only need one set, and so what you get is a combination. The different combinations of those genes make you unique from your siblings.
- o Here's how it works. It was first understood by a monk named Gregor Mendel. We call it Mendelian genetics. He researched genetics in the second half of the 19th century? What years are those?
  - 1851 to 1900
- o He observed the regularity in how traits of what we look like were passed down from parent to children. Mendel noticed this not just in humans but in "parent" plants and "baby" plants.
  - If pollen from a white flower, landed on a purple flower, the distinct genes from those two flowers would make up the genes of a new flower. Some baby flowers from these parents would be purple and some would be white, but it wouldn't be half and half. We're going to look at what in our genes shows which trait from our parents will be in us.
- o I'm using the word, *trait*; it's a distinguishing characteristic. You might have brown eyes. That's a trait. You might be stubborn. That's a trait.
  - For each of those unique things that make people different from one another we carry two pieces of information in our genes.
    - Our bodies do a lot of things in pairs!
    - From those two bits, a child gets one from the mother and one from the father.
      - One half of the gene that gives eye color comes from the mother and one half of the gene that gives eye color comes from the father.
      - It's that way for all of our genetic information that gives us our unique look, personality, and inherited abilities.
      - On the following page there is a picture of how this genetic information gets passed along.

- We use capital letters and lowercase letters to show the two parts of the genetic information for both the mom and the dad.
- You can see that there are four possible ways to combine the two pieces of information from both parents. There are four different outcomes possible in their children, for that one trait.
  - This happens for every single trait, not just hair color but hair texture and hair thickness, etc., so that there are many, many, many overall combinations of how all the traits could come together.
- Look at the chart. Each parent flower's gene for color has two parts, shown by the uppercase and lowercase Bs.
- Each box shows what gene combination from the mom and dad was received. It's shown by the two Bs and by the picture.
- Make observations. What's different about the genetic information that makes the one flower different?

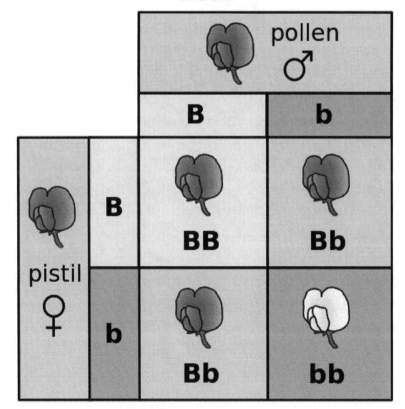

- The white flower has two lowercase letters. All of the others have an uppercase letter.
  - We call the uppercase letter the *dominant* trait. It dominates. It's the most powerful and influential. If it's present, that trait is what you will get.

- The lowercase letter represents the *recessive* trait. It occurs more rarely because both pieces of genetic information have to be the same.
  - We will continue with trait charts on Day 90.
  - Recall: What letter represents the dominant trait? the capital letter; If the dominant trait is present in the gene, what happens? That trait will be present in the flower or the person or whatever.
  - Explore more: Learn about Mendel.

V. Social Studies
  - We are going to continue to study the nations. Learn the locations of some more countries on the map for Day 89.
  - Also practice the locations of the map from Day 88 and also the Middle East map from Social Studies Review 10.
  - On Day 90 you will be quizzed. (Don't memorize number locations because I will change the numbers! Learn the country names for the given locations.)

VI. Discussion
  - Where do you get your physical traits from? Whose eyes do you have? Whose nose? Whose hair?

VII. Writing
  - Use the discussion question as a writing prompt.
  - Get a high five and/or hug if you can use a vocabulary word or spelling word that you've learned.
  - My first essay in college was during a placement test. My essay was called "My Father's Nose." I think we had to write about someone influential in our lives, and I wrote about ways I was like my father. I placed out of two required writing courses based on that essay. I followed the five paragraph structure. I had a point and supported it with three paragraphs that each had a main topic sentence and then details. How you write matters! Always do your best!

Day 90

I. Read Genesis 23:1-2.

II. Memory Verse
- o Hebrews 11:1
- o Now faith is the assurance of things hoped for, the conviction of things not seen.
- o Review last week's memory verse.
  - • Job 19:25
  - • As for me, I know that my Redeemer lives,
    And at the last He will take His stand on the earth.

III. Language
- o Spelling/handwriting
  - • Today you can write your memory verse.
  - • Test yourselves on the words from Days 86-89.
    - ▪ two, stretch, against, wood
    - ▪ thicket, caught, provide, mount
    - ▪ declare, Abraham, second, seashore
    - ▪ eight, knives, sensational, tremendous
- o Vocabulary
  - • Test yourselves on the words from Days 86-89.
    - ▪ altar – an elevated surface where religious rites are performed, especially the offering of sacrifices
    - ▪ thicket – a dense group of shrubs, bushes or small trees
    - ▪ declare – to state clearly, to make known publicly
    - ▪ omniscient – all knowing
- o Hebrew
  - • Review Genesis 1:5.
    - ▪ va yikRA eloHEEM la or yom ve la KHOshekh kaRA LII-la va yeHEE Erev va yeHEE VOker yom ekHAD
  - • Trace the words on the Hebrew Writing 10 page. They are the words I used to introduce the new letters, so there are two letters on the page you haven't learned yet.

IV. Science
- o Today we're going to continue with how our genes determine our traits, our characteristics, the things that make each of us unique.
- o What is DNA's job?
  - • DNA is the boss of each cell. He gives the instructions.
- o What is RNA?
  - • RNA is the messenger.
- o Who gets the message?
  - • ribosome
- o What does ribosome do?
  - • He's the builder. He builds the protein, the robot worker.
- o The protein does his job, the one specific job he was built to do.

- o Chromosomes are long strips of DNA. Do you remember what DNA looks like?
  - • double helix shape
  - • Where are chromosomes?
    - ▪ They are tightly wound up in the nucleus of the cell (every human cell with a nucleus).
- o Genes are what we called each segment of the DNA.
  - • Genes are the instructions the DNA gives out. The RNA is actually a copy of the gene. It copies the gene, the instruction, and delivers it.
- o Each gene has at least two variations. For instance, there are two genes that control eye color. One gene says either brown or blue, and one gene gives the instructions for either blue or green. Your eye color is the result of which of the two variations of each of those genes your instructions carry.
  - • You can also remember that dominant genes are at work as well. If there is the brown-eyes gene present, then your eyes will have brown coloring, even if there is a blue-eye-color gene present as well.
  - • Genetics is very complex. There are billions and billions of people on the earth and each one is different. Even something as seemingly simple as eye color scientists don't fully understand how the genetics work beyond the basics.
- o Let's do one example of genetics at work. We'll do more during the review week.
- o Use the Science Review 12 page to determine the genetic makeup of your new, pet dog.
  - • (Note: Below are notes for the parent. Don't read them out loud.)
  - • They will first design a mom and a dad dog.
  - • Then they will choose randomly odd or even.
  - • Then you can explain to them what traits their puppy will have using the guidelines below.
  - • For the trait that they chose odd for, the mom trait chosen will be the dominant trait. For the traits that they chose even for, what was chosen for the dad will be the dominant trait.
    - ▪ As an example, for ears, if they chose long for dad and short for mom, and they chose "odd," then mom's trait, the short ears will be what the baby has.
- o Explore more: Make a chart for eye color showing the dominant and recessive traits and possible outcomes.

V. Social Studies
- o Complete Social Studies Review 11. There are three maps.

VI. Discussion
- o What personality traits have you gotten from your parents or grandparents? Do you laugh like your mother? Can you build things like your grandfather?

VII. Writing
- o Choose one of your writings from Days 87-89 to edit.
- o Use your checklists and ask someone else to edit it as well.
- o Make a final draft.

Day 91

I. Read Genesis 23:3-11.

II. Memory Verse
- o John 11:25
- o Jesus said to her, "I am the resurrection and the life; he who believes in Me will live even if he dies."

III. Language
- o Spelling/handwriting
  - verse 11
  - words to know: mourn, burial, burying, approach
  - Spelling tips:
    - The word <u>mourn</u> has the same vowel combination as mount.
    - The word <u>burial</u> has three vowels and no Es.
    - The word <u>burying</u> starts just like burial.
    - The word <u>approach</u> is the words app and roach put together. There is a double letter.
- o Vocabulary
  - Review: sojourn (a temporary stay somewhere)
  - Then what's a sojourner? (verse 4) (someone who temporarily stays somewhere)
  - mourn (verse 2)
  - to feel deeply saddened about a loss
- o Hebrew
  - Your new Hebrew letter is Hei.

 The word on the left is vohu from Genesis 1:2. Do you see the V sound at the beginning of the word (on the right)? That's the Bet without a dot sounding like a V. You may have noticed that the last letter is making the U vowel sound. It's not a separate vowel letter of the alphabet. That dot is added to the letter to turn it into the U sound. We haven't gotten to that letter yet.

IV. Science
- o Abraham is wanting to buy a cave. We read before about Lot and his daughters hiding out in a cave.
- o How are caves formed inside of mountains? It's related to something we've already learned about. What do you think?
  - Caves can form in different ways, but they are basically made by erosion. Can you think of any ways that erosion could form caves?

- Waves can pound away at a rock, and water (along with gritty sand) can erode away in cracks until the cracks become caves.
  - Wind can do the same thing, carry along gritty sand that wears away in already existent cracks, until eventually there is a cave.
- Most caves or caverns are formed near the water table. Some rock can be dissolved by the groundwater. Many caves are made of a rock called limestone because it can be dissolved. Water can just eat away at it to open up caves.
- Why does Mount Sodom have caves? (hint: What is it made of?)
  - It's made of salt and salt dissolves in water. Little by little exposure to water wears away at the mountain. Water gets into cracks and opens it up more and more.
- Water can also create caves inside of *glaciers*, which are like floating ice mountains. Since there is water flowing around glaciers, water can wear away at it.
- What do you know about volcanoes?
  - *Lava*, which is hot, melted, liquid rock, flows out of an opening in the earth's crust. What happens to the lava once it is outside and no longer near its heat source?
    - It cools. What happens to a liquid when it cools enough?
      - It forms a solid.
- Lava cools and hardens into rock.
  - If there is a lot of lava, the lava on the outside, touching the air, cools and hardens first, but there could be a layer of still flowing lava under it, which rushes through and out, leaving a cave opening.
  - One final note on caves. One feature that caves are famous for are stalactites and stalagmites. Stalactites, with a T, are on Top. And stalagmites, with a G, are on the Ground. Take a look at the picture.

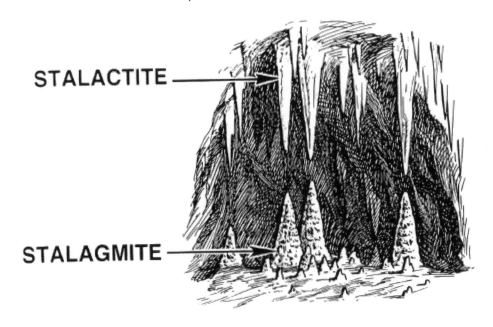

STALACTITE

STALAGMITE

- o These cave features are mostly formed with water as well. Maybe you've seen an icicle hanging outside of your house. How did it get there?
  - They are formed by dripping water. But it's so cold outside, that the water freezes before it can fall to the ground.
  - Another drip of water comes along and starts rolling down the icicle, but again, freezes before the drip falls off.
  - Drip by drip the icicle gets bigger.
- o How do you think this happens in rock caves to form a rock that hangs like an icicle?
  - In caves where the rock dissolves, drips of water get in through cracks and dissolve some of the rock as it makes its way through. The sediment, the little bits of rock and things that are in the water, is left behind as it drips from the ceiling of the cave or when it drops to the cave floor. Little by little the sediment deposits build up.
- o Recall: How does water create caves? It creates caves through erosion. It can batter away at a rock or dissolve it. How can lava form a cave? When the lava on top hits the air and cools, lava underneath can keep running, leaving a tunnel inside the rock. What are glaciers? large hunks of floating ice; How are stalagmites formed? when water carrying sediment drips to the ground over and over again in the same spot
- o Explore more: Learn about limestone stalactites and stalagmites. What does carbon dioxide have to do with them?

V. Social Studies
- o Today I am going to write about mourning. There are personal ways that we mourn, how we feel and express our sadness at a loss, but there are also cultural expressions of mourning.
- o How are people supposed to mourn in your country? How are people supposed to act at a funeral when someone dies?
  - Are people expected to cry?
  - Are people expected to wear black?
- o Christians sometimes call funerals "homegoing celebrations" and may wear "happy" colors instead of the traditional black. It's still normal to be sad and cry, even if you know someone is in heaven. And, it's okay not to cry.
- o In many cultures there are different traditions for mourning.
  - Among the Roma we lived with in Macedonia, they had different cultural ideas about mourning. Roma are better known as Gypsies.
    - For the first twenty-four hours professional mourners were hired. Their job was to wail, loudly, so everyone knows how much the person was loved. (It doesn't make any sense to me, but it does to them.)
    - They also had special ceremonies on the 7th, 40th and 52nd day after the person died where people gathered and were fed and a Muslim leader read a long poem, Mevlit, praising the Prophet Mohammed.
  - In Ghana, in Africa, they throw parties to celebrate the person who died. People eat, drink, and dance the night away. People donate money to the family of the deceased.
  - In Europe there are some cultures that expect a widow to mourn by wearing black, even for the rest of her life, or for at least two years.

- In many cultures black is the color of mourning, and it is customary to bring food to the family in mourning.
- In Turkey people are expected to bring sweets to the family and stay and sit with them.
- In both Hinduism and Islam, it's considered wrong to be excessive in showing grief. They think it will bother the dead person.
  - In America we collectively show that we are mourning by hanging the American flag at half-mast.
  - Recall: What are some differences in ways people morn? celebrating and hiring professional wailers
  - Explore more: Learn about burial practices around the world.

VI. Discussion
  - Have you ever mourned the loss of someone or something? Was there anything or anyone who helped you through it?

VII. Writing
  - We've talked a little bit about past tense. It's when things happened before. Some verbs have a regular past tense. How would you say these verbs happened yesterday?
    - kick (kicked)
    - play (played)
    - tickle (tickled)
    - cry (cried)
  - Those are regular past tense verbs. What about some irregular ones. How would you say you did these things yesterday?
    - throw (threw)
    - drink (drank)
    - sing (sang)
    - read (read) They are spelled the same!
    - sweep (swept)
  - Last week we worked on lay verses lie. What about those in the past tense. This is crazy. Ready?
    - lay (laid)
    - lie (lay)
      - He just lay there all day yesterday.
      - It sounds weird because people say it incorrectly all the time.
  - Complete Writing Sentences 15 in your workbook and fill in the correct past tense of the word.

Day 92

I. Read Genesis 23:12-16.

II. Memory Verse
- o John 11:25
- o Jesus said to her, "I am the resurrection and the life; he who believes in Me will live even if he dies."

III. Language
- o Spelling/handwriting
  - verse 12
  - spelling tips:
    - The word <u>sight</u> uses the I-G-H spelling pattern. It is also another homophone. This is the type of sight that talks about seeing, not a web site.
    - The word <u>answer</u> has a silent letter.
    - The word <u>price</u> has a C for the S sound.
    - The word <u>people</u> has an unusual letter in the middle. You just have to learn that it's there.
- o Vocabulary
  - commercial (verse 16)
  - intended for profit (adjective)
- o Hebrew
  - Can you say Genesis 1:1-5? (You can find it on the Hebrew page in the back of this book.)
  - Trace Hei on the Hebrew Writing 11 page in your workbook.

IV. Science
- o Silver is weighed out as a measure, "commercial standard." That means there is a standard weight used in selling.
- o When my family lived in Istanbul, we had a bazaar set up on our street every Sunday. Poles held up tarps for blocks and two rows of wooden tables lined the two sides of the street. There were clothes and school supplies for sale, but the majority of the bazaar sold food. Some things were sold by item, for instance six TL (Turkish Lira) for one tub of butter, but mostly, food was sold by weight.
  - You would ask for a kilogram of apples or whatever you wanted to buy. Some would give you a bag and you would choose your own. Others would choose for you. Always look for the booths where you can choose your own!
  - They would put your apples on the one side of the balance scale.

- They would put their commercial standard weight on the other side of the balance.
  - Weights could be for a half kilo, or for one or two kilos. A kilo is short for kilogram. It's a little more than two pounds.
- Then there are two types of sellers.
  - One would throw in an extra apple to tip the scale in your favor. The heavier side will be lower than the other. They didn't want to wait for the scale to be perfectly balanced, but they made sure you got your money's worth.
  - The other type of seller would work really hard to balance the scale. They would take out the big, beautiful apple that you chose carefully, and they would grab a smaller bruised one and throw it in to balance the scale out. They wanted to make sure you didn't get more than you paid for.
  - Watching the balances always make me think of Bible verses like this one.
    - A false balance is an abomination to the LORD, but a just weight is His delight (Proverbs 11:1).
    - What do you think is a "just" weight or balance?
      - It's one that measures accurately.
      - If they chipped a little off of their weight, then it would weigh less and you wouldn't get as much as you were paying for. I'm sure people have through the years thought of many ways to cheat.
- In science we use the metric form of measurement: kilograms and meters, not pounds and yards. I'll show you why.

10 millimeters = 1 centimeter

10 centimeters = 1 decimeter

10 decimeters = 1 meter

1000 meters = 1 kilometer

COMPARE

1 inch is made up of 16 parts
12 inches = 1 foot
3 feet = 1 yard
1,760 yards = 1 mile

It's not hard to see why the first is much better when you have to do calculations. It's logical and orderly and full of zeros to make it easy to do the math.

Here are the metric weights.

10 milligrams = 1 centigram
10 centigrams = 1 decigram
10 decigram = 1 gram
1000 grams = 1 kilogram

- We will do a worksheet to practice using metric weights during next week's review.
- Recall: What tool is used in weighing? a scale or balance scale; What's the word for the measurement that equals 1000 meters? kilometer; What weighs 1000 grams? kilogram
- Explore more: Build a balance scale. Hint: If you can't figure out a stand, it can be hung.

V. Social Studies
- There's another experience that's common at the bazaar. It's *haggling*, discussing the price to try to get the best deal for yourself.
- There's a conversation between Abraham and Ephron. They don't haggle. Abraham says he will give the price of the land. Ephron tells him it's 400 shekels of silver. Ephron makes it sound like it's nothing, "What is that between me and you?" Abraham doesn't argue the price, but he pays the 400 shekel weight in silver.
    - The word shekel is related to the Hebrew word for weighing.
    - We think of a shekel as a currency. It was eventually a standard coin, but at first it was a weight.
        - To pay 400 shekels of silver, you put 400 shekels, the weight, on one side of the balance. On the other side of the scale you would put as much silver as was needed to balance the scale.
- If I was ever offered a price by a smooth talker like Ephron, I would have haggled. In many parts of the Middle East, it is expected. You aren't told the "real" price. They expect you to make a lower offer. In some places the tourist books will tell you to offer one third of the price you were told. So if they said 30 dollars, you would say 10. They would say 25. You would say 15. Then you could agree on 20.
    - It's not that simple of course. You go back and forth. They say what great quality it is. You say you can get it cheaper elsewhere. They say it's beautiful. You say there are others just like it.
- Sometimes they will be staunch on their price and then you have to decide if you want to pay it. Sometimes you will get the lower price and they will look defeated!
    - This reminds me of another Bible verse.

- Proverbs 20:14 says: "Bad, bad," says the buyer, but when he goes his way, then he boasts.
    - What happened in this verse?
        - The buyer haggled. They said it was of poor quality and got a better price. But then he bragged on what a good deal he got.
        - It is fun to walk away from haggling with a good price!
- In America we don't haggle much, but it still happens. We make deals if we are going to be buying a lot of something in order to get the best price. The seller gets guaranteed business out of the deal.
- Another time it happens in America is with buying cars. Some places advertise that the price is clearly marked and there is no haggling. It can be stressful to haggle and no fun to wonder if you are getting cheated by the seller.
- One problem with haggling is that the sellers judge you by your appearance and decide how much you should pay. Whenever we are told the price in euros, instead of the local currency, we always walk away. They judged us as tourists and thought they could get more money from us.
    - In fact walking away is always a good haggling technique. Show them you are willing to walk away. They will lose the sale if you do. Delaying is another tactic. If they see you are unsure, they will lower the cost to help you decide to buy.
        - That's a trick you can use on websites. On some sites, if you click to close the page, it will offer you a discount. It's the same principle at work.
- Recall: What does it mean to haggle? to argue the price of something to try to get the better deal (or just a fair deal)
- Explore more: Read about haggling practices around the world.

VI. Discussion
- What type of seller would you be? Making sure it's even or tipping the scale in favor of the other person?

VII. Writing
- Use the discussion question as a writing prompt.

Day 93

I. Read Genesis 23:17-20.

II. Memory Verse
- ○ John 11:25
- ○ Jesus said to her, "I am the resurrection and the life; he who believes in Me will live even if he dies."

III. Language
- ○ Handwriting/Spelling
  - • verse 15
  - • words to know: confines, worth, four, weigh (some words are from the previous reading)
  - • spelling tips:
    - ▪ Fourth was an earlier word.
    - ▪ The word four is a homophone. Today you are spelling the number four.
    - ▪ The word weigh is another homophone. You are spelling the word that tells how much gravity is pulling down on your mass, how much you weigh. Not the path you should take.
- ○ Vocabulary
  - • approach (verse 23:8)
  - • to come near, or to speak to someone about something for the first time (verb)
  - • How is the word used in verse 8? (The second definition.)
  - • Approach could also be a noun. My approach to schooling is different than yours. Approach can mean a way of doing things.
- ○ Hebrew
  - • Find the letter Hei in Genesis 1:2-3. Circle them in the verses on your Hebrew Writing 11 page in your workbook.
  - • I found 11. There are similar looking letters. Look closely. (There are more H's in the transliteration of the Hebrew than in the Hebrew because they are combined with K to make KH, which is one sound and one letter in Hebrew.

IV. Science
- ○ Today we're going to learn about the biome of fields. Do you remember the word biome? Do you remember what it means?
  - • A biome is the broad characteristic of a major habitat, such as mountains are a biome and forests are a biome and fresh water is a biome.
  - • Do you remember what a habitat is?
    - ▪ It's the home of a plant or animal.
- ○ Abraham's in a field, so we're going to look at fields as a habitat.
  - • I don't know what Abraham's field was like, specifically.
  - • We've already looked at the desert as a biome. Today we'll look at grasslands as a biome.
  - • Grasslands get a medium amount of precipitation. What's precipitation?

- rain or snow (or sleet or hail)
- Grasslands get more rain than a desert, which enables the grass to grow, but they get less rain than a forest, which keeps trees from growing there.
- Israel is semi-arid land. Arid means dry, so semi-arid means partly dry. Around the country it gets between 10 to 70 centimeters of rain each year (about 4 inches to 2 feet).

○ Fields are a type of grassland, the major biome. What do you know about fields or grasslands?
- Obviously, they have grass.
- Because they are in between forests and deserts in the amount of rainfall they receive, they are often between forests and deserts. Grasslands often border deserts.
- There is grassland on every continent except Antarctica.
- Grasslands are used for farming, so in some areas, there is not much free, wild grassland.
- What animals live in the grasslands depends on where in the world you are. There could be zebras and lions and cheetahs and elephants if you are on the African *savannah*. Or foxes and prairie dogs and mice and skunks and deer in the American *prairies*. Grasslands have different names depending on where in the world you are.
  - Historically, bison ruled the prairies of America. They were hunted for food and for sport (just for fun) by those traveling west on the Oregon Trail. Bison roamed in huge herds making target practice easy. It's estimated that more than 20 million once roamed free in America. Now it's estimated that there are only 5,000 living in the wild in America. There are others in protected herds to keep them from dying out. (Note: If your little kids think 5,000 is a lot, then you can explain that means that for every 1 buffalo we have now in the wild there used to be 4,000. You can pretend that everyone in the room is a bison. That's how it is today in America. Before there would have 16,000 of you in the room – if there are four of you. Multipy how many people by 4 and add "thousand.")
  - Along with those animals are hundreds of bird, bug and plant species.

○ One striking event in the grasslands is fires during the dry season. They can be started on purpose by man, but lightening can also start fires in the grasslands. It's a part of the life cycle of the grasslands.
- Fires clear away crowding plants and make room for plants to grow when the wet season comes in the grasslands.
- I told you that the roots of a tree are often just as big as the system of branches at the top of the tree. In prairie plants the roots can be even bigger than the plant is tall.
  - Some grasslands are known as short-grass prairies. Others are known for their long grass, even up to 11 feet tall!
  - Sometimes two-thirds of the plant is underground. (If you hold up three fingers and they were the parts of the plant, two of your fingers would be the roots and the other finger would be what you saw

above ground.) Their strong root system keeps the prairie alive through fires and harsh winters.

- o Recall: What are the grasslands in Africa called? savannah What are the grasslands in America called? the prairie; How does the amount of precipitation that falls determine the area of the grasslands? less rainfall would make a desert, more rainfall would make a forest; Name animals on the savannah and on the prairie. answers will vary (zebras, elephants, lions…foxes, mice, deer…)
- o Explore more: Learn about the flora of the grasslands.

V. Social Studies

- o I told you how the savannah is the name of the grasslands in Africa and the prairie is the name of the grasslands in America. People living in grasslands are away from urban, city centers. What type of lifestyle do you think people have who live on the grasslands?
  - In some areas they are farmers. In some areas they are herders, living off of animals such as cows.
- o There are some other famous grassland areas in the world named the Pampas and the Steppes.
  - The Pampas are in Argentina and Uruguay in South America. You can find them on the Day 20 South America map.
  - The Steppes stretch across Asia and Europe. We'll look at maps of this area today.
  - Grasslands are usually found between forests and what?
    - deserts
  - Parts of the Eurasian Steppe were part of a famous trade route. Why do you think the steppes would make a good route for travelers who wanted to sell and buy goods?
    - Grasslands, like the Steppes, made for easier travel than forests or deserts.
  - Take a look at the maps for Day 93. The blue routes are the water routes for traders. We talked before how traders used rivers as highways. The red lines are what is known as the Silk Road.
    - You can see the Himalaya Mountains on the second map. The trade route had to make it past the highest obstacle in the world. You can also see a desert right in the path of the route.
    - Although the Steppes can have fierce winter winds, it still provided a better travel alternative to the desert or the mountains.
- o During the Han Dynasty in China, the Silk Road was established. It happened about a century before the time of Anno Domini, the year of Christ's birth according to the calendar.
  - Silk was a product of China. For a long time they kept the secret of how the fabric was made. Traders took it west from China all the way to Turkey.
- o The Silk Road developed over time. It wasn't just one road. Several branches developed. And silk wasn't the only thing traded on the route, but it was a startling new material for those who encountered it in the west.

- o The Silk Road not only enabled the trade of goods to previously disconnected areas but also enabled the trade of ideas. It opened up the way for religions to spread. It allowed Buddhism to spread from India to China. Contact was being made between cultures in new ways.
- o The Silk Road was at its prime in the mid-8th century AD. Around what year would that be?
  - • 750 AD
- o Recall: What is the name of the long strip of grasslands across Asia and Europe that enabled trade to be carried out over land? the Steppes; Why is The Silk Road remembered? It enabled the exchange of goods and ideas over previously disconnected areas.
- o Explore More: There were several factors in the decline of the use of The Silk Road by around 1400 AD.
  - • The Ming Dynasty, newly ruling in China, cut themselves off from the outside. Islam was growing and Islamic leaders rejected trade from some regions. There was no longer any dominant ruler and the area became fragmented.
  - • Learn about the Han and Ming dynasties.

VI. Discussion
- o What is it like where you live? How would you describe your habitat?

VII. Writing
- o Use the discussion question as a writing prompt.
- o Get a high five and/or hug for cheerfully completing your writing.

Day 94

I. Read Genesis 25:1-11. (We're skipping the next story but will come back to it.)

II. Memory Verse
- o John 11:25
- o Jesus said to her, "I am the resurrection and the life; he who believes in Me will live even if he dies."

III. Language
- o Spelling/handwriting
  - verse 12
  - words to know: satisfied, hundred, commercial, standard (some from the previous readings on Abraham buying the field and cave)
  - spelling tip:
    - The word <u>satisfied</u> starts with sat and is. Satisfy ends with a consonant Y. What needs to happen to add the ED?
    - Hundredth was an earlier word, so <u>hundred</u> should be easy.
    - The ending of the word <u>commercial</u> starts with a C.
    - Pronounce <u>standARd</u> with an exaggerated ending to remember how it is spelled.
- o Vocabulary
  - I chose today's word from the story of Abraham buying the field for 400 shekels of silver, commercial standard.
  - standard (adjective)
    - accepted as normal
  - standard (noun)
    - something used as a measure to compare other things against
    - a level of quality
  - Because the word can be used as a noun and an adjective you could say, "The standard standard." Would the first or the second "standard" be the adjective?
    - the first
- o Hebrew
  - Say Genesis 1:1-5.
  - Trace and write the letter Hei on the Hebrew Writing 12 worksheet.

IV. Science
- o We're going to use the story of Abraham buying the field and cave for today's lesson.
- o Abraham pays for the field with silver. Look for silver on your periodic table. If you need a hint, it's in a group, which are the columns, with other metals used for payment. Some refer to this group as the coin metals.
  - It's just above gold on the chart and just under copper, both metals used as coins in history.
  - Silver is number 47 on the periodic table. What is its symbol?
    - Ag; It comes from the Latin, *argentum,* which just means *silver.*

- Silver, like the other metals, is mined from the earth. It is dug up and found inside rock.
- Like gold it is a malleable metal, you can bend and shape it.
- It can be melted and poured into molds.
  - The *melting point* is the temperature at which a solid turns to a liquid.
  - Silver's melting point is 961.78 °C, 1763.2 °F.
  - Did you notice how precise it is? Every metal has a melting point. Every mineral has a melting point. *Minerals* are the natural substances that make up what we call rock.
  - Do you remember that lava is melted rock?
    - The name of the melted rock under the earth's crust is *magma*. It's called molten rock or semi-molten rock.
      - *Molten* just means that it's reached its melting point. Molten rock is liquefied rock. Semi-molten rock is rock that is starting to liquefy. It's moving like a really thick liquid.
    - Under the earth's crust is the *mantle* and it's made up of magma.
      - The mantle is the thickest layer of the earth. It is around 1800 miles (2900 kilometers) deep.
- Here's an image of the layers of the earth. Maybe you'd like to build your own model with clay.

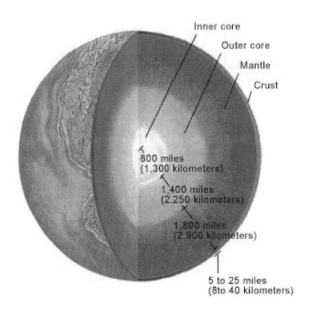

- "The inner core is in the centre and is the hottest part of the Earth. It is solid and made up of iron and nickel with temperatures of up to 5,500°C. With its immense heat energy, the inner core is like the engine room of the Earth. The outer core is the layer surrounding the inner core. It is a liquid layer, also made up of iron and nickel. It is still extremely hot, with temperatures similar

352

to the inner core." (from
http://www.bbc.co.uk/schools/gcsebitesize/geography/natural_hazards/tectonic_plates_rev1.shtml)

- o (Note: A really astute student will see there seems to be a problem with one core being liquid and one being solid. We'll explain that on Day 98.)
- o Recall: Define magma, molten and mantle.
- o Explore: There are layers to the mantle that behave differently. What are they? Do you remember the word viscosity? What does it have to do with the mantle?

V. Social Studies

- o You learned about the word commercial and how it's related to profit, to buying and selling. We looked at a commercial trade route, the Silk Road. We looked at the bazaar marketplace and the practice of haggling. I wanted to look a little at the history of commerce.
    - We believe we saw commerce in the ancient boat picture from Mesopotamia. The rivers were used as highways to transport goods.
    - We looked at the commercial standard, the weight that decided how much you paid of a certain metal, such as the coin metals like silver and gold and copper.
    - How do you think people paid for goods before there was a "commercial standard?"
        - People bartered for things. *Bartering* is trading. You make a deal. If you'll give me that, I'll give you this.
- o Can you think of reasons why coins and then paper money are preferable?
    - I can think of a few reasons. For one, it set a standard of how much things are worth.
    - Maybe you are a leather worker, and you want a basket, but the basket maker doesn't want any leather. It made trade easier because everyone wanted what you had, money.
    - And also it was easier. Carrying around money is easier than hauling around an animal or 50 pounds of fruit or something!
- o And speaking of easier, that's how paper money began, with a desire to make things easier.
    - Paper money was first used in the Tang Dynasty in China, at the height of the Silk Road in the 7th century. It was an IOU, meaning the person held onto the paper and then could trade it in for the metal coins later. It was the metal coins that had value.
        - Now our money is not backed by precious metals. It's backed by a guarantee by the government. It's worth something just because we've decided it's worth something.
    - Here's an image of ancient copper Chinese coins. Why do you think paper money would be easier?

- What if you were buying something very big and expensive? Those coins could get really heavy.
- The hole in the coin served two purposes from what I understand.
  - They were lined up on a square rod that would hold them in place so the edges could be sanded smooth.
  - Then the coins were threaded onto a string for easy carrying.
- This reminds me of the women in the Muslim areas of the world I've lived in. The woman is given gold when she marries. It's hers. Her husband is not allowed to ask her to sell it. She will wear it at all times. Some of it is in the shape of a small coin that is pinned on.
  - Recall: Who first used paper money? the Chinese; How did people buy before money? bartering; What are some reasons why money is preferable? standard, easier to carry around, wanted/accepted by everyone
  - Explore more: Read about the history of money.

VI. Discussion
- The Bible says that the love of money is the root of all sorts of evils (1 Timothy 6:10). What kinds of evil do you think comes out of the love of money? Do you ever find yourself loving money? How you can combat that to keep from falling into evil?

VII. Writing
- Use the discussion question as a writing prompt.
- Get a high five and/or hug if you do your writing cheerfully.

Day 95

I. Read Genesis 25:12-26.

II. Memory Verse
- John 11:25
  - Jesus said to her, "I am the resurrection and the life; he who believes in Me will live even if he dies."
- Review last week's memory verse.
  - Hebrews 11:1
  - Now faith is the assurance of things hoped for, the conviction of things not seen.

III. Language
- Spelling/handwriting
  - Today you can write your memory verse.
  - Test yourselves on the words from Days 91-94.
  - mourn, burial, burying, approach
  - sight, answer, price, people
  - confines, worth, four, weigh
  - satisfied, hundred, commercial, standard
- Vocabulary
  - Test yourselves on the words from Days 91-94.
  - sojourner, mourn, approach, commercial, standard
- Hebrew
  - Use the Hebrew Writing 13 page of your workbook.
    - In Genesis 1:1-5 find all of the letters you have learned so far.
    - Aleph, Bet, Gimmel, Dalet, Hei

IV. Social Studies (We're doing a double social studies lesson today.)
- Abraham's home town is Ur. It's a city in southern Mesopotamia. The area is the oldest urban center of the world.
  - Where is Mesopotamia?
    - You can find it on the maps for Day 16.
    - What rivers is it between?
      - the Euphrates and the Tigris
  - What does urban mean?
    - city
  - What was the time period called when technology moved Americans and Europeans from agricultural society to an urban society?
    - the Industrial Revolution
  - We're not looking at that today. That happened around the turn of the 18th century AD. Today's lesson is from around the 20th century BC.
    - What does BC stand for?
      - before Christ
    - What year is the last year of the 20th century mark BC?
      - 2000

- In BC, because we are counting down, the 20th century is 2100 to 2000. In AD it's the opposite because we're counting opposite, but it's still true that the last year of the 20th century AD is also the year 2000.

o We're going back in time today to before Abraham. Abraham started out in Ur. You can look at the Day 47 map to find Ur.

- Ur was a city in Sumer, which covered that whole area across the rivers and to the Persian Gulf. What modern day country is that area? (Look at the map for Day 16 if you need help.)
  - Iraq

o Ancient Sumer is the oldest urban center.

o Sumerians developed city-states, which were cities and their surrounding areas each ruled by their own governments.

- The city was walled off and centered around a temple. Priests of whatever gods they worshipped held considerable power and were the most educated.
- The outlying areas around the walled city were farming areas that supplied the city with food.
- The set up created the first ruling, elite classes of people.
- Ur was one of the city-states.

o The Sumerians are maybe most famous for their writing system, called *cuneiform*. They wrote by making marks in a wet clay tablet. It would then be dried and would harden.

- Writing began out of necessity. They could track commerce, the buying and selling of things.

o Their writing system changed over time.

- It began with numbers, using a system of 10s like we have today.
- It also began as written from top to bottom in columns. It used pictures as symbols for words.

- Later it switched to being written from left to right and phonetic letters were added, symbols for sounds, like a modern alphabet where the symbol D makes the sound "duh."
  - It developed into a way to keep records.
    - We can read in the Sumerian script about the creation of man and about the great flood and about the time when languages were confused.
    - Tablets with fragments of this story date back to 2000 BC. (date from http://www.icr.org/article/noah-flood-gilgamesh/)
  - Recall: What is the name of the writing system developed by the Sumerians? cuneiform; What modern-day country occupies the land of the ancient Sumerians? Iraq; What time period are we looking at today? around 2000 BC

V. Social Studies continued
  - We know Abraham lived around the year 2000 BC. (I date him as being born in 1918 BC.) The city of Ur is where he lived until God sent him out to the land of Canaan. Here's a bit of history from this period.

    > Sumerian civilization revived, including rule in the city of Ur by a king called Ur-Nammu, who, around the year 2050, created the first known code of laws. Ur-Nammu created retribution and punishment in the form of fines, superseding the justice of an eye for an eye and tooth for a tooth. He was described as having removed the "grabbers" of the citizen's oxen, sheep and donkeys, as having established laws that guarded an orphan or widow from anyone who might wish to exploit them, and as having guarded the poor from the rich.
    > (from http://www.fsmitha.com/h1/ch03.htm)

  - Who created one of the earliest codes of law?
    - Hammurabi, and he comes into the area soon.
  - The Sumerians are attacked by the Elamites and the Amorites in 1950 BC.
    - Is 1950 BC come later or before 2050 BC?
      - later, BC is a countdown until Christ's birth.
  - Genesis 10:22 tells that Elam, the father of the Elamites, was the son of Shem.
    - Do you know who Shem was?
      - a son of Noah
    - The Day 50 map shows the kingdom of Elam at one point.
    - Genesis 10:15-16 says that the Amorites were descendants of Canaan.
      - Canaan was the son of Ham. Who was Ham?
        - another son of Noah
    - Amos 2:9 (God speaking) Yet it was I who destroyed the Amorite before them, though his height was like the height of cedars and he was strong as the oaks; I even destroyed his fruit above and his root below.
    - Always remember, history is full of real people. These are descendants of Noah. These are contemporaries of Abraham (meaning they lived at the same time). These aren't just stories. This was real life for real people.
  - In the 18th century BC, in the 1700s BC, there was a king of the Amorites named...Hammurabi.
    - He conquered the neighboring cities and brought them under his control instead of each having its own government. They paid taxes to him, and he offered protection.

- He ruled from the Persian Gulf to Haran. Find that on the Day 47 map of Abraham's travels.
- He ruled from his capital city, Babylon.
- Hammurabi built roads and canals, waterways. Easier transportation enabled him to more easily connect and rule over the various cities. It also enabled the development of a postal system, which means he made a way for mail to be delivered.
- And of course he's credited with building what engineering feat in Babylon?
  - the hanging gardens of Babylon
- Not all of his progress was positive.
  - He established class distinctions, declaring certain people more important than others. He is famous for his laws, but he divided his laws so that different classes of people were treated differently.
  - There were the nobles, the merchants, the farmers, and the slaves. The law treated them each different.
  - The nobles were the ruling class. The merchants were the sellers and traders.
- Recall: What people were the first to develop urban living? Sumerians; Who ruled after the Sumerians? Amorites; What famous king united the city-states under one ruler? Hammurabi; In what area did all this take place? Mesopotamia
- Explore more: Learn more about Sumer and Sumerians.

VI. Discussion

- What do you think are the greatest accomplishments of your current president? What do you think are the greatest accomplishments of any leader of your country? What are some of the worst decisions of the current leader? What is one of the worst decisions of all time of any president from your country?

VII. Writing

- Choose one of your writings from Days 92-94 to edit.
- Use your editing guidelines and ask someone to edit your work as well.
- Create a final draft.

Day 96 (check Materials List)

I. Read Genesis 25:27-26:5.

II. Memory Verse
- o Review Joshua 24:15.
  - • [If it is disagreeable in your sight to serve the LORD,] choose for yourselves today whom you will serve: [whether the gods which your fathers served which were beyond the River, or the gods of the Amorites in whose land you are living;] but as for me and my house, we will serve the LORD.
- o Say Genesis 1:1 from memory.
  - • In the beginning God created the heavens and the earth.

III. Language
- o Spelling
  - • Complete Spelling Review 11 in your workbook.
- o Hebrew
  - • Review Genesis 1:1.
  - • Remember that you can look these up in the back of the book and listen to them online by going to the Online Support page of our site.
  - • We're going to learn the letter R in Hebrew since you've already practiced writing it. The letter is Resh. Here's what it looks like.

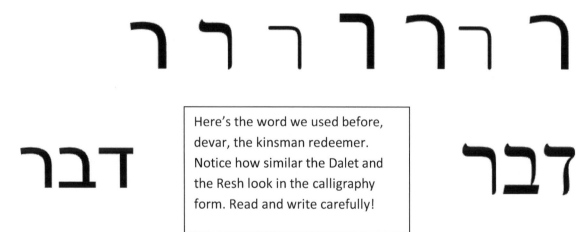

ד ר ר ר ר ד ר

דבר

Here's the word we used before, devar, the kinsman redeemer. Notice how similar the Dalet and the Resh look in the calligraphy form. Read and write carefully!

דבר

IV. Science
- o Today we're going to review simple machines with some simple experiments.
- o Simple machines are tools that make work easier. Let's start with a review of the definitions. Do you remember the science definition of work?
  - • Work is force moving an object. The force has to move the object. If there is no distance traveled, then no work was accomplished.
- o What are some forces?
  - • gravity, pushing, pulling…
- o What is the definition of force?
  - • Something that affects the movement of an object.

- o We figure out how much work was done by seeing how much force was used and over how much distance it was used.
    - Let's take an example: move a feather around the block.
        - Would that be a big force or a little force used to move a feather?
            - little
        - Would that be a little distance or a big distance?
            - It's relative, but I would say it's a big distance.
    - Here's another example. Let's say I need to move my full bookcase over to make room for a lamp.
        - Would it take a big force or a little force?
            - big
        - Would it be a little distance or a big distance?
            - little
    - They could be the same amount of work. Work equals the amount of force times the distance the work is applied over, which means a little force used over a big distance can be equal to a big force used over a little distance.
        - It's like in math that 1 + 10 = 11 and 10 + 1 = 11. You switch the big and little numbers, but the answer stays the same.
- o Let's try this out with our wheel and axle simple machine. Simple machines make work easier in different ways. Wheels and axles make work easier by making it so that less force is required. We don't have to use as much muscle to move an object when we use a simple machine.
- o Set up your experiment.
    - You'll need a broom, a table that a broom can reach across, string, a bucket or basket with handle, a BIG book or heavy object that fits in the bucket/basket.
        - Lay a broom over a table with the broom part off the table on one side and the handle sticking off the end on the other side.
        - Tie a string to the broom handle and to the basket handle.
            - Tie the string tight and tape it to the broom handle after you tie it. We need it to wind around the broom handle when we turn it.
        - Put something heavy in the basket.
- o Here's a picture of our set up. We used a long-handled scrub brush.

- What's the axle?
  - the broom handle
  - We're going to use the broom end as the wheel.
- Holding the broom handle, turn it to try to lift the heavy basket.
- Now, hold onto the broom. If it has a plastic top across it, hold that. Otherwise, you need to create something to hold onto that's significantly wider than the handle. You could tape on a ruler or wooden spoon.
  - Turn the broom using your "wheel."
  - Is it easier? Why?
    - Both ways you are accomplishing the same work. You are moving the basket up.
    - With the wheel, you are turning over a greater distance so less force is needed to get the same work done.
  o Now we are going to try another way to lift the book or whatever heavy object you are using. I'm going to say book.
    - Put the big book flat on the table. Try to lift it with one finger, enough so that you could hold onto the binding. You can't use a finger nail to get under it. That would be using a wedge, a simple machine!
    - Now we are going to try to lift the book with a wedge. Do you remember what a wedge does?
      - It's a simple machine that makes work easier by concentrating the force into one place and by changing the direction of the force.
    - Choose a wedge such as a long fork or a long spoon with a thin edge.

- Slide it under the book. You are pushing in and the wedge is lifting the book up, even if just a little, but it's what you needed in order to lift the book.

V. Writing
  - Write for two minutes. Start writing a story.
  - Time yourselves. Just write and write and don't stop. I'll give you a word to start with to get your brain activated. Use that word in your first sentence to get you going.
  - Today's word is URGE. (Note: I'm using vocabulary words for these. Make sure everyone knows what the word means.)
  - You can always share these with each other and get speaking practice by standing up and reading them aloud.

Day 97 (check Materials List)

I. Read Genesis 26:6-11.

II. Memory Verse
- o   Review 2 Peter 3:9.
    - • The Lord is not slow about His promise, as some count slowness, but is patient toward you, not wishing for any to perish but for all to come to repentance.
- o   Say from memory Psalm 150:6.
    - • Let everything that has breath praise the Lord. Praise the Lord!

III. Language
- o   Spelling
    - • Complete Spelling Review 12 in your workbook.
- o   Hebrew
    - • Review Genesis 1:2.
    - • Trace the Resh on the Hebrew Writing 14 page in your workbook.

IV. Science
- o   Today we're going to review the periodic table and some chemical processes.
- o   Do you remember the name of the chemical process where oxygen combines with other atoms? (Hint: OXYgen)
    - • oxidation
    - • We saw oxidation in fires and in fermentation. A common result of oxidation is hydrogen atoms gaining oxygen atoms. Do you remember what is formed when two hydrogen atoms combine with an oxygen atom?
        - ▪ water (H_2O)
- o   Do you remember what exothermic means? (Note: If not, ask what EX means in exit and exterior-out. Also ask what THERM means in thermos and thermometer-heat.)
    - • Exothermic means it produces heat; it gives out heat.
    - • In an exothermic chemical reaction, the chemicals combine to make something new and to release energy, which is the heat we observe.
- o   We're going to do an experiment to observe an exothermic chemical reaction but before that, complete Science Review 13 on the periodic table.
- o   Now for your experiment.
    - • Your materials are a glass, a thermometer only if you have one that can record room or outside temperature (my digital thermometer couldn't register the low temperature), hydrogen peroxide and dry yeast (or as an alternative vinegar and steel wool).
    - • Place ½ cup hydrogen peroxide (or steel wool) in a bowl.
        - ▪ Take its temperature if you can and record it. My digital thermometer just said, "L" because the temperature was too low.
    - • Add ½ teaspoon dry yeast (or cover the steel wool with vinegar).
        - ▪ The yeast will make it bubble up. It won't instantly feel hotter.

- If you are using the vinegar, let it soak one minute and then take the steel wool out and squeeze out the excess. Put it in another cup and cover it. (You could use aluminum foil or plastic wrap.)
- Observe what happens.
  - Observe with all your senses. Make sure to feel the cup. Our cup did feel warmer after a minute or two.
- If you have a thermometer, after a few minutes take the temperature of the new substance.
  - Did an exothermic reaction take place? How do you know?
- Make sure you've completed Science Review 13 in your workbook.
- Explore more: You can adjust the amounts to get the greatest increase in temperature and make a chart of your data. You could write up a full lab report with your findings.

V. Writing
- Write for four minutes. Start writing a story.
- Time yourselves. Just write and write and don't stop. I'll give you a word to start with to get your brain activated. Use that word in your first sentence to get you going.
- Today's word is JEST. (Note: I'm using vocabulary words for these. Make sure everyone knows what the word means.)

Day 98 (check Materials List)

I. Read Genesis 26:12-22.

II. Memory Verse
- Review Job 19:25.
  - As for me, I know that my Redeemer lives,
    And at the last He will take His stand on the earth.
- Say from memory Acts 17:28.
  - For in Him we live and move and exist, as even some of your own poets have said, "For we also are His children."

III. Language
- Spelling
  - Complete Spelling Review 13 in your workbook.
- Hebrew
  - Review Genesis 1:3.
  - Find the Resh on your Hebrew Writing 14 page in your workbook. Can you find a word that you know all of the letters for?
  - Note: I found three. Bara, the second word, is one we've learned all the letters for.

IV. Science
- Today we're going to review some of what we've learned about the earth.
- What are two things that can cause erosion? (Hint: Both start with W.)
  - water and wind
- What are some things that erosion can form?
  - caves, sand
- Do you remember what we call the outer layer of the earth?
  - the crust
  - What do you know about the crust?
    - It's the dirt and water under our feet.
    - Do you remember what the water table is?
      - The water table is underground and is where we get well water from and includes slow flowing rivers that move water to the oceans. Why does water always flow towards the oceans? (Hint: Sea level has an elevation of zero. It's at the bottom.)
        - Gravity pulls the water down from higher elevations to lower elevations.
    - The crust is the thinnest layer but we've never gone below it.
  - Do you remember that the crust comes in pieces? Do you know what those pieces are called?
    - tectonic plates
- Do you remember the next layer of the earth?
  - the mantle
  - What do you know about the mantle?

- It's semi-liquid or semi-solid (depending on how you look at it ☺). It's melted rock. What makes something melt?
  - heat
  - The inside of the earth is incredibly hot.
- What's the melted rock in the mantle called?
  - magma
  - Can you think of when it is that some people get to see magma?
    - in lava flows
- We only quickly mentioned the other two layers called the inner and outer cores, which they believe are both made of iron and nickel, two metals.
  - The outer core is hot liquid, not hot like boiling water, hot like you can't imagine.
  - The inner core, amazingly, is solid.
- The inner core and the outer core are both made of the same metal and are both about the same temperature (though the inner core is probably hotter), yet the outer core is liquid and the inner core is solid. What seems to be the problem?
  - What have we learned causes something to change from a solid to a liquid and back again?
    - temperature
- Do you remember what happens to the molecules as they heat up?
  - They get excited and move around.
- Here's a picture of how molecules act in different states. Molecules in a solid move, just very little. They move more and more as they get hotter and change into a liquid and then into a gas. (image from Wikimedia.org)

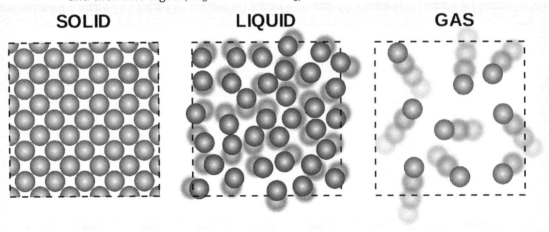

SOLID   LIQUID   GAS

- Now look at the picture of the solid and think about what would happen if that box around it couldn't be penetrated. What if the molecules were stuck inside? If they heated up, could they go anywhere?
  - No, and that's what's happening in the inner core. Both parts of the core are the same metals and around the same temperature. Where the inner core begins is where there is so much pressure (literally the weight of the world) that the molecules are pressed into place and squeezed together so that they stay in solid form.

- o Make a model of the layers of the earth. The mantle and the outer core are about the same thickness. The inner core is about half of that. The crust is very thin in comparison.
- o Now take a skewer or toothpicks and poke through your earth to make an axis. (The toothpicks can just stick out the two ends, if they can't reach all the way through.)
  - Tilt your axis and demonstrate its orbit around the sun showing how the seasons change with the light hitting the earth in different ways throughout the year.

V. Writing
- o Write for SIX minutes. Start writing a story.
- o Time yourselves. Just write and write and don't stop. I'll give you a word to start with to get your brain activated. Use that word in your first sentence to get you going.
- o Today's word is DECLARE. (Note: I'm using vocabulary words for these. Make sure everyone knows what the word means.)

Day 99 (check Materials List)

I. Read Genesis 26:23-35.

II. Memory Verse
- o Review Hebrews 11:1.
    - • Now faith is the assurance of things hoped for, the conviction of things not seen.
- o Say from memory Romans 3:23.
    - • For all have sinned and fall short of the glory of God.

III. Language
- o Spelling
    - • Complete Spelling Review 14 in your workbook.
- o Hebrew
    - • Review Genesis 1:4.
    - • Trace and write Resh on Hebrew Writing 15 in your workbook.

IV. Science
- o Today we're going to review genetics. Complete the three pages of Science Review 14 in your workbook.

V. Writing
- o Write for EIGHT minutes. Start writing a story.
- o Time yourselves. Just write and write and don't stop. I'll give you a word to start with to get your brain activated. Use that word in your first sentence to get you going.
- o Today's word is COMMERCIAL. (Note: I'm using vocabulary words for these. Make sure everyone knows what the word means.)

Day 100

I. Read Genesis 27:1-14.

II. Memory Verse
- ○ Review John 11:25.
  - • Jesus said to her, "I am the resurrection and the life; he who believes in Me will live even if he dies."
- ○ Say from memory 1 Corinthians 10:13.
  - • No temptation has overtaken you but such as is common to man; and God is faithful, who will not allow you to be tempted beyond what you are able, but with the temptation will provide the way of escape also, so that you will be able to endure it.

III. Language
- ○ Spelling
  - • Complete Spelling Review 15 in your workbook.
- ○ Hebrew
  - • Review Genesis 1:5.
  - • Practice writing words on the Hebrew Writing 16 page in your workbook.
  - • Read the words.

IV. Science
- ○ Today we're going to review several things. (Note: The kids will use their Science Review 15 page while you work through this lesson. They can go there now.)
- ○ Here's a review of the metric distance measurements.

  10 millimeter = 1 centimeter;
  100 centimeters = 1 meter;
  1000 meters = 1 kilometer

- ○ To find conversions you just look at how many zeros you need to add or take away. It's like scientific notation. You just move the decimal.
  - • To get from meters to centimeters, do you need to add or take away zeros?
    - ▪ add
  - • How many zeros do you need to add?
    - ▪ 2
  - • So to figure out how many centimeters is 4 meters, we just add 2 zeros. 4 meters equals 400 centimeters.
  - • To go backwards to get from centimeters to meters, do we need to add or take away zeros?
    - ▪ take away
  - • How many zeros need to be taken away?
    - ▪ 2
  - • So to figure out how many meters is 900 centimeters, we take away two zeros. 900 centimeters equals 9 meters.
- ○ Students can now try it in their workbooks.
  How far is 300 centimeters in meters? 3 meters
  Older kids, in millimeters and kilometers? 3000 mm, .003 km
  How far is 7 meters in centimeters? 700 centimeters

Older kids, in millimeters and kilometers? 7000 mm, .007 km
- o Replace meter with gram and you have metric weights. What would be 1 kilogram in grams?
  - 1000 grams
- o Label the parts of the eye (Day 71) on your workbook page. The pupil is what opens to let in light. The retina is what receives the focused light to send the signals to the brain. The cornea is the part that refracts the light just right. Write in pupil, retina, and cornea.

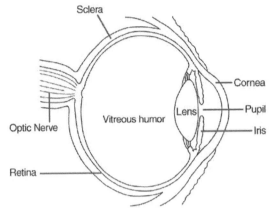

- o Which part shows the color of your eyes? (Hint: surrounds the pupil)
  - The iris is the colored circle around your pupil.
- o Do the last section of Science Review 15, the matching activity page.

V. Writing
- o Write for TEN minutes. Start writing a story.
- o Time yourselves. Just write and write and don't stop. I'll give you a word to start with to get your brain activated. Use that word in your first sentence to get you going.
- o Today's word is THICKET. (Note: I'm using vocabulary words for these. Make sure everyone knows what the word means.)

Day 101

I. Read Genesis 27:15-29.

II. Memory Verse
- o Review 1 John 1:9.
  - • If we confess our sins, He is faithful and just to forgive us our sins and to cleanse us from all unrighteousness. (KJV)
- o Say from memory Joshua 24:15.
  - • [If it is disagreeable in your sight to serve the LORD,] choose for yourselves today whom you will serve: [whether the gods which your fathers served which were beyond the River, or the gods of the Amorites in whose land you are living;] but as for me and my house, we will serve the LORD.

III. Language
- o Grammar
  - • Complete Grammar Review 6 in your workbook.
  - • (Note: This is like Mad Libs. When they are ready, you will read this paragraph with their words in the blanks.)

  I had a 1. _____ idea.

  I was going to 2. _____ .

  I never 3. _____ before, but I had seen it on the Olympics, and it looked 4. _____ .

  I got my 5. _____ together and headed out the door. I ran down the street to 6. _____ 7. _____ 8. _____ .

  It had a 9. _____ 10. _____ .

  I 11. _____ my 12. _____ firmly on my 13. _____ and took off down the 14. _____ .

  It lasted about 15. _____ 16. _____ .

  I 17. _____ .

  I was not as 18. _____ as the 19. _____ on TV like 20. _____ .

- o Hebrew
  - • Review Genesis 1:1.
  - • Learn the letter L in Hebrew since you've already practiced writing it. Its name is Lamed. Here are some examples of how it's written.

 Here's the word we used before, goel, the kinsman redeemer.

IV. Social Studies
- o In the early 19th century, America was quickly changing. They were in the middle of the Industrial Revolution. What was that?
  - It was a change in culture from an agricultural society to an urban society where people lived and worked in cities instead of farming.
- o New technology was bringing people to Lowell, Massachusetts, where factory growth exploded between 1820 and 1840.
  - The factories produced cotton thread and cotton fabric. Before this time people may have only owned two shirts. Factories were making cotton fabric cheaper and more easily available to people.
  - It was all possible because of machines. Machines cleaned the cotton, picking through it to take out sticks and seeds and such. Machines spun the cotton into threads. Water wheels (huge wheels on axles turned by a flowing river) were the tools that powered the machines in the factories.
  - On the next page is a picture of a water wheel that's not used any more.

- Tens of thousands of job were available in the factories and people moved to the city, developing urban living.

- Among those flocking to the cities were women.
- By working in factories, women were able to earn money on their own.
  - However, they were paid half of what men earned for the same work.
  - They weren't satisfied with what they were given and started the first women's union. Do you remember what a union is?
    - It's an organized group of workers who have joined together to make sure they are treated well by their employers.
  - The Lowell Mill Girls union organized strikes, where they would encourage as many women as possible to stop working until the bosses agreed to their demands.
    - They were eventually successful in getting limits on how many hours they could work each day and they stopped their bosses from cutting back how much money they earned.
- On your Social Studies Review 12 page, draw a star on Lowell, Massachusetts.

- We're going to label that map in your workbook to show the growth of America. On the page after the America map, you'll find a list of when each state was *ratified*, or became official, as a state. I have already labeled the original 13 colonies and when they became states. Delaware was the first. I drew a line to the smaller states from a state labeled with the same year they were ratified.
  - Today write in the years for numbers 14 through 24 on the list of states. They are listed in chronological order, from the earliest to the latest.
  - This was at the height of the Industrial Revolution and when factories were first being built in Lowell.
  - You can use the map of America on Day 77 to help you find states you are unsure of.
  - Just a note: It mentions Kentucky and Maine seceding. The land which became those two states was originally part of the state each seceded from. They each parted into two states by agreement.

V. Writing
- Write for eleven minutes. Start writing a story.
- Time yourselves. Just write and write and don't stop. I'll give you a word to start with to get your brain activated. Use that word in your first sentence to get you going.
- Today's word is DISTRESS. (Note: I'm using vocabulary words for these. Make sure everyone knows what the word means.)

Day 102

I. Read Genesis 27:30-40.

II. Memory Verse
  - Review Romans 6:23.
    - For the wages of sin is death, but the free gift of God is eternal life in Christ Jesus our Lord.
  - Say from memory 2 Peter 3:9.
    - The Lord is not slow about His promise, as some count slowness, but is patient toward you, not wishing for any to perish but for all to come to repentance.

III. Language
  - Vocabulary
    - Complete Vocabulary Review 6 in your workbook.
  - Hebrew
    - Review Genesis 1:2.
    - Trace the letter Lamed on the Hebrew Writing 17 page of your workbook.

IV. Social Studies
  - In the first half of the 19th century, America was expanding its abilities and production through invention and industry, but America was also expanding its borders.
  - America gained a third of its size through the Louisiana Purchase in 1803 and Lewis and Clark were sent out by President Jefferson to explore the west and look for ways to open it up to settlement.
  - In 1836 the first wagon trains started heading west on the Oregon Trail. Dozens of families, many strangers to each other, joined together in what we call a train to head west together. There was protection in numbers. Do you remember some of the dangers of the trail?
    - The biggest threat was disease, especially cholera.
    - There was also the threat of drowning in river crossings.
  - At the same time Lowell was at its height of cotton production, the wagons were rolling on the Oregon Trail, headed west over the prairies and over the mountains. Their jumping off point was Independence, Missouri.
    - Oxen pulled wagons loaded down with household goods and only one out of every four people lived to establish their home in the west.
    - People headed west for their own reasons. Some wanted the adventure. Some wanted to get away from encroaching towns. Some wanted the free land offered to those willing to settle it. Some wandered west to evangelize those on the trail or the Native American tribes.
    - While some desired to help the Native Americans by sharing the gospel, other settlers shot at them out of fear and ignorance.
  - We're going to work on the map of America. Use the map on the Social Studies Review 12 page in your workbook.
    - Put a star on Independence, Missouri.

- Label the states with the year they became ratified as an official state of the United States of America starting with the year 1836 when the wagon trains first started rolling. Do numbers 25 through 34, which is just before the Civil War began.
- Lightly color in the area purchased from France in the Louisiana Purchase.
- Draw as best you can the Oregon Trail.
- Use the Day 77 maps to help you.

V. Writing
- o Write for twelve minutes. Start writing a story.
- o Time yourselves. Just write and write and don't stop. I'll give you a word to start with to get your brain activated. Use that word in your first sentence to get you going.
- o Today's word is SEIZE. (Note: I'm using vocabulary words for these. Make sure everyone knows what the word means.)

Day 103

I. Read Genesis 27:41-28:5.

II. Memory Verse
   o Review Genesis 1:4.
      • God saw that the light was good; and God separated the light from the darkness.
   o Say from memory Job 19:25.
      • As for me, I know that my Redeemer lives,
        And at the last He will take His stand on the earth.

III. Language
   o Grammar
      • Complete Grammar Review 7 in your workbook.

   o Hebrew
      • Review Genesis 1:3.
      • Find the letter Lamed on the Hebrew Writing 17 page of your workbook.
         ▪ That's Genesis 1:1-5 on the page. What word is repeated in every verse? It has an L sound in it.

IV. Social Studies
   o We've been reviewing what we've learned about what was happening in America during the first half of the 1800s, the early 19th century.
   o Take a look at the maps for Day 103 and see what else was growing in America during these years. These maps show the railroads in America in 1830, 1840, 1850, and 1860.
      • What observations can you make?
      • Do you see how dense the railroads are around Lowell?
      • What were Lowell factories producing?
         ▪ cotton thread
         ▪ Where did all that cotton come from?
            • The cotton came from large farms in the south called plantations that used slaves to pick their cotton.
   o Now take a look at the next page in your map book for Day 103. This map shows America divided into groups. There are states that don't allow slavery, which we call free states, and states that do allow slavery, which we call slave states.
   o What observations can you make?
      • In fact, all southern states were slave states, states where slavery was allowed.
      • While Massachusetts was a free state, they didn't have a problem benefiting from slave labor. It was the slaves working on southern plantations that made the Lowell Mills possible and so successful.
      • The plantations produced a constant supply of cotton that the factories spun into threads and then wove into fabric.
   o The American Civil War was fought from April 12, 1861 – April 9, 1865. Only one new state was added during this time; Nevada was added toward the end of the war.

- In the middle of the war, Abraham Lincoln, the president, wrote the Emancipation Proclamation, an executive order issued on January 1, 1863. It declared all slaves free. When the North won the Civil War, that law was enforced and southern plantation owners had to pay their workers and allow them the freedom to leave if they wanted to.
- In the fall of the same year, 1863, President Abraham Lincoln made the annual national holiday of Thanksgiving, when we, as a nation, would thank God for all He has done for us.
- On your American map, color in the slave and free states lightly so that you can still see your year numbers. Use the example map in your Map Book for Day 103.
  - You can add in the rest of the years if you are interested. What were the last two states added, long after the rest?
- I said that only one state was added during the years of the war. That's only sort of true. Our state list says that during those years West Virginia *seceded* from Virginia, which means it separated itself from Virginia. Virginia was a slave state and that part of Virginia wanted to join the northern free states in the war. Abraham Lincoln and those in charge in the North I'm sure were happy to acknowledge them as a state on their side.
- Explore More: Learn the terms Union and Confederacy. Where was the capital of the confederacy and who was the president of it? How did the railroads affect the Civil War?

V. Writing
- Write for thirteen minutes. Start writing a story.
- Time yourselves. Just write and write and don't stop. I'll give you a word to start with to get your brain activated. Use that word in your first sentence to get you going.
- Today's word is STANDARD. (Note: I'm using vocabulary words for these. Make sure everyone knows what the word means.)

Day 104

I. Read Genesis 28:6-17.

II. Memory Verse
- o Review Genesis 26:4.
  - • I will multiply your descendants as the stars of the heaven, and will give your descendants all these lands; and by your descendants all the nations of the earth shall be blessed.
- o Review Hebrews 11:1.
  - • Now faith is the assurance of things hoped for, the conviction of things not seen.

III. Language
- o Vocabulary
  - • Complete Vocabulary Review 7 in your workbook.
- o Hebrew
  - • Review Genesis 1:4.
  - • Trace and write the letter Lamed on the Hebrew Writing 18 page in your workbook.

IV. Social Studies
- o There was one more war we mentioned in our lessons, World War II. We learned a little about two historical events, The Battle at Midway and the bombing of Hiroshima and Nagasaki.
- o Midway is an island in the middle of the Pacific Ocean, about midway between America and Japan. It's too little to really see on a map of the world.
  - • On our America map we've been working on (SS Review 12), it shows Hawaii as a string of islands. It puts them at the bottom of the map, along with Alaska, because they wouldn't be seen on the map otherwise.
  - • The Hawaiian Islands are in the middle of the Pacific Ocean.
    - ▪ Those islands would just be the size of a dot on a world map.
    - ▪ There are actually about 150 islands that make up Hawaii.
  - • Midway is an island a little farther out from the last island in that string shown on your map, toward the top left.
- o Japan surprised America by dropping bombs on the war boats America had stationed in Honolulu, Hawaii. If you look at the America map, the island, second from the top, on the southern side of the island is where it happened.
  - • You can also see on your Social Studies Review 12 page that Hawaii wasn't a state yet. It was one of America's territories, like many states were before they were ratified and made official.
- o The attack on the US navy happened specifically at a place called Pearl Harbor. A harbor is where boats are docked. It was attacked on December 7, 1941.
  - • It shocked America.
  - • President Roosevelt (the one who moved Thanksgiving to give us more shopping time) declared war on Japan after the attack.

- One of the ways America retaliated, got back at Japan, was to send in the Doolittle Raiders, which I mentioned before. The raid took place on April 18, 1942.
  - They were pilots who were sent in to do strategic bombing, meaning they had orders to drop bombs on specific locations in Japan.
  - The Pacific Ocean is huge. Large ships called aircraft carriers took planes out into the ocean. There was a runway on the deck of the ship for the planes to take off.
  - One big problem with flying over so much ocean is that planes ran out of fuel. The aircraft carriers could get them closer to their targets.
- The Japanese then wanted to get back at the Americans. They made a plan. They wanted to take control of the Island of Midway to have a base for their operations in the middle of the Pacific.
  - Again, that's a lot of ocean to fly over every time you want to do something. It would help to be able to land and refuel in the middle.
  - The Americans were able to learn Japan's plan of attack. Japan was using secret code messages, but the Americans figured out the code.
  - Americans were able to attack the Japanese before the Japanese attacked them.
    - The Japanese had four of the massive ships that carried aircraft to battle. The Americans sunk all four.
    - The Americans brought three and lost one, the one that had already been badly damaged in another battle.
    - The Japanese had been considered to have never lost a battle at sea, a naval battle, so it was a deep blow to them. We call it a turning point. Things turned around in America's favor on that day, June 4, 1942, within 6 months of the attack on Pearl Harbor.
- Pearl Harbor was the attack that shocked America. Hiroshima was the attack that shocked Japan.
  - On August 6, 1945, after three more years of fighting, the Americans dropped the first atomic bomb. Instead of a bomb destroying part of a building, this bomb destroyed a whole part of a city. Everything was destroyed. The majority of people within a mile around the bomb were killed, around 100,000 people all at once.
  - America repeated the event on August 9, 1945, in the city of Nagasaki. Then Japan surrendered and the war was over.
  - These atomic bombs have never again been used in war.

V. Writing
- Write for fourteen minutes. Start writing a story.
- Time yourselves. Just write and write and don't stop. I'll give you a word to start with to get your brain activated. Use that word in your first sentence to get you going.
- Today's word is VINDICATION. (Note: I'm using vocabulary words for these. Make sure everyone knows what the word means.)

Day 105

I. Read Genesis 28:18-29:8.

II. Memory Verse
- Review 2 Corinthians 1:20.
  - For as many as are the promises of God, in Him they are yes; therefore also through Him is our Amen to the glory of God through us.
- Say from memory John 11:25.
  - Jesus said to her, "I am the resurrection and the life; he who believes in Me will live even if he dies."

III. Language
- Grammar
  - Complete Grammar Review 8 in your workbook.
- Hebrew
  - Review Genesis 1:5. Can you say all five verses?
  - Write words from Genesis 1:1-5 on the Hebrew Writing 19 page of your workbook.
  - Try to read the words. Sound them out and add in the vowel sounds.

IV. Social Studies
- Let me ask a few questions today to see what you remember. (Note: There are ten questions. You could play basketball, give them a shot with each right answer, or have them just pass the ball to someone to answer the next question.)
  - Where was the first paper money made?
    - China
  - What trade route was begun by the Han Dynasty in China?
    - the Silk Road
  - What was used before money was standard in order to buy goods?
    - bartering
  - What's it called when you argue over the price of something to get the better deal?
    - haggling
  - What are the four branches of the US military?
    - army, navy, air force, marines
  - When the patriarch of a family dies, what is the person called who receives the inheritance, the money and things left behind by the person who dies?
    - the heir
  - What is capital punishment?
    - the death penalty, being killed as the punishment for your crime
  - What was the name of the writing system developed by the Sumerians?
    - cuneiform
  - What do we call people who flee from their country?
    - refugees
  - What are some ways we worship God?
    - singing, dancing, giving, obedience

- (Bonus: What did you learn about your state history?)
  - Today complete Social Studies Review 13 in your workbook.

V. Writing
  - Write for fifteen minutes. Start writing a story.
  - Time yourselves. Just write and write and don't stop. I'll give you a word to start with to get your brain activated. Use that word in your first sentence to get you going.
  - Today's word is INTEGRITY. (Note: I'm using vocabulary words for these. Make sure everyone knows what the word means.)
  - (Note: You might want to save this in your child's portfolio.)

Day 106

I. Read Genesis 29:9-20.

II. Memory Verse
- o Learn Jeremiah 29:11.
- o "For I know the plans I have for you," declares the Lord, "plans to prosper you and not to harm you, plans to give you hope and a future."

III. Language
- o Handwriting/Spelling (Note: The words this week come from various places in Genesis.)
    - • verse 20
    - • words to know: grief, envied, defiance, thirty-seven
    - • spelling tips:
        - ▪ The word <u>grief</u> follows the spelling pattern I before E except after C.
        - ▪ Envy is spelled with the letter Y at the end. Today we are writing it in the past tense, <u>envied</u>. The word envy is spelled E-N-V-Y. Does a vowel or a consonant come before the Y?
            - • a consonant
            - • That means we have to change the Y to an I. Then we can add on our E-D for the ending.
        - ▪ The word <u>defiance</u> ends with the same letters as countenance and advance.
        - ▪ The word <u>thirty-seven</u> is two words made into one with a hyphen.
- o Vocabulary
    - • envy (verse 26:14, envied)
    - • to be upset over what someone else has that you don't (verb)
    - • As a noun, the word envy means jealousy. It's the feeling of being upset over what someone else has.
- o Hebrew
    - • We're going to learn the letter Vav. This is the letter V. You've already learned a letter that can make the V sound, but this also makes the V sound.
    - • Vav is the letter that is used to write va and ve. Remember that they aren't writing the vowels, so just a Vav writes va and ve. Since it's only one letter by itself, it just links onto the word that comes after it.

- • Above is Genesis 1:1 in Hebrew. I underlined Eloheem for you. What word comes next in the verse?

- et
  - I circled the two "et"s. Why does the second look different?
  - What word comes before et?
    - ve
    - That's ve and et combined into one word when written.
- Trace the letter Vav on the Hebrew Writing 20 page in your workbook and circle the Vav in Genesis 1:1.

IV. Social Studies

- We're just going to travel around the globe this week, visiting a continent each day. Today we'll go to Africa. Find Africa on the map of the world in the front of your Map Book.
- Take a look in your Map Book for Day 106. Find where you think the areas of East, West, and Central Africa would probably be. Find the Horn of Africa. (Hint: Find yellow Somalia over on the right.)
- What African countries can you name? Can you find them on the map?
- The first African country we'll look at is Chad.
  - Chad is located in the center of Africa. You can find it on the map under Libya, which is on the northern coast of Africa.
  - It is a large, landlocked country.
  - The northern part of Chad is part of the Sahara Desert and gets little rain. The central part is part of what is called "the Sahel," a dry area with mostly thorny bushes, but with more rain than the Sahara. The southern part of the country has grassland good for grazing animals.
  - Lake Chad is a large lake in western Chad, on the edge of the Sahara, that is surrounded by four countries including Chad.
  - There are a lot of well-known African animals, such as lions, giraffes, hippos, rhinos, elephants, and crocodiles, living in Chad, but only in small numbers because of poaching.
  - Chad has about 14 million people, but they are not spread evenly over the country; most people live in the south, while the north is almost empty.
  - Chad's capital city is called N'Djamena.
  - There are over 200 ethnic groups, or tribes, in Chad, each with its own language and customs. Chad is a place where the black African tribes and the Arab Africans of the north meet.
  - There are many languages spoken in Chad, but the two official ones are French and Arabic. Many people learn the Chadian version of Arabic as a second language to communicate between the different tribes.
  - There are several different religions practiced in Chad. A little over half of the people are Muslim; about 22% are Catholic; about 18% are Protestant; and many Chadians practice their ancient traditions involving belief in spirits. There are many missionaries in Chad, both Christian and Muslim. The different groups generally get along without serious problems here, unlike in neighboring Nigeria.
  - Chad is a very poor country. About 80% of the people live in extreme poverty.
  - Education is a problem here; only about 25% of the people are literate. That means that three out of every four people cannot read.

- Chad has a problem with violence based on politics or ethnic differences. Innocent women and children are often victims. There are also hundreds of thousands of refugees from wars in neighboring countries living in refugee camps in Chad.

o The next country we'll look at is a tiny, little-known but very beautiful country that is completely surrounded by another country!

- The land of Lesotho is unusual in several ways among African countries. Its name is pronounced "Leh-SOO-too."
- Lesotho is not only landlocked, it's surrounded entirely by only one country: South Africa. You can find them both on the map at the southern tip of the continent.
- Lesotho is the highest country in the world; it's the only country in the world that lies entirely above 1000 meters (3,281 feet) above sea level. Because of its high mountains and cool climate, it is sometimes called "the Switzerland of Africa."
- Lesotho's climate is quite a bit cooler than other places at a similar latitude because of its high elevation. Summers in the capital city can be as warm as 86 degrees Fahrenheit (30 degrees Celsius). But during the winter it can get down to 19 degrees Fahrenheit (-7 Celsius) in the capital and much colder in the higher mountains. Snow is common during the winter, which lasts from May to September (remember this is the southern hemisphere!).
- The capital of Lesotho is called Maseru.
- Lesotho only has about 2 million people. It is unusual among African countries in that there is only one ethnic group or tribe, called the Basotho.
- The two official languages of Lesotho are English and Sesotho, which is the language of the Basotho people. The language uses a complicated system of changes in tone of voice, which change the meaning of words.
- Because of the cold climate, the traditional clothing of Lesotho revolves around a thick wool blanket, which can be seen everywhere, in every season, and is worn differently for men and for women.
- About 90% of the people of Lesotho consider themselves Christian. The sad fact, though, is that it seems that for many people this is a part of their culture but doesn't really impact their lifestyle. Lesotho has possibly the highest rate of violence against women in the world, and one of the highest rates of infection with the HIV/AIDS virus: about a quarter of the people are infected, and half of the younger women in the cities.
- Because of the very high rates of HIV/AIDS, life expectancy is only 42 years in Lesotho. There are also about 100,000 orphans, which is a huge number for such a small country.
- About 40% of the people live in extreme poverty and only about 5% of the people use the internet.

o One of the most well-known African countries is Kenya. You can see Kenya's flag on the map page. The green stands for their rich natural resources. It is a rich reminder that Africa is not a poor continent. It is extremely wealthy in many ways. It suffers from corruption, which means that people with power have hurt the continent.

- Natural resources such as diamonds, gold, oil, gas, etc. are stolen or used to only make a few very wealthy instead of letting them enrich the whole country and continent.
- There are thoughts of Africa as if it never rained there, that there is always a famine, and that there is a lack of resources and know-how to make it on their own.
  - These are all utterly false. Africa is a beautiful continent with much to offer the world. Of course, it rains in Africa! They have suffered from droughts and famines, but poor governments are to blame, not the land or the people.
  - Western governments make it worse by providing aid, giving the locals things for free, so that local businesses cannot sell!
  - What Africa wants most is to be left to govern themselves and to participate in the world economy, meaning they want to buy and sell and work freely without governments interfering.
- Our friends from Kenya taught us this simple bread recipe. They eat it daily. It's called Ugali.
  - 4 cups of water
  - 1 cup of yellow cornmeal
  - Mix and boil.
  - Stir and mush constantly until it pulls away from side of pan without sticking.
  - Cover and let stand.

V. Discussion (from your reading over the review weeks)
  - What is your birthright as a Christian? (What is birthright?)
  - Do you take advantage of your position?

VI. Writing
  - Today you are going to practice with commas. You are going to add in a comma after an introductory phrase.
  - A phrase is a group of words. The introduction is the beginning. An introductory phrase is the group of words that comes at the beginning of a sentence.
    - You don't have to always have a comma, but it's more likely to be expected than not. You can say the sentence out loud and see if it sounds better with a pause.
  - Here are some examples of introductory phrases that you can add a comma after.
    - Finally, (comma) they were able to make their way home.
    - After the sudden burst of rain, (comma) the sun came out.
    - On March 13, 1954, (comma) my father was born.
    - Thinking she knew the answer, (comma) Sarah raised her hand.
    - If you begin your sentence with the word if, (comma) then you need a comma after the first part of your sentence.
    - When you begin a sentence with the word when, (comma) then you also use a comma after the first half of your sentence.
  - Complete Writing Sentences 17 in your workbook.

Day 107

I. Read Genesis 29:21-30.

II. Memory Verse
- o Practice Jeremiah 29:11.
- o "For I know the plans I have for you," declares the Lord, "plans to prosper you and not to harm you, plans to give you hope and a future."

III. Language
- o Handwriting/Spelling
  - verse 22
  - words to know: descend, console, deceitful, violently
  - spelling tips:
    - The word <u>descend</u> has a similar spelling to the word ascend.
    - The word <u>console</u> ends with a silent E.
    - The word <u>deceitful</u> is another one to practice putting I before E except after C. Does I or E come first in this word?
    - What part of speech is <u>violent-LY</u>?
      - adverb
      - It describes how he trembled.
- o Vocabulary
  - noun, deceit – the act of lying
  - verb, deceive – to lie, to trick someone
  - adjective, deceitful – describing someone who lies
  - adverb, deceitfully – describing how someone lives, acts or speaks with deceit
- o Hebrew
  - Trace and write the Vav on the Hebrew Writing 21 page of your workbook.
  - Practice saying Genesis 1:1.
  - Look at the word vohu that you have seen before. What letter is making the V sound? What letter is making the U sound?

  - The Bet, without the dot, is making the V sound. The Vav, with that extra dot, is making the U sound. We'll also see the Vav taking on other vowel sounds.
  - It's just another function of the letter Vav. You'll have to accept it! Before you complain...English is the worst when it comes to letters saying crazy things. Just read these words: sew/new and now/tow.

IV. Social Studies
- o We're traveling around the globe this week, visiting a continent each day. Today we'll go to Asia. Find Asia on the map of the world in the front of your Map Book.

o   Take a look at Asia in your Map Book for Day 107. There are two maps. The first doesn't include Turkey which is to the far left, bordering Iran. Find where you think the areas of Southeast Asia, Central Asia, and the Middle East would probably be.

o   Asia is very diverse. There are northern countries such as Kazakhstan and Mongolia, the islands of Southeast Asia such as Indonesia and the Philippines, and the desert nations of the Middle East such as Saudi Arabia.

o   Let's learn a little about Asian nations.

o   I lived in Turkey for about seven years, so I think we should start there. You can find it on the far left of the second map.

- Turkey is a large and ancient country. Some say even part of the Garden of Eden was located there. In fact, several parts of the Bible can be mapped in Turkey, including the early churches and where Noah's ark landed.

- Turkey is a "bridge" from Europe to Asia. The city of Istanbul is divided by water and part of the city stands on each continent.

- Turkey has always been a desirable country because it is surrounded on many sides by water. It has a long history of being invaded.

- Turkey became a Muslim nation when the Ottomans attacked and took control in 1299.

- The language in Turkey is called Turkish.

- Their money is called the Turkish Lira. One lira is about 60 US cents, though it changes constantly. This is their new money. They changed from their old system where one dollar equaled more than one million lira!

- The crescent moon and star on Turkey's flag are symbols of Islam.

- While almost everyone in Turkey says they are Muslim, Turkey is officially a secular country. There is a deep divide between religious and secular Turks. Currently there are laws which protect the secular state such as forbidding government workers from covering their heads. College students also can't cover their heads, whereas conservative, religious Muslim men and women wear head coverings as a sign of devotion to Islam.

- The evil eye charm is three concentric circles always including the color blue. It is found everywhere in Turkey and in a lot of Islamic cultures.

o   My favorite recipe I learned in Turkey is lentil soup.

- One onion

- One carrot, grated

- One cup red lentils

- Tomato paste

- Salt

- Chop onion. Cook onion in a tablespoon of oil for a few minutes. Add a tablespoon of tomato paste. Continue to stir for a couple minutes. Pour in six cups of water. Add red lentils and grated carrot. Cover and boil over low heat about an hour. Salt to taste.

o   The eastern part of Asia is mostly Islamic. Asia is the birth place of the largest religions of the world. Muslims, Christians, and Jews all consider Jerusalem in Israel to be a sacred place to their religion. Everything we've been reading about in Genesis has taken place in Asia. Genesis will end in Egypt. What continent is Egypt on?

- Africa

- America has been at war in the Islamic Middle East a number of times, vying for power and control. America has fought in Afghanistan, Iraq, and Kuwait.
- In the opposite corner of Asia, there is the opposite type of government. Where Islamic countries force their religion on its citizens, even killing those who convert to other religions like Christianity, these countries are Communist and say all religion is wrong.
  - Maybe they aren't so different in that these countries have killed those who have converted to Christianity as well.
- One of the communist countries of Asia is Laos.
  - Laos is located in southeast Asia. Look for it on your maps. It's between Vietnam and Thailand under (south of) China.
  - It's a small, mountainous country composed of lots of different ethnic groups speaking a variety of languages.
  - The capital of Laos is Vientiane. It's a small, relatively peaceful city.
  - About 50% of the people of Laos are Lao. That's the name of their ethnic group. Their language is also called Lao and is closely related to Thai, spoken next door in Thailand. The Lao people are the dominant ones in Laos and often tend to look down on the other ethnic groups.
  - Other well-known ethnic groups in Laos are the Hmong and the Khmu. There are actually a lot of Hmong in certain parts of the US. They came as refugees during and after the Vietnam War.
  - Most of the people of Laos are Buddhists. There are many Buddhist temples throughout Laos, and the sight of Buddhist monks dressed in their orange robes is common. Every Buddhist male is expected to serve as a monk for a period of time.
  - There are a smaller number of animists (believing in spirits and magic) and Christians in Laos. Most areas of Laos have some Christian churches. Even though it is a communist country and Christianity is restricted, churches are allowed to operate under the watchful eye of the government.
  - Laos is a very poor country. Many of the people rely on small-scale farming to support themselves.
  - The US was involved (sometimes secretly) in Laos during the Vietnam War in the 1960s and early 1970s. Laos has the sad distinction of being the most-bombed country in the world, ever. The US dropped the same total number of bombs on Laos as it dropped in all of Europe and Asia during all of World War 2. Many innocent people were killed and continue to be killed to this day as farmers still sometimes accidently set off unexploded bombs and landmines found on their land.

V. Discussion
- Laban really seems like a cheat. Have you ever been cheated? What happened? What did you do about it?

VI. Writing
- Use your discussion question as a writing prompt?
- Get a high five and/or hug for any adverbs you use.

Day 108

I. Read Genesis 29:31-30:8.

II. Memory Verse
- o   Practice Jeremiah 29:11.
- o   "For I know the plans I have for you," declares the Lord, "plans to prosper you and not to harm you, plans to give you hope and a future."

III. Language
- o   Handwriting/Spelling
  - •   verse 6
  - •   words to know: flock, almond, continue, distance
  - •   spelling tips:
    - ▪   <u>Flock</u> has the same spelling pattern as clock.
    - ▪   <u>Almond</u> ends like the word pond.
    - ▪   <u>Continue</u> ends like the word blue.
    - ▪   <u>Distance</u> ends like the word dance.
- o   Vocabulary
  - •   feeble (verse 30:42)
  - •   weak (adjective)
- o   Hebrew
  - •   We're going to learn to write another letter today, the letter Tav. It has the T sound.
  - •   It looks a little similar to the Hei. Notice the difference here. The Tav is on the right.

  - •   Trace the Tav on the Hebrew Writing 22 page of your workbook and circle the letter Tav in Genesis 1:1 as well.
  - •   (Note: There are three. In English we write Arets with a T, but in Hebrew there is a separate letter that makes the TS sound.)

IV. Social Studies
- o   We're traveling around the globe this week, visiting a continent each day. Today we'll go to South America.
- o   Find South America on the map of the world in the front of your Map Book. Then look at South America in your Map Book for Day 108.
- o   The first country we'll look at is Brazil. It's huge, covering nearly half of South America's land area.

- Brazil is the largest country in South America, and the fifth largest country in the world both in size and in population. Over 206 million people live there.
- Brazil is the home of the Amazon River, the world's second longest.
- There are a variety of different climates in Brazil. The northern part is mostly tropical rain forest; the central part is more grassland; and the southern part is mountainous and some areas have cool winters and even snow.
- Scientists estimate that there are nearly 4 million different types of plants and animals in Brazil. Some especially interesting animals include jaguars, sloths, capybaras (the world's largest rodent), the anaconda (the world's largest snake), the Goliath spider (second largest spider), pink dolphins, poison dart frogs, and about 75 different species of primate, apes and monkeys.
- Brazil's capital is Brasilia. Its largest city, though, is Sao Paulo, with a population of over 12 million people. There are many other large cities as well.
- Brazil is estimated to have over 50 native tribes which are uncontacted (meaning they have little or no contact with the outside world), living mostly in the Amazon region.
- Brazil has the world's largest population of Catholics; about 65% of the people claim to be Catholic. About 22% of the people are Protestant, and their numbers are growing.
- The official language of Brazil is Portuguese, which was brought over to the New World by the explorers from Portugal who settled here. Portuguese is similar to Spanish. There are also about 180 languages spoken by the native tribes.
- Unfortunately, Brazil has a very high violent crime rate and a relatively large percentage of the population is very poor.

o Another country of South America, one which touches Brazil, is Paraguay.
- Paraguay is located very centrally in South America, and is sometimes referred to as the "Heart of South America" in Spanish.
- The land is mostly grassy plains, wooded hills, or marshes.
- The weather of Paraguay is influenced by winds. Between October and March, warm winds blow from the Amazon region to the north; from May to August, cold winds blow from the Andes mountains to the northwest.
- The population of Paraguay is only about 7 million. Its capital city is called Asunción and has only about half a million people. Most of the people of Paraguay live in the eastern half of the country.
- Spanish is the official language of Paraguay, along with a native language called Guarani. Paraguay is different from other Latin American countries in that about 90% of the people speak this native language.
- Paraguayan culture is a mixture of European and native.
- About 90% of the people are Roman Catholic.
- The people of Paraguay are known for being very happy and easygoing.
- A relatively high percentage of the population is very poor.

o Recipe from Brazil – Moqueca de Peixe – Brazilian Fish Stew
- 2 lbs white fish (ex: tilapia) 1 ½ T salt 2 T lime juice 2 T garlic, mashed 3 tomatoes, seeded* 1 onion 2/3 c cilantro 1/3 c scallions 2 T palm oil 1 can (~1 c) coconut milk

- Mix the salt, garlic, and lime juice and rub over the fish. (You can use either fish fillets or cuts with bone.) In a small bowl or on a large cutting board, mix the seasoning: thinly slice the tomatoes and onions, and chop the cilantro and scallions. Mix together and mash slightly to release the flavors. In a larger bowl or casserole, layer the fish and seasoning: place the fish in single layers with the tomato/onion mix spread between each layer. Cover tightly and let marinade for at least 30 min. Heat the palm oil in a large pan (or Dutch oven) over medium heat. Add all the fish and seasoning, cover, and simmer until fish flakes easily (10-20 min). Remove from heat and gently stir the coconut milk into the broth that has formed (stir around the fish to avoid flaking). Serve with white rice.
- *Note: It really is necessary to seed the tomatoes; otherwise, the final dish will be too watery.

V. Discussion (from the review weeks)
- It would seem that Jacob was the one who was supposed to receive the blessing. He becomes the father of the nation of Israel. Did Rebekah do the right thing or the wrong thing?
  - This is tricky stuff. God can use even sinful actions of men (or women) to accomplish His goals. It doesn't make their actions right, though.
  - What maybe could she have done differently to ensure Jacob received the blessing? Was it her responsibility to make sure Jacob was the one blessed?
  - What about Jacob? He had the choice between disobeying his mother and lying to his father. Is it okay to disobey when someone asks you to sin? Did he do right or wrong? What do you think he should have done?

VI. Writing
  - Use the discussion question as a writing prompt.
  - Get a high five and/or hug for using a semi-colon or comma and conjunction to combine two sentences.

Day 109

I. Read Genesis 30:9-24.

II. Memory Verse
- o   Practice Jeremiah 29:11.
- o   "For I know the plans I have for you," declares the Lord, "plans to prosper you and not to harm you, plans to give you hope and a future."

III. Language
- o   Handwriting/Spelling
  - •   verse 24
  - •   words to know: embrace, gracious, prevail, wrestle
  - •   spelling tips:
    - ▪   The word <u>embrace</u> has the word brace in it. The letter C makes the S sound.
    - ▪   <u>Gracious</u> comes from the word grace which has the same spelling pattern as brace. In the word gracious, you take off the letter E at the end, and add an I before the ending.
    - ▪   <u>Prevail</u> ends like the word rail as in railroad.
    - ▪   The word <u>wrestle</u> has a few silent letters. Do you know what it starts with?
- o   Vocabulary
  - •   droves (verse 32:16)
  - •   a large crowd; here it's a herd being moved (noun)
  - •   prevail (verse 32:28)
  - •   to win, to be widespread or more frequently occurring (verb)
- o   Hebrew
  - •   Trace and write Tav on the Hebrew Writing 23 page of your workbook.
  - •   Practice saying Genesis 1:2.

IV. Social Studies
- o   We're traveling around the globe this week, visiting a continent each day. Today we'll go to Europe.
- o   Find Europe on the map of the world in the front of your Map Book. Then look at Europe in your Map Book for Day 109. There are two maps. The one has writing that's too small, but it shows how many countries there are very clearly.
- o   The first country of Europe we'll talk about is one that our family visited. We got to spend some time living in a small house far from any towns in the beautiful land of Finland.
  - •   Finland is located in the northern part of Europe in the region known as Scandinavia.
    - ▪   It's way up north next to the peninsula of Norway and Sweden. What's a peninsula?
      - •   Land surrounded by water on three sides.

- The population of Finland is about five and a half million people. Most of them are known as Finns and speak a language called Finnish. It is very different from other European languages.
- The capital of Finland is called Helsinki. It is the second most northern capital city in the world, after Iceland's capital.
- The country is mostly flat and covered with coniferous forests called taiga. There are about 168,000 lakes and 179,000 islands in Finland.
- Much of Finland has long, cold winters and short summers.
- The northern part of Finland is called Lapland. Reindeer are common there.
- Finland is a member of the European Union, or the EU, and uses the euro (the same currency used by many other European countries).
- The system of education in Finland is considered to be one of the best in the world. Some of its characteristics include: less homework, more play time, more independent exploration, more individual attention from teachers…sounds a little like homeschooling, doesn't it?
- Finland also has one of the highest standards of living in the world, meaning the country's people are generally very prosperous compared to other countries, including the US.
- One of the most important parts of Finnish culture is the sauna, a room in the house or a log cabin where you sit to enjoy the heat from steam that comes from water being thrown onto hot stones. This has a relaxing and healing effect on the body and mind. When the heat gets too uncomfortable, you jump into a lake or a swimming pool, take a cool shower, or (in the winter) even roll in the snow to cool off, and then begin the cycle over again in the sauna. Saunas are considered a necessity in Finland and are part of the people's national identity. Most people try to go to the sauna at least once a week, if they don't have one in their home.

o Now let's look at another, smaller country in Europe. This is a place I lived in for about six years, and I like to call it my favorite place in the world. I'm talking about Macedonia.

- Macedonia is located in southeastern Europe, just north of Greece. It is on the so-called "Balkan Peninsula."
  - Try to find it on the map. Macedonia is just above Greece, which is the peninsula to the east (right) of Italy.
- Macedonia is only about the size of Vermont and only has about two million people (less than Houston, Texas).
- Macedonia is landlocked (surrounded on all sides by land). It is mostly mountainous and generally has warm, dry summers and cold, moderately snowy winters. Some high mountain areas have long winters with lots of snow.
- The capital city of Macedonia is called Skopje, which is pronounced "SKOPE-yeh." It has about half a million people.
- The population of Macedonia is diverse. The majority of the people are ethnically Macedonian, but there is a large minority of ethnic Albanians and smaller minorities of Turkish and Roma (Gypsy) people.

- They are all citizens of Macedonia, but they have their own ethnic identity and their own languages. There is a lot of hatred and mistrust between different ethnic groups.
  - The official language is Macedonian, which is written in the Cyrillic alphabet like Russian. All citizens have to learn it, even if they have their own language in their own communities.
  - The ethnically Macedonian people are Eastern Orthodox Christian, but the Albanian, Turkish, and Roma people are mostly Muslim.
  - Macedonia was part of a larger communist country called Yugoslavia until 1991, when Yugoslavia broke up into a bunch of smaller countries such as Croatia, Slovenia, Bosnia, Serbia, and later Kosovo and Montenegro, in addition to Macedonia.
  - It's important to realize that the northern part of Greece is also called "Macedonia" by the Greeks. The people of Greece and Macedonia argue quite a bit over the name and who it should belong to. When you cross the border to or from Greece there are signs on both sides of the border saying "Welcome to Macedonia." In other words, both sides claim the name.
  - Our family mostly lived and worked with the Roma people. On the edge of Skopje is the largest Roma settlement in the world. It's like a different world!
  - If you spend time with people in Macedonia, you'll quickly realize that relationships are more important to them than time. Just going to get your hair cut or get an oil change can take a long time (hours even) because people like to take their time and talk, drink tea or coffee, talk some more...
  - o Here's a recipe from Macedonia.
    - "Selsko Meso" (Village Meat)
    - Two medium onions
    - Half pound stew meat
      - I use two pounds for 10 of us (7 are adults/teens).
    - Use a wide and deep pan. Use plenty of oil. I use olive oil. Turn it up to high heat on the stove.
    - Brown mushrooms in oil and remove.
    - Chop onions and cook in oil to brown a little. Remove.
    - Add half a pound of stew beef and let brown.
    - Add two drinking cups of water.
    - Bring to boil and simmer for about two hours. Check to make sure water doesn't all disappear.
    - Add a tablespoon of chopped parsley at the end. Salt to taste. They use lots! Actually, they use Vegeta.

V. Discussion (from your reading over the review weeks)
- o Do you see God's blessing as important as Jacob did? What do you have in your life because of God's blessing? Is there anything that we have because of ourselves and not because God first gave to us?

VI. Writing
- o Use the discussion question as a writing prompt.
- o Get a high five and or hug for using a spelling or vocabulary word.

Day 110

I. Read Genesis 30:25-35.

II. Memory Verse
- o Test yourselves on Jeremiah 29:11.
- o "For I know the plans I have for you," declares the Lord, "plans to prosper you and not to harm you, plans to give you hope and a future."

III. Language
- o Handwriting/Spelling
  - Test yourselves on words from Day 106-109.
  - grief, envied, defiance, thirty-seven, descend, console, deceitful, violently, flock, almond, continue, distance, embrace, gracious, prevail, wrestle
- o Vocabulary
  - There was a good vocabulary word in a passage that's been skipped for now; it's odious. It's related to the word odor.
  - odious (verse 34:30)
  - repulsive, offensive (adjective)
  - Shechem, Simeon and Levi all acted odiously.
  - Test yourselves on words from Day 106-109.
    - envy – jealousy; being upset over what someone else has and you don't
    - noun, deceit – the act of lying
      - verb, deceive – to lie, to trick someone
      - adjective, deceitful – describing someone who lies
      - adverb, deceitfully – describing how someone lives, acts or speaks with deceit
    - feeble – weak
    - droves – a large crowd; here it's a herd being moved
    - prevail – to win, to be widespread or more frequently occurring
- o Hebrew
  - o Trace the words on your Hebrew Writing 24 page in your workbook.
  - o Say/read the words as you write them.

IV. Social Studies
- o We're traveling around the globe this week, visiting a continent each day. Today we'll go to North America.
- o Find North America on the map of the world in the front of your Map Book. Then look at North America in your Map Book for Day 110.
- o The first North American country we'll be talking about is the southern neighbor of the US: Mexico.
  - The official name of Mexico is the "United Mexican States."
  - Mexico is a large country crossed north to south by mountain ranges which are extensions of the Rocky Mountains in the US.
  - Mexico has a variety of climates as well as great biodiversity, meaning lots of different types of plants and animals.

- Mexico has a large population, with over 120 million people.
- Mexico is made up of 31 states, plus Mexico City, which forms its own state.
- Mexico City is the capital and is huge, with about 9 million people.
- Spanish is the official language of Mexico, and there are also many American Indian languages used by millions of people.
- Most Mexicans are Catholic, and Mexico is the world's second largest Catholic country after Brazil.
- Some well-known advanced civilizations thrived in Mexico before the arrival of the Spanish explorers in the 16th century, including the Aztecs and the Mayans. Many people still speak languages that descend from the ancient languages. (Note: In another year of the curriculum, they will learn about the Aztec and Maya.)
- One very important holiday in Mexico is the "Day of the Dead," which begins on October 31 and ends on November 2. On this day people build small altars in their homes to honor those who have died, and may visit graves to bring gifts to the dead. A common symbol of the holiday is a skull.

o The next country we'll be talking about might surprise you: Nicaragua! You may be thinking, "But that's not in North America!" Well, technically it is...Nicaragua is a small country in what we call Central America, which is not actually a continent, but is part of the North American continent.

- Nicaragua is the largest country in Central America.
- Nicaragua is surrounded by Honduras to the north, Costa Rica to the south, the Caribbean Sea to the east and the Pacific Ocean to the west.
- The country is full of amazing natural beauty. About a fifth of the country is protected land, as in national parks and nature reserves.
- Nicaragua has lots of mountains and at least 19 active volcanoes.
- The capital and largest city of Nicaragua is called Managua.
- Spanish is Nicaragua's official language. Some people of African descent on the eastern coast speak English or English Creole (which means English mixed with other languages).
- Nicaragua has a population of about 6 million. The people are a mixture of European, Native Americans, Africans, and even Asians.
- About 5% of the people are members of the Miskito Native American tribe and speak their own language.
- Most of the people in Nicaragua are Roman Catholic. Catholic bishops have a lot of influence in the country, and most towns honor patron saints, who are believed to talk to God on behalf of the people.
- There are annual fiestas, or celebrations, honoring the patron saint of a particular area. The most important religious festival all over the country is called La Purisma; it is a week of festivities in early December dedicated to the Virgin Mary. Fancy altars are built to honor her in homes and businesses.
- The currency used in Nicaragua is called the cordoba. The symbol used for this currency is C$.
- The cuisine of the west coast of Nicaragua uses a lot of local fruits and corn; the cuisine of the east coast uses a lot of seafood and coconut. Corn, rice, and beans are very common ingredients. Most people eat meat only on special holidays, since most people cannot afford it.

- Nicaragua is a very poor country. It is the second poorest country in the Western Hemisphere after Haiti.
- Nicaragua faces dangers from earthquakes, volcanic eruptions, landslides, and hurricanes.
- The Nicaraguan people especially value family and politeness. They are often very eager to avoid offending anyone.
  - o Look at the next page in the Map Book and find each continent and about where each country is that you've learned about this week: Kenya, Sudan, Turkey, Laos,...

V. Discussion

- o Jacob was faithful for many years but is getting fed up. What are his good qualities? Would he make a good husband?
- o What qualities would make a good husband? (Boys can think of these for themselves, who they need to become to be good husbands, or you can flip it around and say what qualities you should look for in a wife.)

VI. Writing

- o Edit something you wrote this week.
- o Use your guidelines.
- o Look for problems with punctuation and grammar.
- o Have someone else edit.
- o Make a final draft.

Day 111

I. Read Genesis 24:1-9. (We've jumped back to the story we skipped. It's the story of Rebekah.)

II. Memory Verse
- o Learn Deuteronomy 31:8.
- o "The LORD is the one who goes ahead of you; He will be with you. He will not fail you or forsake you. Do not fear or be dismayed."

III. Language
- o Handwriting/Spelling
  - • verse 1
  - • words to know: age, thigh, beware, concern
  - • spelling tips
    - ▪ The word <u>age</u> ends just like your spelling word image.
    - ▪ The word <u>thigh</u> has the I-sound spelling pattern of night and light.
    - ▪ The word <u>beware</u> ends with a silent E.
    - ▪ The word <u>concern</u> has two letter Cs.
- o Vocabulary
  - • concerning (verse 9)
  - • related to a subject (preposition)
  - • Other definitions: to worry about something (adjective)
- o Hebrew
  - • This week we'll learn those two other letters in eloHEEM.
  - • Today we'll learn the Yod (pronounced yode). It's our letter Y.
  - • Here are examples of how it is written. It's the one that looks like an apostrophe to us.

- • Trace the Yod on the Hebrew Writing 25 page of your workbook.

אלהים

> The Yod can sound like the Y in the word yes, but in eloHEEM the Yod is part of the EE sound in the word. We use the letter Y that way too, like in the word family.

V. Science
- o There was a body part mentioned in today's reading. What was it?
  - • thigh
- o Today we're going to do some *anatomy*, the study of the structure of living things.
- o We have learned a little human anatomy. Do you remember where your femur is?
  - • It's your thigh bone.

- Why did we learn its name? What makes it special?
  - It's the longest bone in the body.
- We learned bicep. Can you flex your biceps?
  - Those are muscles.
- Do you remember where Achilles was weak?
  - It was in the back of his heel.
  - Your Achilles tendon is that hard line that comes up from your heel.
- Do you remember what tendons do?
  - They connect bone and muscle.
- Do you remember how muscles move?
  - The muscle fibers stack up when the muscle contracts (which pulls on the tendon, which pulls on the bone).
- On the next page is a human skeleton drawing with some labels.
- How many can you learn? We also have already mentioned the ribs, the vertebrae (which are the bones that make up your spine down the middle of your back), and the humerus, your funny bone. You can find this in your workbook on Science Review 16.
  - Practice today with finding these on yourself:
    - cranium, mandible, sternum, clavicle (collar bone), scapula (shoulder blade), humerus, femur, patella, carpals, metacarpals, phalanges
    - (Note: Try calling the name and having the children point to it on themselves, and then try pointing to it and having them call out the name. You could do this after telling them the first four, then again after doing the arm and leg bones, and then after the wrist and hand bones. You could practice each group of bones and then all together.)
- Recall: What's the study of the structure of living things? anatomy
- Explore More: Learn all of the bones here. Find the ones I removed the labels for. There are hundreds more you could learn.

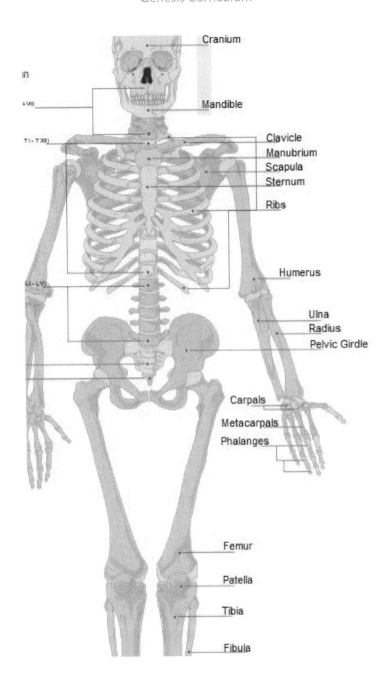

V. Social Studies
- o Today we're looking at some cultural things again. What does Abraham make the servant do while his hand is under Abraham's thigh?
  - Verse 9 from today's reading says: So the servant placed his hand under the thigh of Abraham his master, and swore to him concerning this matter.
  - The servant was taking an oath, making a strong promise.
- o In literally placing a part of himself under Abraham, he was submitting himself to the wishes of Abraham.
- o How do we take an oath today?
  - Some people put their right hand over their heart. In legal proceedings they put their hand over a Bible.

- o Do you know what the New Testament says about oaths?
  - James 5:12 says "But above all, my brethren, do not swear, either by heaven or by earth or with any other oath; but your yes is to be yes, and your no, no, so that you may not fall under judgment."
  - We are supposed to speak what is true and mean what we say. People should be able to trust us to do what we say we will do.
- o There's another cultural oddity in today's reading. Abraham wants his son, Isaac, to only marry a relative. In America there are laws about how close a relative you can marry. Part of it has to do with genetics. A relative is likely to carry a similar recessive gene (the lowercase one) and some unwelcome trait might show up in their children. Remember that different disorders that people have are carried in their genes as well.
  - However, in some places in the world, it's still not only common but considered preferable to marry a relative. We have friends from Pakistan who will marry their cousins.
  - It's hard for us Americans to accept that because we view it as wrong and just plain weird!
- o Another thing that's weird for us westerners is to have an arranged marriage. Isaac is not involved in this discussion at all, and they are talking about his wife.
  - I know women who have arranged marriages. They just accept it and believe that their father (or eldest brother if the father isn't alive) knows what's best for their family.
  - It's in many ways an economic transaction. They want their daughter to move up in the world if possible.
- o I had a neighbor who met her husband one time before they agreed to marry. Both of their families got together and they were allowed to see each other and greet each other. They each then had the opportunity to say no. You'll have to believe me that she did not agree because of his looks! but only because her family said it was a good idea.
- o Arranged marriages are statistically way more long-lasting than what they call "love" marriages. I read that the divorce rate in India is just over 1% where most marriages are arranged.
  - In comparison, the divorce rate in America is around 50%!
- o Why do these arranged marriages last? Why do you think?
  - I would think it has to do with the whole culture surrounding it. The foundation of their marriage is the decision to submit to their elders to commit to this marriage and to stay committed to it.
  - There is also a different expectation for marriage. They are a committed partnership, not people acting on feelings that come and go.
- o Recall: What does it mean to take an oath? make a strong promise; What does the Bible say about making oaths? Say what you mean and mean what you say.
- o Explore More: What else can you learn about oaths and pledges in different cultures or arranged marriages and dowries?

VI. Discussion

- o What do you think about arranged marriages and love marriages? Is one better than the other? Is there a way to combine the two?

VII. Writing
- We've talked about proper nouns, those nouns that start with a capital letter because they are names: names of people, names of places, or names of things.
- Today we're going to practice capitalizing titles.
  - A title is the name of a thing: a book, a song, a movie, etc.
- There are a few differences, though, in how we capitalize a title. When we capitalize the name of a person, we capitalize every part of the name, such as Martin Luther King, Jr. That has four capital letters. In a title, we sometimes leave certain words lowercase.
  - We always capitalize the first and last words of a title. We capitalize most words, but we leave lowercase insignificant words like "the" and "a" and most prepositions (those words we've been practicing this year such as in, on, between, from, of, at, and about).
- Give it a try on the Writing Sentences 16 page in your workbook.

Day 112 (check Materials List)

I. Read Genesis 24:10-21.
    *Note: Did you notice that God sent Rebekah before the servant even finished his prayer?

II. Memory Verse
- o   Learn Deuteronomy 31:8.
- o   "The LORD is the one who goes ahead of you; He will be with you. He will not fail you or forsake you. Do not fear or be dismayed."

III. Language
- o   Handwriting/Spelling
  - • verse 20
  - • words to know: quickly, lower, shoulder, emptied
  - • spelling tips:
    - ▪ For the word <u>quickly</u>, the letter Q is basically always followed by the letter U.
    - ▪ The word <u>lower</u> has the same vowel spelling as your spelling word flow.
    - ▪ The word <u>shoulder</u> seems like it should have the word old inside of it. It almost does, but with an extra letter. Even though it has the O sound, that sound is spelled with the two vowels in your spelling words ground, mount, mourn, and four.
    - ▪ Do you remember the rule about spelling plurals when a word ends in Y? (Note: This is for the word <u>empty</u>.)
      - • If the letter Y at the end of a word comes after a consonant, then the Y turns into an I and you add E-S.
    - ▪ In the word emptied we are writing the past tense, but we do the same thing.
      - • The word empty ends in the letter Y. Does the Y come after a consonant?
        - o   Yes, it comes after the letter T. What happens to the Y?
          - ▪ It changes to the letter I.
          - ▪ Then we can add E-D onto the end to make it past tense.

- o   Vocabulary
  - • Today for our vocabulary word, we're going to learn adverb.
  - • It's the part of speech we've not covered yet.
  - • Adverbs are words that describe verbs or adjectives.
  - • What do adjectives describe?
    - ▪ nouns
  - • Our spelling word quickly is an adverb. It tells us how she emptied her jar. She emptied it quickly. The adverb quickly describes the verb, to empty.
  - • Adverbs end in the letters L-Y a lot of the time but not all of the time.
    - ▪ Take the following sentence as an example.

- He often hastily does his chores because he eagerly wants to play.
  - What are the L-Y adverbs in that sentences?
    - hastily; What does hastily describe?
      - how he does his chores
    - eagerly; What does eagerly describe?
      - how he wants to go play
  - There's one other adverb that describes when he hastily does his chores. Listen to the sentence again and try to find it. "He often hastily does his chores because he eagerly wants to get to play."
    - It's often. Adverbs can tell us how often or how much something is done like "daily doing his chores" or "completely doing his chores."
    - Often is hard to spot because it doesn't have L-Y at the end, but it still is telling us something about how his chores are done.
- Hebrew
  - Trace and write the Yod on the Hebrew Writing 26 page of your workbook.
  - Practice saying Genesis 1:1-5.

IV. Science
- In today's reading, we read about the servant and the camels taking a drink. We learned about several of the body's systems earlier this year, but let's learn another today, the digestive system.
- The *digestive system* is the body system that takes in food and drink, uses it in our bodies, and discards waste from our bodies.
  - What is the first part of the digestive system if what it does is take in food and drink?
    - Our mouths are the first part. What different things are happening in your mouth when you eat that are helping you swallow and continue on the digestive process?
      - There are teeth chewing the food, a tongue moving around the food, and *saliva*, your spit, is at work breaking down your food and making it easier to swallow.
- Once you swallow food, where does it go?
  - Down your throat, right? When you breathe in through your mouth where does the air go?
    - Down your throat. There are two different paths down from your mouth. One leads to the lungs and one leads to the stomach.
    - If you've ever choked on food, it's because a piece started heading down the lung path, which we call the wind pipe. When you cough, that air is pushing out whatever you got stuck in your wind pipe.
  - The path down to your stomach is your *esophagus*. There are muscles that act as gatekeeper to keep air out of the stomach and food out of the lungs.
    - We can swallow air when we eat. Do you know what happens when you swallow air?
      - You burp it out.

- o We've moved from the mouth through the esophagus down to the stomach. What do you think happens in your stomach?
  - The stomach stores food while it's being broken down further into a mushy, liquidy mixture.
  - That breaking down of food is a chemical process. There is an acid in your stomach (like vinegar and lemon juice are acids); it's called gastric acid, and it eats at the food to break it down. It also can kill harmful bacteria that might have been eaten.
  - Once the food is ready (in maybe 2 to 5 hours depending on what you ate), it is moved on to your intestines.
- o Do you know where your stomach is?
  - It's not in your belly. That's where your intestines work.
  - Your stomach is actually just a little ways below your heart. Here's a picture.

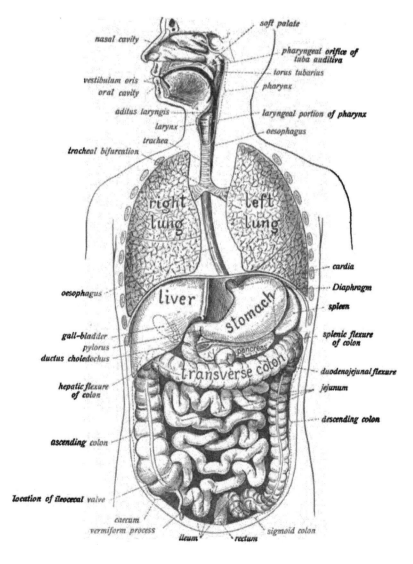

- o As I said, what's in your belly is your intestines. There are two, the large and the small intestines.

- In the picture we see the word colon. The colon is the tube part of the large intestines. You can see that it wraps around the small intestines.
- What you can't see is how long those squiggly tubes are. Want to make a guess?
  - The large intestine is much shorter. It's about five feet long and four inches around. (nearly 10 centimeters around and 1.5 meters long)
  - The small intestine is smaller only in that it's about two inches around (4 centimeters), but it's about 22 feet long by the time you're an adult. (about 6.5 meters)
  - Measure out 22 feet. That's what is wrapped up inside of you. Amazing isn't?
  - The small intestine comes first. Your food can spend about four hours there as it turns into a very watery mixture. This allows the nutrients from your food, all the good stuff, the vitamins, minerals and proteins to get absorbed into your blood, making your blood healthy.
  - What's leftover, the stuff your body can't use, is passed onto your large intestines. There's one last chance in the colon for any leftover liquid to be absorbed into the blood. If all of the liquid is being absorbed, what's leftover?
    - Poop. It's what is produced at the end when the digestive system has completed its job.
  - We're going to do a double science lesson today because there's a lot more we haven't gotten to.
  - Recall: What's the scientific word for spit? saliva; What's the esophagus? the tube that carries food from the mouth to the stomach; What's the body system that takes in and uses food? digestive system
  - Explore More: Why does some food stay longer than others in the stomach?

V. Science continued
  - We're going to next learn about what they say is the largest internal organ in the body. It's the liver. It weighs in at about three and a half pounds (1.6 kilos).
  - You can see it in the picture on the previous page. It's tucked up under your ribcage opposite your stomach.
  - It has a number of jobs.
    - It's actually your blood that gets shipped through the liver, not your food. The nutrients from your food get into your bloodstream and then the liver cleans the blood before it gets sent to the rest of your body.
    - It breaks down medicines enabling them to be passed through the bloodstream to get where they are needed.
    - It stores some nutrients and sends on what nutrients are needed at the moment.
    - It produces something called *bile* which goes into your small intestines and helps with the absorption of fats into the blood stream.
    - Your liver also transforms glucose into a form usable by the body for energy.
      - Do you remember what glucose is?
        - It's the sugar we get from our foods like bread and fruit.
        - Our bodies can create more energy stores by using the glucose in our food.

- Do you remember what we call the body's energy source, where energy is stored in our bodies?
  - ATP
  - The liver not only transforms the glucose but also stores it in the liver for when your blood sugar gets low and sends out the glucose for energy when we need it.
  - It also produces a protein whose job it is to clot blood; it's what stops the bleeding when you get a cut.
- Livers can be damaged by high-fat and high-sugar diets and especially from alcohol. Too much alcohol can damage the liver. There is no medical treatment that can replace a liver at this time.
- The bile produced by the liver helps digestion in the intestines, and the extra bile produced is stored in the gallbladder.
  - The gallbladder is small and tucked in under liver, near the diaphragm.
    - Do you remember where the diaphragm is and what it does?
      - It is a muscle that helps pull air into the lungs and then force it out.
- Another organ called the pancreas produces a juice to aid the body in digesting fats as well as proteins.
  - Find the pancreas in the digestive system picture.
- There's another piece of the digestive system called the appendix. For a long time people thought it served no purpose. But if you believe God created humans, then you know God must have created it for a reason.
  - Now doctors see the appendix as being a storehouse for good bacteria, the kind our bodies need after fighting off the bad bacteria from a sickness.
    - The appendix is just a small, skinny bag tagged onto the colon, the tube part of the large intestines.
- Recall: The small intestines have the help of three organs to aid digestion. What are they? the liver, the gall bladder and the pancreas; What's the largest internal organ? the liver
- Explore More: Why does some food stay longer than others in the stomach? Learn about the gall bladder.

VI. Discussion
- Learning how hard your body has to work to digest and how what you eat and drink goes into your blood (which supplies every other part of your body with what it needs to function), does it make think twice about how you eat?
  - What foods do you think make your body function best?
  - What foods do you think hinder how your body functions?

VII. Writing
- Use the discussion question as a writing prompt.
- Get a high five and/or hug for any adverb you use.

Day 113

I. Read Genesis 24:22-32. What story are we in the middle of? What's happening?

II. Memory Verse
- o Practice Deuteronomy 31:8.
- o "The LORD is the one who goes ahead of you; He will be with you. He will not fail you or forsake you. Do not fear or be dismayed."

III. Language
- o Handwriting/Spelling
  - verse 28
  - words to know: camel, lodge, bracelet, guide
  - spelling tips:
    - The word <u>camel</u> is the word came with one extra letter.
    - The word <u>lodge</u> ends with the same spelling pattern as your spelling word judge.
    - The word <u>bracelet</u> is the words brace and let combined.
    - The word <u>guide</u> doesn't follow a normal pattern for the sound of the vowels. You can think of it as there being a silent U stuck in after the G, like with words starting with Q.
- o Vocabulary
  - lodge (verse 25)
  - to stay a short time in a place such as a home or hotel (action verb)
  - Other definitions (action verb):
    - to provide a place to stay for a short period of time
    - to become stuck in something
- o Hebrew
  - Today we're going to learn the letter Mem. It's the M sound.
  - There are five letters in the Hebrew alphabet that take on a special shape when at the end of the word. Use the word eloHEEM to figure out which of these lines shows the Mem in the middle of a word and which shows the Mem at the end of the word.

  - Trace the Mem on the Hebrew Writing 27 page of your workbook.

IV. Science
- o The scene we have been reading in Genesis this week has been taking place by a spring.
- o What do you remember about springs? What is a spring?
  - It's where water naturally comes out of the ground.
- o Where does the water come from?
  - It comes from the water table, where water collects and pools up underground. It happens where the water can't travel any father. It could be because the ground is saturated, or full, and can't take in any more water, or maybe the water has hit rock and can't get through.
- o How does spring water come out of the ground?
  - Erosion allows water to break through. Water can push through cracks in rocks. The hole gets bigger by erosion and lets more and more water break through.
- o Do you remember what an artesian well is?
  - It's where water shoots up into the sky. Do you remember what force causes the pressure that pushes the water out so strongly that it shoots up?
    - ▪ gravity
    - ▪ The water table is above the hole where the water is shooting out, so the water is being pushed down through its underground passageway, but where it comes out of ground it points up, shooting it out of the ground.
  - There's another time pressure causes water to shoot up out of the ground. I'm going to tell you about *geysers,* where water and steam periodically shoot up out of the ground. This is different from an artesian well where water continually comes out of the ground.
- o As I describe how a geyser works, draw a diagram of it. Make a picture of how you think it would look. Ready?
  - We know that it gets warmer the deeper you go under the earth. Water that is miles down underground can be heated by the mantle. Cracks in the rock and pressure from the heat below can push this water upwards. This heated water can get into a small open area underground ground where water pools up.

- Added to the hot water is cold water coming from regular sources. This water also fills up the underground pool of water that is part of the water table.
- The more water there is, the more pressure there is. That's like the center of the earth is not liquid because of all the pressure, the weight of all that water creates pressure that keeps the water from boiling.
- That's true to a point. The hot water keeps getting heated from the hot rock underneath and the hot water keeps mixing with the cold water making it warmer and warmer.
- Eventually all of the water gets hot enough for it to start boiling.
- When some of the water escapes as steam, it relieves the pressure and then in a flash, all of the water can boil and all at once a lot of the water turns into steam and shoots out of the opening forcing the rest of the water out with it.
- Then the process starts over again, and water starts filling the empty space underground.
- Look at the picture below. Which is the geyser? What is different about it that would cause water and steam to shoot out?

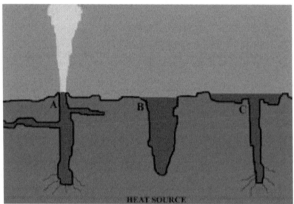

http://www.photovolcanica.com/VolcanoInfo/Yellowstone/Yellowstone.html

- The difference is the small opening. We talked about that before. If you use a hose and make the opening smaller, water shoots out farther because you are forcing the same amount of water out of a smaller opening.
- The most famous geyser in America is named Old Faithful. It is called that because it erupts predictably. It shoots up water and steam about every thirty to ninety minutes as the pressure is relieved and then builds again.
  o If the opening on the surface is not a small hole but a pool area, then the water doesn't erupt. It rises up to the surface in a small pool, like in picture C above. That's called a *thermal spring*. It always has a supply of hot water warming it.
    - We used a thermal spring for baptisms in Macedonia. The water is warm all winter long even though it was up on a mountainside.
  o Recall: How does water in a geyser get hot? It is heated by hot rocks found deep below the surface. What kind of spring has hot water in it? thermal spring
  o Explore More: Learn about pressure and boiling points. Learn about how much pressure there is under water.

V. Social Studies

- o Today we're going to make a family tree. You can use your worksheet page for this.
- o God, Adam, Eve, Seth, Cain, Abel, (under Seth but with a … break from Genesis 5 add) Methuselah, Lamech, Noah, and his sons: Shem, Ham, Japheth
  - From Japeth we get the tribes of Gog and Magog.
  - From Ham come the Canaanites and Amorites.
  - From Shem come the Elamites and a son named, Arphaxad, who is the great, great, great, great, great grandfather of Terah.
- o Terah is the father of Abraham, Sarah (by a different mother), Nahor and Haran.
- o Can you add Hagar, Ishmael, and Isaac?
- o Haran has Lot and Milcah and Iscah.
  - From Lot come the Moabites.
- o Can you use today's reading to add on Rebekah and Laban? (The Nahor mentioned in verse 24 is Abraham's brother. Nahor marries Milcah and they have Bethuel.)
- o Then you can add Jacob and his sons.
- o Explore More: What else can you fill in?

VI. Discussion

- o Your lineage starts with Adam and Noah as well. We are all related. If you were related to the orphan or the widow or the homeless man, how would you treat them? Is there someone you don't like? Can you see them as part of your family?
- o When we become Christians, we become part of God's family. Do you see yourself as one family with other believers?

VII. Writing

- o Use the discussion question as a writing prompt.
- o Get a high five and/or hug for any adverb that you use.

Day 114

I. Read Genesis 24:33-49. We're continuing the story of Rebekah today.

II. Memory Verse
- o Practice Deuteronomy 31:8.
- o "The LORD is the one who goes ahead of you; He will be with you. He will not fail you or forsake you. Do not fear or be dismayed."

III. Language
- o Handwriting/Spelling
  - verse 36
  - words to know: business, successful, blessed, down
  - spelling tips:
    - Three of your words today, <u>business</u>, <u>successful</u>, and <u>blessed</u>, have a double S in them. The word successful has two different double letters.
    - The word <u>down</u> ends with the word own.
- o Grammar
  - We're going to look at adverbs in today's reading.
  - Here are some phrases from today's reading. Find the adverb or adverbs that tell us more about the verb.
    - The Lord has <u>greatly</u> blessed
    - deal <u>kindly</u> and <u>truly</u>
    - will not eat <u>until</u>
  - The first examples tell us how God blessed and how they are going to deal with him, but the last one tells us about when he's going to eat.
  - They are all adverbs.
- o Hebrew
  - Trace and write the Mem on the Hebrew Writing 28 page of your workbook.
  - Remember that the closed one comes only when used at the end of a word. The other is used everywhere else.
  - Practice saying Genesis 1:1-5.

IV. Science
- o Since we looked at anatomy earlier this week, I want to do it again. What's anatomy?
  - The study of the structure of living things.
- o We have three body parts in today's reading. Do you remember any of them?
  - The nose is the most memorable because Rebekah gets a ring for her nose from the servant.
  - She also gets bracelets for her wrists and carries the water jug on her shoulder.
- o I'm assuming you know where all those body parts are. Let's learn a little more about them though.
- o The nose is made of bone and *cartilage*. The cartilage is what divides your nose into two nostrils. You can stick your thumb and forefinger into your nostrils and wiggle the cartilage a little.

- Cartilage doesn't heal the way the rest of our body is able to heal on its own, so don't be rough with your nose!
  - You also have a nose bone that's the bone running down the top middle of your nose.
  - Can you guess where else you might have cartilage in your body?
    - Your ear has cartilage. Your ear also has bones, but cartilage is in the outside part of your ear, the part of the ear you can see.
    - Can you feel it in there?
  - There are a few other places. One surprising place is your rib cage. Each rib ends with a small length of cartilage.
  - A main function of cartilage is found in our joints. Do you remember what a joint is?
    - It's where two bones connect.
    - Some joints allow for a lot of movement. Where are some joints that allow for a lot of movement?
      - fingers, wrists, shoulders, ankle, hip, etc.
    - Some joints have more limited movement such as knees and elbows.
    - Some joints don't allow for movement such as bones in your skull.
  - In our story we read about shoulders and wrists. They are both joints and both have cartilage. The cartilage makes for a smooth surface to make it easier for the joints to move.
  - The shoulder is actually two joints.
    - Swing your arm around in a large circle. That's one joint working.
    - Hold your arm out to the side and rotate it back and forth. That's another joint working.
  - From the bones you learned the other day, what bones do you think are connected at the shoulder?
    - the humerus, the clavicle and the scapula
    - What are those bones?
      - upper arm, collar bone, shoulder blade
  - What bones are being connected by joints in your wrist?
    - The carpals are connected with the metacarpals in your hand and the ulna and radius in your forearm.
  - How do those joints let your hand move?
  - Recall: What is the name of the material that covers joints for easy movement and which makes up part of our noses and ears? cartilage
  - Explore More: There are three main types of joints. What are they and what are the differences?

V. Social Studies
  - Today's lesson is in answered prayer.
  - What does the servant pray in our Bible story?
  - Who does the servant's prayer affect?
    - It affected Rebekah, Isaac, their families, their future children Esau and Jacob and all of Israel that comes from Jacob, including Jesus.
  - Some prayers we may never know the impact of.
    - I'm going to tell stories of answered prayers today.
  - I told you one example earlier about George Washington Carver. Do you remember his prayer?

- Of course, he prayed lots of things over his lifetime, but one thing he specifically prayed and asked God was why He created the peanut. He would get up at four in the morning and ask God, "What do you want me to discover today?"
- He discovered three hundred uses for the peanut and one hundred uses for the sweet potato.
  - Why is that a big deal?
    - Cotton farming had ruined the soil in southern America. All of the nutrients were taken out of the soil and crops weren't growing well. Freed slaves often just kept growing cotton because that's all they knew.
    - George convinced these farmers to grow peanuts and sweet potatoes so that they would have nourishing food from what they grew and because those crops would put nutrients back into the soil.
    - The problem was that no one wanted to buy their crops. With his discoveries he was able to create a large demand for their crops. Factories wanted peanuts instead of just cotton because they could make so many products out of them such as oil, flour, and soap.
  - People agree that George Washington Carver did more than anyone else to restore the South after the terrible Civil War. He especially helped former slaves, like himself, to create a living.
    - He was born a slave. When he was a baby, his mother was kidnapped and he never saw her again. He was raised as the child of his owners.
    - His prayers affected a whole country and the families of former slaves not only those alive then but their children and grandchildren. And who knows how having a successful farm affected those future generations?
    - This is what was written about George Washington Carver when he died. "He could have added fortune to fame, but caring for neither, he found happiness and honor in being helpful to the world."
  - And by his prayers he helped his whole world.
  - How about another George, George Müller. He lived in England in the 1800s.
    - He became a Christian in college. His father refused to continue to pay for his schooling because he wanted to become a missionary. George prayed and asked God to provide the money for tuition to continue at school.
      - An hour later he was offered a job tutoring. It paid his expenses.
    - George Müller is most famous for running orphanages, taking in Britain's street children. He cared for more than 10,000 orphans during his life.
    - He prayed for everything, for the building, for the furniture, for the food, for the clothing, etc. but on the first day, no children showed up. He realized he had taken that for granted! He prayed for children, and they came. The rest, as they say, is history.
  - The most famous story of his answered prayers comes from a time when the orphanage ran out of food.
    - George ordered all of the children to go and sit in the dining room anyway. They prayed and thanked God for their meal. There was a knock on the door. A baker hadn't been able to sleep the night before thinking that the orphans needed food and had gotten up and made bread for the children. Then there was someone else at the door. A milk delivery wagon broke in front of the

orphanage. The milk was given to the children so it wouldn't spoil. The children were fed.

- o How many lives were affected by George Muller's prayers? We can never know. All of those ten thousand orphans, what would have become of them if they had lived on the street? Their lives changed direction completely and who knows what they each went on to contribute to the world.
- o Recall: Who were the two men whose prayers changed the world? What did they do? George Washington Carver, George Muller, helped save the southern economy and raise African Americans up from poverty, took care of more than 10,000 orphans
- o Explore More: Read biographies on these two great men.

*At the end of the lesson I included two stories of answered prayer just because. ☺ There are millions of stories of answered prayers. These stories are from the site praybold.org and are printed with permission from their site.

VI. Discussion
- o What are your family's stories of answered prayer?
- o We discussed before how an act of obedience can change the world. What about a prayer? If you believed your prayers could change the world, what would you be praying for?

VII. Writing
- o Use the discussion question as a writing prompt.
- o Get a high five and/or hug if you use an adverb.

STORIES OF ANSWERED PRAYER

This first story is a story reported by an Overseas Missionary Fellowship missionary at his home church in Michigan.

While serving at a small field hospital in Africa, I traveled every two weeks through the jungle to a nearby city for supplies. This required camping overnight halfway. On one of these trips, I saw two men fighting in the city. One was seriously hurt, so I treated him and witnessed to him about the Lord Jesus Christ. I then returned home without incident.

Upon arriving in the city several weeks later, I was approached by the man I had treated earlier. He told me he had known that I carried money and medicine. He said, "Some friends and I followed you into the jungle knowing you would camp overnight. We waited for you to go to sleep and planned to kill you and take your money and drugs. Just as we were about to move into your campsite, we saw that you were surrounded by 26 armed guards."

I laughed at this and said, "I was certainly all alone out in the jungle campsite." The young man pressed the point, "No sir, I was not the only one to see the guards. My five friends also saw them, and we all counted them. It was because of those guards that we were afraid and left you alone."

At this point of the church presentation in Michigan, one of the men in the church stood up and interrupted the missionary. He asked, "Can you tell me the exact date when this happened?" The missionary thought for a while and recalled the date.

The man in the congregation then gave his side of the story. He stated, "On that night in Africa, it was day here. I was preparing go play golf. As I put my bags in the car, I felt the Lord leading me to pray for you. In fact, the urging was so great that I called men of this church together to pray for you. Will all of those men who met to pray please stand?"

The men who had met that day to pray together stood - there were 26 of them.

A LITTLE GIRL'S PRAYER

(As told by Helen Roseveare, a doctor missionary from England to Zaire, Africa)

One night I had worked hard to help a mother in the labor ward; but in spite of all we could do she died leaving us with a tiny premature baby and a crying two-year-old daughter. We would have difficulty keeping the baby alive, as we had no incubator (we had no electricity to run an incubator) and no special feeding facilities.

Although we lived on the equator, nights were often chilly with treacherous drafts. One student midwife went for the box we had for such babies and the cotton wool the baby would be wrapped in. Another went to stoke up the fire and fill a hot water bottle. She came back shortly in distress to tell me that in filling the bottle, it had burst. Rubber perishes easily in tropical climates.

"And it is our last hot water bottle!" she exclaimed.

As in the West it is no good crying over spilled milk, so in Central Africa it might be considered no good crying over burst water bottles. They do not grow on trees, and there are no drugstores down forest pathways.

"All right," I said, "Put the baby as near the fire as you safely can; sleep between the baby and the door to keep it free from drafts. Your job is to keep the baby warm."

The following noon, as I did most days, I went to have prayers with many of the orphanage children who chose to gather with me. I gave the youngsters various suggestions of things to pray about and told them about the tiny baby. I explained our problem about keeping the baby warm enough, mentioning the hot water bottle. The baby could so easily die if it got chills. I also told them of the two-year-old sister, crying because her mother had died.

During the prayer time, one ten-year-old girl, Ruth, prayed with the usual blunt conciseness of our African children. "Please, God," she prayed, "send us a water bottle. It'll be no good tomorrow, God, as the baby will be dead, so please send it this afternoon."

While I gasped inwardly at the audacity of the prayer, she added by way of corollary, "And while You are about it, would You please send a dolly for the little girl so she'll know You really love her?"

As often with children's prayers, I was put on the spot. Could I honestly say, "Amen"? I just did not believe that God could do this. Oh, yes, I know that He can do everything. The Bible says so. But there are limits, aren't there? The only way God could answer this particular prayer would be by sending me a parcel from the homeland. I had been in Africa for almost four years at that time, and I had never, ever received a parcel from home.

Anyway, if anyone did send me a parcel, who would put in a hot water bottle? I lived on the equator!

Halfway through the afternoon, while I was teaching in the nurses' training school, a message was sent that there was a car at my front door. By the time I reached home, the car had gone, but there, on the verandah, was a large twenty-two pound parcel! I felt tears pricking my eyes. I could not open the parcel alone, so I sent for the orphanage children. Together we pulled off the string, carefully undoing each knot. We folded the paper, taking care not to tear it unduly. Excitement was mounting. Some thirty or forty pairs of eyes were focused on the large cardboard box.

From the top, I lifted out brightly colored, knitted jerseys. Eyes sparkled as I gave them out. Then there were the knitted bandages for the leprosy patients, and the children looked a little bored. Then came a box of mixed raisins and sultanas-that would make a nice batch of buns for the weekend. Then, as I put my hand in again, I felt the... could it really be? I grasped it and pulled it out-yes! A brand-new, rubber hot water bottle! I cried. I had not asked God to send it; I had not truly believed that He could.

Ruth was in the front row of the children. She rushed forward, crying out, "If God has sent the bottle, He must have sent the dolly, too!"

Rummaging down to the bottom of the box, she pulled out the small, beautifully dressed dolly. Her eyes shone! She had never doubted!

Looking up at me, she asked, "Can I go over with you, Mummy, and give this dolly to that little girl, so she'll know that Jesus really loves her?"

That parcel had been on the way for five whole months! Packed up by my former Sunday school class, whose leader had heard and obeyed God's prompting to send a hot water bottle, even to the equator. And one of the girls had put in a dolly for an African child-five months before -- in answer to the believing prayer of a ten—year—old to bring it "that afternoon."

Day 115

I. Read Genesis 24:50-67. Today we're finishing the chapter and the story of Rebekah's marriage to Isaac.

II. Memory Verse
- o Test yourselves on Deuteronomy 31:8.
- o Find it in the Bible.
- o "The LORD is the one who goes ahead of you; He will be with you. He will not fail you or forsake you. Do not fear or be dismayed."
- o Do you know what Genesis 1:1-5 is?

III. Language
- o Handwriting/Spelling
  - • Test yourselves with words from Days 106-109.
    - ▪ age, thigh, beware, concern
    - ▪ quickly, lower, shoulder, emptied
    - ▪ camel, lodge, guide, bracelet
    - ▪ business, successful, blessed, down
- o Vocabulary
  - • Test yourselves with the words from Days 106-108.
    - ▪ concerning – related to a subject
    - ▪ adverb – word that describes how something is done
    - ▪ lodge – to stay a short time in a place such as a home or hotel
- o Hebrew
  - • Practice writing words with Yod and Mem on the Hebrew Writing 29 page of your workbook.
  - • Can you read ve et? Can you read through shamayim? You need to add in the vowel sounds.

IV. Social Studies
- o We're going to talk a little more about George Washington Carver. This is an important lesson, so we're doing a double social studies lesson today.
- o Carver was the name of the family who owned George's mother. He was treated well, raised like a son in their home after George's mother was kidnapped and sold.
  - • He chose the name Washington himself when he wasn't receiving mail. He had to distinguish himself from a white man named George Carver who kept getting his mail. He named himself after the first president of the United States.
- o He learned to read and write at home, but wanting to go to school, he had to move west to Kansas from his home in Missouri to find a school that taught black children.
  - • He worked as a cook and by doing housework, whatever it took, to be able to attend these schools, while he was still a kid.
  - • He graduated from a high school in Kansas even though he constantly faced discrimination, people treating him wrongly because his skin was dark.
  - • He was accepted at a college in Kansas. He was turned away when he showed up because they saw that he was an African American.

- He became the first black student at Iowa State College. He had to sleep in an office and eat in the basement with the kitchen staff to maintain segregation from the white students. He started a laundry business to put himself through school.
  - Why did Carver work so hard to go to school? Why did he take jobs and work just to be able to go to school? Why did he not give up when the college rejected him? Why did he not give up when he was treated poorly compared to the other students? Why was education that important to him? Any thoughts?
  - Slaves were freed right around the time George Washington Carver was born. It was good timing for George to be born, but of course, it was God was behind it. George had the chance to go to school. Before slaves were freed, there had been a law that made it illegal for anyone to teach a slave to read.
    - Why? Why wouldn't they want a slave to be able to read? Why was it important to them to have uneducated slaves?
    - Why do you think it would be easier to control slaves who were uneducated?
  - George Washington Carver got his master's degree and became a professor. He eventually accepted a position at a school for only African American students. It was called Tuskegee University. The students there were required to build their own buildings.
    - Why? What benefit would that bring?
  - Here's an excerpt from the autobiography of Booker T. Washington. He was the founder of Tuskegee University. He explains why students had to build their own buildings. (excerpt from Booker T. Washington. Up from Slavery: An Autobiography. 1901. X. A Harder Task Than Making Bricks Without Straw)

FROM the very beginning, at Tuskegee, I was determined to have the students do not only the agricultural and domestic work, but to have them erect their own buildings. My plan was to have them, while performing this service, taught the latest and best methods of labour, so that the school would not only get the benefit of their efforts, but the students themselves would be taught to see not only utility in labour, but beauty and dignity; would be taught, in fact, how to lift labour up from mere drudgery and toil, and would learn to love work for its own sake. My plan was not to teach them to work in the old way, but to show them how to make the forces of nature—air, water, steam, electricity, horse-power—assist them in their labour.

At first many advised against the experiment of having the buildings erected by the labour of the students, but I was determined to stick to it. I told those who doubted the wisdom of the plan that I knew that our first buildings would not be so comfortable or so complete in their finish as buildings erected by the experienced hands of outside workmen, but that in the teaching of civilization, self-help, and self-reliance, the erection of the buildings by the students themselves would more than compensate for any lack of comfort or fine finish.

I further told those who doubted the wisdom of this plan, that the majority of our students came to us in poverty, from the cabins of the cotton, sugar, and rice plantations of the South, and that while I knew it would please the students very much to place them at once in finely constructed buildings, I felt that it would be following out a more natural process of development to teach them how to construct their own buildings. Mistakes I knew would be made, but these mistakes would teach us valuable lessons for the future.

During the now nineteen years' existence of the Tuskegee school, the plan of having the buildings erected by student labour has been adhered to. In this time forty buildings, counting small and large, have been built, and all except four are almost wholly the product of student labour. As an additional result, hundreds of men are now scattered throughout the South who received their knowledge of mechanics while being taught how to erect these buildings. Skill and knowledge are now handed down from one set of students to another in this way, until at the present time a building of any description or size can be constructed wholly by our instructors and students, from the drawing of the plans to the putting in of the electric fixtures, without going off the grounds for a single workman.

Not a few times, when a new student has been led into the temptation of marring the looks of some building by leadpencil marks or by the cuts of a jack-knife, I have heard an old student remind him: "Don't do that. That is our building. I helped put it up."

- How did they learn to love work?
  - They learned by working. Working gave them valuable tools for life, and it gave them pride in what they accomplished.
- Read this first sentence again and listen for what else they were required to do besides build the buildings. "From the very beginning, at Tuskegee, I was determined to have the students do not only the agricultural and domestic work, but to have them erect their own buildings."
  - They did the agricultural and domestic work.
  - That means the students also did their own farming to produce their own food and did all the cleaning and such around the university campus.
- Why were the students willing to work so hard to be able to go to school?
- What makes education so valuable?
- What makes education so dangerous that it had to be kept from slaves?
  - Do you have answers?
  - Every piece of information is power. Every word you learn how to use is a tool for persuasion. Every math concept you learn is a tool for discovery. Every history lesson learned is a tool for freedom. Every science lesson learned is a tool for creating. Every piece of art and music explored is a new way of thinking opened in your mind.
  - Education is power.
- I told you that when the Communists came to power, they killed off many of the educated people in the population. They were seen as a danger to the new government.
- The official, political church of the Middle Ages forbade Christians from having and reading a Bible! William Tyndale was killed for translating the Bible into English so that people could read the Bible for themselves.
- Why?
  - Knowledge is power. That church wasn't God's Church. It wasn't made up of God's family. They were in power, and they wanted to keep it.
  - One example is that the Catholic Church told people they had to pay the church money to have their sins forgiven. If people read the Bible for themselves, they would see that wasn't true!
  - They would lose the power they held over people.

- o These are just some examples. Tyndale lost his life to give people knowledge of God's Word. Other missionaries have done the same. The knowledge of God's Word is the most powerful of all. It's the power to be saved!
- o Explore More: The reading was from Booker T. Washington's autobiography, *Up from Slavery*. You may want to read it or a biography on him.

VI. Discussion

- o Do you see education as valuable? Do you see education as dangerous to those in power? Are you taking advantage of your education?
- o Maybe not everything interests you, but you learn all you can, and then you take the things that interest you and learn everything possible. Become a master at it. Change the world.
- o Get a high five and/or hug if you decide you want to change the world. ☺
- o Do you want more explanation about the value of education?
  - • Words are tools for persuasion. Abraham Lincoln credited an author for starting the Civil War by writing her book *Uncle Tom's Cabin*, which showed the cruelty of slavery.
  - • Math is a tool for discovery. Math shows us patterns. It can help us uncover faults and scams, and it can reveal to us future direction by following the outcome of those patterns.
  - • History is a tool for freedom. The saying goes, "Those who don't know history are bound to repeat it." Knowing history frees us to make better choices.
  - • Science is a tool for discovery. George Washington Carver is an example of that.

VII. Writing

- o Choose one of your writings from Days 107-109 to edit.
- o Use your editing checklist and have someone else edit it as well.
- o Create a final draft.
- o (Note: You might want to save this in your child's portfolio. It would be a good time to save an example of math as well and to write down what your child has been reading.)

Day 116

I. Read Genesis 37:1-11. (We're moving into Joseph's story now.)

II. Memory Verse
   o Learn Romans 8:28.
   o And we know that God causes all things to work together for good to those who love God, to those who are called according to His purpose.

III. Language
   o Handwriting/Spelling
     • verse 11
     • words to know: bind, erect, rebuke, jealous
     • spelling tips:
       ▪ The word <u>bind</u> has the same spelling pattern as the word kind.
       ▪ The word <u>erect</u> is spelled just like it sounds if pronounced carefully.
       ▪ The word <u>rebuke</u> ends with a silent E.
       ▪ The word <u>jealous</u> has the same vowel spelling pattern for its first syllable as your spelling word heaven.
   o Vocabulary
     • rebuke (verse 10)
     • to scold; to tell someone their behavior is wrong in a sharp manner (action verb)
     • As a noun, a rebuke is the words expressed when someone scolds.
   o Hebrew
     • This week we'll learn the last two letters we need to write all of Genesis 1:1.
     • Today we'll learn the Shin. It's our sound SH. We don't have an individual letter for this sound in English. This is the letter you wrote in shaMAyim, heaven.
     • Trace the Shin on the Hebrew Writing 30 page of your workbook.

IV. Science
   o Joseph is given a varicolored tunic. Here's a picture of a *tunic*. It's basically like a short dress, but it was masculine, manly attire back then. Why do you think men wore dresses, robes, etc. Why didn't people wear pants?
     • My guess is that it was a lot simpler to make. They didn't have sewing machines. Pants have to be fitted and kept up. They weren't using buttons and zippers. They were also probably cool in the desert heat.

- o What does it mean that Joseph's tunic was varicolored?
  - • It had a variety of colors. What do you think was special about that?
  - • Most clothing was probably just the color it came as. It was a lot of work to dye cloth or thread, and a lot of work means it was expensive. This was not even just a dyed tunic. It was woven together with a variety of colors or it was sewed together from a variety of cloths. It was not something any of his brothers would ever own.
- o Today we're going to learn a little about dying cloth in the ancient world. People have been dying cloth for all of recorded history. Why do you think people like to wear colors?
  - • I think it affects how people feel.
  - • We've talked about turning cotton into thread and turning wool into yarn. That thread and yarn can get color from dying, or it can be made into clothing and then dyed.
- o Dying cloth, up until the Industrial Revolution was in full swing, meant taking a color found in nature and applying it to the cloth.
- o Let's say you decide you want to turn your shirt brown and you choose a brown chocolate chip cookie as your dye.
  - • What happens if you smear a chocolate chip cookie on your clothes?
    - ▪ Some of it would just brush off as crumbs. Some of it would turn your clothes brown in that spot.
    - ▪ What happens after it is washed (hopefully)?
      - • The brown comes out.
- o One problem with using a chocolate chip cookie is that it only colored your shirt in a small area. When you dye cloth, you want to dye the whole thing.

- o Can you think of things people had to figure out in order to dye clothing? What were two other problems they had to overcome? (Note: Think of the results of rubbing chocolate chip cookie on your shirt.)
  - They had to find color that would stick to the fabric.
  - They had to find color that wouldn't just come off when it got wet.
  - So, they had to get the dye color to stick and to stay stuck.
- o Where do you think their dye came from?
  - It came from plants and animals.
  - Did you ever peel and grate carrots and end up with orange fingers?
- o The first dyes were just plants rubbed into wool. (They had sheep. They didn't have cotton farms. Wool was the main source for threads for fabric.)
- o Later dyes were boiled in water with the textile. This enabled the whole cloth to be more evenly dyed.
- o Boiling was done with animal dyes such as the purple that came from sea snail.
  - You may know that purple is considered the color of royalty. Can you guess how a color might have come to be worn only by royalty? (Hint: It could be worn by anyone wealthy.)
    - It was really expensive to make. Supposedly it took 12,000 snails to make enough dye to color the trim on the edge of a cloak.
  - This kind of dye was special because the color remained and even was said to get better with age instead of fading.
- o Do you remember the two problems people had to overcome in order to dye clothing?
  - They had to make it stick and stay.
- o Most dyes didn't stay as well as the royal purple color. They needed what we call a *mordant*.
  - Modern day mordants include alum if you want to try this at home.
  - Ancient mordants included old urine. When mixed with the dye, the color would then stick and stay on the wool.
- o Recall: What were two problems that cloth dyers had to overcome?
  - making the color stick and then keeping it there so it wouldn't be washed out
- o Explore More: What's the chemistry behind dying cloth? What did they use to keep color dyes from washing out of cloth? Urine was also used in laundering. You could look into that.

V. Social Studies
- o What did Joseph do in verse two from our story today?
  - He was a tattletale. He told on his brothers. Did he do what was right or not?
  - If his father asked him to report on what they were doing, then he did right. If not asked, when is it right to tell on others?
    - If someone is doing something wrong, you should remind them to do what is right.
    - You need to tell on them, though, if they are doing something dangerous. That could be dangerous to themselves or to someone else.

- Sinning and lying about it to cover it up are dangerous to someone because they need to confess and repent to be forgiven and to be right with God.
- Teasing or making a mess are not dangerous even if you think the person is doing wrong.
- So, answer the question, when is it right to tell on others?
- There are times when adults tell on each other. Just like with kids, there are times they should tell and times this shouldn't happen.
  - Sometimes people tell on homeschoolers, reporting that their kids aren't in school.
  - There are some famous circumstances, though, where adults do share secrets for the benefit of everyone.
  - When someone in an organization sees that something immoral or illegal is going on and reports it to the public or the police, we call that person a *whistleblower*, not a tattletale.
- Right now there is a website dedicated to whistleblowing called Wikileaks. We call it a *leak* when information is sneaked out. People release documents online that they have found that tell us about the operations of governments. Governments are often the ones being told on. Here are some examples from America.
  - "The Pentagon Papers" were given to newspapers and revealed that President Johnson was lying to the public about the Vietnam War.
  - President Nixon ended up leaving his job as president because a whistleblower, who hid his identity by calling himself "Deep Throat," gave information to two journalists which proved Nixon had cheated to get elected.
- People blow the whistle on businesses too. A famous instance of this happening is when someone made known to the public that a company was giving a false impression of its success. The company was called Enron. People were investing millions of dollars in the company because the company always made it seem that they were doing really well. Someone told the public that they were really losing money and the whole company crashed. Its leaders were taken to court for lying.
- Recall: What's a whistleblower? What is a leak?
  - someone who reveals secrets about an organization
  - when information is leaked out
- Explore More: A recent whistleblower is Edward Snowden who leaked documents about PRISM. What did he expose?

VI. Discussion
- What do you think? Do you think whistleblowers do the right thing?
- Sometimes they end up in jail. Sometimes they are killed. Sometimes they spend years in hiding. Sometimes they are treated like heroes.
- Do you think you could be brave enough to be a whistleblower? What things are important enough for you to speak up against?

VII. Writing
- o Today you are going to practice sentences that don't need commas. When you use a word like because, since, when and if in the middle of your sentence, you don't use a comma.
- o You don't use a comma before a conjunction if it couldn't be a separate sentence on the other side.
- o You never, ever put just one comma between the subject and the verb. (Note: See what I just did there? Rules were meant to be broken, sometimes.)
- o Complete Writing Sentences 18 in your workbook.

Day 117 (check Materials List)

I. Read Genesis 37:12-21.

II. Memory Verse
- o Practice Romans 8:28.
- o And we know that God causes all things to work together for good to those who love God, to those who are called according to His purpose.

III. Language
- o Handwriting/Spelling
  - • verse 15
  - • words to know: pasture, pasturing, welfare, devour
  - • spelling tips:
    - ▪ The word <u>pasture</u> starts with the word past and ends with a silent E.
    - ▪ When you write the word <u>pasturing</u>, the letter I in ING, replaces the letter E at the end of pasture.
    - ▪ The word <u>welfare</u> does not have a double letter and ends with a silent E.
    - ▪ The word <u>devour</u> ends with the word our, as in our house.
- o Vocabulary
  - • devour (verse 20)
  - • to eat up <u>hungrily</u>; to beat or to destroy <u>completely</u>; to consume <u>quickly</u> (verb)
  - • I used three adverbs in my definitions. What are they?
- o Hebrew
  - • Trace and write the Shin on the Hebrew Writing 31 page of your workbook.
  - • Practice Genesis 1:5. Say it and think about what the words mean.

IV. Science
- o There's an imaginary wild beast in today's reading. What wild beasts would have lived where they were? What do you think?
  - • Some animals that Joseph might have encountered are goats, lions, antelopes, bears, crocodiles, ostriches, cheetahs, ox, and deer.
- o Which of those animals do you think would have been willing to eat Joseph?
  - • lions, bears, crocodiles, cheetahs
- o Let's look at lions today. Let's start with their scientific classification. What is scientific classification?
- o It's the way we organize living things into categories.
  - • What kingdom would lions belong to? (hint: bacteria, plants...)
    - ▪ animal kingdom
  - • Is a lion a vertebrate or an invertebrate?
    - ▪ vertebrate
    - ▪ What does that mean?
      - • It means that the animal has a spine, a backbone.
  - • What class does a lion belong to? (hint: not reptile, not fish, not bird...)
    - ▪ mammal

- What order does a lion belong to? (hint: What does it eat? not a herbivore)
    - carnivore
- What family does a lion belong to? (hint: not canine...)
    - feline (cat)
- A lion's genus is panther.
- The species of lion we're talking about today is the Persian Lion or the Asiatic Lion.
    - Can you guess where Asiatic Lions live? (Note: If they can't guess, you could show them the word. It's easier to see the connection than to hear it.)
        - Asiatic means of Asia.
  - Right now, these lions only live in India. They are *endangered*, meaning there are not many left.
  - The species is in danger of going *extinct*, not existing anymore, but they are protected now. There were fewer than 200 left, but their numbers are increasing.
  - Take a guess at how tall and long an Asiatic lion can be.
    - Asiatic lions can stand three and a half feet tall, to the shoulder (over 100 cm), and can be nearly ten feet (3 m) long, including the tail.
    - Stand up and figure out about how big that would be.
  - Guess how much a lion weighs?
    - The male weighs around 400 pounds (175 kilos) and the female weighs around 250 pounds (115 kilos).
  - What do you think they eat besides Josephs?
    - Lions are carnivores, so they eat meat, other animals.
    - They hunt in groups and work together to get meals of deer, antelope, boars, bulls, and many other animals.
    - It's the female lions that do most of the hunting.
  - The male lions are the ones with manes, the hair around their heads. They defend their territory and their family.
    - Like other animals, lions mark their territory with urine. The scent lets other animals know it's not their turf and to stay away.
  - Lions live in *prides*, like fish swim in schools. A pride is a family group. It can have a few males and several females and then all of their cubs.
    - Lions are the only felines that live in family groups.
  - Recall: What carnivore, vertebrate, mammal were we learning about today? What is the name of their family group? What do we call animals that are in danger of becoming extinct?
    - Asiatic lions
    - a pride
    - endangered
  - Explore More: Compare and contrast the African lion with the Asiatic lion.

V. Social Studies
  - Joseph walks to Shechem and then to Dothan. How far was he walking? How long did it take? Instead of just looking at maps, today we're going to make a map to scale and figure out the answers to those questions.
  - On the next page is a map of what's happening in Genesis 37.

- o Verses 14 and 17 tell us the three locations of this story. What are they?
  - • the valley of Hebron, Shechem, and Dothan
- o The distance from Hebron to Shechem is about 50 miles or about 80 kilometers.
- o Draw a map of Israel. You can just draw a piece like the map I have on the next page. See the directions below for how big to make it.
  - • Include the Dead Sea, the Sea of Galilee and the Jordan River. They are all pictured on the map. The Dead Sea is the bigger one and they are connected by the river. You could label them on your map.
    - ▪ Measure 14 centimeters from the middle of the Dead Sea to the middle of the Sea of Galilee for their distance
  - • Place Hebron on your map. Draw a dot and write its name (with an N at the end, not like on the map).
  - • Measure eight centimeters from Hebron north to Shechem. Put a dot at Shechem and label it.
  - • At the bottom of your map, draw a line one centimeter long. Under the left end of the line, write a zero. Under the right end of the line, write 10 kilometers or 6.2 miles. (Note: I'm using kilometers because it makes math easier.)
    - ▪ Now you have a key to your scale. That shows people that every distance of one centimeter on your map is equal to ten kilometers in real life.
  - • What is the distance from Hebron to Shechem? Use your scale.
    - ▪ about 50 miles or 80 kilometers
- o Now we're going to add Dothan to our map.
- o Dothan continues north but a little to the east as well. This is about another 20 kilometers or twelve and a half miles.
  - • Use your scale to measure the distance and place your dot. Label Dothan.
- o Why are maps to scale helpful?
  - • Full size maps are too big! And a map that only showed the direction something was in, wouldn't tell you how far away it is. That would be a problem if you decided to walk to the arctic because it didn't seem so far on the map!
- o Since we know how far Joseph walked, let's think about how long it might have taken him. He walked about 100 kilometers or 62.5 miles. (We're going to use kilometers to make the math easier.)
  - • If you can walk 1 kilometer in 7 minutes, how long would it take for Joseph to walk from Hebron to Dothan?
    - ▪ 7 minutes times 100 kilometers equals 700 minutes. Do you want to figure that out in hours and minutes?
      - • 11 hours and 40 minutes.
    - ▪ Do you think he did it in one day?
- o Recall: What is a map drawn to scale? It's a map that shows distances.
- o Explore More: You could add more to your map. Can you make your seas and river to scale?

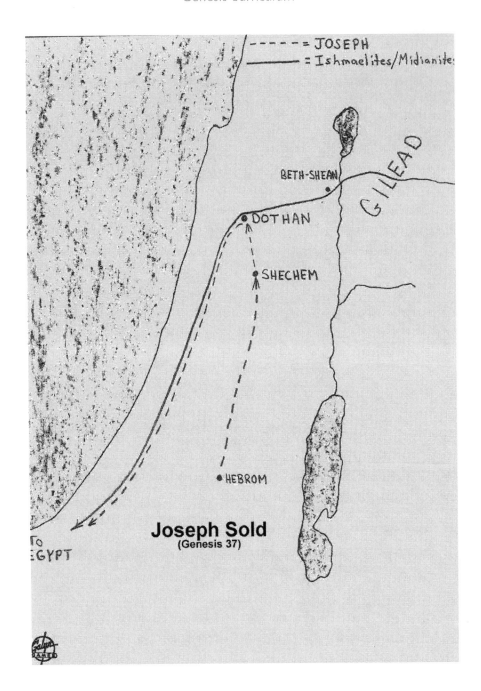

Joseph Sold
(Genesis 37)

VI. Discussion
- o Just a note of something I wanted to share with you: I told you that lions live in prides. Fish swim in schools. We call it a pod of whales. The most fascinating is a murder of crows!
- o If you could travel anywhere in the world, where would it be? Why?

VII. Writing
- o Use your discussion question as a writing prompt.
- o Get a high five and/or hug or any adverbs you use.

Day 118

I. Read Genesis 37:19-25. (Starts with the end of the previous reading.)

II. Memory Verse
- o Practice Romans 8:28.
- o And we know that God causes all things to work together for good to those who love God, to those who are called according to His purpose.

III. Language
- o Handwriting/Spelling
  - • verse 21
  - • words to know: rescue, further, balm, stripped
  - • spelling tip:
    - ▪ The word <u>rescue</u> ends with the same vowel spelling pattern as the word blue.
    - ▪ The two vowels used in rescue are also used in <u>further</u>.
    - ▪ The word <u>balm</u> is probably new to you. It is spelled similarly to calm and palm.
    - ▪ The word <u>strip</u> needs an extra letter P before adding the letters E-D onto the ending. Why?
      - • Otherwise it would be striped because the E would make the I say its name.
  - • A little grammar note today: We say farther when we can measure the distance to the thing that is farther away. We say further when we can't measure the distance, such as in "You couldn't be further from the truth," or "We'll need to take you in for further questioning."
    - ▪ You can remember which one means distance because farther has the word far in it. Use that when you are talking about how much more distance you need to cover.
- o Vocabulary
  - • balm (verse 25)
  - • a cream used for medicine, a sweet smell, or anything that heals or soothes (noun)
- o Hebrew
  - • Today we're going to learn the letter Tsade. Read those vowels like you would for a Hebrew word.
    - ▪ It's the sound TS at the end of Arets.
  - • There are five letters in the Hebrew alphabet that take on a special shape when at the end of the word. We learned that with the Mem. The Tsade is another one. The first row below is the regular version. The second row is the ending version that's only used at the very end of a word.
  - • Trace the Tsade on the Hebrew Writing 32 page of your workbook.

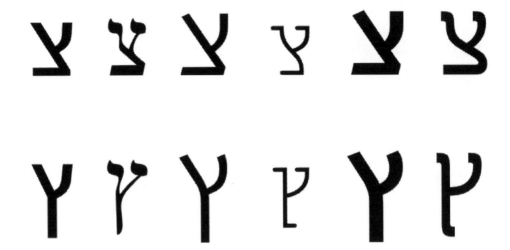

IV. Science

- o In our reading today, there are traders bearing aromatic gum and balm and myrrh. Let's learn what we can about those things.
- o For one, they all can be very fragrant, sweet smelling.
- o Balms are often thought of as medicine, but it could be a sweet smelling lotion or even a kind of plant that is used in seasoning.
- o When it says gum, it's not talking about bubble gum, but it does usually refer to a sticky substance. In other translations, instead of "aromatic gum" it says "spices."
- o This gum is taken from trees, and in fact, myrrh is a type of gum. It's used as a perfume, or in medicine, or to burn to produce a sweet smell.
- o Since we're talking about aromatics, things that give off fragrant or sweet-smelling aromas, let's learn about smell. What are we actually smelling? How does a smell get from something into our noses? Where do those smells come from? Any ideas?
- o What goes into our eyes that allows us to see?
  - light
- o When we smell, we are taking in molecules. We breathe in molecules that are in the air. That's the beginning of our body's *olfactory system*, what we know as our sense of smell.
  - Molecules of the scent are in the air we breathe.
    - Those molecules could be in something like smoke that is carrying them into the air.
    - Those molecules could also be in what's evaporating off of substances.
      - Evaporation is happening in the oven when dinner is cooking, which is why we smell it after a while.
    - Why don't we smell windows?
      - They aren't releasing anything into the air.
- o Most of your nose is dedicated to cleaning the air before it gets to your lungs, but a small portion of it, about 5%, (remember that's five balloons out of the hundred) is dedicated to smells.
  - But in just that small location in our noses, we have 40 million neurons ready to receive molecules. We call those neurons olfactory receptor neurons.

- Each smell triggers a different set of neurons.
  - People can distinguish between thousands and thousands of smells.
- Those neurons are part of our nervous system which means those olfactory receptors send their signals straight to the brain.
  - In the brain different reactions are triggered.
  - What are different reactions to smells that you can think of?
    - There's disgust and wanting to flee away from it.
    - There's a delicious smell that can literally trigger your body to make your mouth start watering.
    - There's a sweet smell that makes you feel good and warm inside.
    - Smells can trigger feelings. They can make us feel peaceful or excited.
    - Smells can also trigger memories. Your brain can connect a smell today to a memory from years before.
- We can get used to smells. Since smells trigger so much activity in our brain, if we continue to smell something, our neurons will stop sending signals to our brain about it, so we aren't overwhelmed by the continuous reaction to it.
  - The smell hasn't gone away. You've just gotten over it.
- You could try some smell experiments. You can test each other's sense of smell by blindfolding each other and putting out things for each other to smell and guess what it is. Make sure you don't mix smells. Keep things separate. You could also put out three shirts that have been worn for at least a few hours and see if you can tell which one is yours by the scent. (We each have a unique scent, like a fingerprint!)
- Recall: What are we breathing in that enable us to register a smell? What system takes in molecules and identifies them as scents?
  - molecules
  - olfactory system
- Explore More: Learn more about the olfactory system and the centers in our brain that are triggered by scents.

V. Social Studies
- Reuben hears his brother's plot to kill Joseph and stops it. This reminds me of what we've touched on about a big break in World War II.
  - I want to talk more about codes and code breaking in World War II.
- People who figure out codes are called *cryptologists*.
- The Americans were able to break the Japanese codes during World War II.
  - The man who put the final pieces of the puzzle together was Lieutenant Francis Raven.
- The Americans had to keep it a secret that they had figured out Japan's code.
  - Actually, the first time they broke the code the Japanese found out and then just changed their methods of *encryption*, or making a coded message.
  - The next time the American cryptologists decoded Japanese encryption methods, they kept it secret.
    - While the information they decoded was used to stop some attacks, they had to let other attacks occur, so it didn't look like they knew everything the Japanese were planning.
- Information is power. That's why we value education, right? Information won the war for the Allies, the Americans and British and those on their side.

- o Can I tell you one more thing about World War II codes? The Americans had their own unbreakable code.
  - They used Native Americans. We call them the Navaho Indian Code Talkers.
    - They spoke languages that were unwritten.
    - No one else in the world knew them. No one could study them without coming to America and living with them.
  - The Navaho Indian Code Talkers were a secret weapon of the Americans. They protected America's information.
- o Wars are full of spies and secrets. Communication is necessary, and messages had to get where needed. Encryption was one method of passing information secretly. Another method was pigeon.
  - Pigeons were trained to carry messages. They could get into dangerous areas. Homing pigeons are trained pigeons that always know how to find their way home.
  - There were more than a quarter of a million pigeons used during World War II.
- o Centuries earlier, secret messages were written in invisible ink that could be revealed by holding it up to a fire. The heat would cause a reaction and reveal the message.
- o Recall: How did Americans code messages?
  - They used Native Americans.
- o Explore More: You could learn about the Enigma and Alan Turing.

VI. Discussion

- o The Americans were able to decipher the Japanese plans for attacks but had to let some attacks happen in order to keep it a secret that they could read the enemy's plans.
- o What is the right decision? Is there a right decision? Was it right to let attacks happen when they could have been prevented? What does it mean that a short-term loss is worth a long-term gain? Does that apply when lives are involved?

VII. Writing

- o Use the discussion question as a writing prompt.
- o Get a high five and/or hug for using an adverb.

Day 119

I. Read Genesis 37:25-28. We're continuing our story. Do you remember where Joseph is? (in the pit)

II. Memory Verse
   - Practice Romans 8:28.
   - And we know that God causes all things to work together for good to those who love God, to those who are called according to His purpose.

III. Language
   - Handwriting/Spelling
     - verse 26
     - words to know: aromatic, myrrh, Joseph, caravan
     - spelling tips:
       - You spelled the word aroma before. The word <u>aromatic</u> is related. They both have to do with smell. The word aromatic has the word aroma inside of it.
       - The word <u>myrrh</u> is spelled in an unusual way. There are no regular vowels in it. It ends in a silent letter. It has a double consonant.
       - The word <u>Joseph</u> is a name, so it has to begin in a certain way. It ends with two letters making the final sound.
       - The word <u>caravan</u> begins with the word car and ends with the word van.
   - Vocabulary
     - profit (verse 26)
     - to get a benefit, often refers to money (verb)
     - As a noun it means the thing you got, such as an advantage or the money you made.
   - Hebrew
     - Trace and write the Tsade on the Hebrew Writing 33 page of your workbook.
     - Remember that the form of the letter at the bottom of the page is only used at the end of a word. That form hangs down below the line (like our letter p does).

IV. Science
   - Our Ishmaelite traders are traveling by camel. Let's learn about the camel today.
   - We talked about desert plants before. What's special about the plants that are able to survive in the desert?
     - They have to be able to live without a lot of water. What are some of the ways they do that? Do you remember what helps the cactus?
       - Plants, like the cactus, have a really large stem to store lots of water.
       - Plants have scales instead of open leaves to slow evaporation.
   - How do you think a camel is like a cactus?
     - Did you say that they both store water? This is a trick question! Many people believe that camels store water in their hump. That's not true, though. Their

humps are fat. I'll tell you about that in a second. So, how is a camel like a cactus?

- The cactus and the camel were both created to limit evaporation.
  - That hump of fat keeps all of the camel's fat away from its body. Why do walruses have fat, blubbery bodies?
    - It keeps them warm with insulation. Camels don't need help staying warm in the desert. Keeping the fat away from their bodies keeps them cooler so they don't sweat and lose water.

o Camels are mammals. Are mammals warm blooded or cold blooded?
  - warm blooded
  - What does that mean?
    - Its body temperature doesn't depend on the temperature of the air surrounding it.
  - When you get hot, you sweat to cool off. The sweat evaporates off of you.
  - When your body temperature goes up a degree, how do you feel?
    - sick
  - Camels are quite unique in that their body temperature can go up over ten degrees during the day (6 degrees Celsius). He doesn't need to sweat to cool off because his body is okay with its temperature rising to that extent.

o Camels can go months without drinking. When they get the chance to drink, they can drink and drink and drink and drink and drink! But it's not being stored, just replacing all the water they've used up.
  - Their digestive system conserves water. Their intestines take out all of the water until the camel's poop comes out completely dry. This is convenient for their owners who can use it as fuel for their fires.

o Camels get water from plants that they eat, but they aren't herbivores. They are omnivores. In fact, they are everything-ores. They can and will eat just about anything. They've been known to eat their owners' tents.
  - They can eat cactus and other thorny desert plants. Their mouths are so tough that thorns don't poke through the skin in their mouths.

o Let me tell you one last way camels were created to survive in the desert. They have an extra eyelid. It moves across the eye horizontally. It is *transparent*, which means that the camel can see through it. Why do think that eyelid might be needed by a camel?
  - It protects the camel's eye from sand. It can help clear sand out too, if it's already gotten in there.

o Recall: What's in a camel's hump? Why doesn't a camel sweat easily? What does a camel eat? Why is the camel's extra eyelid transparent?
  - fat
  - It can handle a raised body temperature.
  - most anything
  - so they can see through it

o Explore More: What are the two main types of camels we have today? Turn their starting letters (capitals) on their sides to help you remember which has one hump and which has two. Where in the world do they live? What makes camels good pack animals for carrying people and goods? What's the word for camel in Arabic? (This is another trick question!)

V. Social Studies

- ○ The traders in our story today are Ishmaelites. Who did they descend from?
  - • Ishmael
- ○ They are coming from Gilead. You can see where that is on Day 117. Do you remember what balm is?
  - • It's a cream or something that can be used for healing.
- ○ There is a song called, "There Is a Balm in Gilead." Here's a little about it from Wikipedia.

> This is a well-known traditional African-American spiritual. The "balm in Gilead" is a reference from the Old Testament, but the lyrics of this spiritual refer to the New Testament concept of salvation through Jesus Christ. The Balm of Gilead is interpreted as a spiritual medicine that is able to heal Israel (and sinners in general). In the Old Testament, the balm of Gilead is taken most directly from Jeremiah chapter 8 v. 22: "Is there no balm in Gilead? Is there no physician there? Why then is there no healing for the wounds of my [God's] people?"

- • Here are the traditional lyrics for its chorus:
  There is a balm in Gilead
  To make the wounded whole;
  There is a balm in Gilead
  To heal the sin-sick soul.

- ○ What we know as spirituals are the songs created and sung by slaves in North America. They encouraged themselves with music. The music was a balm to them.
- ○ When slaves became Christians, they became more obedient to their masters, but it helped the slaves as well. Not only did it save them from hell, but it empowered them. They got a new identity in Christ and the power to live above their circumstances. It also made them seem "human" to those who didn't want to see them that way before.
- ○ While many spirituals were an expression of their new faith; some are believed to be expressions about their life, trials, and hope of escape.
- ○ Here is a famous spiritual. What do you think it is referring to? Maybe it has more than one meaning.
- ○ This is *Swing Low, Sweet Chariot.* You can probably find versions online to listen to.

> Chorus:
> *Swing low, sweet chariot*
> *Coming for to carry me home,*
> *Swing low, sweet chariot,*
> *Coming for to carry me home.*
> I looked over Jordan, and what did I see
> Coming for to carry me home?
> A band of angels coming after me,
> Coming for to carry me home.
> *Chorus*

Sometimes I'm up, and sometimes I'm down,
(Coming for to carry me home)
But still my soul feels heavenly bound.
(Coming for to carry me home)
Chorus
The brightest day that I can say,
(Coming for to carry me home)
When Jesus washed my sins away.
(Coming for to carry me home)
Chorus
If you get there before I do,
(Coming for to carry me home)
Tell all my friends I'm coming there too.
(Coming for to carry me home)
Chorus
(lyrics from Wikipedia, http://en.wikipedia.org/wiki/Swing_Low,_Sweet_Chariot)

- o What do you think the song is about? Is it about going to heaven or escaping to freedom? Or both?
- o Recall: What do we call the songs of the African American slaves?
  - • spirituals
- o Explore More: Learn more about spirituals.

VI. Discussion
- o What songs give you hope? What songs encourage you?
- o If you were to write a spiritual, what would it be about?

VII. Writing
- o Use the discussion question as a writing prompt.
- o Get a high five and or hug for writing a compound sentence or using a semi-colon.

Day 120

I. Read Genesis 37:29-36.

II. Memory Verse
- o Test yourselves on Romans 8:28.
  - • And we know that God causes all things to work together for good to those who love God, to those who are called according to His purpose.
- o Find it in the Bible.
- o Review Jeremiah 29:11.
  - • "For I know the plans I have for you," declares the Lord, "plans to prosper you and not to harm you, plans to give you hope and a future."

III. Language
- o Handwriting/Spelling
  - • Test yourselves on words from Day 116-119.
  - • bind, erect, rebuke, jealous, pasture, pasturing, welfare, devour, rescue, further, balm, stripped, aromatic, myrrh, Joseph, caravan
- o Vocabulary
  - • Test yourselves on words from Day 116-119.
  - • rebuke, profit, devour, balm
- o Hebrew
  - • Trace Genesis 1:1 on the Hebrew Writing 34 page of your workbook. You'll be tracing the printing font. I wrote it with the calligraphy font for you to see as well.
  - • For your next lesson, we will work on reading it.

IV. Science
- o Joseph is thrown into a pit. It's a dried up well. Why is it dry? Why is there lots of rain in some parts of the world and practically none in others? Any guesses? Let's see what we can find out.
  - • Before we can talk about rain, we need to remember what we've learned about water.
- o What makes up a water molecule?
  - • Hydrogen and oxygen atoms, specifically two hydrogen atoms and one oxygen atom. How do you write a water molecule with the symbols for hydrogen and oxygen?
    - ▪ H_2O
- o What are the solid, liquid, and gas forms of H_2O?
  - • ice, water, and water vapor
  - • Ice is made up of water molecules. The water you drink is made up of water molecules. The clouds are formed with water molecules. It's all the same water molecules.
- o What is different about the water molecules that make them appear solid sometimes or a gas sometimes?
  - • The difference is in the temperature and how much the molecules are moving.

- When molecules have a lower temperature, are they moving faster or slower?
  - slower
    - Are they in a solid or a gas when they are moving very slowly?
      - solid
- When molecules get warmer, they start moving more, and the solid becomes a liquid.
- When the temperature gets even higher, the molecules get really excited and start moving around a lot. Then what form do they take?
  - a gas

o A little side note: Why doesn't your kitchen table get up and float away into the clouds on a hot day along with the water vapor?
  - Different materials have different temperatures at which they melt or evaporate.
    - It never gets hot enough for your table to turn into a gas so it could float away.
  - The outer core in the middle of the earth is made in part of melted iron, but we don't worry about our steel skyscrapers melting in the summer. You may remember that steel is an alloy of iron, a mix of iron and carbon.
  - Why does iron melt inside the earth but not in summer?
    - Skyscrapers need a really high temperature to melt. It never gets that hot in the summer, not even close. It's super hot in the middle of the earth, so metal can melt there.
    - Do you remember why the inner core of the earth is solid even though it's so hot?
      - The weight of the world pushes inward with so much pressure that it holds those excited molecules in place.

o Back to water, water heats up and enters the air. Do remember the word that we use to describe how much water is in the air?
  - humidity
  - At 100% humidity it rains. The air is full of water. We feel sticky when it's humid out because our sweat can't evaporate easily since the air is already so full of water. It's dense. There's not much room left to squeeze in more water vapor.

o So the water is in the air, where does warm air go?
  - Hot air rises.
  - What happens when it gets high enough?
    - It cools. What happens when water molecules cool?
      - They slow down and condense into a solid. What happens when those solids get together?
        - It rains.

o Study the water cycle picture on Day 120 in your Map Book. It may use a little different terminology, but there should only really be one new thing on there, the word sublimation. I've mentioned it. I just never told you that word. Sublimation is when a substance skips the liquid phase and goes straight from solid to gas. I told you that evaporation happens even from ice. That's sublimation.

- Once you've followed all the arrows on your water cycle diagram, look at the map on the next page. It shows how much precipitation, mostly rain and snow, each country gets.
  - Those two countries with the most rainfall are Colombia, in South America, and Papua New Guinea.
  - Make observations.
- Recall: What's humidity? a measure of the amount of water in the air; What happens to water molecules when they evaporate? They turn into water vapor and are in the air. Warm air rises. When it gets higher and cools, it condenses and forms back into water droplets. There's no end! It's a cycle! The droplets collect and then gravity pulls them down as rain (or snow).
- Explore More: We're going to continue this lesson...

V. More Science...
- We haven't answered our questions yet, so we need to keep going. Why do some areas of the world have rain daily and other parts of the world hardly ever get rain?
- Where does rain come down from?
  - clouds
- What decides where those clouds form?
  - The water vapor rises up, so there would have to be water in the area to evaporate first to form the clouds.
- When you look at clouds, do they stay still? What moves them?
  - The wind moves the clouds. Clouds are water droplets in the sky. Wind can carry rain towards a dry area, but maybe it's too hot there and the water drops evaporate before they can fall as rain.
- Can you think of anything else that might affect where the clouds go?
  - On the news the weatherperson might talk about high and low pressure systems.
    - Remember that pressure is how something is being pushed. If you press hard on something you are applying a lot of pressure, high pressure; if you are pressing lightly, you are applying low pressure.
    - Pressure systems push clouds (and the rain with them) in a certain direction.
- Clouds can be blocked by other things. What tall things might block a cloud?
  - Mountains and even skyscrapers can affect the weather. Clouds are things. They are water molecules. They can't go through mountains or buildings. They have to go up over them. The wind is air and that air has to go up and over too. How would that affect rainfall? Think about the answer.
    - When air goes up, what happens?
      - It reaches cooler air and more water condenses.
  - When the air goes up the side of the mountain, it cools, condenses and rains. Then the other side of the mountain doesn't get any rain.
  - It's called the shadow effect, and it can even happen in large, tall, modern cities.
- There's one last map for Day 120. Look at the mountains. Do you think there is a connection to the mountains and the areas of deserts?
- Compare the precipitation map to the biome map.

- o Recall: What is it called when one side of a mountain gets all the rainfall? the shadow effect; What causes it? The air is forced up over a mountain, and as it rises it cools, condenses, and rains. The sky empties before the air makes it over the mountain.
- o Explore More: Maybe you'd like to learn about some of the biomes that are unfamiliar to you. Or maybe you'd like to research more about high and low pressure systems.

VI. Discussion
- o Do you believe God controls the weather specifically or generally? Did He create the weather patterns and set them in place and then let His creation do its thing, or does He control specific weather each day? Or does He do both? When? Do you know stories of when God seemed to specifically control weather? (We know in the Bible how God speaks to the storm and it stops at that moment. Matthew 8)

VII. Writing
- o Choose one of your writings from Days 116-119 to edit.
- o Look for problems with capitalization, punctuation, and word choice.
- o Add adverbs and adjectives.
- o Make a sentence longer with a semi-colon or comma and conjunction.
- o Have someone else edit your work too.
- o Create a final draft.

Day 121

I. Read Genesis 39:1-9. (Note to parents: I've been trying to not skip, but I couldn't do it. I skipped Tamar. If you haven't had "the talk" with your older kids, you can use chapter 38. I've left it out.)

> *Note if you want to explain: Potiphar's wife is sinning. She is an adulteress, a woman who wants to act like she's married to someone she's not. She sinned when she first desired for him to lie in bed with her. That's called lust. None of us are to lust after anyone we aren't married to. We guard our eyes from immodesty, and we take thoughts captive so that we won't desire what isn't ours. In the day the Lord gives you a husband or wife, you will be free to look at them and touch them and kiss them and have all the pleasure of a husband and wife. And after we marry, we keep our eyes and our touches for our husband or wife only. Joseph refuses and knows he wouldn't only be sinning against Potiphar but against God.

II. Memory Verse
- o Learn Micah 6:8.
- o He has told you, O man, what is good;
     And what does the Lord require of you
     But to do justice, to love kindness,
     And to walk humbly with your God?

III. Language
- o Handwriting/Spelling
  - • verse 3
  - • words to know: officer, desire, handsome, appearance
  - • spelling tips:
    - ▪ The word <u>officer</u> starts with the word off.
    - ▪ The word <u>desire</u> has no Z and ends with a silent E.
    - ▪ <u>Handsome</u> is the words hand and some together.
    - ▪ The word <u>appearance</u> starts with the word appear.
- o Vocabulary
  - • prosper (verse 3)
  - • to succeed financially or physically (action verb)
- o Hebrew
  - • Today we are going to read Genesis 1:1 in Hebrew. You can find it in your workbook on the Hebrew Writing 34 page.
  - • Here it is below as well.
  - • Remember that in Hebrew you don't have to write the vowel marks. They are in some writings for clarity, but I haven't taught you those since they are not normally used. You have to learn what the words look like based on the letters you've learned. Think of Hebrew like a puzzle. You have to figure out how the letters come together to make a word, or words. The one word you should definitely learn to be able to recognize, is eloHEEM. It's in every verse that you've learned. Find it the verse shown.

בְּרֵאשִׁית, בָּרָא אֱלֹהִים, אֵת הַשָּׁמַיִם, וְאֵת הָאָרֶץ.

(TS) R A H T E V M Y M (SH) H T E M Y(EE) H L E A R B T Y(EE) SH E R B

- (Note: I tried to write the English equivalent of the Hebrew letters above, but just ignore them if it doesn't help.)
- Remember to read right to left.
- First say Genesis 1:1.
  - be reSHEET baRA eloHEEM et ha shaMAyim ve et ha Arets
- Those are the words we are looking for. I already showed you how the ve just attaches to what comes next since it's just one letter. What other words look like they might do the same?
  - be, et, and ha
  - be and ha will do the same and combine with other words.
  - The word et is written with two letters, the Aleph and the Tav. The Aleph gives a place for a vowel to come first in a word.
- Start with the first two words, be reSHEET, our "in the beginning." They appear as one word in the verse. The Bet just gets tagged onto the beginning of reSHEET. Look for the Bet (B), the Resh (R), next comes the Aleph (the silent letter-don't fuss about that. English has lots of silent letters!), the Shin (SH), the Yod (making the EE sound), and the Tav, followed by an ordinary comma.
- Practice reading be reSHEET.
- The next words should be easier. baRA comes next and then eloHEEM followed by a comma and the word et.
- The next word is ha shaMAyim. The ha is connected to make one word. It starts with the Hey. Then you'll see the Shin, both forms of the letter M and the Yod, which sounds like the letter Y this time.
- Then comes ve et as one word.
- Then you'll read ha Arets as one word.
- Say Genesis 1:1 in Hebrew, and then say it while you read it.
- Then read it several times without looking at the transliteration.

IV. Science and Social Studies
- We're going to learn about ancient Egypt for a couple of days. Let's look at where we are in history. In a few weeks we'll work on a timeline of what we talked about this year.
- Abraham was around 2000 BC. What does BC stand for?
  - before Christ
- Does the time of Joseph's story come after or before Abraham's story?
  - after
- Are the year numbers of when Joseph lived going to be smaller or bigger than 2000?
  - The year numbers will be smaller. Before Christ we count down the year numbers to 1 BC. Then we just jump to 1 AD and start counting up again.
- There are a lot of dates out there about Egypt and Joseph. It seems his story fits into Egypt's Middle Kingdom in the years from 2000-1550 BC.

- Let's back up a little. Before the Middle Kingdom was the Old Kingdom.
  - Abraham sojourns in Egypt during the Old Kingdom years. This was the time when pyramids were first built. But let's go further back.
- Before all that there were people living in the area. Where did people live during early civilizations?
  - They lived near water sources. What's the main water source in Egypt?
    - The Nile river, which is one of the longest rivers in the world, flowing over 4000 miles (over 6400 km).
    - Do you know what makes the land surrounding the Nile good for agriculture?
      - It floods once a year and deposits sediment from the river, making rich soil just ready for the planting.
- Sometimes the Nile wouldn't flood much. Sometimes it would flood too much. Either way it could cause disaster. What do you think Egyptians did to try to control the annual flood?
  - They worshiped false gods. They developed systems to try to control what, of course, they couldn't control. They acknowledged a creator but also worshiped the sun and moon and the god of the Nile. They made up rituals and sacrifices trying to make the world work as they wanted.
  - Their belief system developed along with the rest of their civilization.
- Again, there are many dates surrounding Egypt. Answers in Genesis puts its founding around 2200 BC, saying it was founded by Noah's grandson, Mizraim, the son of Ham.
  - Their dates are taken from counting the ages given in the Bible and just adding them up.
- Okay, so back to the Old Kingdom. What do you think is the most famous feature of Egypt?
  - You probably said the pyramids because even if you didn't know anything else, you probably knew about the pyramids.
    - Do you know the name of the most famous pyramid?
      - The Great Pyramid of Giza
- The pyramid of Giza was built during the Old Kingdom period, during Abraham's time and before Joseph's time.
  - Here's a description from Answers in Genesis about The Great Pyramid of Giza and Abraham.
    - The Great Pyramid of Giza, built for Pharaoh Khufu of the fourth dynasty, is "the largest and most accurately constructed building in the world." This pyramid required advanced optical, surveying, mathematical, and construction techniques, an impressive leap beyond the technology demonstrated in earlier pyramids.

      Abram's visit to Egypt may explain Egypt's sudden advance. Abram grew up in the advanced but idolatrous culture of Ur about three centuries after the Flood. Josephus wrote that Abram "communicated to them arithmetic, and delivered to them the science of astronomy; for before Abram came into Egypt they were unacquainted with those parts of learning; for that science came from the Chaldeans into Egypt."

- The Bible doesn't give us this account. They are talking about Josephus, a Jewish historian born shortly after Jesus was resurrected.
  - What was so special about the pyramid in Giza?
    - Earlier pyramids were what we call step pyramids. When you build a pyramid out of Legos or blocks, they are step pyramids. If your legs were long enough, you could walk up the pyramids like steps.
    - Do you know what was different about this Great Pyramid?
      - Its sides were smooth.
        - It was covered in completely smooth limestone, fitted exactly to keep the slope of the pyramid.
      - It was the tallest man-made object in the world for thousands of years. It was about 480 feet tall (147 meters). It was an astonishing engineering feat.
        - Its cap was covered in gold.
  - The pyramids weren't like your block towers. They were open on the inside. They had rooms and passageways. They were built as tombs for the Pharaohs, the kings of Egypt.
    - Pyramids are famous for housing mummies, the bodies of the dead Pharaohs.
      - They had an elaborate ritual where they took out organs from the dead body and dried them out to preserve them, just like we have dried herbs. It keeps them from going bad. The heart is left in the body because they thought they would need it later.
        - Do you remember what the word decompose means?
          - It means to breakdown. Plants and animals decompose and breakdown into bits. It's part of what helps soil stay healthy for planting.
          - Drying or *dehydrating* things keeps them from decomposing by taking all of the water out of them.
      - The body is also dried and then rubbed with oils and all the dried organs are put back in along with things like sawdust and leaves to stuff it and make it look more normal.
      - It's then wrapped in cloths and many superstitious items are placed inside with the wrappings that were supposed to protect the dead person.
      - A wooden board was placed over the body which was then placed in a coffin and then that coffin was placed in another coffin.
    - They believed in life after death and thought they could take things with them, so they filled their pyramids with stuff. It made the pyramids targets for robbers over the years.
  - The pyramids have also attracted archeologists, those who study the past from what we can still physically find of it.
    - A big find was in 1922 when the tomb of the famous King Tut was found. King Tutankhamen was a pharaoh of the New Kingdom, coming after the days of Moses.

- He died young and left no heir and his general took over. He's famous because his gold-covered tomb was found. He was buried with many pure gold objects. His outer coffin was pure gold. And a wonderfully preserved mask that was placed over him was preserved and is displayed for the world.
  - We'll continue with ancient Egypt. Following are some pictures of King Tut.
  - Recall: What biblical patriarch lived when the pyramids were first built? What is the name of the pyramid that was made with smooth sides?
    - Abraham
    - The Great Pyramid of Giza
  - Explore More: Learn about King Tut and the pharaohs. (Explanation: It is said that the date discrepancy between our dates and secular dates is that they stacked up all the pharaohs end to end and added up their reigns. The mistake is that some were rulers over only part of Egypt and ruled at the same time as others.)

The pictures following:

1. Howard Carter, the archeologist who found King Tut's tomb, carefully cleaning off the inner coffin which was ornately made to look like the Pharaoh.

2. A pharaoh in maybe the 1300s BC, King Tut was a boy king whose gold-encrusted tomb fascinated the world. The picture is of the gold mask that he was buried with.

V. Discussion
- o   Have you ever been filled with desire for something you can't have? What did you do about it? What choice do you have in such a situation? How can you prevent being in that situation?
- o   It's a common trick of the enemy to cause us to feel addicted to something. We feel we just have to have it. We never need anything but Jesus, so when you feel that way, remember it's the devil's trick. Don't let him trick you. Wise up. Repent, which means change your mind, and ask God for help. Confess your struggle to your parents who will pray for you and encourage you. It's not sin to be tempted, but it's sin when you let it control you. Taking the steps of confessing and repenting are the first steps to getting free from a controlling desire.

VI. Writing
- o   Today you are going to use quotation marks.
- o   Quotation marks mark quotations. ☺
- o   A quotation is what someone said. I'm sure you've seen them in books. When someone is speaking, you let the reader know by using quotation marks.
    - •   You put them before and after. It's called opening and closing the quote.

- o Since what the person is saying is part of your sentence, you don't put a period before or after what they say. Let me give you examples. Open your workbooks to see them on the Writing Sentences 19 page.
  - "Let me show you, (comma)" she said.
  - He said, (comma) "Please come with us."
- o The person's quotation starts with a capital letter.
- o Give it a try and use the examples to help you.
- o Complete Writing Sentences 19 in your workbook.

Day 122

I. Read Genesis 39:9-18.

II. Memory Verse
- o Practice Micah 6:8.
- o He has told you, O man, what is good;
  And what does the Lord require of you
  But to do justice, to love kindness,
  And to walk humbly with your God?

III. Language
- o Handwriting/Spelling
  - verse 16
  - words to know: garment, Hebrew, screamed, fled
  - spelling tips:
    - Screamed is the past tense of the verb, to scream. It's formed in the regular way by adding the letters E-D onto the end.
    - Here are some irregular past tense verbs in this reading. What is the present tense of each verb? (Note to parents: Use the pronoun I to help you. I brought. I bring. You could use the future to help as well by saying I will...)
      - brought (bring), went (go), caught (catch), fled (flee), left (leave), spoke (speak)
- o Vocabulary
  - garment (verse 12)
  - a piece of clothing (noun)
- o Hebrew

בְּרֵאשִׁית, בָּרָא אֱלֹהִים, אֵת הַשָּׁמַיִם, וְאֵת הָאָרֶץ.

- Read Genesis 1:1 (above).
- Today we'll write Genesis 1:3. On the Hebrew Writing 35 page, trace Genesis 1:3.
- Find eloHEEM.

IV. Science and Social Studies
- o We're going to continue with ancient Egypt. We were talking about pyramids and pharaohs. We know that the Israelites were slaves in Egypt, so many people think the pyramids were built by slaves. Some of them may have been, but others were built by workers.
  - Workers were paid in bread and beer, basically they worked for their dinner. Slaves would have to be fed as well, so I'm not sure what the distinction is between them! The beer was healthy and didn't contain as much alcohol as today's beer.
    - A little side story: Guinness beer, one of the most successful and prosperous beer brands in the world today, was first made by a

Christian in Ireland. The man, Arthur Guinness, along with other Christians, brewed beer to combat drunkenness that plagued their country. The beer they brewed was healthier and had much less alcohol than the drinks offered at the bars. The water was unclean and gave people diseases, and so people needed a safer, healthy alternative.

- This was taking place in the 1700s in Ireland. The Guinness family was influenced by the teaching of John Wesley to "Earn all you can. Save all you can. Give all you can." Their family was an influence for change for God's kingdom.
- Okay, back to Egypt.

o Tens of thousands of workers could have worked on such a huge undertaking as the Great Pyramid of Giza.

- There were huge workforces involved.
- When the Israelites were slaves in Egypt, there were millions of them.
  - We are given the number that there were 600,000 men of age to fight in their army (Numbers 2:32). Certainly there were just as many women which would put the number over a million. One child per person would put the number over two million.

o Let's move past the pyramids. What else do you know about ancient Egypt? Do you know what hieroglyphics are?

- Do you remember the form of writing we learned about that was used by the Sumerians in Mesopotamia?
  - cuneiform

o Hieroglyphics are written with hieroglyphs. They are picture words. They were written on all sorts of surfaces in the early years of the pharaohs.

- Hieroglyphs have been found on bones, pottery, and walls.

o Like cuneiform, and all languages, it simplified over time.

- Pictures represented words, but over time a simplified symbol came to represent a sound, so that words could be formed by putting the sounds together.

o This simplified writing was able to be written on their form of paper. Do you know what it was?

- It was made from papyrus, a plant found along the Nile.
  - The stalks of the plant were slightly decomposed in water and then layered upon each other and smashed together and then dried.
- Other cultures bought papyrus paper from the Egyptians. What are some of the reasons that paper would be better than clay tablets for writing on?
  - It wouldn't break when dropped. It was lighter to carry. It was easier to store as it didn't take up as much space.

o According to Mr. Donn, papyrus was also used to make "baskets, sandals, mats, rope, blankets, tables, chairs, mattresses, medicine, perfume, food, and clothes." (egypt.mr.donn.org/papyrus.html)

- Papyrus could grow ten feet tall. Can you picture how it could be used for some of those purposes? Which ones can't you imagine?

o The Egyptians invented more than papyrus paper for writing. They were an agricultural society, so they made ways to make their farming work easier.

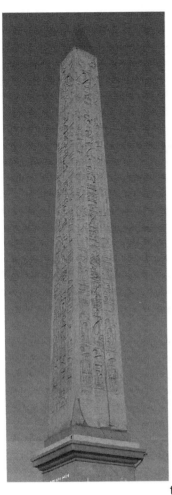

- They used irrigation ditches that carried water from the Nile to their farmland. They invented a simple tool, a bucket on a pole weighted at the other end, that would make getting water out of the Nile and into those ditches easier.
  o They had a tool that would measure the level of the Nile flood and made a plow that could be pulled by oxen. You saw picture of it when we learned about oxen (Day 77).
  o They also invented different types of clocks.
    - They made obelisks (ob-e-lisks) which were basically just straight, four-sided statues. Here's a picture (by David Monniaux). (The Washington Monument in Washington, D.C. is this shape.)
    - How do you think it helped tell time?
      ▪ It cast shadows. It's like a sun dial. Over time it developed and markings were made around it to show where the shadow would fall throughout the day.
    - A nighttime clock was also developed. It was a water clock. It was a bowl with rows of holes in it. How do you think it worked?
      ▪ The water ran out of the holes. As the water lowered in the bowl, you could see by the markings how many hours had passed since it had been filled.
    - Why is this a better nighttime clock than daytime clock?
      ▪ I would think evaporation in the heat of the day would throw off the timing.
  o Let's visit pharaohs one last time before we finish with ancient Egypt. The pharaoh was the king. He eventually was considered one of the gods. He owned everything in Egypt. Everything belonged to him: your land, your home, even your clothing.
    - Under him was his *vizier*. (Say it vizzeer.) He was the man in charge of actually running the country.
    - Under the vizier were the other government officials and the high priests.
  o Temples were built to various gods. (There were gods for everything. They even had a god of beer.)
    - Temples were run by the priests whose job it was to make the gods happy.
      ▪ Another side note: That's another difference between Christianity and false religions. False religions rely on man to do certain things to earn the god's approval. In Christianity, we can't earn God's approval on our own. We are all sinners. We are only saved by grace. The only reason we can please God is because He sent His Son to die for us so that we can be forgiven, and He gives us His Spirit so that we can live in a way that pleases Him.
      ▪ I don't know a lot about some religions, but Islam, for example, is all about earning God's favor through your works.
  o Continuing down the order of ancient Egyptian society are the educated scribes who knew how to read and write.

- Under the scribes came the merchants, those selling goods. Those were the men who would have traveled to buy goods from other places and brought them back to sell.
  - Then came the craftsmen. Those who could make the baskets and the shoes and the other items needed for daily life.
  - Finally came the peasants, the farmers, and under them the servants and the slaves.
- In the story of Joseph we will see him rise from slave to vizier.
- Recall: What were some of the Egyptians' inventions?
  - clocks, agricultural tools (plow drawn by oxen), papyrus paper
- Explore More: Learn about King Menes, the first pharaoh. Learn about the differences between the Old, Middle and New Kingdoms of Egypt.

V. Discussion

- Joseph had to endure a lot of temptation. Sometimes it's necessary to flee from temptation. Joseph ran away when he had to.
- Do you face a strong temptation? You might be pulled to the TV, internet, video games, or snacks, for instance. You never want something controlling your actions. If you have strong urges for something that you give into, then those feelings are controlling your actions. How can you flee that temptation and get it away from you?

VI. Writing

- Use the discussion question as a writing prompt.
- Get a high five and/or hug for starting a sentence with If or When and then using a comma to set off your introductory phrase.

Day 123

I. Read Genesis 39:19-23.

II. Memory Verse
- o Practice Micah 6:8.
- o He has told you, O man, what is good;
  And what does the Lord require of you
  But to do justice, to love kindness,
  And to walk humbly with your God?

III. Language
- o Handwriting/Spelling
  - verse 21
  - words to know: jailer, extend, charge, anger
  - spelling tips:
    - The word <u>jailer</u> is the word jail with the two letters most commonly added onto the end of a word to turn it into a profession, such as with teacher and preacher.
    - The word <u>extend</u> starts with the letters E-X. Do you remember what the prefix, ex, means, like in exit or exterior?
      - It means out. Extend means to reach out.
    - The words <u>charge</u> and <u>anger</u> both have Gs. One uses the soft G and one the hard G even though both are followed by an E.
- o Vocabulary
  - supervise (verse 23)
  - to keep watch over someone while they work (action verb)
- o Hebrew
  - Say Genesis 1:3, va YOmer eloHEEM yeHEE or va yeHEE or.
  - Find Genesis 1:3 on the Hebrew Writing 35 page of your workbook.
  - Then read Genesis 1:3 while you say it. The word light (or) starts with a vowel, so the Hebrew word starts with the Aleph. The va in this verse will attach onto the word that comes after it.
  - Please ignore the hyphen! Just read them as separate words.

וַיֹּאמֶר אֱלֹהִים, יְהִי אוֹר; וַיְהִי-אוֹר.

IV. Social Studies
- o We're going to continue having one long lesson today and Day 124 as well. We're going to learn about the justice system.
- o Why does Joseph get thrown in jail?
  - He was accused of doing wrong.
  - Was it a true accusation?
    - No! But it didn't matter.

- o In the Bible we are given the instruction that no one is to be found guilty on the testimony of just one witness (Deuteronomy 17). That means that you can't assume someone did something wrong just because one person said so. Let's define a few words.
    - guilty and innocent – Do you know what these words mean?
        - Guilty means you did something wrong.
        - Innocent means you didn't do something wrong.
        - However, in the justice system, guilty means it was decided that you did something wrong and innocent means it was decided that you didn't do something wrong.
        - Can you tell the difference?
            - Unfortunately, in any justice system you can be found guilty and actually be innocent and can be declared innocent when you are actually guilty.
- o We learned a little about Old Testament justice. There were laws in place to make sure wrong was punished in order to protect everyone else. Who wrote the justice system code of law that had messy housewives thrown in the Euphrates?
    - Hammurabi
    - His law did have many similarities to God's law given to Moses for the Israelites, but it didn't have justice for all. Different people were treated differently under the law. What was considered just and fair was determined by your rank in society.
    - In America that isn't supposed to happen. They say justice is blind. What do you think that means?
        - It means that laws apply to everyone, no matter who you are.
- o Before we get to America's legal system, let's take a quick look at other legal systems around the world.
- o In some Muslim countries such as Saudi Arabia and Libya, they follow rules called Sharia. That is the law instituted by the Koran. There are various levels of crime. The most serious crimes are considered crimes against their god. They consider theft to be one of these crimes. If there are four witnesses to your stealing, you will have your hands or feet cut off. Another offence is apostasy, leaving true Islam. Anyone who becomes a Christian is an apostate under Sharia law. The punishment is death. Various Muslim groups are often killing each other because they accuse each other of leaving true Islam. It would be like Catholics and evangelical Christians killing each other because they believe differently. An unmarried woman found to be pregnant is also put to death.
    - There are Muslim groups fighting to instill this type of law in more countries, and in areas in other countries where a majority of Muslims live.
        - One group you may know about is ISIS. Many Muslims say ISIS members are violating, not obeying, the Koran, but they say they are acting in the name of Islam. They force men to pray at the prescribed prayer times each day and force women to wear Islamic coverings, where they are covered in black except for their eyes. Where I lived there are many women who even have their eyes covered with a black see-through veil. This group, ISIS, even recruits people to fight with them from my neighborhood. I've seen them drive down the

streets with their flag out the window of the car and they would call out to people. They advertise on YouTube for people to come and fight with them and they do. Why? Why do people want to kill others? Why do they want to beat people who don't do what they say?

- I don't think they care that much about Islam. I think that violence gives their lives meaning. If you feel like your life doesn't matter, then killing someone, or controlling people through intimidation, gives you power and significance. Your life matters all of a sudden. You have an impact on the world around you.
- We find our meaning through being a child of God. He created us and we matter to Him. God tells us He has a plan for our lives. That makes our lives important. At the same time we believe God's the important one, not ourselves, and being able to serve Him gives our lives significance. It makes us important to the world. Even if we only serve God in our neighborhoods, we are all part of the body of Christ and are all, together, part of doing His work on earth.

o Back to the justice system...so Sharia law is a justice system. Some of the laws have set punishments. Some punishments are determined by judges. Crimes against Muslims are considered worse than crimes against non-Muslims, so Sharia law is not blind, as we say.

o Many justice systems in the world have laws set by their federal governments with set punishments for breaking those laws. This is called Civil Law.

- That's not the type of law America has. America has what is known as common law.

o Common law is not set by laws handed down by the central government in Washington, D.C. Judges make decisions on cases based on previous cases, what has been decided before in such situations.

- There are also local laws that are different in different areas of the country, and all laws and decisions made by judges must obey the highest law of the land which is the US Constitution.

o We're going to spend our next lesson learning about the Bill of Rights, a part of the US Constitution.

- But before we get there, let's learn a little about how the justice system works in America.

o What happens when you get arrested in America?

- You are told what your rights are in a language you understand and are taken to jail.
- You wait for a trial, up to six months.
- The trial is between you and whoever is accusing you of wrongdoing. There are lawyers speaking for each side.
- A jury listens to the lawyers and to the witnesses and decides the verdict, guilty or innocent.
- If the verdict is guilty, then the judge gives the *sentencing*, meaning decides what the punishment will be.

- o Okay, act out a trial. You need a judge, lawyers, and jury. Use a stuffed animal for the *defendant*, the person accused of the crime, and you can add stuffed animals to the jury if you like. Act out multiple roles if necessary.
  - The prosecutor, the lawyer for the accuser, should accuse the defendant of the crime and tell the jury why they think the defendant is guilty.
  - The lawyer for the defendant should tell the jury why the defendant is innocent.
  - The jury decides the verdict, whether guilty or innocent.
  - If the defendant is found guilty, the judge decides the sentence, the punishment.
- o Recall: Go over these words if necessary: verdict, guilty, innocent, sentence, justice, trial, jury.
- o Explore More: Learn more about justice systems in other countries. Are they really "just" systems?

V. Discussion

- o Are you responsible enough to not be supervised like Joseph? Do you get your chores and schoolwork done thoroughly and on time so that no one has to come and check and remind you what needs to be done?
- o That should be a goal: to be known as responsible. Do you think an employer would want to hire someone with a reputation for being responsible to get his work done well and on time?

VI. Writing

- Use the discussion question as a writing prompt.
- Get a high five and/or hug for putting a comma after an introductory phrase.

Day 124

I. Read Genesis 40:1-4.

II. Memory Verse
- o Review Micah 6:8.
- o He has told you, O man, what is good;
  And what does the Lord require of you
  But to do justice, to love kindness,
  And to walk humbly with your God?

III. Language
- o Handwriting/Spelling
  - verse 2
  - words to know: furious, officials, baker, confinement
  - spelling tips:
    - The word <u>furious</u> has one letter two times.
    - The word <u>officials</u> has a double letter and another letter used twice.
    - The word <u>baker</u> has no letter used more than once, but it ends with those two letters most often used to turn a verb into a profession.
    - The word <u>confinement</u> has one letter used twice and another used three times.
- o Vocabulary
  - confinement, confine (verse 4)
  - confine – to put restrictions on someone or something (action verb)
  - Confinement is the noun form. It's being confined.
- o Hebrew
  - We're going to learn the last letters needed to read Genesis 1:2.
  - ve ha Arets haaTAH TOhu vaVOhu ve KHOshekh al pnaa teHOM ve RUakh eloHEEM meraKHEfet al pnaa ha MAyim
  - We don't know what makes the KH sound. We need to learn the P and the N sounds, and we don't know the letter that starts the word "al;" it's a letter like the Aleph. It doesn't have a sound, but it gives a place in the word for a vowel sound to attach to it.
  - Let's start with that one, the Ayin. It has no sound on its own. Here's the word "al" in Hebrew. It's the Ayin and the Lamed.

עַל עַל עַל

  - Trace the Ayin on the Hebrew Writing 36 page of your workbook.

IV. Social Studies
- o We're going to continue our study of the justice system in America. The first thing I mentioned on Day 123 about being arrested was that the police officers would tell

458

you your rights, such as your right to remain silent and to not answer any questions until you have a lawyer with you. Those rights are known as Miranda rights.

- Miranda is someone's last name. He was the defendant in a trial. His lawyers won the case and it became the rule that you have to be told your rights.

○ After you've had a trial, if you think the judge and jury in your trial didn't find the truth, especially if you think they didn't follow the Constitution, you make an *appeal*. Then you go to a higher court. If you don't think that court made the right decision, then you can appeal to the Supreme Court. They are judges appointed by the president. Their decisions become common law. What they decide is then used in courts all over the country as the precedent for what decision to make.

- Miranda was arrested and didn't know his rights under the Constitution. The police could use that to their advantage instead of letting him know he could get a lawyer to help him.
- His case was appealed to the Supreme Court, and they sided with Miranda. Now every arrest begins with making sure the suspect is aware of the basic rights.

○ So why is it our right to remain silent and to not answer questions? That's today's lesson. We get that right from the Fifth Amendment to the Constitution, the 5th addition to what the founders of America first wrote as the law of our land.

○ There are twenty-seven amendments, additions, to what was first written in America's Constitution, but the first ten amendments are known as the Bill of Rights.

- They were proposed shortly after the Constitution was written in 1787. They became official in 1791.

○ Let's start learning those first ten amendments, the Bill of Rights. They were written to protect the freedom of the people, to protect them from their government.

○ The First Amendment may be the most important of all. It says that the government cannot establish a religion, and it can't stop anyone from practicing their religion. It also says that we have the right to gather together peacefully in protest and to say and write what we want without the government stopping us.

- Where I lived in the Middle East for a number of years, the government would arrest people who said anything bad about it. Many journalists were thrown in jail for just reporting the truth about the government. While the American government shows favor to news people who are nicer to them, they can't stop people from complaining about them.
- The First Amendment was used to take prayer out of schools in America. School children used to begin their day with prayer, Christian prayer. It was argued that prayer in school was a violation of the First Amendment. Schools are run by the government and therefore cannot establish a religion.
  - I don't agree with this, but I understand the argument. We know, however, that's not how our nation's earlier leaders understood that amendment. When Washington was inaugurated as the first president, the first thing that happened was the church bells rang to call everyone to pray for him and the new country.
  - Abraham Lincoln established a day of prayer and fasting for everyone to confess America's sins and to ask God for mercy.

- The Second Amendment says that no one can stop people from owning guns. Every state has further laws about guns and who can buy them and the process you have to go through to buy one and where you can keep them.
- The Third Amendment just says that you can't be forced to have a soldier stay in your home.
- The Fourth Amendment says that the police or government agent can't search your home and can't take anything from you without a *warrant*, a special permission that can only be given if there is good reason to search your home, like maybe you are a suspected thief and they want to search your home for what was stolen.
- The Fifth Amendment states several things.
    - One is that you can't be made to be a witness against yourself. They can't ask you if you did it or not unless you decide you are willing to answer their questions.
    - The Fifth Amendment also ensures what we know as *due process*. That just means that you have to be accused and have a trial and be found guilty before giving out a sentence. They can't just put you in jail without having gone through the justice process.
- Let's take a pause there and look at a law created by the American government. They call it the Patriot Act. It says that homes can be searched without a warrant and that people can be put in jail indefinitely without a trial. What's wrong with that?
    - It violates the fourth and fifth amendments to the Constitution. The law was challenged and many parts were found unconstitutional and were changed.
- It is being challenged by lawmakers and in the courts.
    - It takes years for court cases to get to the Supreme Court, and the Supreme Court then gets to pick and choose which cases it wants to hear.
- We're halfway through. Should we keep going?
- The Sixth Amendment is about trials.
    - You have to have your trial within six months or they have to drop your case and let you go free. That's in every case except a murder trial.
    - You have to have a jury that hasn't already made up their mind about you being guilty or innocent. They have to assume the person is innocent until they are proven guilty.
        - That's part of justice being blind. One of discriminations that African Americans faced before they had the right to vote is that they were not on juries. Only voters are on juries. They didn't have the right to vote until the Fifteenth Amendment. When blacks were on trial, they had all-white juries. It seemed like the blacks were always guilty, and the whites were always innocent when they committed a crime against blacks. Justice wasn't, and still isn't, blind, but we have made improvements.
    - The Sixth Amendment is also the one that gives you the right to have a lawyer.
- The Seventh Amendment ensures a trial by jury and that a judge can't overrule a decision by the jury.
- The Eighth Amendment protects against excessive fines and the use of cruel punishment against prisoners.

- The Ninth Amendment says there are other rights that need to be protected that aren't each specifically listed in the Bill of Rights.
- The Tenth Amendment says that any power not given the government by the Constitution belongs to the states and the people. This amendment protects people from the government taking too much power.
- Why do we need a Bill of Rights? Do we need to be protected from our government? Remember that these were written by America's government leaders when America was first beginning. They were breaking away from their previous government.
    - There's a famous saying that goes "Power corrupts* and absolute power corrupts absolutely." When people have power to do what they want, they tend to do what they want. That may or may not be good for anyone else. Governments are not morally pure and good. When they have the power to do whatever they want, since they are run by sinful man, they tend to do selfish things, not necessarily thinking about the good of everyone.
    - The Bill of Rights keeps the government from having the power to do whatever it wants. They have to respect the rights of the people.
- Recall: What is an amendment? an addition to the US Constitution; What is the Constitution? What is the Supreme Court? What rights can you name?
    - It is the highest law in America.
    - It is the highest court in America. Its members are appointed by the president. They decide what becomes law by setting precedent, which is then used in courts everywhere in America for how to make a decision in certain cases.
- Explore More: Learn about the Supreme Court.

*Note: One of our vocabulary words was corrupt. Here it is used as a verb. We learned it as an adjective describing someone who would do something bad to get what he wanted. Power corrupts means that power makes you able (and willing) to do something bad to get what you want.

V. Discussion
- If you had the power to do absolutely anything you wanted to do with no fear of punishment in any way, what would you do? After answering that, answer this. Do you believe that power corrupts?

VI. Writing
- Use the discussion question as a writing prompt.
- Get a high five and/or hug for using a semicolon, or comma and conjunction in your writing today.

Day 125

I. Read Genesis 40:5-15. Where is Joseph? (Answer: prison)

II. Memory Verse
- o Say from memory, Micah 6:8.
  - He has told you, O man, what is good;
    And what does the Lord require of you
    But to do justice, to love kindness,
    And to walk humbly with your God?
- o Find it in the Bible.
- o Review Romans 8:28.
  - And we know that God causes all things to work together for good to those who love God, to those who are called according to His purpose.

III. Language
- o Handwriting/Spelling
  - Test yourselves on your words from Days 121-124.
    - officer, desire, handsome, appearance
    - garment, Hebrew, screamed, fled
    - jailer, extend, charge, anger
    - furious, officials, baker, confinement
- o Vocabulary
  - Test yourselves on your words from Days 121-124.
    - prosper – to succeed financially or physically
    - garment – a piece of clothing
    - supervise – to keep watch over someone while they work
    - confine – to place restrictions on someone or something
- o Hebrew
  - Trace and write the Ayin on the Hebrew Writing 37 page in your workbook.

IV. Science
- o Let's learn about dreams. When do you dream?
  - You dream when you are sleeping. We all dream every night even if you don't remember any dreams when you wake up.
- o Scientists have labeled our sleep in different stages.
- o The deepest level of sleep we get to quickly once we fall asleep.
  - Our muscles relax.
  - Much of our brain goes to sleep. We stop thinking things over. Our brain still functions, keeping us alive, but it's not too active.
  - It's hard to wake up someone who is in a deep sleep. If they get woken up, they may feel all confused for a bit.
  - This is when you grow too. While you are in a deep sleep, your body builds bone and muscle and does repairs.
  - We do dream during this phase of sleep, but it's not very exciting. Usually we dream about doing the things we did during the day. This is when sometimes some people sleep walk or talk. They are replaying activities they did during

the day. Our brain decides what's important to remember and what we can forget.
- We spend about 75% of our sleep in the deep sleep stage.
○ About every hour and a half...how long is that in minutes?
○ About every 90 minutes, we enter what is known as REM sleep. The word REM, written R-E-M stands for Rapid Eye Movement.
- Our eyes move really fast under our eyelids, but the rest of our body doesn't move at all. We are paralyzed. Our muscles don't work. Maybe this is to keep us from sleep walking and acting out the crazy dreams of REM sleep!
- While our brains have less activity during deep sleep, the brain during REM sleep is almost as active as a waking brain. There is one part of the brain that is still asleep. It's the part of the brain that makes connections to predict what's going to happen.
- That's part of what makes REM dreams seem crazy. In real life we know that if this happens, then this is the outcome, but without that knowledge during sleep, our brains can let unpredictable things occur.
○ Our dreams are actually important. They help in a few ways.
- Dreams let us process our emotions. It's important to handle our emotions. Replaying the emotion we are feeling in a different situation allows our minds to detach the strong emotion from what we experienced in real life.
- Dreams are strongly associated with memory and emotions. Scientists can scan people's brains and see what parts of the brain are most active. We are remembering things that are important and letting go of things that aren't important during our dreams.
- Dreams can also help us solve problems. Our crazy dreams let us try out different situations and see how to solve our problems.
  - Studies have shown that when people are presented with a puzzle to figure out, those who are allowed to nap are more likely to figure it out than those who just keep thinking about it, trying to figure out the puzzle.
  - People who learn something new are more likely to remember it twelve hours later if they learned it in the evening and then slept than those who learned it in the morning and tried to recall it at the end of the day.
  - When trying to make a decision or to solve a problem, it might be really good advice to "sleep on it."
- In a related way, dreams can help us solve problems we haven't had yet. We can practice what we would do in a certain situation and figure out the best response, even if we aren't aware we are doing it. It's just in our brains somewhere.
○ We do know that God can speak through dreams, but we all dream every night, and every dream isn't from God. He made our bodies and mind to work through things in our dreams in a way where our "thinking" brain can't get in the way. In that way we can learn from our dreams.
○ Mendeleev came up with the form of the periodic table in a dream. It was on his mind. He had been working and working on it. His brain was able to put the pieces of the puzzle together while he slept.

- o Recall: What is the stage of sleep called when we have crazy dreams and aren't sleeping as deeply? REM sleep
- o Explore More: Learn more about sleep cycles.

V. Social Studies
- o We learned about dreams today. They are our brains at work, rehearsing life and helping us figure out our memories and emotions.
- o Even though the characters and scenes in our dreams may seem random, the emotions are not. The emotions in the dreams are real, even if everything else isn't.
- o Even though most dreams are not direct messages from God, there are some standard ideas about what some types of dreams mean.
- o There are actually very common dreams that most people experience at some time. Here are some things that seem to happen in many people's dreams.
  - Falling: Have you ever fallen in a dream? I'll give you a common interpretation of each type of dream event.
    - ▪ Maybe you are falling because you feel out of control of a situation or maybe you need to let go and stop trying to control something that you can't.
  - Flying: How well you fly in your dream may show how confident you are that you will achieve your goals.
  - Being chased: This may mean that you are trying to avoid some problem in life.
  - Being naked: Maybe you are feeling guilty or ashamed or maybe you feel like a fake and are afraid of being exposed.
  - Being unprepared: Maybe you aren't feeling up to the task you need to accomplish.
  - Babies: These usually mean something new is beginning.
  - Teeth falling out: Maybe you feel like you are not in control and are losing confidence in how you can handle things.
  - Water: The state of the water, clear and calm or dark and stormy, may show the state of our emotions.
  - Vehicles: If we are driving a car or something in our dream, it may show how well we think we can handle what's going on in our lives.
- o These are just some typical ideas.
- o I know a Christian, a Syrian refugee, who had a dream she didn't understand. She was walking up steps and Jesus was at the top of the steps. He didn't speak, but He made a symbol with his hands that looked like an upside down A.
  - When I heard the dream, I knew just what that was. That morning it had dawned on me that our word alphabet was probably related to Aleph and Bet, and I researched the origins of the alphabet.
  - The original letter for the Aleph was an upside down A, just like she described.
  - Jesus said that He was the Alpha and the Omega, the beginning and the end, so I told her that the symbol probably meant beginning.
  - It's a couple of months later now, and she and her husband have moved to a new city where he's pastoring a church for Syrian refugees. A new beginning.

- o Another woman I know had a dream about Jesus. There was a huge table set with the largest fruit on it she had ever seen. He said to her, "Come and eat." I was able to show her the verse, ""Every one who thirsts, come to the waters; and you who have no money come, buy and eat. Come, buy wine and milk without money and without cost." (Isaiah 55:1) She was homeless. She lived in a shack in a trash dump. It was very meaningful to her that Jesus called to those who have no money to come, buy, and eat. I could explain to her that He paid the price. His gifts to us are free. She believed and was baptized and is no longer homeless.
- o Explore More: I would be careful in exploring more about dream meanings. I don't want to encourage you to take every little thing in your dreams as a serious symbol. If God wants to get your attention with a dream, I'm sure He knows how to do it.

VI. Discussion
- o What dreams do you remember having? Do you think they had a meaning? Can you relate them to any of the descriptions from the lesson?

VII. Writing
- ▪ Use one of your writings from Days 122-125 to edit.
- ▪ Use your editing sheet and read it out loud.
- ▪ Let someone else edit it as well.
- ▪ Create a final draft.

Day 126 (check Materials List)

I. Read Genesis 40:16-23.

II. Memory Verse
- o Learn Psalm 55:22.
- o Cast your burden upon the LORD and He will sustain you; He will never allow the righteous to be shaken.

III. Language
- o Handwriting/Spelling
  - verse 23
  - words to know: sorts, basket, favorably, chief
  - spelling tips:
    - Sorts has the word OR inside of it, as in either or.
    - Basket does not end with the word it.
    - Favorably starts with the word favor.
    - I before E, except...after C...will help you spell chief. The word weird is spelled E-I, and when E and I are used to make the A sound, they are used E-I. There are always exceptions to rules!
- o Vocabulary
  - interpretation (verse 18)
  - the explanation of something's meaning (noun)
  - The action verb form of the word is interpret. You can interpret a dream or interpret the meaning of a phrase in another language.
  - Someone who interprets is an interpreter, which is also a noun, a person. The interpretation is a noun; it's a thing.
- o Hebrew
  - Today we're going to learn the letter Pey. This is our P sound. You can see it on the next page.
  - Just like the Bet could have the V sound with no dot, the Pey with no dot has the F sound.
  - The Bet and Pey have a dot.
  - Trace and write the Pey on the Hebrew Writing 38 page of your workbook.

IV. Science
- o We learned a little about grain and yeast earlier. We're going to learn about bread today.
- o Let's try to stretch back and remember about grain. We talked about grain because early Mesopotamian society was an agricultural society. What does that mean?
  - They were farmers.

- Their lives revolved around grain in many ways. Grain was grown, harvested, threshed to knock off the grains of wheat from the rest of the plant, and then winnowed to separate out the pure grain by using the wind to blow the rest away.
- Once you have grain, what do you think needs to happen to make bread?
  - The grain is ground into flour. Some people today do that at home with an appliance in their kitchen, but it can also be done by grinding it between two large flat rocks.
    - That kind of flour is known as whole grain. It's made from the whole wheat grain.
  - To make bread the flour has to be mixed with at least water and then heated to bake. Flour and water (with a little salt) is a very basic cracker. It's the simplest form of bread.
  - In the Bible it's called unleavened bread. Do you know what that means?
- It means that there is no leaven in the bread, nothing to make it rise and not be flat. What do you add to make bread rise?
  - You usually add yeast. You can also add baking soda or baking powder.
- Baking soda is scientifically known as sodium hydrogen carbonate. What elements does it sound like it's made of?
  - It sounds like it's made from a sodium atom and a hydrogen atom and a carbon atom. That's not exactly right, though. It has all of those, but it also has three oxygen atoms.
  - Can you write that in symbols?
    - $NaHCO_3$
  - We often use baking soda in cookies to make them puff up when they bake.
  - The baking soda releases carbon dioxide when it interacts with an acid such as sour cream, lemon juice, or even brown sugar. Those gas bubbles get caught in the dough and cause it to rise and fill kind of like a balloon.
    - You can see carbon dioxide released by mixing baking soda with vinegar. (Note: You can do an experiment on baking soda and carbon dioxide on Day 134 if you chose to do so.)
- Baking powder is just baking soda already mixed with an acid. It just needs a liquid to set off the chemical reaction. The liquid makes the acid and baking soda combine and the reaction of the chemicals releases carbon dioxide. Like blowing up a balloon, the carbon dioxide fills the cake or bread or biscuit dough or whatever with gas, filling it and making it puff up.
  - You can make leavened bread by just mixing flour, water, and baking powder. You can then bake it, or in a yummier way, fry it in a pan covered in oil. I would add a little salt though!
- Yeast works in the same way in that the chemical reaction produces carbon dioxide which fills up the bread dough making it rise. When you punch down bread dough, you are just releasing the trapped carbon dioxide.
  - We mentioned yeast when we learned about fermentation. Do you remember what fermentation is?
    - It's the breakdown of a substance by yeast or other such organism.
    - I said organism. Yeast is alive!

- o Yeast are single cells. They belong to the fungus kingdom, not the animal kingdom. They are alive in the same way mold is alive. They can grow and multiply. One yeast cell can just divide itself into two yeast cells. That's called *mitosis*.
  - Yeast doesn't make carbon dioxide by mixing with acids. Yeast changes sugars, or glucose, into carbon dioxide and alcohol.
  - When the bread is baked, the yeast dies.
- o Recall: What kingdom does yeast belong to? What does baking soda need to react with to produce carbon dioxide? What does yeast use to produce carbon dioxide? What does carbon dioxide have to do with leavened bread, bread that rises and isn't flat?
  - the fungus kingdom
  - acid
  - sugar
  - The carbon dioxide is what causes the bread dough to rise by filling it with gas bubbles.
- o Explore More: Learn about mitosis and/or the chemical equation for the process of baking soda and acid transforming into carbon dioxide and other products.

V. Social Studies

- o We have a fun social studies topic today. It's birthdays. The Pharaoh has a birthday and throws a feast.
- o Think about how Americans celebrate birthdays. How do kids celebrate? How do adults celebrate birthdays?
- o We're going to do a little exploration of some differences surrounding birthdays around the world.
  - My first exposure to a different birthday culture was actually in America. I was volunteering with a ministry to inner city kids. I spent lots of extra time with them, went to their homes, brought them to my home, etc. I found out about one child's birthday and found out that she wasn't having a birthday party. I thought she needed a celebration, so I baked a cake. I later learned that their family had one cake a year to celebrate everyone's birthday because it was too expensive otherwise.
  - Another time I was invited to a birthday party at a roller skating rink. I had been to roller skating parties as a child where a room at the rink is rented out and everything was paid for by the family throwing the party as part of the rink's party deal. I was running late. I needed money and I needed to get the present I bought. I decided I absolutely needed to go pick up the present from home and skipped stopping at an ATM. I was late. Everyone was waiting on me. The grandmother saw my present and took it from me and put it in her car. We all went into the rink. Everyone paid their own way. I had to ask for money for my skate rental. They just skated. There was no rented birthday room, no cake, no presents. It was just a special treat to get to go roller skating together, and it was enough of an expense to pay for the skate rental. The inner city had a different cultural birthday experience than what I was used to in my middle-class upbringing.

- Macedonia
  - A few months into our time living in Macedonia, I mentioned to some neighbors that it was my birthday. They asked me if I was having a party. They all wanted to come over. I told them they needed to throw me a party. In Macedonia you throw yourself a party. You pay all the expense on your birthday if you want a celebration.
- Pakistan
  - When I first started teaching English to some Pakistani refugee neighbors of ours, I wanted to know their names and ages. It seemed simple enough, but after years of knowing them, it's still confusing to me!
  - The girls take their mother's last name, so the brothers had different last names than the sisters. Of course, they didn't speak English enough to explain that to me! It was a mystery I eventually uncovered.
  - They didn't know how old they were! They were correcting each other and confused about when their birthdays were.
  - It's not that birthdays are never celebrated in Pakistan, but it obviously wasn't a big deal to them. They couldn't easily tell me their birthdates or ages, even the teenager. It wasn't the same as in America where kids are counting the days down until it's their turn again!
- In Macedonia and in Pakistan and in much of the world, TV and movies have introduced Western ideas about birthdays. In Macedonia I heard many times the "Happy Birthday" song being sung in English with bad accents because that's what you do on a birthday!
- China
  - If you've ever read the book, *In the Year of the Bull and Jackie Robinson*, you know this fact. There are places (most commonly done in Korea), where you are one when you are born, not zero, and everyone turns a year older on New Year's Day. You may still celebrate your birthday, but it's not the day you turn a year older. In the book, the girl comes to America and is put in a class with kids who are really two years older than her because no one understands the cultural difference. If you were born in December, you could be two years old in China when you would be a month old in America.
- Explore More: What culture are you interested in? While many cultures have adopted American birthday ideas, some cultures, like China, have additional customs and traditions and superstitions surrounding birthdays.

VI. Discussion
- What are your family birthday traditions?

VII. Writing
- Today you are to try to figure out which sentences need a comma. They don't all need one!
  - You will put a comma after an introductory phrase.
  - You will put a comma before a conjunction when both sides of it could be its own sentence.
  - You use commas in a list.
  - You use a comma to separate place names like Philadelphia, Pennsylvania.

- • You use a comma to separate date names and date numbers like Tuesday, March 2nd, 1984.
- • One more place you use a comma is to separate off information that's just extra. We will practice that today with some examples.
  - o Complete Writing Sentences 20 in your workbook.
  - o (Note: You can remind them of this list as they work.)

Day 127

I. Read Genesis 41:1-13.

II. Memory Verse
- o Learn Psalm 55:22.
- o Cast your burden upon the LORD and He will sustain you; He will never allow the righteous to be shaken.

III. Language
- o Handwriting/Spelling
  - verse 5
  - words to know: scorch, captain, stalk, magician
  - spelling tips:
    - The word <u>scorch</u> has the word OR inside of it, just like sorts. There is no letter K or T.
    - When you are trying to spell <u>captain</u>, pronounce it cap-tane to help you.
    - The word <u>stalk</u> ends with the word talk.
    - The word <u>magician</u> starts with the word magic.
- o Vocabulary
  - gaunt (verse 4)
  - scrawny looking, especially looking thin from hunger (adjective)
- o Hebrew
  - Trace and write the letter Pey on the Hebrew Writing 39 page of your workbook.

IV. Science
- o In Pharaoh's dream he saw fat cows and gaunt cows. Let's learn about cows today. Cows are the cousin of what animal we already learned about?
  - oxen
- o Cows are in what kingdom?
  - the animal kingdom
- o Do you think they are vertebrates or invertebrates?
  - vertebrates, meaning they have a backbone
- o What class do you think they belong to? (For example: reptile, insect, mammal, fish, bird...)
  - They are mammals.
- o Some people say that cows have four stomachs. This isn't really true, but they do have four compartments in their digestive system.
  - Two of those compartments can hold massive amounts of food. I read 50 gallons. (That's nearly 200 liters.) One of the compartments is called the rumen. When we ruminate on something, we're thinking long and hard about it.
    - They can eat forty pounds (18 kilos) of food and drink a bathtub worth of water each day.
    (from https://www.aipl.arsusda.gov/kc/cowfacts.html)
    - What do you think cows eat?

- They eat things like grass, hay, and corn.
- Are they carnivores, herbivores, or omnivores?
  - They are herbivores. They only eat plants.
- Food gets into the digestive compartments through the esophagus. Do you remember what your esophagus is?
  - It's the tube that takes food down from the mouth.
- Cows will also send partially digested food back up the esophagus and will keep chewing on it.
  - This is called chewing the cud and cows can chew the cud for a lot of the day.
  - Food can get through our digestive system in a few hours; it can take a couple of days for food to work through a cow's digestive system.
- Dairy cows provide more than 90% of the world's milk supply. One cow can give up to 25 gallons of milk a day. (That's nearly 100 liters.)
  - What other food do we get from cows?
    - beef
- Cows are an honored animal in the Hindu religion. They have festivals where they decorate cows and celebrate them as symbols of their religion and there are laws about killing cows.
- Recall: Do cows have four stomachs? What does it mean that cows chew their cud? Why are cows so important to the world?
  - No, they do have four compartments to their digestive system.
  - They spit up into their mouth food that was already partially digested and keep chewing it.
  - They make the milk we drink.
- Explore More: You could learn about cow cloning.

V. Social Studies

- Pharaoh calls together all the wise men of Egypt, and none of them can tell him what the dream means.
- Do our leaders today have "wise men?" The American president does have his own collection of wise men. They are called the *Cabinet*. Their job is to give the president advice.
- The Cabinet is a group of people chosen by the president to oversee various aspects of the country. Let me list them for you. This list has grown over the years.
  - The Department of Education is one of the areas that has a Cabinet member in charge of it. The person in charge of a *department* is called the *secretary*.
    - This department is, of course, in charge of schools, laws regarding schools, money involving schools, etc.
    - Now, the Secretary of Education isn't actually in charge of schools and doesn't make the laws about schools, but his or her job is to advise the president about education issues.
  - The Secretary of State is in charge of international relations. They talk to leaders of other countries and try to reach compromises.
    - That's the Department of State. Sometimes you'll hear about State dinners. That means that some world leader is visiting, and they are holding a fancy dinner at the White House.

- The Department of the Treasury is in charge of giving advice about banking and taxes and money stuff.
- The Department of Defense looks over what happens in the military.
- The Department of Justice is in charge of watching over the judicial system. They might be called upon to offer advice as to whom different judge jobs should be given to.
    - A member of the Supreme Court can stay there until they die or until they decide to retire. The president appoints the new judge to replace the one leaving. The Secretary of Justice would be ready with recommendations for the job.
- The Department of the Interior is in charge of making sure America's natural resources are protected.
- The Department of Agriculture is over what?
    - They give advice on laws concerning farming.
- The Department of Commerce is over what?
    - Commerce is buying and selling. The Secretary of Commerce watches over the business world.
- The Department of Labor looks out for employees. They are giving advice about unions, minimum wage, worker's rights, unemployment, etc.
- The Department of Health and Human Services is over health care.
- The Department of Housing and Urban Development looks over cities and housing, especially making sure housing is available in cities for low income families.
- The Department of Transportation is probably one you can guess what they are in charge of. What things do they watch over?
    - The Department of Transportation is over things like highways, trains, planes, and buses. They look over the snow plows in the winter and are over the place where you go to get your driver's license.
- The Department of Energy is over well, energy. The Secretary of Energy gives the president recommendations involving energy such as electrical plants, solar panels, coal mining, nuclear power plants, etc.
- The Department of Veteran's Affairs is over veterans, the men and women who were previously in the military.
- Finally, the Department of Homeland Security. This is a newly created department. They are supposed to be keeping America safe by keeping terrorists out of America.
    - A little note: The only way to truly be safe is to be in Christ.
  - I can tell you one last thing about the Cabinet. The members of the Cabinet are all in line for the presidency. If the president dies, then the vice president becomes president. This has happened several times. If the vice president dies, then there are two others in line. This has never happened. If those people died, then the members of the Cabinet, in a specific order, would be in line to become president. That is, of course, until the next election where a new president would be chosen instead of inheriting the job.
  - Recall: Collectively, what are the president's wise men called? Are they all men? What is the title given someone on the Cabinet? Can you name three departments?
    - the Cabinet

- no
- secretary
  - Explore More: Learn more about a department you are interested in.

VI. Discussion
  - Which department do you think is the most important? Why?

VII. Writing
  - Use the discussion question as a writing prompt.
  - Get a high five and/or hug for using a comma after an introductory phrase.

Day 128

I. Read Genesis 41:14-32.

II. Memory Verse
- Practice Psalm 55:22.
- Cast your burden upon the LORD and He will sustain you; He will never allow the righteous to be shaken.

III. Language
- Handwriting/Spelling
  - verse 26
  - words to know: subsequent, famine, unknown, abundance
  - spelling tips:
    - The word <u>subsequent</u> is spelled just like it sounds. How many syllables does it have?
      - 3
        - Say each one as you spell it.
    - The word <u>famine</u> has the word mine in it.
    - The prefix to the word <u>unknown</u> is UN. It means not. Unknown means not known.
    - The word <u>abundance</u> ends with the word dance.
- Vocabulary
  - subsequent (verse 31)
  - coming after something, following (adjective)
- Hebrew
  - Today's letter is the Nun. It's our letter N.
  - Look at the N. This is one of those letters that looks different when it comes at the end of a word. The second line shows the ending Nun.
    - The ending form looks like the Vav. One way to tell the difference is that this would only be at the end of the word. I'll also show you a comparison between the two. What's the difference?
      - The Nun is another long letter. It hangs down below the line (like our letter p does).
  - Trace the Nun on the Hebrew Writing 40 page of your workbook.

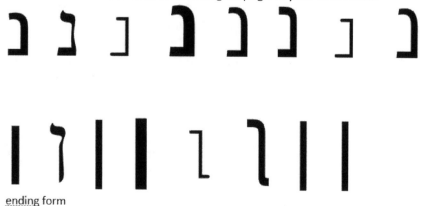

ending form

475

Nun   Vav   Nun   Vav

IV. Science
- o In Pharaoh's dream he's told of a time of abundance and a time of famine.
- o Do you remember any of the causes of famine?
  - It could be a crop failure. What would cause crops to fail and not grow properly?
    - extreme weather (droughts—Do you know what a drought is? flooding, severe storms)
    - disease
    - bugs (like the boll weevil that ate cotton plants)
  - A crop failure might mean there wasn't enough food for everyone or that since there was less food available it cost too much for poorer people to buy any.
- o Now let's look at abundance from a scientific perspective. If disease, extreme weather and bugs could cause famine, what do you think would cause abundance, lots and lots of crops, plenty of food for everyone?
  - Let's look at the opposite of each of the things that would cause famine.
- o Disease-What's the opposite of disease?
  - health
  - If disease can cause a crop failure, then healthy plants would be part of an abundant crop.
  - What do plants need to be healthy?
    - sun, water, good soil full of nutrients
    - Healthy soil would contribute to healthy plants.
  - Fertilizers are used to create soil that plants thrive in. Some people make healthy soil by creating *compost*.
    - You make compost by mixing soil with dead leaves and grass and any leftover vegetable and fruit scraps that you have. You can add in other food trash such as egg shells.
    - It all decomposes and breaks down into the soil. All of the nutrients from the food gets into the soil and then can get into the plants.
      - Some fertilizers are made from chemicals, but then the chemicals can get into the plants which then get into our bodies when we eat them. They might make nice looking food, but it's not necessarily the healthiest food.
- o We have healthy plants living in healthy soil. The next cause of a crop failure is extreme weather. What would be the opposite of extreme weather?
  - The opposite would be regular intervals of rain and sun, neither too much.
    - When there isn't enough rain, then farmers use irrigation techniques. We've used that word before. Do you remember what irrigation is? The ancient Mesopotamians used irrigation ditches.

- Irrigation is getting water to your crops. They dug ditches to make waterways from the rivers to their crops.
- Now farmers use pipes to carry water and sprinkler systems to simulate rain falling.
  - ○ The last on the list was bugs. Bugs can be bad for crops if they eat them, especially if swarms of a certain type of bug eat only a certain type of plant, and they all come together to the same part of a country at the same time. It can devastate a crop.
    - It would seem the opposite of bugs would be no bugs, however, bugs can be good for crops. Earthworms are good for soil. They are practically making their own compost down there.
    - Ladybugs, especially baby ladybugs, are good for gardens. They only eat bugs that eat plants. They are guardians of gardens.
    - Centipedes do the same and hunt only bugs that eat and harm plants.
      - Why is a centipede called a CENTipede?
        - There are 100 CENTs in a dollar. There are 100 years in a CENTury.
        - CENT means 100, so centipedes have 100 legs.
  - ○ Recall: What is compost? What is irrigation? What are some things that make for an abundant crop?
    - It's soil mixed with natural things that would make it healthier such as grass and banana peels, natural things that have decomposed.
    - watering crops
    - perfect weather, healthy soil, helpful bugs
  - ○ Explore More: I wrote that since less food was available it cost too much. Learn about the law of supply and demand.

V. Social Studies
  - ○ We looked before at how governments can cause famines. When Mao Zedong became leader of China as the head of the Communist party, he called it the "Great Leap Forward."
    - What really happened was that they confiscated crops from farmers around the country. They demanded so much from the farmers that the farmers didn't have enough food left for their families. People starved.
    - Now why would a government do that?
  - ○ Governments want control. People, all people, want power. It was the first sin. Satan told Eve that she would be like God. People want to be like God. They want the power. That's why people love money. It gives them power.
    - How would confiscating the crops of farmers give power to the government?
      - People would have to rely on the government for food.
      - Do people in America have to rely on the government for food?
        - It was reported that 20% of Americans were on food stamps in 2013. That means that the government helped those families buy food. If those balloons were 100 people, 20 of them would have relied on the government for some of their food.

- When the Soviets, what the Russians were known as in earlier days, had control over many of the countries surrounding Russia, they wanted to keep their power over those countries.
  - Ukraine was one of the controlled countries.
- They feared the Ukrainians would try to rebel and break free from the Soviets. They wanted to close down all Ukrainian farms and establish government farms. The food would feed the workers at government factories. It could also be sold overseas to earn money for the government.
  - The Ukrainians didn't want to do it. Farmers were arrested as well as anyone considered a threat to Soviet control, basically any leader of the people, anyone who could speak out against the Soviets and lead Ukraine if they broke free.
  - The result was a forced famine in the Ukraine. You could be arrested if you even acknowledged that there was a famine in the Ukraine.
  - This was in the 1930s. In 1991 Ukraine became an independent country.
- This has happened other times as well.
- In Ethiopia in the 1980s a similar thing was tried. They forced farmers onto collective farms. They had to work for the government instead of for themselves. At the same time, they declared the areas they took the farmers from as areas of famine; crops weren't growing as there were no farmers! Aid came in to the government to help with the famine.
  - The government controls the food, and then people have to rely on the government. The government then has power over the people. The government gets to decide who eats and who doesn't.
- The international banking system has also caused poverty in Africa. They keep Africa indebted to them. When you are in debt to someone, they have a power over you. That's a good reason to keep out of debt.
- America isn't free from causing problems. America's aid to Africa also causes problems. All of the free clothing and food provided puts out of business people in the community who would be making and selling those things.
- We read on Day 66 the lesson called "The Great Thanksgiving Hoax." The Pilgrims created an abundant harvest, in part, by allowing families to reap the benefits of their own labor.
  - People in general produce more when they get the benefit of their hard work.
- You may hear phrases like "free market." That means that people are allowed to buy and sell without interference from the government, or at least not a lot of interference.
  - Some believe that is the best way to create abundance for everyone.
- Recall: How do governments create famines?
  - They take away people's ability to feed themselves.
- Explore More: What can you learn about famine in Somalia? What were the factors behind it?

VI. Discussion
- As Christians we can trust God to meet all of our needs. We never have to be powerless, and we can always rely on Jesus.

- o We also need to remember that no government acts on its own. God is in control. God can bring about abundance and prosperity. God can bring about poverty and famine. Either way, God is acting in love! When God brings hard times, it's a way to turn us to Him.
- o You can discuss how a government can bring blessing or curse on a country and what we can do about it, or you can discuss giving.
  - I mentioned how giving could enable poverty. What do you think would be a better way to give to poor nations or individuals?

VII. Writing
- o Use the discussion question as a writing prompt.
- o Get a high five and/or hug for starting a sentence with if or when and using a comma after the introductory phrase.

Day 129

I. Read Genesis 41:33-40. This starts with Joseph talking to Pharaoh. He just finished giving the dream interpretation.

II. Memory Verse
- o Practice Psalm 55:22.
- o Cast your burden upon the LORD and He will sustain you; He will never allow the righteous to be shaken.

III. Language
- o Handwriting/Spelling
  - verse 37
  - words to know: proposal, exact, discern, inform
  - spelling tips:
    - The word <u>proposal</u> can be spelled how it sounds if you pronounce the ending -all.
    - The word <u>exact</u> is ex and act put together.
    - The word <u>discern</u> has two S sounds and one S.
    - The word <u>inform</u> is the words in and form put together.
- o Vocabulary
  - discern (verse 39)
  - to be able to recognize or to see something and distinguish what it is (verb)
- o Hebrew
  - Say Genesis 1:4-5.
  - Trace and write Nun on the Hebrew Writing 41 page of your workbook.
  - The bottom of the page shows the end form of the letter Nun. It's one of those letters that looks different at the end of the word.

IV. Science
- o Joseph is going to store up grain during the years of abundance so that there will be food during the years of famine.
- o Today we're going to learn about food storage. We learned about Egyptians storing organs from bodies by dehydrating them.
- o Let's look first at dehydration as a storage technique. To *dehydrate* is to take the water out of something. It's the opposite of hydrating. You hydrate yourself when you drink water. You are dehydrated when you are in need of a drink of water.
  - The dried herb seasonings you have in your kitchen are dehydrated. That's how they can sit on your shelf for months without going bad.
  - The tea leaves in your tea bags are dehydrated leaves.
  - Raisins are dehydrated grapes. Grapes go bad. Raisins don't.
- o So what keeps the dehydrated food from spoiling?
  - It must have to do with the lack of water.
  - Living things need water.
  - Yeast is a living thing right? It's in the fungus family and so is mold.
  - Mold is the stuff that grows on old food that you let sit around too long. It's a living thing, and it's working on eating your food, decomposing it.

- o Mold, yeast, and other fungi such as mushrooms are called *decomposers*. Their job is to break down things that have died.
  - Decomposing things that have died makes them useful to our world. It brings them down into the soil, and then they can be used again by plants and in turn by the animals who eat plants.
  - Remember how everything is interdependent? We all rely on each other. We rely on decomposers to make our soil richer for better plants which we animals then eat.
- o Since decomposers, such as mold, are living things too, they need water. Without water, they can't live. Dried food doesn't make a good habitat for them.
- o We've talked about living things needing water. We've talked about plants needing water, sun, and soil (its food), but we haven't mentioned the obvious. Living things need air.
  - Food can be packed in tightly so that little air is present. Without air, living things will die.
  - One storage technique is vacuum packing. It sucks the air out of the container so that those little living cells of the fungus kingdom can't get at the food.
- o What about Joseph's grain storage?
  - We aren't told how he did it, but huge silos have been found among ancient Egypt's remains. A *silo* is a large cylindrical building, like a huge can for holding grains. The ones found in Egypt are 20 feet across and 25 feet tall (6 meters/7.6 meters).
    - If you can't imagine that, it's like four tall kids lying end to end and then five tall kids standing on top of each other.
  - Silos are still used. It's an efficient way to store grain.
  - Even without extra special techniques, why was Joseph's attempt at storing massive amounts of grain successful?
    - We're told repeatedly that God blessed everything that Joseph did.
- o Recall: What are two types of techniques used for preserving food? Why do those techniques keep food from decomposing? What is the name of the type of building that is often used to store grain?
  - dehydration and vacuum packing
  - They make the food an unfit habitat for the decomposers like mold that spoil food.
  - silo
- o Explore More: Learn more about preservation techniques. How does canning work?

V. Social Studies
- o Before we begin, what's an amendment?
  - It's an addition to the US Constitution.
- o Joseph taxes the grain production and stores it up to have it for everyone when they need it.
- o Let's look a little bit at taxes and savings.
- o Let's start with the federal income tax. Tax Day in America is April 15th. Everyone has to submit their taxes by then.

- The Sixteenth Amendment to the U.S. Constitution says that the government has the right to collect taxes to use the money for the common defense and welfare, meaning for everyone's good.
- Every American who earns more than $400 in a year is supposed to pay taxes. You may fall into that category as a teenager.
- It's a complicated process. How much you pay in taxes is relative to how much you earned.
  - If you earn a lot, then you give a larger percent of your money to the government.
- There are all sorts of what they call tax breaks. You can pay less in taxes if you are going to school or had a lot of medical needs. Even having kids provides a tax benefit. You can also pay less in taxes if you give money away to churches and charities.

o Now let's look at savings. Joseph saved lives by saving up. Do you remember the Guinness family motto? Earn all you can; save all you can; give all you can. They got that from a famous preacher, John Wesley.
  - Giving all you can and saving all you can seem like they contradict in a way.
  - Here's what Jesus said about saving: "Do not store up for yourselves treasures on earth, where moth and rust destroy, and where thieves break in and steal. But store up for yourselves treasures in heaven, where neither moth nor rust destroys, and where thieves do not break in or steal; for where your treasure is, there your heart will be also." (Matthew 6:19-21)
  - Colossians 3:17 says, "Whatever you do in word or deed, do all in the name of the Lord Jesus, giving thanks through Him to God the Father." So whether we are working or saving or giving, it should be done in Jesus' name, to His glory and not for ourselves.

o When we save money in a bank, we are hoping to get interest, which is earning money from the money we put in. When you open a bank account, you will know what amount of interest you will earn with your money. It's not very much, but you earn it without working!

o The bank uses our money to invest. You can invest too. *Investing* is giving your money to someone or something that you think will earn money. You can invest by buying a house because you may be able to sell it at a higher price. You can invest by giving your money to a company like Walmart or Facebook and they use your money to run their business, and if they make money, then you make a little money too.
  - Investment is a venture. Do you remember what venture means? To do something risky or daring. There is always a risk with investing. It may not turn out how you had hoped.

o When you save, you are only putting aside a small amount. Over time it becomes a big amount, and if you need it, then it's ready for you. That's a better way to live than spending all of your money and going into debt when you need something.
  - *Debt* is when you owe something to someone. You aren't free when you are in debt. You have to pay back your debt plus pay extra money for having the debt.

o If you saved 10 dollars a month, you would have one hundred and twenty dollars in a year, and you'd have a little more than that if you were earning interest.

- o However, if you bought something for $1000 with a credit card and went into debt because you didn't really have $1000, you could end up paying more than $1500. That's $500 more than it cost! You have to pay that extra money to the credit card company. They pay the $1000 when you buy whatever it is, and then you pay them for paying.
  - It's much better to save and spend what you have than to pay so much extra for something because you hadn't saved.
  - Credit cards aren't bad. When I am in America, I use a credit card for everything, but every single month I pay the credit card bill in full, so that I am never in debt and never pay more for things than what they actually cost.
- o Recall: What is investing? What is debt?
  - giving your money to someone or something that you think will earn money
  - owing something to someone
- o Explore More: Below is what I started writing for this lesson and then switched. What can you learn about communistic tactics? Look up communist propaganda. What was its aim? Why did it work?
  - Let me tell you what Joseph does. He collects a tax of grain during the years of abundance. Everyone gives a percentage of what they grow and it is stored. During the famine, those people will need grain and will come to Joseph and ask for it. Joseph will sell it to them. They will be grateful. They will run out of food and come back to buy more. When they run out of money, they will sell their possessions and their land. By the end of the famine, Pharaoh will own everything! In fact, they even sell themselves, saying they will be Pharaoh's slaves.
  - Do you see what happens? Pharaoh takes peoples food, sells it back to them, and they thank him for it. Not only that, but they sell everything to do it. In the end, Pharaoh owns it all.
    - Personally, I think many a leader has tried to replicate this or dreamed they could.
  - In the Bible this is all part of God's plan. Israel ends up as slaves in Egypt because of this event in history. God's deliverance from Egypt is the biggest display of God's power to save us in the Old Testament. Their deliverance gives us a picture of the Passover, a picture of Christ's sacrifice and covering for us. It all starts with Joseph getting on his brothers' nerves! God is always doing more than we can imagine!

VI. Discussion
- o Are you a saver, a spender or a giver?
- o What do you think you could be doing now to earn all you can, save all you can, and give all you can?

VII. Writing
- o Use the discussion question as a writing prompt.
- o Get a high five and/or hug for using a comma appropriately after an introductory clause.

Day 130

I. Read Genesis 41:41-49.

II. Memory Verse
- o Say from memory Psalm 55:22.
  - • Cast your burden upon the LORD and He will sustain you; He will never allow the righteous to be shaken.
- o Find it in the Bible.
- o Review Micah 6:8.
  - • He has told you, O man, what is good; and what does the Lord require of you, but to do justice, to love kindness, and to walk humbly with your God?

III. Language
- o Handwriting/Spelling
  - • verse 41
  - • Test yourselves on the words from Days 126-129.
    - ▪ sorts, basket, favorably, chief
    - ▪ scorch, captain, stalk, magician
    - ▪ subsequent, famine, unknown, abundance
    - ▪ proposal, exact, discern, inform
- o Vocabulary
  - • Review your words from Days 126-129.
    - ▪ interpretation – the explanation of something's meaning
    - ▪ gaunt – scrawny looking, especially looking thin from hunger
    - ▪ subsequent – coming after something, following
    - ▪ discern – to be able to recognize or to see something and distinguish what it is
- o Hebrew
  - • Say Genesis 1:1-5.
  - • Write the words al pnaa, ben and ven on the Hebrew Writing 42 page of your workbook.
  - • Can you read the words?

IV. Science
- o We're going to review what we've learned of simple machines and look at one of them in a new way.
- o What are simple machines? What do they do for us in general?
  - • Simple machines are tools that make work easier.
- o Do you remember the scientific definition of work?
  - • It's a force moving an object.
  - • Is picking up a piece of paper work?
    - ▪ Yes, the force applied by your hand is moving the paper.
  - • Is throwing a ball up in the air work?
    - ▪ Yes, the force applied by your hand is moving the ball.
  - • Is the ball falling back down work?

- Yes, the force of gravity is moving the ball down.
- Is your whole family pushing against the side of your house trying to get it to move work?
  - No, the house doesn't move, so no work was accomplished on the house. No work is accomplished if an object isn't moved.
- We learned about the wheel and axle, the wedge, and the screw.
- We learned about the wedge when Abraham used an ax to split wood. Can you draw a wedge shape? (Parent note: It's basically a skinny triangle.)
  - How does an ax help us cut wood?
    - It puts all of the force into a small edge, so all of the force is concentrated and hits the wood in just one spot.
    - Its wedge shape changes the direction of the force. We swing down and the wedge shape pushes out on both sides. That's what splits the wood.
- When we learned about the wheel and axle, we looked at wells. Can you draw how a wheel and axle is used in a well?
  - On a well you turn the big wheel which turns the axle the rope is around, and it makes work easier by reducing the amount of force we need to lift the heavy bucket of water.
  - How does a wheel and axle make lifting the bucket feel lighter? Why is less force needed when we use the simple machine instead of just lifting the rope and bucket?
    - The force is less because the distance is greater. The bigger the wheel, the less force is needed.
    - Lifting the bucket of water straight up would be really heavy and require a lot of strength or force.
    - Turning the wheel requires more arm movement, that's the greater distance, but it requires less effort, less force.
      - Do you remember how the wheel and axle made lifting the bucket or basket easier when you did the experiment?
- The screw was the first simple machine we learned about, and we didn't talk about how it made work easier. Let's see if you can figure it out.
  - We learned that the screw can carry water, but mostly we use screws to put together pieces of wood. When we use a nail, we have to use a lot of force and hit it hard. Do we use more or less force putting in a screw compared to hammering in a nail?
    - less
    - We don't have to hit it hard to get it in. We just push on it.
  - So if a screw uses less force, what does it need to use more of to complete the same work of getting down into the wood?
    - distance
    - How does a screw use distance to make up for using less force and still get the work done?
      - We turn it around and around and around. That's our distance traveled making the work easier by requiring less force from us.

o Today we read about Joseph getting to ride in a chariot. Here's a picture of a chariot. What simple machine that we've learned about is at work?

- • the wheel and axle
- • The work is done by the horse pulling the chariot. The horse applies the force. The bigger the wheel the less force would be needed to pull the chariot right?
  - ▪ Now look at the picture of the old bicycle. Why is the wheel so big?

- • Did you say it required less force to go the same amount of distance?
  - ▪ That's true, but it also did something else.

- If they applied the same amount of force then what would happen?
  - They would go so much farther for the same amount of force.
  - The distance increased and the force stayed the same meaning this bicycle allowed them to go really fast.
- Recall: What does a simple machine do?
  - makes work easier
- Explore More: Explore more Learn about how a car's axles work. How are they connected? How are they steered? What can you learn about the basic construct of a car?

V. Social Studies

- The chariot was a symbol of power. Rulers rode in chariots. Warriors rode in chariots.
- Here are verses 42 and 43 from today's reading.
  - Then Pharaoh took off his signet ring from his hand and put it on Joseph's hand, and clothed him in garments of fine linen and put the gold necklace around his neck. He had him ride in his second chariot; and they proclaimed before him, "Bow the knee!"
- When people are told to bow before Joseph, what does that symbolize?
  - Bowing symbolized their respect for and submission to Joseph.
- Pharaoh had Joseph dressed in expensive clothing and a gold necklace. What does that symbolize?
  - I would say wealth and power.
  - There's an expression, "The clothes make the man." What do you think that might mean?
    - Not only do people respond to us differently depending on how we dress, but we respond differently too.
    - When we get really dressed up, we behave differently than when we are in jeans and sweats.
  - Workers wear uniforms because it gives them respect for their position. People respond differently.
  - People give more respect to people in white lab coats, like a doctor would wear, even if the person isn't a doctor.
  - Even more interesting, people act smarter (as in scoring better on activities) when wearing what they believe is a doctor's lab coat.
  - When people saw Joseph, they responded to his new attire. It made him look important, and he was treated as someone important.
- Pharaoh also gives Joseph a signet ring. The symbol on the ring was Pharaoh's own. It meant that Joseph had Pharaoh's authority.
  - The signet ring was a symbol of authority.
- Can you think of any symbols today? What do you picture when you picture someone with authority and power? What do they look like? What do they have?
- How is this a symbol of authority?

- o Recall: Why might it a good idea to get dressed in the morning instead of trying to do your school work in your pajamas? What did Joseph's wearing Pharaoh's signet ring mean to people?
    - We act differently depending on how we are dressed.
    - It meant that Joseph had Pharaoh's authority.
- o Explore More: What are symbols of power? Why do presidential candidates wear red ties? Look at pictures of the president speaking or presidential candidates. What symbols are present?

VI. Discussion
- o Do you judge people by how they look? Do you think the same about someone who looks homeless and someone who is dressed beautifully?
- o James 2:2-4 For if a man comes into your assembly with a gold ring and dressed in fine clothes, and there also comes in a poor man in dirty clothes, and you pay special attention to the one who is wearing the fine clothes, and say, "You sit here in a good place," and you say to the poor man, "You stand over there, or sit down by my footstool," have you not made distinctions among yourselves, and become judges with evil motives?
- o If those two people came to your church one Sunday, would you invite one of them home for lunch?

VII. Writing
- o Choose one of your writings from Day 127-129 to edit.
- o Read it out loud to help look for problems.
- o Correct punctuation and capitalization.
- o Have someone else edit it as well.
- o Create a final draft.
- o (Note: You might want to save this in your child's portfolio.)

Day 131 (check Materials List)

I. Read Genesis 41:50-42:13. During our final review weeks, we're going to read through the rest of Joseph's story to the very end of Genesis.

II. Memory Verse
- o Can you say from memory? Deuteronomy 31:8
- o Find it in the Bible.
  - The LORD is the one who goes ahead of you; He will be with you. He will not fail you or forsake you. Do not fear or be dismayed.
- o Review Joshua 24:5.
  - [If it is disagreeable in your sight to serve the LORD,] choose for yourselves today whom you will serve: [whether the gods which your fathers served which were beyond the River, or the gods of the Amorites in whose land you are living;] but as for me and my house, we will serve the LORD.

III. Language
- o Spelling
  - Complete Spelling Review 16 in your workbook.
  - This uses words from Day 110.

- o Hebrew
  - We need one last letter to read Genesis 1:2 in Hebrew.
  - Today we're going to learn the letter that makes the KH sound. It's the Chet. It looks similar to the Tav. Be careful.

- Trace the Chet on the Hebrew Writing 43 page of your workbook.
- You'll notice I slipped in another letter on your sheet that we'll find in Genesis 1:2. It's also transliterated KH. It's a form of the letter Khaf. Don't worry about learning its name right now. Just be aware that the KH in our Bible verses can be represented by that letter as well. This does look like other letters! See it on the left below. It stands out from the others because it's longer. It hangs below the line when written, like our letter p does.
- The word below is KHOshekh. It begins and ends with these two letters.

IV. Science

- Today we're going to do a science experiment on food preservation. We learned about dehydrating food and about packing food airtight. How do those things help preserve food? How do they keep it from going bad?
  - Decomposers, living things that decompose food, need water and air, like all living things, and these techniques make the food an unwelcome habitat for them.
- The ancient Egyptians dehydrated bodies before wrapping them. They also used a salt-like substance on the bodies, so we will use salt in our experiment as well.
- You will need one apple, salt, cooling rack or cooking sheet, four cups or bowls that you can do without for the week, plastic wrap, paper towels, and tape for sealing the apple in.
- Make sure your hands and tools are clean and dry. Cut the apple into four sections.
  - Place one apple piece into a cup. This will have no preservation technique.
  - Put some folded paper towel into a cup. Place in an apple piece and cover it with salt.
  - Wrap one apple piece in plastic wrap. Wrap it as tightly as you can in overlapping layers to try to keep the air out. Then tape it to seal the edges.
  - Slice the remaining piece as thinly as you can and lay it out in the sun on a cooling rack. These will be your dehydrated apples. Or put them in the oven on a low temperature. You aren't cooking them. You are evaporating the water out of them. When you think they are dehydrated, you can put them in a cup like the others.
- We'll come back to these in a week.
- Today on your Science Review 17 page write in the materials and procedure-what you did. (Materials: apple, salt, plastic wrap, cooling rack, tape, 4 cups; Procedure: no preservation slice, salt apple slice, wrap apple slice, dry apple slice)

V. Social Studies

- We are going to play a little game. Everyone starts with $100. On the Social Studies Review 14 page of your workbook you will keep track of your money.
- Today do something with your money: spend, save, give.
  - If you spend, write in the box what you bought and how much it was. Subtract that amount from your bank total and write the amount left in the "Bank" column for the day.
    - Note: Just make up a price for what they want. Be reasonable, but don't worry about being exact.
  - If you give, write what you gave your money for and how much. Subtract that amount from your bank total and write the amount left in the "Bank" column for the day.
  - If you decide to save, then write your starting total in the "Bank" column for the day.
- We will continue this each day for these two weeks. At the end we'll see the outcome of your decisions. Every decision has an impact.

VI. Writing

- o Write for two minutes. Start writing a story. We are going to keep adding to our story this time.
- o If you would like a word to get started, use the word CONFINE from your vocabulary.
- o Time yourselves. Just write and write and don't stop until the time is up. Just start. Go!
- o Get a high five and/or hug for reading what you wrote aloud, standing before your audience.

Day 132 (check Materials List)

I. Read Genesis 42:14-38.

II. Memory Verse
- o Practice Jeremiah 29:11.
- o Find it in the Bible.
  - • "For I know the plans I have for you," declares the Lord, "plans to prosper you and not to harm you, plans to give you hope and a future." (NIV)
- o Review 2 Peter 3:9.
  - • The Lord is not slow about His promise, as some count slowness, but is patient toward you, not wishing for any to perish but for all to come to repentance.

III. Language
- o Spelling
  - • Complete Spelling Review 17 in your workbook.
  - • This uses words from Day 115.

- o Hebrew
  - • Read Genesis 1:1 and 3.

בְּרֵאשִׁית, בָּרָא אֱלֹהִים, אֵת הַשָּׁמַיִם, וְאֵת הָאָרֶץ.

וַיֹּאמֶר אֱלֹהִים, יְהִי אוֹר; וַיְהִי אוֹר.

  - • Trace and write the Chet on the Hebrew Writing 44 page of your workbook.
  - • The final form of the Khaf (at the bottom of the page) is another letter that hangs below the line like our letter p does.

IV. Science
- o Check on your salted apple. What's happening?
  - • Did you see liquid? It's dehydrating the apple. It's pulling out the water.
  - • You can change the paper towel carefully. Make sure you have clean hands.
- o Today we're going to do a science experiment on dying, as in dying the thread that was woven into Joseph's multicolored coat.
- o We're going to create some dyes and then use them.
- o You can dye cloth, but I am going to do eggs for this experiment.
- o The vegetables require longer cooking than the eggs, so you might want to start with those.
- o Take as many eggs as you would like to use and hard boil them. (Parent supervision required.) Run them under cold water when they are done.
- o Set up dye stations. Each color gets its own cup. The egg should be covered in liquid. Here are some color suggestions.
  - • boiled red cabbage
  - • boiled spinach

- boiled onion skins
- boiled beets
- Other options: carrots, coffee, grass…
  - These each take 30 minutes of boiling and need to be done separately to keep their individual colors. Use two cups of water and a half cup of each of the ingredients below. Keep a good lid on it to keep in the water. Don't let it boil out.
  - Add two or three teaspoons of vinegar to each cup.
    - The vinegar is acting as our mordant. It's going to stick the color to the egg.
      - The acid in the vinegar adds hydrogen that will attach to both the dye and the egg.
    - The calcium in the egg shell will react with the vinegar to create carbon dioxide. You can look for escaping gas bubbles of carbon dioxide.

V. Social Studies

- Today, again do something with your money: spend, save, give.
- If you spend or give, record what you did with your money and how much of it you used.
- If you already spent all of your money, you may go into debt up to $50 at any time. That means that you can spend up to $50 of money that you don't have. Think before you act! Actions have consequences.
- Record the total you have in the bank for the day.
- We will continue this each day. On the 6th day you will get $50 dollars more. At the end of 10 days, we'll see the outcome of your decisions. Every decision you make has an impact.

VI. Writing

- Write for four minutes. Add to your story from yesterday.
- If you would like a word to get you going today, use the word DEVOUR from your vocabulary.
- Time yourselves. Just write and write and don't stop until the time is up. Just start. Go!
- Get a high five and/or hug for reading what you wrote aloud while standing before your audience.

Day 133 (check Materials List)

I. Read Genesis 43:1-22.

II. Memory Verse
- o Practice Romans 8:28.
- o Find it in the Bible.
  - And we know that God causes all things to work together for good to those who love God, to those who are called according to His purpose.
- o Review Job 19:25.
  - As for me, I know that my Redeemer lives,
    And at the last He will take His stand on the earth.

III. Language
- o Spelling
  - Complete Spelling Review 18 in your workbook.
  - This uses words from Day 120.
- o Hebrew
  - Today we're going to read and write the first part of Genesis 1:2.
  - You are going to trace and write on the Hebrew Writing 45 page of your workbook.
  - First say Genesis 1:2. Then reread the section in bold.
  - **ve ha Arets haaTAH TOhu va VOhu** ve KHOshekh al pnaa teHOM ve RUakh eloHEEM meraKHEfet al pnaa ha MAyim
  - Now say it as you follow along with the Hebrew. Let me rewrite the transcription to match how the words are combined in the Hebrew.
    - **vehaArets , haaTAH TOhu vaVOhu**
    - Read and follow along with the underlined portion of the verse.
  - Now just read that part of the verse; this time only look at the Hebrew.

וְהָאָרֶץ, הָיְתָה תֹהוּ וָבֹהוּ, וְחֹשֶׁךְ, עַל פְּנֵי תְהוֹם; וְרוּחַ אֱלֹהִים, מְרַחֶפֶת עַל פְּנֵי הַמָּיִם.

IV. Science
- o Today we're going to build clocks.
- o Do you remember the two types of clocks the Egyptians invented?
  - the water clock and the obelisk, which was a shadow clock
- o To make an obelisk clock you just need something straight.
  - You could stick a stick in the ground, or you could build a Duplo tower, etc.
    - It needs to be where it will get some sun.
    - You'll also need paper with it so you can mark where its shadow falls. Figure out a way to hold down a piece of paper next to your obelisk. It needs to stay in place.
  - Mark its shadow with the time at regular intervals.

- Trace a line along the shadow and write the time at the end of the line.
- To make a water clock you'll need a bunch of paper cups, as well as something to poke through the paper cups, maybe pens.
- How did these types of clocks work?
  - The water ran out the holes in the bowl, and the water level told you how many hours had passed.
- What time of day was the water clock made for?
  - nighttime
  - What made it a better nighttime clock?
    - The sun would speed evaporation and change the time!
- Use any timing source that has seconds and work on making a ten second clock with your cup. Where do your holes need to be?
  - The cup doesn't have to empty in ten seconds, but you should be able to time ten seconds with your cup.

V. Social Studies

- Continue with our game on the Social Studies Review 14 page of your workbook.
- Today do something with your money: spend, save, give.
- Record your actions and final total in the bank for the day.
- We will continue this until Day 140. At the end we'll see the outcome of your decisions.
- Note: You could offer them money for their "bank" for dong jobs around the house. ☺ You could also remind them of the motto, "Earn all you can. Save all you can. Give all you can."

VI. Writing

- Write for six minutes. Continue your same story.
- If you would like a word to get started, use the word ODIOUS from your vocabulary. It means repulsive.
- Time yourselves. Just write and write and don't stop until the time is up. Just start. Go!
- Get a high five and/or hug if you used the word odious in your writing.

Day 134 (check Materials List)

I. Read Genesis 43:23-44:9.

*Does it confuse you that Joseph would hide the cup in Benjamin's bag and accuse him of stealing? He's testing his brothers to see if they had repented, to see if they had changed. Would they be willing to abandon their brother? Did they despise Benjamin, the favorite, the way they despised Joseph?

II. Memory Verse
- o Practice Micah 6:8
- o Find it in the Bible.
  - He has told you, O man, what is good;
    And what does the Lord require of you
    But to do justice, to love kindness,
    And to walk humbly with your God?
- o Review Hebrews 11:1.
  - Now faith is the assurance of things hoped for, the conviction of things not seen.

III. Language
- o Spelling
  - Complete Spelling Review 19 in your workbook. You will need to hold onto these words for Day 138.
- o Hebrew
  - Today we're going to read and write the second part of Genesis 1:2.
  - You will trace and write it on the Hebrew Writing 46 page of your workbook.
  - First say Genesis 1:2 and then today's portion.
  - ve ha Arets haaTAH TOhu va VOhu **ve KHOshekh al pnaa teHOM ve RUakh** eloHEEM meraKHEfet al pnaa ha MAyim
  - Now say it as you follow along with the underlined portion of Hebrew. Let me rewrite the transcription to match how the words are combined in the Hebrew.
    - **veKHOshekh al pnaa teHOM veRUakh**
  - Now read the Hebrew for this part of the verse. Only look at the Hebrew.
  - Now say and read along from the beginning of the verse.
  - Now read the Hebrew for the first two parts of the verse.

וְהָאָרֶץ, הָיְתָה תֹהוּ וָבֹהוּ, וְחֹשֶׁךְ, עַל פְּנֵי תְהוֹם; וְרוּחַ אֱלֹהִים, מְרַחֶפֶת עַל פְּנֵי הַמָּיִם.

IV. Science
- o Today you'll choose which experiment to do.
- o First let's look at the two topics they explore. One experiment will be on chemical reactions that produce carbon dioxide. Do you remember the scientific symbol for carbon dioxide?
  - What's the symbol for carbon?
    - C
  - What element makes up the dioxide?
    - oxygen ,
    - What's the symbol for oxygen?
      - O
  - The official scientific symbol for carbon dioxide is CO_2.
    - How many oxygen atoms are in a molecule of CO_2?
      - 2
- o Here's the symbol for baking soda. What elements are in a molecule of baking soda?

NaCHO₃

- Na = sodium, C = carbon, H = hydrogen, and then three oxygen atoms
- o When you mix certain things with baking soda, the reaction will produce carbon dioxide.
  - Carbon dioxide is a gas, so you will see bubbles to let you know that carbon dioxide is present.
  - This is the gas that fills up our bread and cookies to keep them from being flat.
- o The other experiment has to do with the water cycle. Can you tell the water cycle?
  - Water evaporates, rises as water vapor, cools in the sky, condenses and forms clouds, and when the air is saturated, full of water, it rains, and the cycle begins again.
- o We learned about something called the shadow effect where a mountain or even tall buildings can make it rain on one side and not the other. Can you explain why that would happen?
  - The air can't pass through the mountain or building, so it has to go up and over. As it rises, the air cools and the water condenses causing it to rain before it ever gets to the other side.
- o You can design an experiment that uses $NaCHO_3$ to produce CO_2 (ie. uses baking soda to produce carbon dioxide) OR you could design a shadow effect experiment.
  - Examples:
    - combine baking soda with different things to see what produces carbon dioxide, or the most carbon dioxide – Make sure to try acids! (Day 126)
    - place steaming water on one side of a standing-up book and hold aluminum foil over it with ice on top of the foil (Day 120)
    - These are just some ideas. You design how you are going to do your experiment.
- o Fill out a lab report on Science Review 18.

V. Social Studies
- o Continue with our game on the Social Studies Review 14 page of your workbook.
- o Today do something with your money: spend, save, give.
- o Record what you bought or to whom you gave and how much and then your total left in the bank.

VI. Writing
- o Write for eight minutes. Continue your same story.
- o If you would like a word to get started, use the word SUPERVISE from your vocabulary.
- o Time yourselves. Just write and write and don't stop until the time is up. Just start. Go!

Day 135 (check Materials List)

I. Read Genesis 44:10-34. We're starting with the brothers being accused of stealing.

II. Memory Verse
- o Practice Psalm 55:22.
- o Find it in the Bible.
  - • Cast your burden upon the LORD and He will sustain you; He will never allow the righteous to be shaken.
- o Review John 11:25
  - • Jesus said to her, "I am the resurrection and the life; he who believes in Me will live even if he dies."

III. Language
- o Spelling
  - • Complete Spelling Review 20 in your workbook.
- o Hebrew
  - • Today we're going to read and write the last part of Genesis 1:2.
  - • You will write it on the Hebrew Writing 47 page of your workbook.
  - • First say Genesis 1:2 and then today's portion.
  - • ve ha Arets haaTAH TOhu va VOhu ve KHOshekh al pnaa teHOM ve

    RUakh **eloHEEM meraKHEfet al pnaa ha MAyim**
  - • Now say it as you follow along with the underlined portion of Hebrew. Let me rewrite the transcription to match how the words are combined in the Hebrew.
    - ▪ **eloHEEM meraKHEfet al pnaa haMAyim**
  - • Now read the Hebrew for this part of the verse. Only look at the Hebrew.
  - • Now say the whole verse and read along from the beginning.
  - • Now read the Hebrew for the whole verse, only looking at the Hebrew.

וְהָאָרֶץ, הָיְתָה תֹהוּ וָבֹהוּ, וְחֹשֶׁךְ, עַל פְּנֵי תְהוֹם; וְרוּחַ
אֱלֹהִים, מְרַחֶפֶת עַל פְּנֵי הַמָּיִם.

IV. Science
- o Today you are going to build a car using four wheels and two axles.
- o Choose your materials.
  - • Place the axles through the body. (You can tape toothpicks together to make them longer if necessary.) One axle through the back end and one axle toward the front. Think about how a car looks. Your wheels will attach to the axles.
  - • Put your wheels on. Attach them as best you can.
  - • Test out your car.
    - ▪ You could make a ramp for it to roll down.

- If you have more materials, you can test out different wheel sizes.
  - You could time runs and see the difference in different bodies, wheels, and axle length.
  - How would wheel size affect the car?
- You can look online for how to use a rubber band to power your car.

V. Social Studies
- Continue with our game on the Social Studies Review 14 page of your workbook.
- Today do something with your money: spend, save, give.
- Record what you bought or to whom you gave and how much and then your total left in the bank.

VI. Writing
- Write for ten minutes. Continue your same story.
- If you would like a word to get started, use the word INTERPRETATION from your vocabulary.
- Time yourselves. Just write and write and don't stop until the time is up. Just start. Go!

Day 136

I. Do you remember what a remnant is? It's what's left over. In biblical terms it means that God always has a group of His people. It will never happen that all of the Jews or that all of the Christians will be killed off. God will always preserve a remnant of His people. Read Genesis 45:1-20.

II. Memory Verse
- o Can you say from memory Romans 3:23?
- o Find it in the Bible.
  - For all have sinned and fall short of the glory of God.

III. Language
- o Grammar
  - Complete Grammar Review 9 in your workbook.
  - All of the punctuation and capitalization is missing!
  - (Note: In the answer book, every capital letter and every little punctuation mark is an answer.)

- o Hebrew
  - Read Genesis 1:1-3.
  - You can read it on the Hebrew Writing 48 page of your workbook.

א בְּרֵאשִׁית, בָּרָא אֱלֹהִים, אֵת הַשָּׁמַיִם, וְאֵת הָאָרֶץ.

ב וְהָאָרֶץ, הָיְתָה תֹהוּ וָבֹהוּ, וְחֹשֶׁךְ, עַל פְּנֵי תְהוֹם; וְרוּחַ אֱלֹהִים, מְרַחֶפֶת עַל פְּנֵי הַמָּיִם.

ג וַיֹּאמֶר אֱלֹהִים, יְהִי אוֹר; וַיְהִי אוֹר.

ד וַיַּרְא אֱלֹהִים אֶת הָאוֹר, כִּי טוֹב; וַיַּבְדֵּל אֱלֹהִים, בֵּין הָאוֹר וּבֵין הַחֹשֶׁךְ.

ה וַיִּקְרָא אֱלֹהִים לָאוֹר יוֹם, וְלַחֹשֶׁךְ קָרָא לָיְלָה; וַיְהִי עֶרֶב וַיְהִי בֹקֶר, יוֹם אֶחָד.

1. be reSHEET baRA eloHEEM et ha shaMAyim ve et ha Arets
2. ve ha Arets haaTAH TOhu va VOhu ve KHOshekh al pnaa teHOM ve RUakh eloHEEM meraKHEfet al pnaa ha MAyim
3. va YOmer eloHEEM yeHEE or va yeHEE or
4. va yar eloHEEM et ha or ki tov va yavDEL eloHEEM ben ha or u ven ha KHOshekh

> 5. va yikRA eloHEEM la or yom ve la KHOshekh kaRA LII-la va yeHEE Erev va yeHEE VOker yom ekHAD

IV. Science

- ○ It's time to check on your apples.
- ○ What happened? Why? Make observations.
  - Note: When my family did this, our airtight apple was gross. The problem is that air is everywhere. It's hard to get air out and to keep it out. Maybe you were more successful. Airtight packaging is made with a vacuum seal. It sucks the air out.
  - (Note: there will be mold. Clean up well after the experiment.)
- ○ Finish filling out your lab report on the experiment by completing the Science Review 17 page in your workbook. Write in your observations. Write in your conclusions about whether or not salting, dehydrating, and air-tight packing are effective preservation techniques.

V. Social Studies

- ○ Continue with our game on the Social Studies Review 14 page of your workbook.
- ○ Today you get 50 more dollars. You can enter your new total.
- ○ Enter your new total and then do something with your money: spend, save, give.
- ○ Record what you bought or to whom you gave and how much and then your total left in the bank.
- ○ Complete Social Studies Review 15 in your workbook. It's a review of some different people we've learned about.
  - After they've given it their best, go over each the right answers as a review.

VI. Writing

- ○ Write for twelve minutes. Continue adding to your story.
- ○ If you would like a word to get started, use the word GAUNT from your vocabulary.
- ○ Time yourselves. Just write and write and don't stop until the time is up. Just start. Go!

Day 137 (check Materials List)

I. Read Genesis 45:21-46:16.

II. Memory Verse
- o Practice 1 Corinthians 10:13.
- o Find it in the Bible.
  - • No temptation has overtaken you but such as is common to man; and God is faithful, who will not allow you to be tempted beyond what you are able, but with the temptation will provide the way of escape also, so that you will be able to endure it.

III. Language
- o Vocabulary
  - • Do Vocabulary Review 8 in your workbook.
  - • You will be doing a mix of charades and Pictionary. Everyone should look at their list of words to help them guess.
  - • Note: You can keep track of what words have been used.
- o Hebrew
  - • We're going to skip over Genesis 1:4 and learn the last letter needed to read Genesis 1:5. It's the Qof. (Pronounced Kofe.) It's transliterated as a K in our Hebrew.

- • Can you make a guess at the word above? It's from Genesis 1:5.
  - ▪ It's kaRA.
- • Trace the Qof on the Hebrew Writing 49 page of your workbook.

IV. Science
- o Today we're going to start reviewing our body. Tape together a whole lot of paper and trace the outline of your body. You can each do one or all share one body or just draw a body outline on a single sheet of paper. (Note: You can decide what works best for your family.)
- o Today add in the front part of your olfactory system. What's the olfactory system?
  - • your sense of smell
  - • Draw a nose on your body.
- o How do we smell?

- Molecules in the air get into our noses and attach to our olfactory receptor neurons which send a signal to the brain about what we're smelling.
  - You can also draw on corneas and pupils. What are those?
    - Draw on eyes. The cornea is the outer covering that bends the light to direct it to our retinas.
    - The pupil is the dark center, the hole that lets in the light.

V. Social Studies

- Continue with our game on the Social Studies Review 14 page of your workbook.
- Today do something with your money: spend, save, give.
- Record what you bought or to whom you gave and how much and then your total left in the bank.
- Complete Social Studies Review 16 in your workbook on the Bill of Rights.

VI. Writing

- Write for fourteen minutes. Add to your story.
- If you would like a word to get you going today, use the word PROSPER from your vocabulary.
- Time yourselves. Just write and write and don't stop until the time is up. Just start. Go!

Day 138 (check Materials List)

I. Read Genesis 46:17-34.

II. Memory Verse
- Practice 1 John 1:9
- Find it in the Bible.
    - If we confess our sins, He is faithful and just to forgive us our sins and to cleanse us from all unrighteousness. (KJV)

III. Language
- Grammar
    - Take the words from Spelling Review 19 and place them into piles according to their part of speech. Some could be used in more than one way; you can just pick a pile when that's true.
        - Nouns: officer, appearance, garment, jailer, officials, baker, confinement (more than one part of speech: desire, Hebrew, charge, anger)
        - Verb: fled, extend (more than one part of speech: desire, charge, anger)
        - Adjectives: handsome, furious (more than one part of speech: Hebrew)
    - Think of example sentences for the more-than-one-part-of-speech words that use the word in each way?
- Hebrew
    - Trace and write the Qof and words using the Hebrew Writing 50 page of your workbook.

IV. Science
- Today we're going to add the mouth and esophagus to our body. It's the beginning of the digestive system. Our teeth and saliva start the digestive process, breaking up the food we eat. What is saliva?
    - the spit in our mouths
- What is the esophagus?
    - It's the tube that carries the food down from our mouths and into our stomachs.
- Draw a mouth with teeth and the esophagus.
- Label the esophagus and you can label saliva too!

V. Social Studies
- Continue with our game on the Social Studies Review 14 page of your workbook.
- Today do something with your money: spend, save, give.
- Record what you bought or to whom you gave and how much and then your total left in the bank.
- Complete Social Studies Review 17 in your workbook on the Bill of Rights.

VI. Writing
- o Write for sixteen minutes. Continue your same story.
- o If you would like a word to get started, use the word DROVES from your vocabulary.
- o Time yourselves. Just write and write and don't stop until the time is up. Just start. Go!

Day 139

I. Read Genesis 47:1-19.

II. Memory Verse
- o Practice Romans 6:23.
- o Find it in the Bible.
  - • For the wages of sin is death, but the free gift of God is eternal life in Christ Jesus our Lord.

III. Language
- o Vocabulary
  - • Complete the crossword puzzle on the Vocabulary Review 9 page in your workbook.
- o Hebrew
  - • Today we're going to read and write the first part of Genesis 1:5.
  - • You will write it on the Hebrew Writing 51 page of your workbook.
  - • First say Genesis 1:5. Then reread the first section in bold.
    - ▪ **va yikRA eloHEEM la or yom ve la KHOshekh kaRA LII-la** va yeHEE Erev va yeHEE VOker yom ekHAD
  - • Now say it as you follow along with the Hebrew. Let me rewrite the transcription to match how the words are combined in the Hebrew.
    - ▪ **vayikRA eloHEEM laor yom, velaKHOshekh kaRA LII-la**
  - • Now just read that part of the verse. Say the verse and follow along with the Hebrew.
  - • Then go through it again. Only look at the Hebrew.

וַיִּקְרָא אֱלֹהִים לָאוֹר יוֹם, וְלַחֹשֶׁךְ קָרָא לָיְלָה; וַיְהִי עֶרֶב וַיְהִי בֹקֶר, יוֹם אֶחָד.

IV. Science
- o Today you are going to draw in the pancreas, liver, and stomach. Use the diagram on Day 112 to help you.
- o What body system do they belong to?
  - • the digestive system
- o What does each do? You can review with the science lesson on Day 112.
- o Label your pictures.

V. Social Studies
- o Continue with our game on the Social Studies Review 14 page of your workbook.
- o Today do something with your money: spend, save, give.
- o Now today, and today only, the free market is open.
  - • What is a free market?
    - ▪ There is little government interference in buying and selling.

- You may exchange goods (the stuff you bought in our game), or you may sell those goods for whatever price you can get for them. Keep track of what you have, adjust your lists as necessary and write your bank total by "Free Market."
  - Done? Adjust your bank sheet. Enter your money amount and take off or add things you bought and sold.
  - Now you have to pay taxes.
    - Take the total amount in your bank for the end of today and multiply it by 15% (0.15).
    - Enter your tax amount. You have to pay that amount.
    - Subtract it off of your total and enter the final amount for today's bank.
  - What are some things that your government does with taxes? (Need help? What do we get to use that we don't have to pay for? They're free for everyone.)
    - The government uses taxes to build roads and bridges, to provide schools, to take care of public parks, to provide a police force and army for protection, etc.
  - Use your tax money. As members of a country that has a representative government, you may vote on how to spend your tax money, and your representative (mom-or homeschool teacher) will represent you in making the final decision.
    - Your taxes should be used for the common good.

VI. Writing
  - Write for eighteen minutes. Continue your same story.
  - If you would like a word to get started, use the word ENVY from your vocabulary.
  - Time yourselves. Just write and write and don't stop until the time is up. Just start. Go!

Day 140

I. Read Genesis 47:20-48:4.

II. Memory Verse
- o Practice Genesis 26:4.
- o Find it in the Bible.
  - I will multiply your descendants as the stars of the heaven, and will give your descendants all these lands; and by your descendants all the nations of the earth shall be blessed.

III. Language
- o Grammar
  - Complete Grammar Review 10 in your workbook.
  - Fix the capitalization and punctuation.
- o Hebrew
  - Today we're going to read and write the second part of Genesis 1:5.
  - You will write it on the Hebrew Writing 52 page of your workbook.
  - First say Genesis 1:5. Then reread the section in bold.
    - va yikRA eloHEEM la or yom ve la KHOshekh kaRA LII-la

      ## va yeHEE Erev va yeHEE VOker yom ekHAD
  - Now say it as you follow along with the Hebrew. Let me rewrite the transcription to match how the words are combined in the Hebrew.
    - **vayehee Erev vayeHEE VOker yom ekHAD**
  - Now just read that part of the verse. Say the verse and follow along with the Hebrew.
  - Then go through it again, only looking at the Hebrew.

וַיִּקְרָא אֱלֹהִים לָאוֹר יוֹם, וְלַחֹשֶׁךְ קָרָא לָיְלָה; וַיְהִי עֶרֶב וַיְהִי בֹקֶר, יוֹם אֶחָד.

IV. Science
- o Today you are going to draw on the large and small intestines.
- o Use the picture on Day 112 to help you.
- o Label your drawing.
- o You can keep this and we'll come back to it on Day 146.

V. Social Studies
- o Continue with our game on the Social Studies Review 14 page of your workbook. This is your last day. Enter today's bank total but leave the final amount blank.
- o Once everyone's made their decision, use the directions below to figure out their final amount.
  - Start with the Finish total from Day 140.
  - For every day you were in debt, subtract off ten dollars. Do that even if it takes you into the negative.

- That's the interest you have to pay on your debt, the extra they collect from you.
  - For each thing you bought, add five dollars.
    - Well, maybe you didn't spend wisely, but the things you bought can add value to your home, add enjoyment to your life, maybe could be resold or given away at some point, etc.)
  - For each day you gave, add ten dollars.
    - It's more blessed to give than to receive.
  - For each day you had more than fifty dollars in the bank, add five dollars.
    - That's the interest you earned by keeping your money in the bank.
  - What's your final total?
  - If you end the game in debt, you have everything you bought taken away from you and you end with nothing.
  - Your total isn't just what you have in the bank. You have that plus you gained what you bought and what you were able to give.
  - What would you change about how you played?
- Today's social study review is on cryptology and you have a puzzle to complete. Do you remember what unbreakable code the Americans used during WWII?
  - They had Navajo Indians translate and communicate their messages.
- Do you remember what animal helped deliver messages?
  - pigeons
- Do you remember a battle the Americans were able to win against the Japanese because they had intercepted and decoded their attack plans?
  - The Battle of Midway
    - Where's the Island of Midway?
      - in the middle of the Pacific Ocean
- What attack led America into the war with Japan?
  - the attack on Pearl Harbor
    - Where's Pearl Harbor?
      - Hawaii
- Complete Social Studies Review 18.
  - Use the length of the words as a clue to what the word is. This is something they memorized this year!
  - Note: If they need help, the number 8 is the letter I (eye), and the number 22 is the letter E.

VI. Writing
  - Write for twenty minutes. Continue your same story.
  - If you would like a word to get started, use the word DECEIT (or a form of it) from your vocabulary.
  - Time yourselves. Just write and write and don't stop until the time is up. Just start. Go!
  - (Note: You might want to save this in your child's portfolio. It would also be a good time to save an example of math and to write down what your child has been reading.)

Day 141

I. Read Genesis 48:5-22. Jacob (Israel) is speaking to Joseph.

II. Memory Verse
- o   For the last time, say Genesis 1:1-5.

III. Language
- o   Spelling
  - •   Spell the word seventh. Each in turn say the next letter in the word. If you are wrong, it passes to the next person.
- o   Grammar
  - •   Play the add-on game. Today you will play with nouns. What's a noun?
    - ▪   It's a person, place or thing.
  - •   To play the first person lists something they will bring on their picnic. They will say a noun that starts with the letter A.
    - ▪   Example: "I'm going on a picnic and bringing an Apple."
  - •   The next person says the same thing but has to name something that starts with the letter B.
    - ▪   Whoever wants to make it harder should repeat the whole list each time from the beginning as well as add their new word to the end of the list.
  - •   Continue until you get to Z!
- o   Hebrew
  - •   Read Genesis 1:5. It can be found on the Hebrew Writing 51 page.

וַיִּקְרָא אֱלֹהִים לָאוֹר יוֹם, וְלַחֹשֶׁךְ קָרָא לָיְלָה; וַיְהִי עֶרֶב וַיְהִי בֹקֶר, יוֹם אֶחָד.

  - •   Can you say all five verses?

IV. Social Studies
- o   This is the first of our review week activities. This is the last week of daily assignments. Following this week are projects you can complete as you wish.
- o   This week we are making a timeline.
- o   The Social Studies Review 19 page has all of the possible dates you could include.
  - •   You don't have to include everything. It's not all really important, just the dates that were mentioned over the year.
  - •   If you want to review any of them or need a reminder, the day number where each is introduced is included. They are from the history lesson unless otherwise noted.
- o   You can make the timeline how you like.
  - •   You could work as a team or everyone can make their own.
  - •   Decide how you are going to do it. You could make a big wall one or use an online program.
  - •   You could find some pictures online to print and add to your timeline or you can draw on pictures.
  - •   You can just use key words or write on sentences.

- o I have put in spaces to separate them into 8 groups if you'd like to use my guideline of what to work on each day. You could also put those dates on eight pieces of paper across your wall.
    - If you save your timeline, you can add to it next year. But I can also give you these dates again, and you can decide what you want to include along with your new information from next year.
- o You have five assigned days to work on this. Today I suggest figuring out what you are going to do and get the first section accomplished.
- o About the early dates:
    - We can't know exact years even if we are taking the Bible literally. Think about this: from one day to the next, you become a year older. A day before your birthday you are nine, and one day later you are ten. You aren't really a year older, just one day older, but you gained a whole year to your age. The Bible only gives us ages. We don't know if that is 100 years and 1 day or 100 years and 11 months. Extra months over each generation adds up to years. I've given close estimates to what I found using the literal method of adding up ages. You can consider early dates to be give or take a few decades, but it's helpful to have a general timeline of events.
    - Many dates are estimates or a general date. For instance, the Guinness family wasn't only influenced by John Wesley for one year. You don't have to draw an exact spot on the timeline. I suggest just writing the information over or under the general area. I gave you a specific year date for each piece of information to help you be confident in placing things on your timeline. An asterisks* marks a specific date.

Day 142

I. Read Genesis 49:1-15.

II. Memory Verse
- ○ You could do sword drills (practice looking up Bible verses quickly). Another idea is having a race using the memory verse list. Run across the room and then say a memory verse before you can run back where they would get another verse. Call out the memory verse address. (Give beginning words if they need help getting started with the verse.) You could do that as a relay race or time each kid how fast they can do it. Find the memory verse list in the back of the book.

III. Language
- ○ Spelling
  - Spell the word abundantly.
  - Each in turn say the next letter in the word. If they are wrong, it passes to the next person.
    - Mix it up: Have them form the letter with their fingers or bodies or air write it.
- ○ Grammar
  - Play the add-on game. Today you will play with action verbs. What's an action verb?
    - It's something we do.
  - To play the first person lists something they will do today at the park. They will say an action verb that starts with the letter A.
    - Example: "Today at the park I'm going to Astound."
  - The next person says the same thing but has to say a word that starts with the letter B.
    - Whoever wants to make it harder should repeat the whole list each time from the beginning as well as add their new word to the end of the list.
  - Continue until you get to Z!
- ○ Hebrew
  - We have one last verse we need to read, Genesis 1:4.
  - We have one last letter to learn in order to be able to read it, the Tet.
  - This has the sound of T, just like the Tav. You can see it below.
  - Trace the Tet on the Hebrew Writing 53 page of your workbook and find it in the verse. What word is it in? Can you figure it out?

IV. Social Studies
- ○ This week we are making a timeline.
- ○ The Social Studies Review 19 page has dates you could include.

- You don't have to include everything. It's not all really important, just the dates that were mentioned over the year.
- If you need a reminder of any of them, the lesson number where each is introduced is included. Remember that the day number refers to the history lesson unless otherwise noted.

o Today you could try to do the second and third sections of the timeline.

Day 143

I. Read Genesis 49:16-33.

II. Memory Verse
- o Quiz each other on memory verses or do sword drills with the memory verse list in the back of this book.
- o (Note: Race if you like, competitively or noncompetitively, depending on what's more fun for your family.)

III. Language
- o Spelling
  - • Spell the word appointed.
  - • Each in turn say the next letter in the word. If they are wrong, it passes to the next person.
    - ▪ Mix it up: Have them form the letter with their fingers or bodies or air write it. They could even spell the word at the same time this way, one letter at a time.
    - ▪ You could write down each letter as it is spelled to help those who can't visualize the word without seeing it.
- o Grammar
  - • Play the add-on game. Today you will play with adjectives. What's an adjective?
    - ▪ It describes a noun.
  - • To play the first person lists something that describes the puppy they saw at the park. They will say an adjective that starts with the letter A.
    - ▪ Example: "Today at the park I saw a puppy that was Amazing."
  - • The next person says the same thing but has to say a word that starts with the letter B.
    - ▪ Whoever wants to make it harder should repeat the whole list each time from the beginning as well as add their new word to the end.
  - • Continue until you get to Z if you can!
- o Hebrew
  - • Today we're going to practice the last letter we're learning this year. Next year we will start with the alphabet and complete it and learn more about it while working on a new Scripture portion.
  - • Go to the Hebrew Writing 54 page and write the letter Tet and the word tov. It is written with the letter Vav in the middle which is taking on the long O sound like it can take on the long U sound.

IV. Social Studies
- o This week we are making a timeline.
- o The Social Studies Review 19 page has the possible dates you could include.
  - • If you would like to review any of them or need a reminder, the lesson number where each is introduced is included. You could also look any up to learn more.
- o Today you could try to do the fourth and fifth sections of the timeline.

Day 144

I. Read Genesis 50:1-11.
*Note: What did they do to Israel (Jacob)? They embalmed him. They made him a mummy!

II. Memory Verse
- o Quiz each other on memory verses or do sword drills with the memory verse list.

III. Language
- o Spelling
  - Spell the word thirty-seven.
  - Each in turn say the next letter in the word. If they are wrong, it passes to the next person.
    - Mix it up: Have them form the letter with their fingers or bodies or air write it. They could even spell the word at the same time this way, one letter at a time.
    - You could write down each letter as it is spelled to help those who can't visualize the word without seeing it.
- o Grammar
  - Play the add-on game. Today you will play with adverbs. What's an adverb?
    - It describes a verb.
  - To play the first person lists how they are going to play at the park. They will say an adverb that starts with the letter A.
    - Example: "At the park I'm going to play Amazingly." (beautifully, creatively, dreadfully, energetically, etc. if you need some inspiration to get going. Basically you can use adjectives and put them in adverb form by adding LY.)
  - The next person says the same thing but has to say a word that starts with the letter B.
    - Whoever wants to make it harder should repeat the whole list each time from the beginning as well as add their new word to the end of the list.
  - Continue until you get to Z if you can!
- o Hebrew
  - Trace and write the word ki on the Hebrew Writing 55 page of your workbook. This is the last thing you need to be able to read and write Genesis 1:1-5.
  - You'll see a new letter that we're not going to learn right now. It's making the K sound. The Yod is making the EE sound.

IV. Social Studies
- o This week we are making a timeline.
- o The Social Studies Review 19 page has possible dates you could include.
  - You don't have to include everything.
  - If you need a reminder of any of them, the lesson number where each is introduced is included.
- o Today you could try to do the sixth and seventh sections of the timeline.

Day 145

I. Read Genesis 50:12-26.

  *Note: Joseph recognizes that God was in control the whole time, even when things
    appeared horribly wrong. He knew that God worked it out so that Joseph could keep his
    family alive through the famine. God always preserves a remnant, right? God was doing
    much more though. One of the truths God spoke to Abraham was that his descendants
    would be strangers in a land that wasn't their own and would be enslaved and oppressed
    there. Joseph's moving his family to Egypt sets the stage for that prophecy to be fulfilled.

II. Memory Verse

  o Quiz each other on memory verses or do sword drills with the memory verse list.

III. Language

  o Spelling

   • Hold a spelling bee. Take turns spelling words. Stand up front and center and
      spell them out loud.

   • (Note: Use the list of all of our spelling words from the year found in the back
      of this book. Try to choose easier and harder words based on age. You can
      also require young children to just give the first two or three letters. A very
      young child could just give the first letter.)

  o Hebrew

   • Read Genesis 1:4 on the Hebrew Writing 56 page of your workbook.

   • va yar eloHEEM et ha or ki tov va yavDEL eloHEEM ben ha or u ven ha
      KHOshekh

   • **vayar eloHEEM et haor, et tov; vayavDEL eloHEEM, ben haor uven
      haKHOshekh**

   • We've seen the word "and" in three ways: va, ve, and u. At first that probably
      seemed really weird, but in Hebrew, they are all written with the same one
      letter.

וַיַּרְא אֱלֹהִים אֶת הָאוֹר, כִּי טוֹב; וַיַּבְדֵּל אֱלֹהִים, בֵּין הָאוֹר וּבֵין הַחֹשֶׁךְ.

IV. Social Studies

  o This week we are making a timeline.

  o The Social Studies Review 19 page has the dates you could include.

   • You don't have to include everything.

   • If you need a reminder of any of them, the lesson number where each is
      introduced is included.

  o Today you could do the final section of the timeline.

V. A final note as this is our last regular day of lessons: Value your education. Education gives you
power, remember? There's a reason homeschooling is against the law in most of the world.
Governments don't want to give the power to the people. The government can create and teach
its own version of truth. But you know that the Bible is the most trusted source of truth there is.
Knowing the Bible, really knowing what it says for yourself, is the greatest gift you can give
yourself, and believing its words and taking them to heart will give you the greatest power, that of
knowing God.

Days 146-155

We skipped over a part of Genesis if you'd like to read them over the coming review weeks. Genesis 29:36 through the end of chapter 36.

The regular lessons have ended. Use these projects to finish up your school year or over your break if you like. This is a time when you can transition to some "summer school" activities. At my home we do things like handwriting, math games, and continued reading practice for those still learning. If you have a school reading time each day, you could continue with a "free reading" time each day. You should also read and review Genesis 1:1-5 in Hebrew. It's on the Hebrew Writing 57 page of your workbook. If you want some more practice, remember that Hebrew4Christians has tracing and copywork on their site. You can find the direct link to their homeschool resources on the Online Support page of our site, genesiscurriculum.com.

These weeks are our science review.

Week 1: Fill in your body drawing!

> Here are the other body systems we learned about. Each day you can add one of these and review them a little. The number by each is where you can find it in the curriculum, but you can look online for pictures as well. You won't be able to fit in everything. Show parts of each system. Use the things we learned about specifically.

> circulatory system (13)
> muscular system (36-37)
> skeletal system (16, 106)
> respiratory system (12)
> immune and nervous systems (for these you could draw in a brain for the nervous system and a zoom-in of some cells for the immune system, 78)

Week 2: Science project

> Create a science project. You will choose a topic and demonstrate it with a model of some kind. You can be creative in how you do it.

> When you are done, you could send me a picture of it, and I'll put it on our website. Maybe you can find somewhere to display your work or find some people to show it off to and explain it to, or take a video of it and send it to the grandparents. Do something with your work!

> You can use the internet for ideas if necessary, but here are some topics we looked at this year that you might be interested in doing a project on.

> solar system, water cycle, spring/geysers/water table, genetics, simple machines (wheel and axle, wedge, screw), lots of different animals, light/rainbows

Days 156-165

Time for our social studies review. You could work all together, or split up and do different ones; whatever strikes your fancy. Here are some ideas for what you could do. There are some helpful links on our Online Support page for creating a newspaper and writing a play.

Week 1: Newspaper

Write a newspaper: Ancient Egypt Times, newspaper put out by the Lowell Mill Girls describing their conditions and demanding their rights, Hammurabi's Post, Isaac's Inquirer, etc. You could do news articles that give facts about the time period, made up news articles about things that could have happened in the time period, advertisements, pictures, opinions, etc.

Week 2: Play

Put on a play: life in ancient Egypt or Mesopotamia, the story of Abraham or Noah or all of Genesis!, life in the Industrial Revolution (87), traveling the Oregon trail (77), etc.

Days 166-180

Finish off your year with a writing project. Choose between fiction and non-fiction. You can go to the Online Support page on our site for helpful links for writing research reports or novels.

Non-fiction:

You will follow the guidelines for writing an essay, but you should add in more paragraphs into the body. You can use the essay planning sheet to help you.

1. Gather facts, lots of facts. Spend days researching.
2. Organize facts into categories.
3. Each category that has at least three facts will become a paragraph.

Fiction:

Write a story. You could write a whole book! Here's what you'll need.

1. Main character

   The more you know about the character the better your story will be. What does your character look like, act like, etc.

2. Setting

   Decide where and when your story will take place.

3. Problem

   Your main character has to have a problem that he/she/it will try to overcome during the course of your story. What is it? This could be that something is lost and needs to be found, or he has recently moved and has no friends, or she didn't qualify for the regional chess tournament but her goal is to win nationals, or the robot was broken somehow and can't find its way home.

4. Plot

   This is how the main character is going to solve the problem. It would be boring if it were easy. To make it exciting you need to keep making up things that get in the way of solving the problem. This is where the bad guy often comes in. You don't have to have a bad guy though. It could be things like: he makes a friend but it turns out he's a fake friend, or she finds a great partner to practice with but then her partner can't meet with her anymore, or the robot gets rusted in the rain. The more it looks like the main character can't solve the problem, the more exciting it will be.

5. Solution

   This is the end. How is the story going to end? How is the main character going to finally solve the problem and win the championship and get friends and get home, etc?

Course Descriptions – Genesis Curriculum – The Book of Genesis

Language Arts:
Students will grow in their knowledge and understanding of the English language through the study of grammar, vocabulary and spelling. Daily practice will ensure the student's progress in learning spelling tips and tricks, including the spelling of plurals, both regular and irregular, and knowing the differences between homophones. Vocabulary is introduced through the daily reading and then practiced and reviewed. Word roots and related words are used to help students discover the meaning of new words. Students are tested weekly on spelling and vocabulary acquisition. Grammar is focused on learning the parts of speech and how to write proper sentences of varying structure. Students learn to identify subjects, predicates and the objective case and will apply that knowledge to writing well-structured sentences with correct word choice. Capitalization and punctuation is taught and practiced. All of their work culminates in student-produced writing several times a week. Weekly editing exercises put their knowledge to use, and the students create a final draft of one of their written pieces each week. Students will produce both fiction and non-fiction works and will have the opportunity to read their work aloud in front of an audience.

Hebrew:
Students will learn Genesis 1:1-5 in Hebrew. They will be able to read, write and speak it. Students will learn the grammar necessary to understand the sentence construction.

Science:
Students will discover new things as they explore the sciences of biology, physics, chemistry and earth science. In biology the students will learn zoology and anatomy. They will study the body's systems and how energy makes it all run. They will explore the way DNA makes us each unique and have fun practicing genetics. They will dig deep and learn about what's inside our cells and how our amazing bodies work. They will understand the animal classification system and learn the characteristics of major animal groups as well as fascinating facts of specific animals. In chemistry students will explore the periodic table and understand how to read it. The elements will be shown as atoms and in combinations as molecules. They will understand and experiment with chemical processes. Oxidation is one focus of the study of chemical processes. In physics students will study light, gravity, and the way forces produce work. Students will experiment with simple machines to understand how they make work easier. In earth science students will learn about what's inside the earth and out in the heavens. They will act out orbits and build models. They will understand our changing sky and seasons. Student will appreciate the greatness of a God who created all these marvelous things.

Social Studies:
Students will discover their heritage as one people born through Adam and Noah. They will trace the lineage of Abraham and find new meaning and understanding from the Scripture. Students will learn about the Cradle of Civilization and how societies developed in ancient Mesopotamia. They will learn about the development of trade, bartering, and money systems including modern economics. Students will learn the geography of Israel and the ancient world, but they will also study the nations of the world. Students will learn to locate countries from every continent. Students will study world biomes, religions, people groups, and poplulations through the use of maps. Students will see God working through history as they learn about not only ancient events but modern history including the study of such topics as the Industrial Revolution, slavery, and the Civil War, as well as the war between the Japanese and Americans in World War II. Many other topics are covered as students learn about their own culture and of cultures around the world. Students will learn how different types of governments affect their citizens. Students will be challenged to think, examine, and form opinions. Primary sources used in the lessons include maps, a proclamation, autobiography excerpt, and first-hand accounts of life in the Middle East.

Memory Verses

Day 1

Genesis 1:1   In the beginning God created the heavens and the earth.

Day 6

Psalm 150:6   Let everything that has breath praise the Lord. Praise the Lord!

Day 11

Genesis 1:2   The earth was formless and void, and darkness was over the surface of the deep, and the Spirit of God was moving over the surface of the waters.

Day 16

Romans 3:23   For all have sinned and fall short of the glory of God.

Day 21

1 Corinthians 10:13   No temptation has overtaken you but such as is common to man; and God is faithful, who will not allow you to be tempted beyond what you are able, but with the temptation will provide the way of escape also, so that you will be able to endure it.

Review Week

Day 31

Genesis 1:3   Then God said, "Let there be light"; and there was light.

Day 36

1 John 1:9   If we confess our sins, He is faithful and just to forgive us our sins and to cleanse us from all unrighteousness. (KJV)

Day 41

Romans 6:23   For the wages of sin is death, but the free gift of God is eternal life in Christ Jesus our Lord.

Day 46

Genesis 1:4   God saw that the light was good; and God separated the light from the darkness.

Day 51

Genesis 26:4   I will multiply your descendants as the stars of the heaven, and will give your descendants all these lands; and by your descendants all the nations of the earth shall be blessed.

Day 56

2 Corinthians 1:20   For as many as are the promises of God, in Him they are yes; therefore also through Him is our Amen to the glory of God through us.

Review Weeks

Day 71

Joshua 24:15   [If it is disagreeable in your sight to serve the LORD,] choose for yourselves today whom you will serve: [whether the gods which your fathers served which were beyond the River, or the gods of the Amorites in whose land you are living;] but as for me and my house, we will serve the LORD.

Day 76

2 Peter 3:9   The Lord is not slow about His promise, as some count slowness, but is patient toward you, not wishing for any to perish but for all to come to repentance.

Day 81

Job 19:25   As for me, I know that my Redeemer lives,
And at the last He will take His stand on the earth.

Day 86

Hebrews 11:1   Now faith is the assurance of things hoped for, the conviction of things not seen.

Day 91

John 11:25   Jesus said to her, "I am the resurrection and the life; he who believes in Me will live even if he dies."

Review Weeks

Day 106

Deuteronomy 31:8   The LORD is the one who goes ahead of you; He will be with you. He will not fail you or forsake you. Do not fear or be dismayed.

Day 111

Jeremiah 29:11   For I know the plans I have for you," declares the Lord, "plans to prosper you and not to harm you, plans to give you hope and a future. (NIV)

Day 116

Romans 8:28   And we know that God causes all things to work together for good to those who love God, to those who are called according to His purpose.

Day 121

Micah 6:8   He has told you, O man, what is good;
And what does the Lord require of you
But to do justice, to love kindness,
And to walk humbly with your God?

Day 126

Psalm 55:22   Cast your burden upon the LORD and He will sustain you; He will never allow the righteous to be shaken.

Review Weeks

Spelling

Day 5 review   formless, void, darkness, moving, dry, expanse, separate, seas, brought, vegetation, yield, bearing, light, heaven, sign, season

Day 10 review   fruitful, multiply, fifth, which, creature, beast, ground, kind, rule, image, likeness, over, subdue, surface, earth, sky

Day 15 review   shrub, sprouted, creation, mist, breathed, nostrils, breath, being, third, fourth, flows, river (just for fun—Tigris, Assyria, Euphrates), cultivate, garden, Eden, continent

Day 20 review   reason, join, slept, ashamed, sewed, themselves, touch, coverings, presence, enmity, whistle, bruise, stationed, guard, direction, flaming

Day 25 review   Cain, wanderer, field, blood, great, driven, vagrant, vengeance, father, dwell, tents, birth, lyre, implements, speech, striking

Day 40 review   countenance, crouch, receive, vengeance, beautiful, daughter, whomever, forever, inclination, regretted, faithfully, thoughts, violence, gopher, pitch, destroy, wives, alive, seven, hundredth

Day 45 review   decreased, mountains, subsided, recede, abundantly, twenty-seventh, families, dried (words ending in Y), require, cease, aroma, account, successive, generations, descendants, covenant

Day 50 review   journeyed, scattered, thoroughly, building, possessions, pitched, acquired, Lot, donkeys, woman, Egypt, escorted (plurals of words ending in Y), belonged, number, formerly, exceedingly

Day 55 review   priest, sandal, enemies, except, heir, pigeon, prey, shield, children, Egyptian, conceive, maid, authority, against, east, yourself

Day 60 review   throughout, foreigner, twelve, ninety-nine, appeared, opposite, bowed, measure, denied, advanced, appointed, difficult, righteousness, command, judge, forty-five

Day 75 review   inhabitants, surrounded, rained, urged, escape, punishment, dawn, seize, pillar, toward, smoke, technique, ascend, preserve, remember

Day 80 review   frighten, innocence, prophet, nation, womb, wander, thousand, pieces, laughter, Isaac, weaned, borne, maid, listen, die, angel

Day 85 review   swear, therefore, falsely, army, ewe, complain, oath, Philistine, son, said, there, planted, lamb, burnt, worship, knife

Day 90 review two, stretch, against, wood, thicket, caught, provide, mount, declare, Abraham, second, seashore, eight, irregular plurals, sensational, tremendous

Day 95 review   mourn, burial, burying, approach, sight, answer, price, people, confines, worth, four, weigh, satisfied, hundred, commercial, standard

Day 110 review   grief, envied, defiance, thirty-seven, descend, console, deceitful, violently, flock, almond, continue, distance, embrace, gracious, prevail, wrestle

Day 115 review   age, thigh, beware, concern, quickly, lower, shoulder, emptied, camel, lodge, guide, bracelet, business, successful, blessed, down

Day 120 review   bind, erect, rebuke, jealous, pasture, pasturing, welfare, devour, rescue, further, balm, stripped, aromatic, myrrh, Joseph, caravan

Day 125 review   officer, desire, appearance, handsome, garment, Hebrew, screamed, fled, jailer, extend, charge, anger, furious, officials, baker, confinement

Day 130 review   sorts, basket, favorably, chief, scorch, captain, stalk, magician, subsequent, famine, unknown, abundance, proposal, exact, discern, inform

Vocabulary

Day 5 review   void – completely empty
expanse – a large, wide, open area of land or water
yield – to produce
govern – to rule, to be in control over a group of people

Day 10 review   swarm – to abound, teem, to be overrun
creep – to move slowly and carefully, especially to avoid notice
dimension – measurement, or an aspect of something
subdue – to bring under control

Day 15 review   mist – a low lying cloud
midst – in the middle of
divide – to separate into parts
cultivate -- to prepare and use land for crops

Day 20 review   fashion – to take materials and make them into something
crafty, shrewd, vulpine -- clever at using deception to get what you want
enmity – being actively opposed to someone or something
station – to put in a position in a particular place for a particular purpose

Day 25 review   my brother's keeper – to mind others
vagrant – a person who wanders from place to place, living by begging
presence – being there, whether seen or not, or a group or people all together in a particular place for a particular reason, or an impact made by being there
implement – tool made for a particular use, put a plan into action

Day 40 review   strive – to make a great effort to achieve something or to struggle

526

corrupt – being willing to do something wrong to get something for yourself

establish – to create something intended to last

righteous – doing what is right

Day 45 review   recede – to go back or gradually diminish

abate – to lessen, reduce, remove

intent – purpose, what someone is determined to do

successive – coming after another

Day 50 review   mortar – a mixture used to bind bricks or stones together

accumulate – gather or get more and more

severe – intense, extreme

sustain – support physically or mentally

Day 55 review   array – dress someone in particular clothing

heir – the person who will inherit property, money, or position title after a person leaves a position or dies

obtain – to get or acquire

affliction – pain and suffering

Day 60 review   sojourn – a temporary stay somewhere

tender – easy to cut or chew

appointed - designated, pre-arranged, scheduled

venture – to undertake something risky or dangerous

Day 75 review   urge – to strongly persuade someone to do something

jest – to speak or act jokingly

inhabitant – one who lives in a place

ascend – to go up

Day 80 review   integrity – the character quality of holding to strong moral principles

vindication – being shown innocent of an accusation of wrong doing

wean – to gradually get used to not having something you've become dependent on

distress – to cause extreme sorrow or worry

Day 85 review   posterity – descendants of a person, or all future generations

seize – to take hold of suddenly and forcibly

offering – a gift, something offered

arose – stood up or emerged

Day 90 review   altar – an elevated surface where religious rites are performed, especially the offering of sacrifices

thicket – a dense group of shrubs, bushes or small trees

declare – to state clearly, to make known publicly

omniscient – all knowing

Day 95 review   mourn – to feel deeply saddened over a loss

approach – come near, to speak to someone for the first time about something

commercial – intended for a profit of money

standard (adjective) accepted as normal, standard (noun) something used as a measure to compare other things against, a level of quality

Day 110 review envy – jealousy; being upset over what someone else has and you don't

noun, deceit – the act of lying, verb, deceive – to lie, to trick someone

adjective, deceitful – describing someone who lies

adverb, deceitfully – describing how someone lives, acts or speaks with deceit

feeble – weak

droves – a large crowd; here it's a herd being moved

prevail – to win, to be widespread or more frequently occurring

odious – repulsive, offensive

Day 115 review concerning – related to a subject

adverb – word that describes how something is done

lodge – to stay a short time in a place such as a home or hotel

Day 120 review rebuke – to scold; to tell someone their behavior is wrong in a sharp manner

devour – to eat up hungrily; to beat or destroy completely; to consume quickly

balm – cream used for medicine, or anything that heals or soothes

profit – get a benefit, often refers to money

Day 125 review prosper – to succeed financially or physically

garment – a piece of clothing

supervise – to keep watch over someone while they work

confine – to place restrictions on someone or something

Day 130 review interpretation – the explanation of something's meaning

gaunt – scrawny looking, especially looking thin from hunger

subsequent – coming after something, following

discern – to be able to recognize or to see something and distinguish what it is

Hebrew

Find helpful links for listening, pronouncing, and writing at genesiscurriculum.com.

Pronunciation Guide:

a	as in "say <u>ah</u>" at the dentist	aa	long a, as in d<u>ay</u>
e	short e, as in red	ee	long e, as in be
i	short I, as in hit	ii	long I, as in l<u>ie</u>
o	long o, as in go		
u	long u, as in m<u>oo</u>		
r	if you can, roll your R a little with a flicker of your tongue		
kh	Make the sound k. It's in your throat. Try to make it deeper down your throat. Add a hard h sound, as in horse. It's one sound. Practice making the k and h sounds together.		
k	This is the Q sound. Practice Q words such as "quite" and concentrate on isolating the q/k sound. Q is made farther back in the throat than the K.		

1   eloHEEM   God
2   shaMAyim   heaven
3   Arets   earth
4   reSHEET   beginning
5   Review
6   baRA   created
7   be reSHEET baRA eloHEEM et ha shaMAyim ve et ha Arets
    "be" is the "in" in the sentence
8   "ha" is the "the" in the sentence
9   "ve" is the "and" in the sentence
10 Review, "et" shows that what follows is a direct object
11 TOhu vaVOhu   chaos
12 KHOshekh   darkness
13 pnaa   face
14 teHOM   deep
15 Review
16 haaTah   was
17 al   upon
18 practice
19 practice
20 Review: ve ha Arets haaTAH TOhu vaVOhu ve KHOshekh al pnaa teHOM
21 MAyim   waters
22 RUakh   spirit
23 meraKHEfet   moving
24 practice
25 Review: ve RUakh eloHEEM meraKHEfet al pnaa ha MAyim
26 – 35 Review words and Genesis 1:1-2.
1:1   be reSHEET baRA eloHEEM et ha shaMAyim ve et ha Arets
1:2   ve ha Arets haaTAH TOhu vaVOhu ve KHOshekh al pnaa teHOM ve RUakh
       eloHEEM meraKHEfet al pnaa ha MAyim
36   Genesis 1:3 va YOmer eloHEEM yeHEE or va yeHEE or   Read and make observations.
37   va YOmer   and + the imperfect form of the word to say (translated: and said)
     (I'm teaching you how it is in the verse. The vowel sound changes from YOmar to
     YOmer when va comes before it.)
38   va   and, ve changes to va in front of Y
39   va yeHEE   and + imperfect; it's also the command form of the verb to be
     (translated: let there be / there was—This part of the verse could be translated, "Light
     be and light is.")
40   or   light
41   tov   good
42   va yar   and + imperfect form of the verb to see
43   va yavDEL   and + imperfect form of the verb to divide (translated: to
     separate)
44   ki   that (also can be when, if, because)
45   Review
46   ben, ven   between
47   u   and
48   va yar eloHEEM et ha or ki tov

49	va yar eloHEEM et ha or ki tov va yavDEL eloHEEM ben ha or u ven ha KHOshekh	
50	Review	
51	yom	day
52	LII-la	night (hyphen only for clarity between the Is and the L)
53	kaRA, va yikRA	called
54	le, la	to, to the
55	Review: va yikRA eloHEEM la or yom ve la KHOshekh kaRA LII-la	
56	Erev	evening
57	VOker	morning
58	eKHAD	one
59	yom eKHAD	one day (literally, day one)
60	va yikRA eloHEEM la or yom ve la KHOshekh kaRA LII-la va yeHEE Erev va yeHEE VOker yom ekHAD	

א בְּרֵאשִׁית, בָּרָא אֱלֹהִים, אֵת הַשָּׁמַיִם, וְאֵת הָאָרֶץ.

ב וְהָאָרֶץ, הָיְתָה תֹהוּ וָבֹהוּ, וְחֹשֶׁךְ, עַל פְּנֵי תְהוֹם; וְרוּחַ אֱלֹהִים, מְרַחֶפֶת עַל פְּנֵי הַמָּיִם.

ג וַיֹּאמֶר אֱלֹהִים, יְהִי אוֹר; וַיְהִי אוֹר.

_____

ד וַיַּרְא אֱלֹהִים אֶת הָאוֹר, כִּי טוֹב; וַיַּבְדֵּל אֱלֹהִים, בֵּין הָאוֹר וּבֵין הַחֹשֶׁךְ.

ה וַיִּקְרָא אֱלֹהִים לָאוֹר יוֹם, וְלַחֹשֶׁךְ קָרָא לָיְלָה; וַיְהִי עֶרֶב וַיְהִי בֹקֶר, יוֹם אֶחָד.

1. be reSHEET baRA eloHEEM et ha shaMAyim ve et ha Arets
2. ve ha Arets haaTAH TOhu va VOhu ve KHOshekh al pnaa teHOM ve RUakh eloHEEM meraKHEfet al pnaa ha MAyim
3. va YOmer eloHEEM yeHEE or va yeHEE or
4. va yar eloHEEM et ha or ki tov va yavDEL eloHEEM ben ha or u ven ha KHOshekh
5. va yikRA eloHEEM la or yom ve la KHOshekh kaRA LII-la va yeHEE Erev va yeHEE VOker yom ekHAD

If you find a mistake in any of our books, please contact us through genesiscurriculum.com to let us know.

Thank you for using the Genesis Curriculum. We hope you had a great year of learning together.

Genesis Curriculum also offers:

GC Steps: This is GC's preschool and kindergarten curriculum. There are three years (ages three through six) where kids will learn to read and write as well as develop beginning math skills.

A Mind for Math: This is GC's elementary school learning-together math program based on the curriculum's daily Bible reading. Children work together as well as have their own leveled workbook.

Rainbow Readers: These are leveled reading books. They each have a unique dictionary with the included words underlined in the text. They are also updated to use modern American spelling.

Look for more years of the Genesis Curriculum using both Old and New Testament books of the Bible. Find us online to read about the latest developments in this expanding curriculum.

GenesisCurriculum.com

Made in the USA
Middletown, DE
10 August 2024

58879591R00296